HTML5 Hacks

Jesse Cravens and Jeff Burtoft

Beijing · Cambridge · Farnham · Köln · Sebastopol · Tokyo

HTML5 Hacks

by Jesse Cravens and Jeff Burtoft

Printed in the United States of America.

Published by O'Reilly Media, Inc., 1005 Gravenstein Highway North, Sebastopol, CA 95472.

O'Reilly books may be purchased for educational, business, or sales promotional use. Online editions are also available for most titles (*http://my.safaribooksonline.com*). For more information, contact our corporate/institutional sales department: 800-998-9938 or *corporate@oreilly.com*.

Editors: Simon St. Laurent and Meghan Blanchette	**Copyeditor:** Audrey Doyle
Production Editor: Holly Bauer	**Proofreader:** Rachel Leach
	Indexer: Judith McConville
	Cover Designer: Mark Paglietti
	Interior Designer: David Futato
	Illustrator: Rebecca Demarest

November 2012:   First Edition

Revision History for the First Edition:

2012-11-09   First release

See *http://oreilly.com/catalog/errata.csp?isbn=9781449334994* for release details.

ISBN: 978-1-449-33499-4

[LSI]

Table of Contents

Preface

HTML5 is the new catchall term for "the Web." Like Ajax and Web 2.0 before, the term can cause confusion when used in different contexts. HTML5 is technically the fifth revision of the HTML markup language, but you will find the term being used to describe an umbrella of next-generation web technology specifications that include CSS3, SVG, and JavaScript APIs.

In order to understand HTML5 in this context, first it is important to understand that HTML5 is not one technology that is applied or added to a web application. There are more than 30 specifications within the HTML5 umbrella, and each is at a different stage of maturity. Furthermore, each specification is also at a different state of adoption and, potentially, implementation, by the major browser manufacturers.

Depending on an application's business requirements, the app's developer will pick and choose the HTML5 features to take advantage of. It is entirely possible that only a handful of the available specifications will be used for the final implementation of a modern web application.

Critics often proclaim it is necessary to wait until HTML5 is 100% supported before you use it in your application. This is simply not true. Many specifications have already reached maturity and are fully implemented by modern browsers. Other specifications are at an early stage of development, or are poorly supported by some of the major browser manufacturers. It's important to know which specification type you are using. Research is helpful, but the only true way to tell is to thoroughly test your apps in all browsers.

For the specifications that are newer or that aren't as strongly supported, some clever developers have produced free and open source code that can be utilized to shim, or *polyfill*, support in older browsers. As defined by Remy Sharp, "A polyfill, or polyfiller, is a piece of code (or plug-in) that provides the technology that you, the developer, expect the browser to provide natively. Flattening the API landscape, if you will." In our opinion, the best polyfill is one that lets you write your code just as you would if the feature were natively supported, and that does the work in the background when necessary, being transparent to both the user and the developer. In most circumstances, each HTML5 specification has a polyfill, or multiple competing polyfills, and is ready to be used today. You will find references to some of the Web's most effective polyfills within this book.

Why HTML5?

A beginning developer might ask, "Why should I care about HTML5?" Unfortunately, there is not a simple answer to this question. Even the most advanced web developers will answer this question differently depending on the features they are most familiar with.

But overall, there are some common trends that span the feature set and on which most developers would agree. Before HTML5, the Web was not considered to be a rival to native desktop and mobile applications. Nearly since its inception, the Web has been considered to be an easily deployable, cross-platform solution. However, it has been hampered due to its lack of highly important business requirements: namely, performance, security, and graphics. The theory has been that if the modern web browser could mature as an application platform, developers would be able to stop creating platform-specific native applications.

The Ajax revolution took the web application world in the right direction by providing asynchronous, background updates to the server via the `XMLHttpRequest` object, JSON transfer format, and an explosion of JavaScript libraries that stretched the boundaries of application development in the browser, many of which continue to make up the basis for polyfill support. However, HTML5 is about the modern browser providing the necessary support to enable sophisticated application development natively. In order to accomplish this, features such as the ability to maintain browser history and bookmarking during asynchronous interactions, cross-domain communication, local storage, offline support, rich graphics, and even new protocols to improve the speed and efficiency of the connectivity layer still needed to be created and improved.

Browser prefixes are most common in CSS. We urge you to read the introduction to Chapter 2 to get a full explanation of how browser prefixes are implemented in CSS.

HTML5 Implementations

As an eager developer ready to move forward with implementing some of the new features available in this text, it will be important to understand that many of the HTML5 specifications are in experimental stages of development. One major challenge in writing a book about evolving specifications is keeping the information fresh and up to date.

The following topics are important considerations when learning experimental web browser specifications.

Browser-specific prefixes

In order for browser makers to be able to implement experimental features (usually implementing specifications before they were completed), browser makers "prefix" that feature with a shorthand that limits its use to each particular browser. A great example of this is the implementation of `requestAnimationFrame`, which is a JavaScript method in the page that aids in animation within the browser. Each browser originally implemented this feature with browser prefixes as follows:

- `requestAnimationFrame`
- `webkitRequestAnimationFrame`
- `mozRequestAnimationFrame`
- `oRequestAnimationFrame`
- `msRequestAnimationFrame`

Browser prefixes are most common in CSS. We urge you to read the introduction to Chapter 2 to get a full explanation of how browser prefixes are implemented in CSS.

Validation with HTML5 Conformance Checker

An HTML validator is a piece of software that parses your web pages against a set of web standards as defined by a particular Document Type Definition (DTD). If you are unfamiliar with a DTD, think of it as metadata that precedes your HTML markup in order to instruct the browser as to what "flavor" of HTML you will be using.

The HTML validator returns a list of errors found, according to the chosen standard. For our purposes, we will assume that we are using the HTML5 Document Type Definition.

The HTML5 Document Type Definition is more lenient than the most recent XHMTL definition, and the output of the W3C's new validator (*http://html5.validator.nu/*) reflects this difference. After all, a validator should not throw exceptions for stylistic issues. It should be focused on validating your HTML markup against a specification.

HTML5 Lint

This means that developers should also be ready to use a lint tool in order to expose stylistic issues within their code. Some of the more common issues to check for are consistent indentation, lowercase tags, and omission of closing tags.

At the time of this writing, we recommend the HTML5 Lint tool (*http://lint.brihten.com/html/*).

References for HTML5 implementation statuses and feature support

We will continue to provide updates as often as possible to the examples provided within this text on our blog (*http://html5hacks.com/blog*).

There are also many great resources around the web to reference HTML5 implementation statuses and feature support of specific browsers.

For all modern browsers:

> *http://caniuse.com/*
> *http://html5test.com/*

For Chrome:

> *http://www.chromium.org/developers/web-platform-status*

For Internet Explorer:

> *http://msdn.microsoft.com/en-US/ie/ff468705.aspx*

For Mozilla Firefox:

> *https://wiki.mozilla.org/Features*

For Apple Safari:

> *https://developer.apple.com/technologies/safari/html5.html*

Why HTML5 Hacks?

The term *hacker* carries a negative connotation within the media, but the term has evolved to describe a number of different technical people. Wikipedia provides three very different definitions for the term *hacker*:[1]

---

[1] *http://en.wikipedia.org/wiki/Hacker*

1. Hacker (computer security), someone who accesses a computer system by circumventing its security system
2. Hacker (hobbyist), who makes innovative customizations or combinations of retail electronic and computer equipment
3. Hacker (programmer subculture), who shares an anti-authoritarian approach to software development now associated with the free software movement

It is in the context of definition 2 that we are using the term *hack*. Among these types of hacks, the term refers to a self-contained proof of concept, similar to agile spikes, or recipes. These quick solutions exercise or validate an API, feature, or technology, and can also serve a very important role, not only in educating the software team, but also in driving the direction of development within a project's life cycle.

Who This Book Is For

HTML5 Hacks introduces readers to the umbrella of HTML5 specifications through 90 hacks. For beginners it can serve as a starting point for building browser-based applications. For intermediate to advanced developers it can serve to quickly fill in the gaps for specifications they have yet to be exposed to.

Nevertheless, this book will be what you make of it.

Contents of This Book

This book consists of 10 chapters, organized as follows:

Chapter 1, Hacking the Semantic Way
    Introduces new key HTML5 markup elements and attributes

Chapter 2, Hacking with Style
    Covers visual expression and behaviors with CSS3

Chapter 3, Multimedia Hacking
    Discusses HTML5 audio and video tags

Chapter 4, Hacking Your Graphics with Canvas and SVG
    Covers working with Canvas and SVG

Chapter 5, User Interactions
    Introduces HTML5 drag-and-drop, editing elements, and other interactions

Chapter 6, Client-Side Data Storage Hacks
Discusses storage and HTML5 application cache

Chapter 7, Geolocation Hacks
Teaches how to work with geolocations

Chapter 8, WebWorker API
Covers taking advantage of the WebWorker API

Chapter 9, Hacking HTML5 Connectivity
Discusses web sockets, cross-document messaging, server-side events, and more

Chapter 10, Pro HTML5 Application Hacks with Node.js
Teaches how to build professional HTML5 applications with Node.js

Conventions Used in This Book

The following typographical conventions are used in this book:

Italic
Indicates new terms, URLs, email addresses, filenames, file extensions, path-names, directories, and Unix utilities

`Constant width`
Indicates commands, options, switches, variables, attributes, keys, functions, types, classes, namespaces, methods, modules, properties, parameters, values, objects, events, event handlers, XML tags, HTML tags, macros, the contents of files, or the output from commands

`Constant width bold`
Shows commands or other text that should be typed literally by the user

`Constant width italic`
Shows text that should be replaced with user-supplied values

This formatting signifies a tip, suggestion, general note, warning, or caution.

Using Code Examples

This book is here to help you get your job done. In general, you may use the code in this book in your programs and documentation. You do not need to contact us for permission unless you're reproducing a significant portion of the code. For example, writing a program that uses several chunks of code from this book does not require permission. Selling or distributing a CD-ROM of examples from O'Reilly books does require permission. Answering a question by citing this book and quoting example code does not require permission. Incorporating a significant amount of example code from this book into your product's documentation does require permission.

We appreciate, but do not require, attribution. An attribution usually includes the title, author, publisher, and ISBN. For example: "*HTML5 Hacks* by Jesse Cravens and Jeff Burtoft (O'Reilly). Copyright 2013 Jesse Cravens and Jeff Burtoft, 978-1-449-33499-4."

All of the code examples are located at *https://github.com/html5hacks*.

You can also keep up with the authors and any updates at *http://html5hacks.com*.

We'd Like to Hear from You

Please address comments and questions concerning this book to the publisher:

O'Reilly Media, Inc.
1005 Gravenstein Highway North
Sebastopol, CA 95472
(800) 998-9938 (in the United States or Canada)
(707) 829-0515 (international or local)
(707) 829-0104 (fax)

We have a web page for this book, where we list errata, examples, and any additional information. You can access this page at:

oreil.ly/HTML5_Hacks

To comment or ask technical questions about this book, send email to:

bookquestions@oreilly.com

For more information about our books, courses, conferences, and news, see our website at *http://www.oreilly.com*.

Find us on Facebook: *http://facebook.com/oreilly*

Follow us on Twitter: *http://twitter.com/oreillymedia*

Watch us on YouTube: *http://www.youtube.com/oreillymedia*

Safari® Books Online

Safari Safari Books Online (*http://my.safaribooksonline.com/?portal=oreilly*) is an on-demand digital library that delivers expert content in both book and video form from the world's leading authors in technology and business.

Technology professionals, software developers, web designers, and business and creative professionals use Safari Books Online as their primary resource for research, problem solving, learning, and certification training.

Safari Books Online offers a range of product mixes and pricing programs for organizations, government agencies, and individuals. Subscribers have access to thousands of books, training videos, and prepublication manuscripts in one fully searchable database from publishers like O'Reilly Media, Prentice Hall Professional, Addison-Wesley Professional, Microsoft Press, Sams, Que, Peachpit Press, Focal Press, Cisco Press, John Wiley & Sons, Syngress, Morgan Kaufmann, IBM Redbooks, Packt, Adobe Press, FT Press, Apress, Manning, New Riders, McGraw-Hill, Jones & Bartlett, Course Technology, and dozens more. For more information about Safari Books Online, please visit us online.

Acknowledgments

We would like to extend a special thank you to both of our families. This book required a lot of evening and weekend hours to complete, and our wives and children are the ones who sacrificed the most.

Jeff would like to thank his wife Carla who encouraged him to step out and write a book, and for allowing their lives to be turned upside down while he worked to complete it. He would also like to thank his children, Chloe, Maddy, and Jude, for being his inspiration for creativity, and for being proud of him in everything he does. Jeff would also like to thank Jesse, his partner and coauthor, for dreaming up ideas like this book, and making them a reality.

Jesse would like to thank his wife Amy for all the support she gave him through the long and late hours he spent on this book; his children, Carter and Lindley, for trying to understand when Daddy had to work weekends and nights; his brother and sister-in-law for providing a quiet place to write and encouragement that it was worth the effort; and his parents for the continued boosts of inspiration to check another item off the bucket list. And finally, he'd like to thank Jeff for having the shared determination to coauthor this book, overcome the adversity associated with an ambitious project, and make it across the finish line.

Guest Hackers

John Dyer (*http://j.hn/*) is the executive director of Communications and Educational Technology at Dallas Theological Seminary. He has been a web developer and technology writer for more than 10 years, and he loves creating tools that make complex tasks easier for other developers. He lives in the Dallas area with his two amazing kids and his lovely wife, Amber.

Alex Sirota cofounded and was the CTO and Head of Product at FoxyTunes, an Internet startup acquired by Yahoo!, where he spent more than four years building media and entertainment web products. Previously, he cofounded Elbrus Ltd., a company that provided software solutions to Philips Medical Systems, IBM, and others. Prior to Elbrus, he was the head of a computer facility in the Israel Defense Forces, and he coauthored a book (published by Wiley) on Mozilla and web technologies. He holds a bachelor's degree in computer science from Technion–Israel Institute of Technology.

Raymond Camden is a senior developer evangelist for Adobe. His work focuses on web standards, mobile development, and ColdFusion. He's a published author and presents at conferences and user groups on a variety of topics. He can be reached through his blog (*http://www.raymondcamden.com*), via Twitter (**@cfjedimaster**), or via email (*raymondcamden@gmail.com*).

Phil Leggetter is a Real-Time Web Software and Technology Evangelist. He has been developing and using real-time web technologies for more than 10 years, and his focus is to help people use these technologies to build the next generation of interactive and engaging real-time web applications.

Alexander Schulze is the founder of the jWebSocket project, as well as an IT consultant and trainer for IT professionals. He is a speaker at various conferences and author of several articles and books.

1

Hacking the Semantic Way

The spirit of HTML5 is simplicity. HTML5 has made it easy to implement web standards that in the past have been difficult to implement. Instead of trying to reinvent the Web, visionary consortiums such as the WHATWG (Web Hypertext Application Technology Working Group) and the W3C (World Wide Web Consortium) looked at the web standards that had evolved and built upon them.

In essence, HTML5 is primarily an update to the HyperText Markup Language (HTML). In this chapter we will start with the basic building blocks of HTML, the semantic elements, to provide a foundation for the simple yet powerful new web browser technologies exposed within this book.

So, open up your favorite code editor, brew a pot of coffee, and get ready to code in the most powerful language the Web has ever seen: HTML5!

HACK 01 Simplify Your Doc with the Right <doctype>

If there's an emblem representing the simplicity HTML5 brings to the markup world, it's the **<DOCTYPE>** tag. The HTML5 **<doctype>** tag is easy to use.

When you open an XHTML document the first thing you see, the first line of the document, is a mess:

```
<!DOCTYPE html PUBLIC "-//W3C//DTD XHTML 1.0 Transitional//EN" "http://
www.w3.org/TR/xhtml1/DTD/xhtml1-transitional.dtd">
```

The **<DOCTYPE>** tag of HTML past, inherited from its SGML foundations, consisted of three main components: the tag name, the public identifier string, and the DTD (Document Type Definition) URL. It's a strange mix of uppercase and lowercase letters, quote marks and slashes, and a URL that brings up an even less readable file. To make it even stranger, the **<DOCTYPE>** tag is unique, as it is the only HTML tag since HTML 4.01 that is in all caps.

HTML5 says farewell to all that, and keeps it simple:

```
<!doctype html>
```

The browser uses the `<doctype>` to know how to render the web page. Most browsers didn't download the DTD from the URL, but they did change their behavior based on the `<DOCTYPE>`. If a browser encountered the preceding code, it would switch to standards mode (as opposed to quirks mode) and apply XHTML transitional formatting.

Given all that, how can HTML5 get away with a basic `<doctype>` such as `html`? The simple answer is that the new `<doctype>` is a "simple answer." The new `<doctype>` was made to trigger a simplified approach to document rendering, not to meet old expectations. Browser makers reached a consensus on how browser-specific functionality should be handled, so there is no need for "quirks mode" page rendering. If all browsers render in a standard manner, the DTD is unnecessary; thus a simple declaration of `html` states that the browser should set aside any DTD and simply render the page.

HTML5 is a simplified version of HTML. The tags are less complex, the features are less complex, and most importantly, the rules are less complex.

However, in most applications you write, you will not yet be servicing a user base that consistently supports HTML5. So how can you switch between `<doctype>`s when the `<doctype>` is supposed to be the first line of the document? This doesn't leave much room for JavaScript trickery or fancy hacks. Well, good news; there is a backward-compatible HTML5 `<doctype>` as well:

```
<!DOCTYPE html>
```

"But wait," you say. "Isn't that the same simple `<doctype>` presented earlier?" Yes, it is! The only key difference is that "doctype" is now in all caps. The HTML5 specification states that the `<doctype>` is case-insensitive; however, previous versions of HTML require an all-caps version of the `<doctype>`. You will find that much of HTML5 is backward-compatible with earlier versions. The vast majority of browsers on the market today will see the new `<doctype>` and recognize it as simply being "standards mode" for page rendering.

Using the backward-compatible version of the `<doctype>` will allow you to start using HTML5 today, while continuing to support browsers of the past!

HACK 02 Adopt Common Structures

Many web documents have similar structures. Take advantage of markup that makes it easier to share styles and expectations.

Web designers and developers have long conformed to structural components on a page. A common high-level page structure may look something like the following:

```
<!DOCTYPE html PUBLIC "-//W3C//DTD XHTML 1.0 Transitional//EN"
"http://www.w3.org/TR/xhtml1/DTD/xhtml1-transitional.dtd">
<html>
<head>
<meta http-equiv="content-type" content="text/html;charset=UTF-8" />
    <title>...</title>
</head>
<body>
    <div id="header">...</div>
    <div id="nav">...</div>
    <div id="article">...</div>
    <div id="footer">...</div>
</body>
</html>
```

Take note of the "structural" `id`s in the page. This reflects well-organized content and a clean structure for the page. The problem with the preceding code is that almost every element in the markup is a `div`. `Div`s are great, but they are of little use in page definition without associating them with an `id`. The problem with using `id`s for role association is that when you want to use them for another purpose—say, to identify a doc tree—you run into problems: as soon as you add a tool such as YUI Grids or WordPress to a page that actually uses the `id` of a `div`, it conflicts with your `div` "roles," and the next thing you know you are adding layers of `div`s just to satisfy your structural needs. As a result, the clean page shown earlier may now look something like this:

```
<!DOCTYPE html PUBLIC "-//W3C//DTD XHTML 1.0 Transitional//EN"
"http://www.w3.org/TR/xhtml1/DTD/xhtml1-transitional.dtd">
<html>
<head>
<meta http-equiv="content-type" content="text/html;charset=UTF-8" />
    <title>...</title>
</head>
<body>
    <div id="header">
    <div id="nav">
        <div id="doc2">
            <div id="wordpress-org-2833893">...</div>
        </div>
    </div>
    <div id="article">
        <div id="doc2">
            <div id="wordpress-org-887478">...</div>
```

```
            </div>
        </div>
        <div id="footer">...</div>
    </body>
```

You can see pretty quickly where this gets messy, yet we don't want to abandon the idea of structural elements that declare page segments—many code readers, such as screen readers and search bots, have come to rely on structural conventions. As with many parts of HTML5, the new structural tags have provided a simple solution to the problem of added complexity. Let's build our page with structural elements:

```
<!DOCTYPE html>
<html>
<head>
    <meta charset="UTF-8">
    <title>...</title>
</head>
<body>
    <header>...</header>
    <nav>...</nav>
    <article>...</article>
    <footer>...</footer>
</body>
</html>
```

Once again we have a simple, clean HTML5 solution that keeps our page easy to work with, and easy to consume by screen readers and search bots. This same code can meet the needs of our third-party products as well, as shown in the following solution:

```
<!DOCTYPE html>
<html>
<head>
    <meta charset="UTF-8">
    <title>...</title>
</head>
<body>
    <header data-yuigrid="doc2" data-wordpress="2833893">...</header>
    <nav>...</nav>
    <article data-yuigrid="doc2" data-wordpress="887478">...</article>
    <footer>...</footer>
</body>
</html>
```

We'll get into the **data-** attributes later in this chapter, but for now you just need to understand that this solution allows you to keep the structural elements of the page and let third-party components apply identifiers to the nodes, while freeing up the **id** attributes for the page author to control. Take note, third-party developers: never assume that the **id** of an element is yours to consume!

All That and More

HTML5 didn't stop at the new tags discussed in the preceding section. Here's a partial list of some of the new HTML5 markup tags to take note of:

`<article>`	`<aside>`	`<figcaption>`	`<figure>`	`<footer>`	`<header>`	`<hgroup>`
`<mark>`	`<nav>`	`<section>`	`<time>`	`<keygen>`	`<meter>`	`<summary>`

A lot of these tags grew out of common use by web developers. The W3C smartly decided to "pave the cow paths" instead of trying to change the behavior of web developers. This way, the tags are generally useful for immediate adoption.

In most cases each tag's intent is pretty obvious. The `<header>` and `<footer>` tags do exactly what they say: they outline the header and footer of the page (or app). You use `<nav>` to wrap your navigation. The `<section>` and `<article>` tags give you options to the overused `<div>` tag; use these to break up your page according to the content (e.g., wrap your articles in the `<article>` tag). The `<aside>` tag acts in a similar way to the `<article>` tag, but groups the content aside the main page content. The `<figure>` tag refers to a self-contained piece of content, and so on and so on. Note that this list is not conclusive and is always changing. Visit the w3schools website for the most complete list I could find (*http://www.w3schools.com/html5/html5_reference.asp*).

HACK 03   Make Your New HTML5 Tags Render Properly in Older Browsers

Don't wait for full HTML5 adoption across the Web. Make HTML5 structural tags render properly in all browsers.

So, now you have this whole new world of HTML5 elements that will let you be both expressive and semantic with your markup. You've been freed from the shackles of **div**s and can show your face at parties again!

Semantic markup is the use of markup in a meaningful way. Separation of structure and presentation leads us to define our presentation (look and feel) with CSS, and our content with meaningful or semantic markup.

You're feeling pretty good about yourself until you remember that some of your visitors are not using HTML5 browsers, and being the web standards elitist that you are, your page has to be backward-compatible. Don't throw those HTML5 tags out the window just yet. This hack will teach you how to write your code once, and use it on all the browsers out there.

Any browser made in the past 10 years will see your HTML5 tags in one of 3 ways:

1. See the HTML5 tag and render it appropriately (congratulations, you support HTML5!).
2. See the HTML5 tag, not recognize it, and consider it an unstyled (which defaults to inline) DOM (Document Object Model) element.
3. See the HTML5 tag, not recognize it, and ignore it completely, building the DOM without it.

Option 1 is a no-brainer: you're in an HTML5 browser. Option 2 is likewise pretty easy to address, as you simply have to set your default display parameters in your CSS. Keep in mind that with option 2, you have no functional DOM APIs for these new tags, so this is not true support for the tags. In other words, using this method to create a `meter` element does not create a functional meter. For our use case of semantic markup elements, however, this should not be an issue.

So, focusing on option 3, you're using IE 6, 7, or 8 and you're loading a page that contains new HTML5 semantic tags. The code will look something like this:

```
<!DOCTYPE html>
<html>
<head>
    <meta charset="UTF-8">
    <title>My New Page with Nav</title>
</head>
<body>
<div>
    <nav class="nav">
    <p>this is nav text</p>
    </nav>
</div>
</body>
</html>
```

There are basically two different ways to handle this lack of support.

The Fallback div

In the preceding code sample, the **nav** element is not recognized and is passed over at render time. Since the DOM does not recognize these elements, option 1 uses a fallback element that the browser does recognize, and wraps each unrecognized element in it. The following code should make this easier to understand:

```
<!DOCTYPE html>
<html>
<head>
    <meta charset="UTF-8">
    <title>My New Page with Nav</title>
</head>
<body>
<div>
    <nav class="nav">
        <div class="nav-div">
            <p>this is nav text</p>
        </div>
    </nav>
</div>
</body>
</html>
```

Voilà! We can now style the element with the **nav-div** class instead of the element with the **nav** class, and our DOM will be complete in all common browsers. Our page will style correctly, and we will have our new HTML5 tags in place for screen readers and search engines that will benefit from the semantic tags.

This method will work, but there are some downsides to this solution. For starters, having duplicate tags negates the benefit in many ways, as we are still using **div**s for every structural element of the page. The biggest problem with this solution, though, is how it corrupts the DOM tree. We no longer have a consistent parent–child relationship from browser to browser. The browsers that do recognize the HTML5 element will have an extra "parent" to the contents of the element, so the trees will differ from one browser to the next. You may think you don't need to care about this, but as soon as you start accessing the DOM with JavaScript (especially if you're using a JavaScript library such as YUI or jQuery) you will run into cross-browser issues.

The Real DOM Hack: The HTML5 Shim (or Shiv)

I'm happy to say there is a second, and in my opinion better, solution to our problem. I believe this "feature" was first discovered by Sjoerd Visscher in 2002 when he switched from `createElement` to `innerHTML` and realized he lost the ability to style unrecognized elements. Fast-forward to 2008, when John Resic realized he could exploit the same bug to make HTML5 elements recognizable in IE; he named the capability the "HTML5 shiv," although it is technically a shim. Here are the details.

Old versions of IE don't recognize HTML5 elements naturally, but as soon as you use `document.createElement()` in the head of the document passing in an unrecognized element, IE will add the element to its tag library and it can be styled with CSS. Let's go back to the markup:

```
<!DOCTYPE html>
<html>
<head>
    <meta charset="UTF-8">
    <title>My New Page with Nav</title>
<style>
.nav {
color: red
}
    nav {
display: block;
background-color: blue
}
</style>
</head>
<body>
<div>
    <nav class="nav">
            <p>this is nav text</p>
    </nav>
</div>
</body>
</html>
```

Figure 1-1 shows how the preceding markup will appear in IE versions 6 through 8.

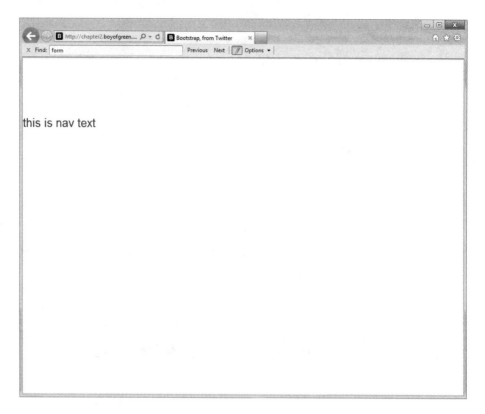

Figure 1-1.
Styled nav element in a browser that doesn't support the tag

Notice that the element didn't pick up the color from the tag name or the CSS class assigned to the tag; it simply ignored it. Now let's throw in our JavaScript and try it again:

```
<!DOCTYPE html>
<html>
<head>
    <meta charset="UTF-8">
    <title>My New Page with Nav</title>
<style>
.nav {
color: red
}
        nav {
display: block;
background-color: blue
}
</style>
```

```
<script>

    document.createElement('nav');
</script>
</head>
<body>
<div>
    <nav class="nav">
            <p>this is nav text</p>
    </nav>
</div>
</body>
</html>
```

Now our markup will pick up the blue background from the tag styles and the red text from the class name; the result will look something like Figure 1-2.

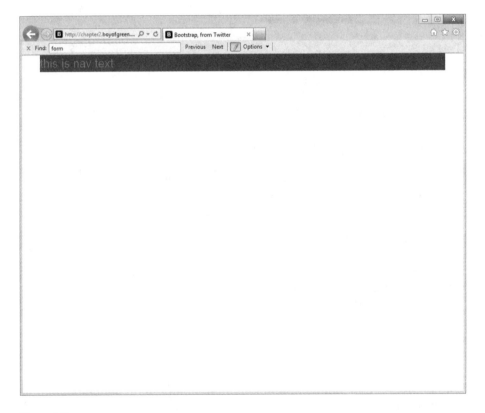

Figure 1-2.
Styled nav element in a browser that doesn't support the tag, but with the JavaScript hack

HACK 04 Bring Back the <input> Tag

HTML5 has breathed new life into the `<input>` tag. It's time to get excited once again about this "age-old" tag.

I have to admit that I was getting a little bored with the `<input>` tag. Before HTML5, any real interaction had to be done outside the tag: whether the interaction involved validation, formatting, or graphical presentation, JavaScript was a necessary polyfill. Well, HTML5 has given us a reason to be excited about the `<input>` tag again.

The `<input>` tag is not truly an HTML5 tag, per se. It's the same `<input>` tag we have had in every previous version of HTML, but HTML5 has added a slew of new features. The good thing about updating an existing tag is that it's naturally backward-compatible. You may code your tag like this:

```
<input type="date" />
```

and non-HTML5 browsers will simply see this:

```
<input />
```

In this hack we'll look at a few new, common features of this wonder of a tag.

Some of the Basics

There are a few basic (but powerful) new features in the HTML5 `<input>` tag that are accessible on almost any input type. We'll start by looking at some of the simple attributes and then move on to some of the more complex ones.

First on the list is the placeholder text, which is a string assigned to the `placeholder` attribute that provides a hint for the input box. Placeholder text is quite useful and quickly becoming commonplace. The text appears when the input value is empty and disappears once the input receives focus. Then it reappears when it loses focus (providing the input box is still empty).

Another common attribute is `autofocus`, which, as you can guess by the name, brings focus to an element once the document is loaded. Simply set `autofocus="autofocus"` (or just add `autofocus` as an attribute) and this will be the default focus element once the page is loaded (as opposed to focusing on the first element of the page).

The `required` attribute is another one of those patterns that has been accomplished through JavaScript for years, but has finally made it into DOM functionality. Simply add the attribute `required="required"` (or simply `required`) to your input and the DOM will not submit the form while the requirements of that field are not satisfied. Let's look at a quick example:

```
<!DOCTYPE html>
<html>
<body>

<form>
  Add your telephone: <input type="tel" name="phone" required /><br />
  <input type="submit" />
</form>

</body>
</html>
```

If you try hitting the Submit button without putting a value in the field, your browser will throw up a default message along the lines of "Please fill out this field." It's not perfect, but it's a start.

The `form` attribute is a feature that has been a long time coming. Have you ever wanted to have a form on your page, but without constraining the form elements to one section of your DOM? Maybe you are on a mobile device and you would like your Submit button to pop up from the bottom of the screen instead of residing in your form area. The `form` attribute lets you create a `form` element for a form, even when it is not a child node of the form. Simply set the `form` attribute to the `id` of the form (it can't be the form name or another attribute, something the W3C needs to address). With this attribute, the preceding example would look something like this:

```
<!DOCTYPE html>
<html>
<body>

<form id="myForm">
  Add your telephone: <input type="tel" name="phone" required /><br />

</form>


  <input type="submit"  form="myForm" />
</body>
</html>
```

Now that we've covered the basics of the `<input>` tag, let's move on to some of the tag's more interesting features.

The autocomplete Attribute

The Web definitely has a fascination with autocomplete. Since we all hate to type, we love it when the **form** element knows what we want to type and just does it for us. So HTML5 comes along and introduces autocomplete as a simple attribute. You set **autocomplete** to **on** or **off** (it's **on** by default) and your work is done! The code would look something like this:

```
<!DOCTYPE html>
<html>
<body>

<form id="myForm">
   Add your telephone: <input type="tel" name="phone" autocomplete="on" /
><br />

</form>


   <input type="submit"  form="myForm" />
</body>
</html>
```

Now, what sucks about **autocomplete** is where it gets its data. To explain this I'll cite the boring old spec from the W3C:

> The user agent may store the value entered by the user so that if the user returns to the page, the UA can prefill the form.[1]

So, the **autocomplete** value comes from the user agent. But who is the user agent? It's not the page developer, or JavaScript, or HTML: it's the *browser*. If I fill out a few forms and always enter the string *email@mail.com* into the input field designated for an email address, the browser remembers that and prefills it for me. So it's great for form elements such as email address and telephone number, but it's not incredibly useful for a developer. The key thing to take away from this discussion is that you can turn off the autocomplete feature when you need to.

Fortunately, all is not lost. HTML5 didn't forget about the other use case. It's actually there in the spec as well, it's just poorly named and even more poorly supported. It's the **list** attribute; at the time of this writing, the only browsers that support this attribute are Firefox 10 and Opera 10.

---

[1] *http://www.w3.org/TR/html5/common-input-element-attributes.html#the-autocomplete-attribute*

The list Attribute

Think of the `list` attribute as being a version of **autocomplete** for developers. The `list` attribute is tied to an `id` of a **datalist** (yes, once again this is not a name or any other type of identifier, it has to be an `id`). It will look something like this:

```
<!DOCTYPE html>
<html>
<body>

<form action="demo_form.asp" autocomplete="on">
  First name:<input type="text" name="fname" /><br />
  Last name: <input type="text" name="lname" /><br />
  E-mail: <input type="email" name="email"  /><br />
  Favorite Animal:  <input type="text" name="animal" list="animals" /><br />
  <datalist id="animals">
   <option value="Dog">
   <option value="Dolphin">
   <option value="Duck">
   <option value="Cat">
   <option value="Bird">
   <option value="mouse">
  </datalist>

  <input type="submit" />


</form>


</body>
</html>
```

The level of interaction is what you would expect from an autocomplete feature: press the "D" key on your keyboard and it should offer you the options from the list of animals that start with D (see Figure 1-3). Once again, don't be surprised if your favorite HTML5 browser doesn't support this; it will in time. Keep in mind that the **datalist** is not visible to the user; it's purely a reference.

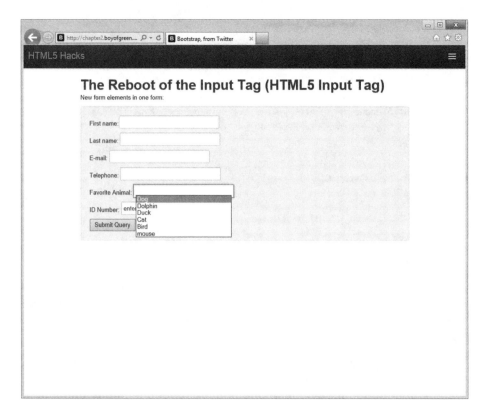

Figure 1-3.
Datalist displaying predefined options

One of the bad things about both `list` and `autocomplete` is that you can't style them. I'll rant about that some more as we get into a few of the more functional input types, such as `date`, but I would expect to be able to style the results with CSS, just as I do any form element.

The pattern Attribute

How many times have you run a regex (or regular expression) against the value of `input` to see if it meets certain criteria? If you're like me, you've done this more times than you can count. This was the inspiration for the `pattern` attribute in HTML5. According to the W3C spec, the pattern should "control" the input value. As you would expect, you utilize this value with the `pattern` attribute set to a JavaScript format regular expression. Let's take a look:

```
<!DOCTYPE html>
<html>
<body>
```

```
<form action="demo_form.asp" autocomplete="on">
  First name:<input type="text" name="fname" /><br />
  Last name: <input type="text" name="lname" /><br />
  E-mail: <input type="email" name="email"  /><br />
  ID Number:
  <input placeholder="enter your 5 digit id number" type="text"
    name="idNumber" pattern="[0-9]{5}" />
  <br />

  <input type="submit" />

</form>

</body>
</html>
```

If you don't meet the pattern criteria the form cannot be submitted, and instead you get a user agent message that says something like "Please match the requested format." One of the big problems with this implementation is its lack of adherence to modern web patterns.

Back in the day (2005 or so) we used to wait until a form was submitted to validate each input field, and if one or more of the fields didn't pass we would return an error message to the user. The W3C's implementation is so HTML 4.01. In HTML5 I would have expected the validation to be on a specified keystroke or on a blur of the field.

Luckily HTML5 has a backup plan for some of these validation shortcomings. The next hack discusses form validation to see how to make it all work for you!

HACK 05 Easily Implement Form Validation Without JavaScript

HTML5 includes powerful form validation that works seamlessly with the slew of new input types.

Form validation is fun again. Well, maybe not fun, but more fun than it ever was before. OK, let's just admit it, form validation sucks. It's not fun, but it is necessary. In the past you would write a form and then run some very custom code to make sure all your inputs contained what they were supposed to contain. This was done in one of two ways: on the server or on the client. For server-side validation you would submit your form and run server-side code to make sure all your requirements were met, and if they weren't you would reload the page with an error or two on it telling the user where the problem was. Client-side validation worked in pretty much the same way, except you would run some JavaScript before the form was submitted to make sure all your conditions were met. For the record, the best kind of validation is when you do both. You should start with validation on the client to give the user an immediate response, and then revalidate on the server to make sure your response wasn't being hacked.

HTML5 isn't going to help you with server-side validation, but it sure will make it easier on the client. HTML5 once again takes a tried-and-true web standard and reinvents it as native browser functionality. Let's dive in!

What Does It Mean to Validate?

In HTML5 every input has the ability to have validation engaged, and a form cannot be submitted if it doesn't validate. In order for the form to validate, every input needs to have its validation criteria met. It's pretty simple: every input has a method you can call to see if it will meet a validation test. Let's look at a form containing an **input** of type **number**:

```
<!DOCTYPE html>
<html>
<body>

<form name="myForm">
  Quantity (between 1 and 5):
  <input type="number" name="quantity" min="1" max="5" value="11" />
  <input type="submit" />
</form>

</body>
</html>
```

Now let's check it with JavaScript:

```
<script>
if(document.myForm.quantity.checkValidity() === false){

alert('fail');
}

</script>
```

When the value of **quantity** is greater than 5 the alert will be fired. Now let's try something a little different. Instead of checking the input itself, let's just check the form. Here is the new JavaScript:

```
<script>
//myForm is the name of the form element
if(document.myForm.checkValidity() === false){
```

```
    alert('fail');
    }

    </script>
```

Notice that the validity state rolled up to the form. If any one of the inputs within the form doesn't meet the criteria for validation, the form rule will return `false` as well. This is a key feature when you have long forms. For instance, if I have a form with 25 input fields that need to be validated, I don't want to have to go through the form with JavaScript and check each input field—this would require 25 different DOM hits. Instead, I'd rather check the form and have it determine whether all the necessary input criteria are met on each of the 25 inputs.

Validation Criteria

So, we know how we can check to see if a form is valid or not, but how do we set the criteria we want to validate against? Well, there are really three ways to do this in HTML5.

The required attribute

First, we can simply add the `required` attribute to an `input`, and the `input` will return a `true` state for its `validity` value only if the element has a value and the value matches the required input criteria. In the following example, the `input` has to be a number between one and five:

```
    <input type="number" name="quantity" min="1" max="5" />
```

The pattern attribute

The new `pattern` attribute is pretty slick, especially for people who like to write regular expressions. In this case you set a regular expression to the `pattern` attribute, and your input will validate against that pattern in order to have the `validity` value return `true`:

```
    <input type="text" name="quantity" pattern="[0-5]{1}" />
```

Notice that the `type` was changed to `text` in order for the pattern to make the input invalid; we need to remove the `number` type, as that will supersede the validation criteria. If the type and pattern conflict (by requiring results that exclude each other), the validation criteria will never be met, and the form will never validate.

HTML5 HACKS

Measurable attributes

Some `input` types have comparative criteria such as `email`, which require a strict input pattern. Other `input` types have attributes such as `min` and `max` that must be satisfied before the input can be considered valid. Let's look at our first input example again:

```
<form name="myForm">
  Quantity (between 1 and 5): <input type="number" name="quantity" min="1"
max="5" />
  <input type="submit" />
</form>
```

In this case the number that is input must meet the `min` and `max` criteria in order to be considered valid. For example, the number 11 would not validate but the number 4 would validate. In a similar manner we have the `email` type:

```
<form name="myForm">
  Enter Your Email: <input type="email" name="myEmail" />
  <input type="submit" />
</form>
```

The `email` type looks for a value that meets traditional email criteria that would match a regular expression such as this:

```
var emailTest = /^[a-zA-Z0-9._-]+@[a-zA-Z0-9.-]+\.[a-zA-Z]{2,4}$/;
```

If the value of the input doesn't have a username, an at sign (@), and a domain, it's considered invalid.

Let's Call This Validation Thing Off

Sometimes you may want to skip validation. A few HTML5 validations allow you to do this. The first is the `formnovalidate` attribute. As you can guess, if you apply this attribute to a button or an input whose `type` is `submit`, the validation does not stop the form from submitting. This attribute can be placed as follows:

```
<form name="myForm">
  Quantity (between 1 and 5): <input type="number" name="quantity" min="1"
max="5" />
  Enter Your Email: <input type="email" name="myEmail" />
  <input type="submit" />
  <button type="submit" formnovalidate>save</button>
</form>
```

Note that the form is still invalid. If you call the `checkValidity()` method on this form, it will still return `false`. In the case of the `formnovalidate` attribute, you simply ignore whether the form is valid or not when you submit.

The second way to escape validation is with the **novalidate** attribute. In a similar manner, the **novalidate** attribute is added to the **form** element itself, and every button and input whose **type** is **submit** will skip the validation stem and submit the form directly:

```
<form name="myForm" novalidate>
  Quantity (between 1 and 5): <input type="number" name="quantity" min="1"
max="5" />
  Enter Your Email: <input type="email" name="myEmail" />
  <input type="submit" />
<button type="submit" >save</button>
</form>
```

The Constraint Validation API

The HTML5 spec makes allowances for us to be more specific with our validation errors. In the previous example form, the user must enter a number between one and five to not receive an error. If we wanted to update the error message to be a little more suitable, we would add a custom message with the **setCustomValidity()** method:

```
<form name="myForm">
  Quantity (between 1 and 5):
  <input type="number" name="quantity" min="1"
   max="5" oninput=  "updateMessage(this)"/>

  Enter Your Email: <input type="email" name="myEmail" formnovalidate />
  <input type="submit" />
</form>

<script>

myForm.quantity. setCustomValidity('looks like your numbers ... between one
and five')

function updateMessage(input){

if(input.value ==""){}
input.setCustomValidity('');

}


</script>
```

Our form will now give us an option for a friendlier, more helpful user error. Notice that we had another method in the `<script>` tag and set it to the `oninput` of the `input`. When you use `setCustomValidity()` you automatically trigger the other portion of your Constraint Validation API to return `false` when you call the `checkValidity()` method. In order to use a custom method and still have the form be considered valid when the criteria are met, you need to throw in some JavaScript to clear out the `setCustomValidity()` method once the validation criteria are met (in this case, once the form is not blank). I still think the W3C has some room to make this even easier for web developers in upcoming versions of the spec. This is functionality you should be able to access without JavaScript.

Developers aren't the only ones using the Constraint Validation API. The user agent uses the same API when it sets up the pseudoclasses for its CSS. With CSS3 we can change visual cues based on the "state" of a validation field. We have access to two pseudoclasses (more on this later) to use for visualizing cues: `:required`, for elements that are marked as required; and `:invalid`, for elements that are marked as invalid. Unlike the form-level validation that occurs when the page submits, the pseudoclasses are based on the current state. This will give users strong visual cues. Let's look at an example with a contact form where the name is required, and the phone number and email address are not required:

```
//our css
<!DOCTYPE html>
<html>
<body>

<style>
input {display: block;
border: 1px solid #ccc;
}


:invalid{
border-color: #DB729C;
  -webkit-box-shadow: 0 0 5px rgba(27, 0, 97, .5);
}

:required{
border-color: #1BE032;
  -webkit-box-shadow: 0 0 5px rgba(57, 237, 78, .5);
}

</style>

//our form
```

```
<form name="myForm" >
 Enter Your Name: <input type="text" name="myName" required >
 Enter Your Phone Number:
 <input type="tel" name="myPhone" pattern="\d\d\d-\d\d\d-\d\d\d\d" />
 Enter Your Email: <input type="email" name="myEmail" />
 <input type="submit" />

</form>
```

Figure 1-4 shows our rendered view.

Figure 1-4.
Form with validation for required field

The CSS in the preceding code snippet adds a red border around the invalid field. The red border will remain until the proper content is entered.

We had to do this in two different ways due to browser support. The easy way was the method we used for the email address. The **input** knows what a valid input address looks like (i.e., the pattern of the address, not whether it works). So once a valid string is set to the proper value, the field will no longer appear with a red border.

The method we used for the telephone number was a little more difficult. Most modern browsers "partially" support the `tel` input type for HTML5. One thing that isn't supported is whether what is entered is indeed a valid telephone number. I could easily type my name into that field and it would validate. Here, we needed to go back to the `pattern` attribute and use a regex to determine whether it was a phone number. This particular regex isn't very useful, as it only checks to see if there is a digit string that matches this pattern: xxx-xxx-xxxx. It doesn't satisfy the use of brackets around an area code, nor does it support any numbers in a format other than that used in the United States. We'd need a more robust regular expression for that.

It would appear that our form is complete and ready to throw onto our website, but there are a few final details to point out. We assigned a `required` state to the `name`, as we desired, but note that a partially filled `input` will stop the form from submitting as well (the form field is invalid but not required, but this form must validate before it can be submitted). Adding `novalidate` to the form allows not only the invalid inputs to submit, but also the required ones as well. There is no clear solution for avoiding this, so let's move forward and address the issue with the user if it becomes a problem.

Before we try this form again, let's go back and update the Enter Your Name field to display a more user-friendly error message:

```
<style>
input {display: block;
border: 1px solid #ccc;
}

:invalid{
border-color: #DB729C;
  -webkit-box-shadow: 0 0 5px rgba(27, 0, 97, .5);
}

:required{
border-color: #1BE032;
  -webkit-box-shadow: 0 0 5px rgba(57, 237, 78, .5);
}

</style>

//our form
<form name="myForm" >
 Enter Your Name:
 <input type="text" name="myName" placeholder="Enter Your Name"
  oninput="updateMessage(this)" required>
 Enter Your Phone Number:
 <input type="tel" name="myPhone" pattern="\d\d\d-\d\d\d-\d\d\d\d" />
```

```
Enter Your Email: <input type="email" name="myEmail" />
<input type="submit" />

</form>

<script>
document.myForm.myName.setCustomValidity("To join our list..., please enter
it here")

function updateMessage(input){

if(input.value ==""){}
input.setCustomValidity('');

}

</script>
```

There we have it. In the past, such validation would have required a good amount of custom JavaScript. Now it can be done with the simplicity of HTML5!

HACK 06 Improve the Usability of Your Forms with New Controls

Your forms just got easier to use. HTML5 browsers include new controls such as the **date** input type, the **<range>** tag, and others.

We've been talking about form elements for the past few hacks now, and they all have a common thread when it comes to reasoning. Many of these simple, easy-to-implement specifications actually replace standards that web developers have been coding to for years. This has made life easier for developers, made pages perform more quickly (browser code instead of JavaScript), and brought uniformity across web applications.

Let's focus on uniformity for a bit. For example, let's look at the **date** input type. In the past, web developers have developed a date picker standard similar to the one shown in Figure 1-5, which is from the popular YUI library.

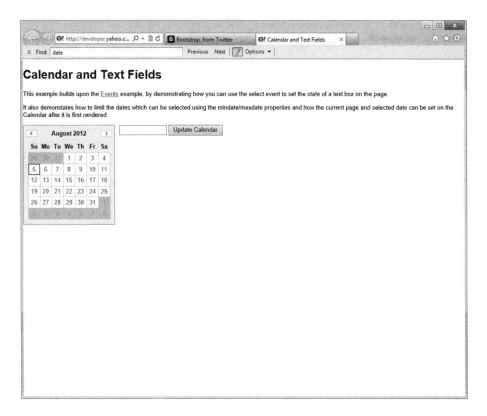

Figure 1-5.
The YUI date picker, which provides a clean interface for date selection

This is a huge improvement over having the user enter the date into an input field and hoping that it meets the required format. With the YUI date picker, we can stylize the component with CSS and make it look like it blends right in with our app. This has served our purposes for years. Whether we are using the Internet Explorer browser or the Firefox browser, our date picker will look the same and the user will always know what to expect.

Along comes mobile. Mobile browsers, for the most part, surf the same Web as our desktops. If you come across this same date picker on an iPhone, this previously great experience becomes difficult. Since the component has no awareness of the native content (it has a small screen in this scenario), it can't adapt to its context. Many keen JavaScript Ninjas have already started to think about how they can use the User Agent Declaration (part of the request) to customize this date picker for the context of each known user agent. This is a great idea, and many of our polyfill libraries, such as YUI, are a step ahead and provide concessions for small screens. Unfortunately, the only way to do this without HTML5 is to add more code. And more JavaScript, more markup, and more CSS equals page bloat and additional memory usage. Let's use that extra code and memory for something spectacular and leave the basic input functionality to the browser. Each of the following form features takes something that used to be hard to do in JavaScript and makes it easy, light, and context-aware.

The date Input Type

The **date** input type is one of my favorites. As in the previous date picker example, a lot of work has gone into creating a successful date selection tool. I can't tell you how many times I've been frustrated with parts of the Web that use date selection tools that are slow and buggy (yes, I mean you, airline and car rental sites).

The HTML5 **date** input type is fairly simple to implement. Out of the box it looks something like this:

```
<form name="dateSelection">

Enter Departing Date: <input type="date" name="departingDate" />
</form>
```

The preceding code results in the simple pull-down box shown in Figure 1-6.

Figure 1-6.
The date input field showing a date selector

In terms of context, here's the great thing about the preceding example. As it stands, the date selector will be pretty tough to use on my iPhone; not only is it hard to see, but also my fingers are pretty fat and those tap zones are pretty small. So in iOS 5 and later, Apple has kindly implemented the date input field shown in Figure 1-7.

Figure 1-7.
The date input field in the iOS 5 Safari browser on an iPhone

Nice job, Apple! Now let's look at some of the other attributes we can add to give this application a functionality similar to those great little polyfill date pickers. Here's the code:

```
<form name="dateSelection">
    Enter Departing Date: <input type="date"  min="2012-03-12" step="1"
                          max="2012-05-12" name="departingDate" />
    <input type="submit" />
</form>
```

Let's look at some of these in more detail:

step

> Increment at which a date can be selected. The spec doesn't clarify all the increment types that a user agent must adhere to, but day, week, month, and year are obvious implementations.

min

> A date value that represents the minimum date the input will consider valid. It's not clear whether the controller will allow you to choose dates below the min date, or whether it limits selection to the valid date range. Implementations differ among browser makers at this point.

max

> A date value that represents the maximum date the input will consider valid.

As is the case with all changes that are powerful, a new set of DOM methods has been added as well:

stepUp()/stepDown()

> Can be called to increment the date that is input to either the next date or the preceding date in the series. stepUp() calls the next day; stepDown() calls the preceding day.

valueAsDate()

> Returns a JavaScript date object, not just a date string.

This might not sound exciting, but you can replace this polyfill:

```
<form name="myForm">
  Birthday: <input type="text" name="bday" value="03/12/2012" />
  <input type="submit" />
</form>
<script>
var myInput = document.myForm.bday.value;
var myDate = new Date(myInput);
</script>
```

with this:

```
<form name="myForm">
  Birthday: <input type="date" name="bday" value="2012-03-12" />
  <input type="submit" />
</form>
<script>
var myInput = document.myForm.bday.valueAsDate();
</script>
```

It's also interesting to note that there are a few variations on the input type of **date**, and each provides noteworthy interface challenges, especially on mobile and touch devices. Here are some similar types to keep your eye on:

- datetime
- month
- week
- time
- datetime-local

The range Input Type

Once again, let's look at one of our great polyfill libraries to get an idea of what the problem is. Figure 1-8 shows a screen capture of the YUI slider utility.

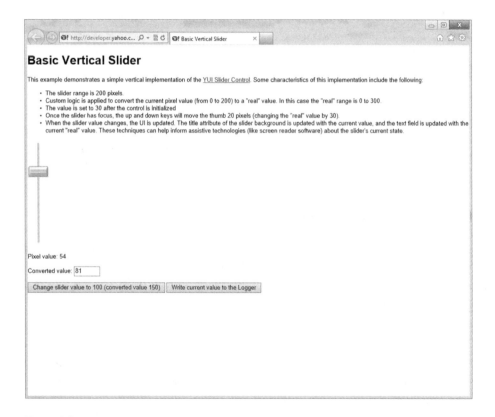

Figure 1-8.
A slider component for YUI (Yahoo! User Interface) library version 3.5

When you're selecting ranges, nothing is worse than typing in values, especially when you're "exploring" what will happen when those ranges change. The slider has become a standard tool on both web and desktop devices. You generally have a bar representing something like numeric values or colors, and a handle that you drag from one end of the bar to the other. Again, let's consider how difficult it may be to make selections on the YUI slider if you're on a mobile device. The handle is small, and what feels like a short amount of movement on a mobile device could be a sizable amount to the slider.

The HTML5 type of `range` allows browser makers to provide a range selection tool with an experience that best fits the context of the device. The pattern for desktop browsers appears to be a slider. Let's jump into the implementation:

```
<form name="myForm">
Shoe size: <input type="range" name="shoeSize" min="0" max="15" step=".5"
value="3" />

<input type="submit" />
</form>
```

All that, with no JavaScript—this polyfill would be hundreds of kilobytes' worth of code. Now let's look at some of the attributes we added to the input:

min/max

> Once again we see the ability to set a `min` and a `max` for the range. These are a bit more profound in the `range` input type because they define the first step (the bottom of the slider) and the top (the top of the slider). If no `min` and `max` are set, the user agent (again, the browser) will assume the range is 0 to 100.

step

> In the preceding example we are selecting shoe sizes that come in half or whole sizes. Therefore, we set the **step** to `.5` so that whole or half sizes can be chosen. This can come in handy in very large ranges as well. Say you are applying for a loan and you're using a range tool to choose your loan amount. For an improved user experience, you may want to round up to the nearest $10,000. Setting the `step` to `10,000` will allow you to do just that.

value

> We've seen **value** hundreds of times when it comes to input: it allows us to set the initial value of that input. It's of particular interest on the `range` input type, because there is no "null" value. Since it is a slider, there is no point at which the value would be undefined, so the user agent will choose a reasonable default value for you—something in the middle of the range. In our example, we chose our

value to be **3** since the most popular shoe size in our little store is size 3. (Yes, we do cater to elves, leprechauns, and small children.) The **value** allows you to choose the "default" value that makes the most sense, not just what's in the middle.

The HTML5 version of the sliders also has the added benefit of being able to match the other browser controls, as shown in Figure 1-9.

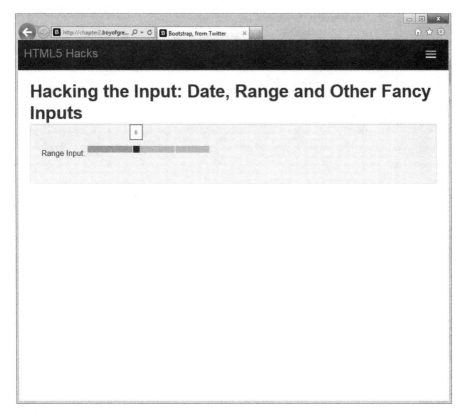

Figure 1-9.
HTML5 range input type from Internet Explorer 10 that matches other form elements on the page

It's also interesting to note that the range tool can be tied to a **datalist** (we discussed this briefly in Hack #04). The **datalist** could include non-numeric values or unequal numeric values that can be selected within the range. I haven't seen any browser makers implement this yet, but it will be interesting to see some possibilities.

The color Input Type

You may not have thought of a color picker as being essential to a user's web experience, but as the Web becomes more of an application environment, complex activities such as picking colors need to be responsive and adaptive. The `color` input type allows you to select a color value from within the input.

Support for this input type is still nascent, and at the time of this writing no user agent supports it. As with all of the other unsupported input types, browsers that do not (or do not yet) support the `color` input type will simply see an input tag as it would appear for an input with the `type` equal to `text`.

The <meter> and <progress> Tags

Moving slightly out of the input space but staying within the HTML5 form, we see two new form components that will quickly become basic building blocks for web applications. The first of the two is the `<meter>` tag. For a clear definition, let's go right to the spec:

> The meter element represents a scalar measurement within a known range, or a fractional value; for example disk usage, the relevance of a query result, or the fraction of a voting population to have selected a particular candidate.

Think of a meter as a bar from a bar chart. It's a graphical representation of one number as part of a greater number. Let's look at a code example:

```
<form name="myForm">
30%: <meter value="3" min="0" max="10"></meter><br />
30%: <meter value="0.3" low="0.4">30%</meter>

</form>
```

The preceding code would result in something like Figure 1-10.

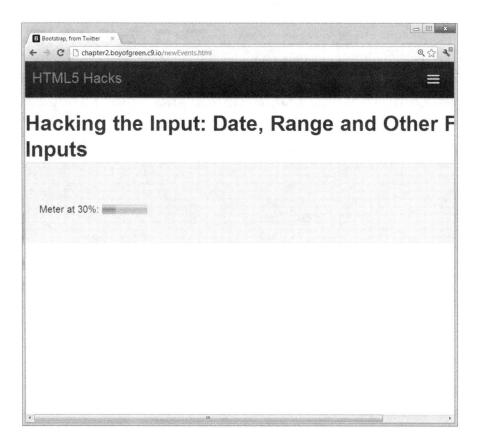

Figure 1-10.
The <meter> tag as it appears in Chrome for Windows

This particular form element has some interesting UI controls. You can see from the preceding example that the meter needs to have a value set, as well as a range, to be effective. The min and max attributes will set the range (the meter is completely empty and the meter is completely full, respectively), and the value will specify the current fill level. If either of the attributes is missing, the form will assume the value—for example, an undefined value will probably be considered zero by most user agents.

Additionally, three other attributes can be added to the meter to control the interface. The optimum value would display a graphical representation of what the ideal value would be. The low and high attributes are for setting thresholds when your meter is below or above the optimal range. The interface should respond accordingly; current browser implementations turn the meter color to yellow for "low" and red for "high."

The <progress> tag is also new for HTML5 forms. Think of the <progress> tag as the bar that pops up when you're downloading a file to tell you how much longer you have to wait. It might look something like Figure 1-11.

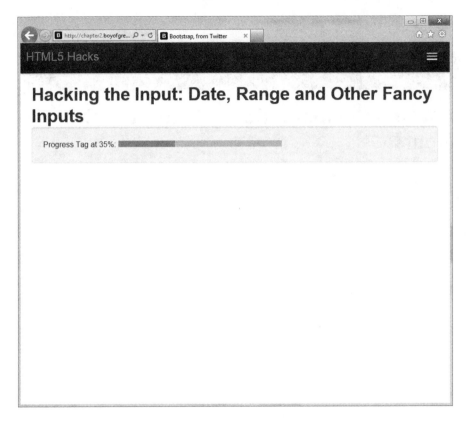

Figure 1-11.
The <progress> tag as it appears in Internet Explorer 10

The code implementation would be as follows:

```
<form name="myForm">
Downloading progress:
<progress value="35" max="100" >
</progress>
</form>
```

The **<progress>** tag has only a few configuration attributes, and both are shown in the preceding code. The first is the **max** attribute that tells you what your progress "goal" is. The **max** value will be the top of your meter; the bottom will always be zero. Your **value** will then specify the progress, and thus, how much of the progress bar is filled.

Once again, these two new tags are examples of web standards that traditionally were implemented with JavaScript and CSS but can now be accomplished directly through HTML5. Each tag should look appropriate for the context of the application.

Form Elements and Making Them Look Good

One thing all form elements have in common is that they look bad. Since I first started working with forms nearly 15 years ago, I've been trying to find ways to make them look better. A perfect example of this is the drop-down menu. Drop-downs look pretty simple. However, it's difficult to do anything special with them, such as adding help text to the options or controlling the width of the menu while it has options with a lot of text in them.

HTML5 and CSS3 bring us some good news and some bad news. The good news is that we can use CSS to control a lot of the treatments we've looked at in this hack. The bad news is that we can't control all of them. Let's look at a few examples.

```
<form name="myForm">

<input type="number" value="5" />
<input type="submit" />


</form>
//css
<style>
input[type=number]::-webkit-inner-spin-button,
input[type=number]::-webkit-outer-spin-button {
    -webkit-appearance: none;
    margin: 0;
}

</style>
```

In the preceding example, we have a **number** input type with some funky spinner buttons on it to increment and decrement the number. We don't want the funky buttons, so in CSS we specify (with browser prefixes) the subcomponents we want to alter. In this case they are `-webkit-inner-spin-button` and `-webkit-outer-spin-button`. We are simply hiding them in this example.

Browser makers are adding flexibility for many form controls. Most browser makers allow you to alter the look of the validation error pop-up windows as well. Some components, such as the **date** *and* **color** *input types, may not have CSS subcomponent controls.*

Keep in mind that this control is both good and bad. It's good when you just don't like the experience presented by the user agent and you need to update the look and feel on your own. In contrast, it's bad to makes changes to these elements because they then lack the ability to adapt to the context in which they are being used. Remember the drop-down menu I complained about earlier? Well, iOS has found a way to turn it into a brilliant user input on the iPad and iPhone. On the iPhone it becomes a spinner input at the bottom of the screen (see Figure 1-12). On the iPad it becomes a drop-down window in the context of the Select Box. In both cases, the input is well suited to its context. If you had CSS overrides on these components, who knows what the experience would be like for the end user on an iOS device.

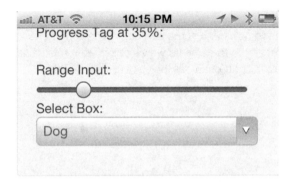

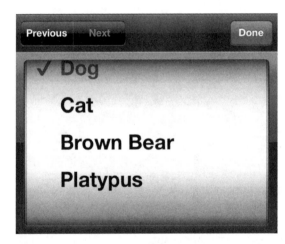

Figure 1-12.
The Select Box displayed in iOS 5 on the iPhone

In Conclusion

Now that we've explored the inner workings of forms, you should be ready to dive into some HTML5 applications. Forms are still the basic building blocks of pages, and to understand forms is to understand HTML5. So let's get going and dig in!

HACK 07 Know What's Going On in Your App with New DOM Events

HTML5 provides a slew of new events for you to latch on to. The world has moved beyond mouse clicks and keyboards. Now the Web has, too.

DOM events haven't changed much in the past 15 years. I think the last new DOM event we got was the mouse scroll (that's what you call that little spinner in the center of your mouse). Even touch events are not officially supported DOM events, although they are much more prevalent (and supported) than `DOMMouseScroll`.

With HTML5 we have tons of new input types to work with. As JavaScript is an event-driven language, it helps to work with a DOM that also natively fires events when actions take place. Some of these actions are directly related to a user interaction (such as the traditional DOM events), whereas others are related to events triggered by the user agent (such as going offline and coming back online). Let's start with a look at some form events.

The oninput, onchange, and oninvalid Events

In the past we have relied on **keydown** and **keyup** events quite often to determine what's going on within form elements. The bad thing about key events is that they don't specifically apply to the input element itself, as technically it's the document, not the input, which is receiving the keystrokes. This led us to trick the DOM, by temporarily adding key events after an input receives focus and removing the key listeners once the blur event of an input is fired. This has been terribly inefficient.

With the **oninput** event, a listener can be placed directly on an input tag (or bubbled up from one) and be associated with the actions of that input only. Let's look at a traditional listener with an **oninput** event instead of an **onkeypress** event:

```
<input id="myInput" type="text" placeholder="enter text">

<script>

document.getElementById('myInput').addEventListener('input',function(e){
  console.log("I just changed an input on:", e.target);
}, false);

</script>
```

Once you begin typing in the input field, the log will be fired. As you can see, the input event is attached to the **myInput** field, so input into any other input field will not trigger this event.

Similarly, we have two additional events that can be attached to the input field: **on change** and `oninvalid`. The **onchange** event fires once the `value` attribute is updated. You may not immediately see the need for an **onchange** event, since we do have `oninput` and numerous other events that can be triggered on an input change. But let's think about some of the new HTML5 elements, such as the input with **type** set to `range`. The range input or slider has no input mechanism; it simply changes. When I drag the handle from one position to another it doesn't fire an `oninput` event, only an **onchange** event. Similar events are required for other input mechanisms, such as date pickers, number wheels, and color pickers. These new input types make the onchange event not just handy, but essential.

The `oninvalid` event is a similar new event that is fired when a form element is deemed invalid. Unlike many of our other validity checks, current implementations do not work on the form element itself, but rather on the individual inputs. Remember a few hacks back when I was complaining about how the form elements weren't validated in real time (such as when you enter data into the input rather than at form submit) and that only the CSS state change was in real time? Let's look at an example of how we can put some of these events together to make the solution to my pet peeve a reality!

Real-Time Form Validation with the oninput/oninvalid Events

In order to validate an input field while the user is entering data into it, we need an event which fires as the user changes the value of the input. In the past we would have to follow troublesome keystrokes, but with the `oninput` event we can easily attach a listener to the input in question, and react to the change.

Once we catch that event we need to do some ad hoc validation checking, so for this we will go back to the `checkValidity()` method (see Hack #06) to get the input to self-validate. This can easily be fired from the `oninput` event. At this point, if the input is deemed invalid the `oninvalid` event will be fired alongside it.

The last thing we need to do is to attach an event listener to the `oninvalid` event, and have it fire a function that will indicate to the user that the value she entered is invalid. We'll follow this up with some CSS to reinforce the state of the input.

Let's take a look at the code:

```
<!DOCTYPE html>
<html>
<body>

<style>
input[type=number]{border: 2px solid green}
input:invalid {border: 2px solid red}
```

```
        </style>

        <form name="myForm">
          Pick a number, any number between 1 and 5:
          <input type="number" name="quantity" min="1" max="5" /> <br />
          <input type="submit" name="mySubmit" />
        </form>

        <script>
        document.myForm.quantity.addEventListener('input', function(e){
                                        this.checkValidity()
                                                }, false);

        document.myForm.quantity.addEventListener('invalid', function(e){
        alert('Your Number needs to be between 1 and five, you chose '+this.value
        +'.')
        }, false);
        </script>

        </body>
        </html>
```

Endless fun, right? We now have the best of both worlds: built-in validation with real-time responsiveness.

Other New Events

While we are on the subject of events, HTML5 is proposing the adoption of a slew of new events similar to the ones mentioned in the preceding section. Most of these events focus on a user action, and they fire before, after, and during the event. Here's a list of events that had not been adopted at the time of this writing, but are likely forthcoming:

onabort	oncanplay	oncanplay through	onchange	onclick
oncontextmenu	oncuechange	ondblclick	ondrag	ondragend
ondragenter	ondragleave	ondragover	ondragstart	ondrop
onduration change	onemptied	onended	oninput	oninvalid
onkeydown	onkeypress	onkeyup	onloadeddata	onloadedmeta data
onloadstart	onmousedown	onmousemove	onmouseout	onmouseover

onmouseup	onmousewheel	onpause	onplay	onplaying
onprogress	onratechange	onreadystate change	onreset	onseeked
onseeking	onselect	onshow	onstalled	onsubmit
onsuspend	ontimeupdate	onvolumechange	onwaiting	

HACK 08 Add Rich Context to Your Markup with Custom Data

HTML5 formalizes the ability to store data directly in the page element. The data is simple to add, and just as simple to access.

Custom data attributes give us the ability to add more richness and depth to our markup than we've ever been able to before. Custom data attributes, often called the `data-*` attributes, are an easy way to add contextual data to HTML5 markup. Just come up with an attribute name, prefix it with "data-", and add it to any HTML markup tag:

```
<ul id="carInventory" >
    <li class="auto" data-make="toyota" data-bodytype="sedan" data-year="2005">
    Light blue Toyota Prism
    </li>
</ul>
```

In the preceding example, we have information we want to present to the user that we include as text inside the tag. We also have contextual information that our app will want to use to provide additional functionality to the user. Before HTML5, this additional data would have been stored in one of two ways. Either we would have hacked up another attribute (such as the `class` attribute or the `id`) with a string that encoded all this information, or we would have kept a separate data source in JavaScript that had a reference to this tag linked to it. Neither of these options is very fun, and both require quite a few lines of JavaScript to become useful.

Being able to place this data in the element itself not only is convenient for access purposes, but also provides rich context. According to the HTML5 spec from the W3C, a custom data attribute is defined as the following:

A custom data attribute is an attribute in no namespace whose name starts with the string "data-", has at least one character after the hyphen, is XML-compatible, and contains no characters in the range U+0041 to U+005A (LATIN CAPITAL LETTER A to LATIN CAPITAL LETTER Z).[2]

In summary, it's an attribute that starts with "data-" and is in all lowercase letters. Now, let's be clear about the purpose of this data. We'll start with how we don't want to use it (let's get all that negative stuff out of the way!).

First, the data attribute shouldn't be used to replace an existing HTML attribute such as class name `id`. For example, if you want to add a unique identifier to an element of which there will only be one on the page, just use the `id`, because that is exactly what it is designed for. Having a `data-id` on all your elements will probably get you a healthy number of complaints from your friends and coworkers. Second, don't use the data element to make your code more "machine-readable." This is what microformatting is for, which we will discuss in depth in a few hacks. Your custom data attribute is intended to provide information that is relevant for your application, not for an external page reader (whether it is human or machine).

Now, on to the fun part! How *should* you use custom data attributes? Simply put, you should use them for "anything you need," with emphasis on the words *anything* and *you*. Anytime you need access to data about a DOM element or to data related to the information that element represents, store it in the custom data attribute.

In the following example we have a table that was built out dynamically in JavaScript from a database. The database has a local key that identifies each row of data, but that key only means something to our application; it doesn't have any value to the user. Before custom data attributes, we had to do something like this:

```
<table width="100%" border="1">
  <tr>
    <th class="key">key row</th>
    <th>Title</th>
    <th>Price</th>
  </tr>
  <tr>
    <td  class="key">323</td>
    <td>Google Hacks</td>
    <td>FREE</td>
  </tr>
  <tr>
    <td  class="key">324</td>
    <td>Ajax Hacks</td>
```

---

[2] *http://dev.w3.org/html5/spec/single-page.html#attr-data*

```
        <td>FREE</td>
    </tr>
    <tr>
        <td  class="key">325</td>
        <td>HTML5 Hacks</td>
        <td>FREE</td>
    </tr>
</table>
```

Then we had to use CSS to hide the first row (with a class name of **key**):

```
.key{
display: none
}
```

Another really bad solution involved using one of the existing attributes to store this data. In the following example the data is stored in the **id** attribute:

```
<table width="100%" border="1">
  <tr>
    <th>Title</th>
    <th>Price</th>
  </tr>
  <tr id="323">
    <td>Google Hacks</td>
    <td>FREE</td>
  </tr>
  <tr id="324">
    <td>Ajax Hacks</td>
    <td>FREE</td>
  </tr>
  <tr id="325">
    <td>HTML5 Hacks</td>
    <td>FREE</td>
  </tr>
</table>
```

There are so many problems with this solution that it's hard to know where to start. First, it's a horrible idea to store data in the **id** attribute. The **id** attribute is meant to be a unique identifier for HTML elements. Since it's associated with our database key, the key will change when the data changes, making it impossible to use that **id** to reference the element, as it's subject to change. Storing the key as a class name is equally bad, for similar reasons.

Now let's turn it around and put that essential data into a custom data attribute:

```
<table width="100%" border="1">
  <tr>
    <th>Title</th>
    <th>Price</th>
  </tr>
  <tr data-key="323">
    <td>Google Hacks</td>
    <td>FREE</td>
  </tr>
  <tr data-key="324">
    <td>Ajax Hacks</td>
    <td>FREE</td>
  </tr>
  <tr data-key="325">
    <td>HTML5 Hacks</td>
    <td>FREE</td>
  </tr>
</table>
```

Here we have simple markup that contains a reference to our database key, without unnecessary markup or prostitution of the **id** or **class** attribute. We didn't even have to write any CSS to make this work.

Accessing the Data

Another important piece of the puzzle concerns accessing the data. The W3C HTML5 spec has a clear method for collecting data in JavaScript. A **dataset** object is available on the HTML5 element that allows you to access your custom values by name:

```
<div id="myNode" data-myvalue="true">my node</div>

//javascript access to value
var nodeValue = document.getElementById('myNode').dataset.myvalue
//nodeValue = 'true'
```

Notice that we don't need the "data-" in front of our value; we just call our value name directly. This access method is great and meets the spec, but like many of our HTML5 features, it only works in HTML5 browsers. Interestingly enough, putting a custom data attribute of **sort** onto an element has worked in browsers for some time (it may not have validated, but it worked), all the way back to IE 6. However, note that the JavaScript access method is introduced with the HTML5 spec, but don't fret—we have a hack for that:

```
<div id="myNode" data-myvalue="true">my node</div>

//javascript access to value where nodeValue = 'true'
var nodeValue = document.getElementById('myNode').getAttribute('data-
myvalue')
```

Before, HTML5 browsers simply recognized the value as an attribute of the element, so a simple **getAttribute** method of the element would retrieve the data. Note that in this method, the "data-" part of the value is required to retrieve the data.

There is one more way to access this data, but it comes with a warning. Most current browsers support a CSS3 pseudoproperty (see Chapter 3 for more about pseudo-classes) on which you can base a style declaration. It looks something like this:

```
<div id='myNode' data-myvalue='true'>my node</div>

/*css declaration */
#myNode[data-myvalue]{
color: red;
}
```

or this:

```
#myNode[data-myvalue='true']{
color: red;
}
```

Now your CSS can style the element based on the presence of the custom data attribute, or by the value of the custom data. Here's your warning: *don't use custom data in place of CSS classes*. Class names are still the definitive way to declare reusable style rules. Remember, custom data is not intended to represent something to the user, but rather to provide context data for your application, which means that, in general, you don't want to use the previously demonstrated pseudoclasses.

`HACK 09` Track User Events with Custom Data

Tracking user events can be difficult on highly dynamic pages with JavaScript alone. It usually requires that you add and remove multiple listeners. With HTML5 custom data, you can have that same rich interaction on dynamic pages with a single listener.

One of the most difficult things about generating HTML markup with JavaScript is managing behaviors. Anyone who has worked with DOM events on a dynamic app knows that managing behaviors can be quite a hassle. This hack shows you a way to use custom data along with JavaScript event delegation to make an otherwise difficult task easy and lightweight.

We're not going to talk too much about event delegation; there are plenty of books and other resources out there that explain the details behind all of that. But it is important to know what event delegation is and why we do it.

Event delegation is the act of passing (or *bubbling*, to use a more accurate term) the captured event from an inner element to an outer element. Think about what happens when you click a button that is inside a list element (`li`). Since the button is inside the `li`, technically you clicked on both elements, so the browser by default passes or "bubbles" that click up from the button to the `li`. First the button executes its **on click** event, and then the `li` executes its own **onclick** event. Event delegation is when you allow your event (in this case, the click event) to bubble up to a parent element (in this case, the `li`), which then fires an event based on the fact that you clicked on the button.

Generally, event delegation allows you to use fewer event listeners on a page, as any one listener can handle an endless number of functions based on the different elements being clicked. Using event delegation generally uses less memory in your page, and makes maintenance of dynamic pages much simpler.

In this hack we will add a tool tip to a list of elements using custom data and only one event listener.

Let's start with our markup:

```
<div class="container">

  <h1>Choose Your weapon</h1>
  <p>
  Click on one of the selections below to find out more info
  about your character:
  </p>

  <ul id="myList">
    <li data-description="Most powerful goblin in entire kingdom" >Ludo</li>
    <li data-description="Ruler over all goblins big and small" >
    Jareth the Goblin King
    </li>
    <li data-description="Only person who can put a stop to the Goblin King" >
      Sarah
    </li>
    <li data-description="Unsung hero of the goblin kingdom" >
    Hoggle
```

```
        </li>
      </ul>
      <p id="displayTarg" class="well"></p>
    </div> <!-- /container -->
```

Figure 1-13 shows the results.

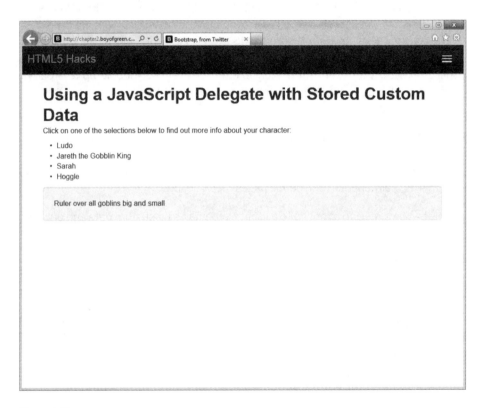

Figure 1-13.
Our simple content

Custom data attributes allow us to "inline" data in our elements by setting a string to the **data-** attribute of the element. (For a more in-depth look at custom data, see Hack #08.)

We are using an HTML5 page "primer" (the base page that we edit to get a quick start on development) called *twitter bootstrap*. It provides us with the clean look and feel for our markup; some of our additional class names come from that framework. Now let's add our listener to the unordered list (**ul**) so that we can take action on any of the items inside it:

```
        var mainElement = document.getElementById('myList');
        var descriptionTarget = document.getElementById('displayTarg');
```

```
mainElement.addEventListener('click', function(e){
    var description = e.target.getAttribute('data-description');
//remember we use getAttribute instead of
//dataset.description due to its backwards compatibility
    descriptionTarget.innerHTML = description;
    });
```

JavaScript event delegation is so much more powerful when you have access to additional data within the DOM element itself. Now imagine that this data was pulled from a database or JSON (JavaScript Object Notation) object and updated in the DOM. The list and markup can be updated, but the JavaScript does not need to change. The same listener can handle this list of four characters or a list of 400 characters, no matter how many times the list changes.

Can It Get Any Easier?

As markup gets more complex and we start to see elements nested inside other elements, finding the right **target** element to pull our description from can get pretty complicated. We are lucky to have many fine frameworks on the market that make event delegation easy to manage. Instead of managing the event target (**e.target** in the previous code) to get ahold of the right element, these frameworks allow us to write a few lines of code to make sure we're working with the right elements. Let's look at a few examples just to see how easy it is:

- YUI (Yahoo! User Interface) Library version 3.0 and later

```
Y.one('#myList').delegate('click', function(e){...}, 'li');
```

- jQuery Library version 1.7 and later

```
$("myList").on("click", "li", function(e) {...});
```

Embrace JavaScript event delegation, and make your markup more powerful with custom data attributes. You'll find yourself writing less code, taking up less memory, and living an overall happier life!

HACK 10 Make Your Page Consumable by Robots and Humans Alike with Microdata

HTML5 microdata provides the mechanism for easily allowing machines to consume the data on your pages, while not affecting the experience for the user.

If you're like me, you believe that in the future, machines will rule over us humans with an iron fist (provided, of course, that the Zombie Apocalypse doesn't get us first). While there isn't anything we can do to help the zombie masses understand the Internet, HTML5 does offer a feature that prepares us for that machine dictatorship. It's called *microdata*, and it's supposed to be for machines only—no humans allowed.

You can tell by now that HTML5 adds a lot of depth to your data, but up to this point the focus has been on your users. Microdata takes you down a slightly different path when you think about consumers who aren't your users. Microdata is additional context you add to your markup to make it more consumable. When you build your page, you can add these additional attributes to give further context to your markup.

Microdata can be added to any page element to identify that element as an "item" or a high-level chunk of data. The content nested inside that item can then be labeled as properties. These properties essentially become name–value pairs when the `item prop` becomes the value name and the human-readable content becomes the value. The relevant code would look something like this:

```
<div itemscope>
    <span itemprop="name">Fred</span>
</div>
```

Sometimes item property data isn't in the format that a "machine" would like, and additional attributes need to be added to clarify what the human-readable data is saying. In that scenario your data would look like this:

```
<div itemscope>
    Hello, my name is <span itemprop="name">Fred</span>.
    I was born on
    <time itemprop="birthday" datetime="1975-09-29">Sept. 29, 1975</time>.
</div>
```

Now imagine how consumable the Web would be for those machines of the future once microdata is utilized on every page!

In this hack we'll use microdata to make sure our contact list is machine-readable. Each contact entry will be identified as an item, and its contents will be labeled as a property. Our first contact will look like this:

```
<li itemscope>
    <ul>
        <li>Name: <span itemprop="name">Fred</span></li>
        <li>Phone: <span itemprop="telephone">210-555-5555</span></li>
        <li>Email: <span itemprop="email">thebuffalo@rockandstone.com</span>
        </li>
    </ul>
</li>
```

As you can see, we have constructed one data item on our page, and when the markup is machine-read it will see the item as something like this:

```
Item: {    name: 'Fred',
      telephone: '210-555-5555',
      email: 'thebuffalo@rockandstone.com'
      }
```

Now let's build ourselves a whole list:

```
<ul>
<li itemscope>
    <ul>
        <li>Name: <span itemprop="name">Fred</span></li>
        <li>Phone: <span itemprop="telephone">210-555-5555</span></li>
        <li>Email: <span itemprop="email">thebuffalo@rockandstone.com</span>
        </li>
    </ul>
</li>
<li itemscope>
    <ul>
        <li>Name: <span itemprop="name">Wilma</span></li>
        <li>Phone: <span itemprop="telephone">210-555-7777</span></li>
        <li>Email: <span itemprop="email">thewife@rockandstone.com</span>
        </li>
    </ul>
</li>
<li itemscope>
    <ul>
        <li>Name: <span itemprop="name">Betty</span></li>
        <li>Phone: <span itemprop="telephone">210-555-8888</span></li>
        <li>Email: <span itemprop="email">theneighbour@rockandstone.com
        </span></li>
    </ul>
</li>
<li itemscope>
    <ul>
        <li>Name: <span itemprop="name">Barny</span></li>
        <li>Phone: <span itemprop="telephone">210-555-0000</span></li>
        <li>Email: <span itemprop="email">thebestfriend@rockandstone.com
        </span></li>
    </ul>
</li>
</ul>
```

To our human friends, the page looks something like Figure 1-14.

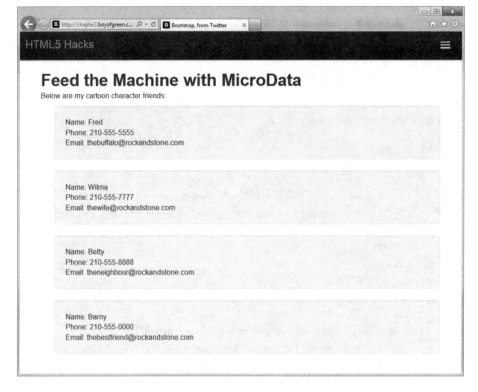

Figure 1-14.
Adding microdata to the page, which does not change the view for users

To our machine friends, the code looks something like this:

```
Item: {    name: 'Fred',
    telephone: '210-555-5555',
    email: 'thebuffalo@rockandstone.com'
    },
Item: {    name: 'Wilma',
    telephone: '210-555-7777',
    email: 'thewife@rockandstone.com'
    },
Item: {    name: 'Betty',
    telephone: '210-555-8888',
    email: 'theneighbor@rockandstone.com'
    },
Item: {    name: 'Barny,
    telephone: '210-555-0000',
    email: 'thebestfriend@rockandstone.com'
    }
```

It's that easy to add microdata to your page without sacrificing the interface for your human friends.

Details, Details!

Microdata is pretty darn easy to implement, and the W3C spec thinks it should be just as easy to read, which is why the W3C added a JavaScript API to be able to access the data. Remember, each of your identified elements was marked with an attribute called `itemscope`, which means the API considers them items. To get all these items, you simply call the following:

```
document.getItems();
```

Now your items can also be segmented by type, so you can identify some of your items as people, and others as cats. Microdata allows you to define your items by adding the `itemtype` attribute, which will point to a URL, or have an inline definition. In this case, if we defined our cat type by referring to the URL *http://example.com/feline*, our cat markup would look something like this:

```
<li itemscope itemtype="http://example.com/feline">
    <ul>
        <li>Name: <span itemprop="name">Dino</span></li>
        <li>Phone: <span itemprop="telephone">210-555-4444</span></li>
        <li>Email: <span itemprop="email">thecat@rockandstone.com</span>
        </li>
    </ul>
</li>
```

And if we wanted to get items with only a specific type of cat, we would call:

```
document.getItems("http://example.com/feline")
```

Thanks to this simple API, your microdata-enriched markup is both easy to produce and easy to consume.

2

Hacking with Style

I remember designing websites without CSS. It was horrible—lots of tables and images and image maps. Back in the day, most sites took several minutes to load because generally they were so overladen with image hacks in an effort to achieve a decent design. Then CSS came along and it was spectacular! Suddenly the Web had standards, you could separate your functionally into your JavaScript, your markup into your HTML file, and your look and feel into your CSS file.

Just as HTML went through a decade without seeing any true updates, CSS followed nearly the same path, which is why I am so excited that the HTML5 revolution brought CSS3 along with it. This chapter focuses primarily on another spec within the HTML5 family of technologies: Cascading Style Sheets version 3.0, a.k.a. CSS3. HTML5 may bring us a whole new world of functionality, but CSS3 blows the doors open on the user experience!

A Word About Browser Prefixes

One important thing to note within this chapter is the use of *browser prefixes* for new CSS3 attributes. In brief, a browser prefix is an extension placed at the beginning of a CSS3 class to be used while that feature is in an experimental stage. For additional information on browser prefixes, see Hack #11.

In my references and code examples, I chose to not utilize browser prefixes, even when the prefix may be required for the example. The reason is simple: browsers are updating at a pace at which a print book cannot keep up. It is very likely that some functionality may require a browser prefix at the time of this writing, but may drop the prefix by the time the book is released.

I suggest that you research the browsers you are supporting with your application to validate which browsers need browser prefixes for which features. It's also good during development, or while implementing one of the examples within this book, to attempt to use the features with the proper CSS3 attribute directly, and then only add the browser prefix if the functionality fails.

CSS3 is a powerful tool, but due to the high level of features it offers in the experimental release phase, it can be difficult to implement at times. Using the hacks in this chapter, however, can bring clarity to this exciting new technology.

HACK 11 Use Experimental CSS Features with Browser Prefixes

Browser makers often give you access to the experimental version of CSS3 features before the specifications are finalized. Browser prefixes enable you to implement some of these experimental features early on in their development.

CSS3 features came on the scene quickly with the rapid adoption of WebKit-based browsers (WebKit is an open source browser layout engine developed by Apple). The CSS feature richness of the WebKit-based browsers encouraged other browser makers such as Firefox, Internet Explorer, and Opera to advance their adoption of CSS3 features as well.

Browser adoption of CSS moved at such an accelerated rate that it literally outpaced the development of the specifications. This led to browser makers implementing features that were still in draft or experimental mode. This resulted in features being implemented differently by different browser makers, as the feature specification was not yet solidified.

To clear up the confusion and allow developers to implement these features while they were still in the experimental stages, browser makers developed browser prefixes. The browser prefix is prepended to the attribute name to limit its implementation to that specific browser. Table 2-1 lists the most common browser prefixes.

Table 2-1. CSS browser prefixes by extension

PREFIX	BROWSER
-khtml-	Konqueror (really old Safari)
-moz	Firefox
-o	Opera
-ms	Internet Explorer
-webkit	Safari, Chrome, Silk, Android, and other WebKit-based browsers

It's common to see CSS3 implemented with a style declaration, and then repeated each time with the browser prefix of each browser that has early support for that feature. Your CSS may look something like this:

```
.testClass {
width: 100%;
color: #fff;
transform: rotate(30deg);
-ms-transform: rotate(30deg); /* IE 9 */
-webkit-transform: rotate(30deg); /* all webkit browsers */
-o-transform: rotate(30deg); /* Opera */
-moz-transform: rotate(30deg); /* Firefox */
}
```

This gives flexibility to the developer to utilize CSS3 features on the browsers that support them and not affect the browsers that don't. Let's assume you're only comfortable supporting the Firefox version of the transform feature, and you want all other browsers to fall back to nontransformed text. Your CSS would look something like this:

```
.testClass {
width: 100%;
color: #fff;
transform: rotate(30deg);
-moz-transform: rotate(30deg); /* Firefox */
}
```

Notice that the traditional **transform** attribute is left in place. Once the specification for the CSS3 transform solidifies, browser makers will drop the prefix and utilize the default attribute. It's usually a good idea for you to add the traditional attribute when using browser prefixes to future-proof your CSS.

The Browser Prefix Controversy

The web development community holds a split opinion on the use of browser prefixes. Browser prefixes have been beneficial for the application of these early supported features. Since the features were implemented before the specifications were finalized, prefixes did allow developers to utilize the experimental version of the functionality without having to worry about writing CSS that would someday stop working.

The negative aspect of browser prefixes was the added flexibility it gave developers. For years, the web development community pushed back on browser makers to be standards-based, encouraging them to build browsers that followed the W3C specifications and guidelines instead of building uniquely supported features. The goal was to write a single code base that rendered properly in any browser. Browser prefixes reopen the door for developers to write code that only works in a subset of browsers.

It's ultimately up to the development community to keep browser prefixes in check. When you write CSS with browser prefixes, consider all browsers that support that feature. Utilize the browser prefixes when necessary, but do your part to not "fork" the Web...again.

HACK 12 Design with Custom Fonts Using Web Fonts

Your web page doesn't have to settle for those plain old "web-safe" fonts anymore. Freshen up your designs with CSS3 web fonts.

Web fonts aren't actually a new concept for CSS. They were originally proposed for CSS version 2.1, but they were dropped before the spec was finalized. Oddly enough, one browser maker did implement the feature early on, and surprisingly, it was Internet Explorer. IE has supported web fonts since IE version 5 back in 1999. However, like most features developed for the Web in the 1990s, web fonts were implemented in a proprietary fashion, only supporting one type of font. IE 5 supported the EOT (Embedded OpenType) font, which was never adopted by other browser makers. Thus, web fonts went the way of the Jedi until their rebirth in CSS3.

Having access to the proper fonts can make or break a design. For decades, web developers had been limited to a small subset of web-safe fonts to work with, and have pushed the limits of Arial and Verdana. Prior to the adoption of CSS3 web fonts (first seen in Safari 3.1), CSS allowed us to specify a list of the font families we wanted to use on our web page, and the browser would cycle through the list of fonts until it came across a font that was installed on the user's machine. The declaration looked something like this:

```
body {
font-family: Verdana,Arial,Helvetica,sans-serif;
}
```

There was no guarantee that the user would have access to the font we wanted to use, so it was customary to list a few fonts in order of preference so that the browser could select the one that best completed our design. The last font in the preceding list, sans-serif, refers to a generic type of font that the browser is sure to support, as it's required to identify a font within its system for each high-level font family.[1]

CSS3 doesn't actually change the way you apply the font-family attribute. You still follow the same pattern of listing your desired fonts in order of preference. Let's restate the CSS rule shown earlier, this time listing our new preferred font first:

---

[1] The generic font families that each browser supports are the following: serif, sans-serif, monospace, cursive, and fantasy.

```
body {
font-family: Radley,Arial,Helvetica,sans-serif;
}
```

Without any additional changes, every browser will apply the Radley font to the body text of the page if it has this font installed. As it's extremely unlikely that a user will have this specific font, the CSS3 `font-face` declaration can be applied to greatly improve the chances of this particular font being available for use. The declaration needs to be made only once per page, and it isn't associated with any particular `font-family` attribute or any CSS rule. It's simply declared:

```
@font-face {
font-family: Radley; src: local('Radley'), url('Radley.woff');
}
```

Once your font is imported, it can be utilized by any CSS declaration. Now, in the preceding example, any browser that supports **@font-face** or that has the Radley font installed will use Radley on the page, and all other browsers will cycle through the fallback chain until they find a font they can use.

Let's look at a specific use of a few imported fonts. In the next example we will use our example page to display a few unique font treatments. Figure 2-1 shows our end product.

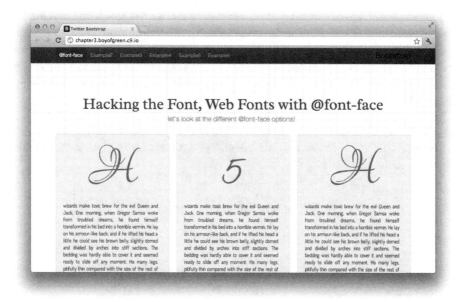

Figure 2-1.
Using web fonts to utilize fonts in our design that a user doesn't have installed on the client machine

We've added three distinctive fonts on this page (in addition to some traditional fonts we used in the primer page). The first thing we want to do is to bring the fonts into the page so that we can access them. This is where the import comes in:

```css
@font-face {
  font-family: 'Radley';
  font-style: normal;
  font-weight: normal;
  src: local('Radley'), url('/f/Radley.woff') format('woff');
}
@font-face {
  font-family: 'Lovers Quarrel';
  font-style: normal;
  font-weight: 400;
  src:local('Lovers Quarrel'), url('/f/quarrel.woff') format('woff');
}
@font-face {
  font-family: 'Dosis';
  font-style: normal;
  font-weight: 400;
  src: local('Dosis Regular'), url('/f/dosis.woff') format('woff');
}
```

Each font has two declarations in the `src`. The first is the local name of the font. It's a good practice to specify this for all your fonts; if the user has this same font loaded locally, we can save the user the payload of loading it from the Web. The second declaration is the `url`. If the browser doesn't find the font locally, it is imported into our page. The `font-family` attribute specifies how we refer to the imported font on the page (the name of the font). The only required attributes are the `font-family` and the `src`.

Our CSS that utilizes the imported font should look pretty familiar. We identify the imported fonts in the same way we have always assigned fonts. Here is the CSS we wrote to customize this page font:

```css
.fontHeader {
    font-family: Radley, Arial, sans-serif;
    }

h2.fontHeader {
    font-size: 12em;
    line-height: 1em;
    font-family: Lovers Quarrel, Arial, serif;
    text-align: center;
    color: #c91c10;
```

```
}

.smallFont {
    font-family: Dosis, Arial, sans-serif;
    text-align: justify;
    }
```

Notice that our fallback fonts are still listed in our `font-family` declaration. If the browser fails to load the font, we want the browser to fall back to its best alternative. With a few imports and a few new CSS declarations, we've given our page that custom design that gives it much needed character, and sets it apart from the rest!

Working with Different Versions of Fonts

A lot of times you have one font that comes in normal, bold, italic, or myriad other variations. Generally, this means loading multiple fonts to support your type. Let's see what the CSS would look like:

```
@font-face {
  font-family: 'Radley';
  src: local('Radley'), url('/f/Radley.woff') format('woff');
}

@font-face {
  font-family: 'RadleyBold';
  src: local('Radley'), url('/f/RadleyBold.woff') format('woff');
}

@font-face {
  font-family: 'RadleyItalic';
  src: local('Radley'), url('/f/RadleyItalic.woff') format('woff');
}

.fontHeader {
    font-family: Radley, Arial, sans-serif;
    }

.fontHeader.bold {
    font-family: RadleyBold, Arial, sans-serif;
    }

.fontHeader.italic {
    font-family: RadleyItalic, Arial, sans-serif;
    }
```

This works just fine; you can access the normal, bold, and italic versions of your fonts. But it's a real mess to implement, and it's prone to human error. Let's go back to those imports and define these same characteristics when we import them:

```
@font-face {
  font-family: 'Radley';
  font-style: normal;
  font-weight: normal;
  src: local('Radley'), url('/f/Radley.woff') format('woff');
}

@font-face {
  font-family: 'Radley';
  font-style: normal;
  font-weight: 800;
  src: local('Radley'), url('/f/RadleyBold.woff') format('woff');
}

@font-face {
  font-family: 'Radley';
  font-style: italic;
  font-weight: normal;
  src: local('Radley'), url('/f/RadleyItalic.woff') format('woff');
}
```

and now the easy implementation:

```
.fontHeader {
    font-family: Radley, Arial, sans-serif;
    }

.fontHeader.bold {
    font-weight: 800;
    }

.fontHeader.italic {
    font-style: italic;
    }
```

By setting the style and weight on the import, we can control the style and weight with simple, familiar attributes. This helps us keep our CSS clean, and since we now build our declarations just like we would with any font, we are a lot less prone to error.

A Few Things to Note: Support and Performance

IE 5 started supporting web fonts more than 10 years ago, yet web developers hadn't really been able to use them until CSS3 support became prolific. Looking back, it might have had something to do with the fact that IE only supported one type of font for the Web (EOT) and no one else supported it. The CSS3 implementation opens up the support model significantly. The CSS3 font-face attribute supports most modern font types: TTF (TrueType fonts), OTF (OpenType fonts), WOFF (web-only font format), EOT (Embedded OpenType, IE only), and SVG-generated fonts. Not all browsers support all font types equally.

It's also key to note that it does take time to load a font. Browsers can still display a web page when it's loading fonts, but most browsers will not show the text utilizing the imported font until the font is loaded. Be cautious, as this could result in a problematic user experience. There is no specified limit to the number of fonts you want to use on a page, or the number of times you want to use each font, but remember that in most cases you need to load that font from the Web, so consider the number of fonts and the size of the fonts you are using on each page.

HACK 13   Use Google Web Fonts for Simple @font-face Implementation

Web fonts are great for your design, but they can sometimes be a hassle to manage. Google Web Fonts makes the implementation simple, and the management even simpler.

> *Special thanks go to Dave Crossland from the Google Web Fonts team for contributing to the content of this hack. Dave is a libre fonts specialist and can be found at @davelab6 on Twitter.*

As you learned in Hack #12, CSS3 web fonts can be a powerful design tool. They allow you to use any font you want, whether the user has that font installed or not. With all the benefits that come along with using web fonts, there are a few drawbacks as well.

I mentioned previously that fonts can sometimes be resource-intensive, and they take time to load from a server and to render on a page. In most browsers (all but Firefox at the time of this writing) this means your user doesn't see any of your web-font-enabled text until the fonts are fully loaded. This could be a less-than-desirable experience for a user who is waiting for a few fancy fonts to load.

There is another problem that can put a damper on "fun with fonts": the legal system. Just because you have access to a font doesn't mean you have the right to use that font in your web application. It definitely doesn't mean you have the permission to distribute the font—and yes, putting a font on a publicly accessible web server can be considered distribution.

Now that I've sucked all the fun out of web fonts, let's look at one very practical solution from the protector of the Internet, Google! Google Web Fonts is a service that provides access to a collection of open source fonts, which you can use freely in your web applications. Here's what Google says about this project:

> The API service runs on Google's servers. They are fast, reliable and tested. Google provides the service free of charge. It is possible to add Google Web Fonts to a website in seconds.[2]

Google's service is fast and, in most cases, delivers fonts even faster than you could yourself. In fact, every font comes with an analysis of the amount of time it will add to your page load if you utilize that particular font. On each font page you'll find a chart that looks something like Figure 2-2.

Figure 2-2.
Font page from Google Web Fonts service displaying the visual impact this particular font will have on your page performance (right side of screen)

---

[2] http://www.google.com/webfonts#AboutPlace:about

The fonts available through the Google Web Fonts service are also open source. This helps you immensely with the legal aspect of font use. Each font you find in the service will already be curated to make sure it is licensed for you to use. This not only helps you avoid any questions about your permission to use the fonts, but it also means you don't have to worry about any issues regarding distribution.

Easy Implementation of Google Web Fonts

Google Web Fonts gives you a few easy ways to implement your web fonts (if you're not familiar with the CSS3 implementation, review Hack #12). To begin, fire up your favorite HTML5 web browser and go to the Google Web Fonts page (*http://google.com/webfonts*). This will land you on the gallery view of the directory. Although you have the option to filter and browse fonts, let's search for a specific one. Enter the font name **Bitter** into the Search box and only one font should come up. Select the Quick Use feature to get more information about how to use the font. There are three main implementation methods: Standard, @import, and JavaScript. Let's look at the Standard version first.

Leave it to Google to make something easy even easier. Standard implementation has you add one line of code to your HTML document:

```
<link href='http://fonts.googleapis.com/css?family=Bitter'
   rel='stylesheet' type='text/css'>
```

When you load this stylesheet, it adds this declaration to your page:

```
@font-face {
  font-family: 'Bitter';
  font-style: normal;
  font-weight: 400;
  src: local('Bitter-Regular'), url('http://themes.googleusercontent.com/
static/fonts/bitter/v4/SHIc
Xhdd5RknatSgOzyEkA.woff') format('woff');
}
```

If you read Hack #12, this might look familiar to you. The stylesheet is simply loading an **@font-face** declaration. Once the font is loaded, it can be used by any CSS declaration on *any* stylesheet. Simply add the name to your styles:

```
h1 {
font-family: Bitter, Georgia, serif; font-weight: 400;
}
```

The second implementation type is @import. To import the font, add this line of code to your stylesheet or to a style block within your HTML page:

```
@import url(http://fonts.googleapis.com/css?family=Bitter);
```

This will load the same stylesheet with the same **@font-face** declaration.

The third option, JavaScript, will load the same CSS stylesheet, but this time it will load it dynamically with a script:

```
<script type="text/javascript">
  WebFontConfig = {
    google: { families: [ 'Bitter::latin' ] }
  };
  (function() {
    var wf = document.createElement('script');
    wf.src =('https:' == document.location.protocol?'https':'http')
    +'://ajax.googleapis.com/ajax/libs/webfont/1/webfont.js';
    wf.type = 'text/javascript';
    wf.async = 'true';
    var s = document.getElementsByTagName('script')[0];
    s.parentNode.insertBefore(wf, s);
  })(); </script>
```

This script dynamically loads a JavaScript file that will in turn dynamically load your CSS file.

Although there are benefits and trade-offs to each of these loading methods, my recommendation is to try each one in your app, and look for the one that yields the best results for your situation.

Now let's say you want to load a few different fonts for your page. Google Web Fonts calls this a *collection*, and will help you do this with as little impact as possible. Let's go back to the Google Web Fonts directory (*http://google.com/webfonts*) and select a few fonts at once. This time click the Add to Collection button. I'm going to search for three of my favorite fonts: Merriweather, Bitter, and Alegreya. Once you have chosen a few fonts, click the Use button and you will be taken to a familiar page that provides you with the code to add this collection of fonts to your pages. You'll notice in Figure 2-3 that my page load meter has gone up since I am loading three fonts instead of one.

Adding a collection is just as easy as adding a single font. I'll choose the standard method:

```
<link href='http://fonts.googleapis.com/css?family=Bitter|Merriweather
|Alegreya' rel='stylesheet' type='text/css'>
```

If we preview the CSS file added to my page, we will see three **@font-face** declarations instead of one:

```
@font-face {
  font-family: 'Alegreya';
  font-style: normal;
  font-weight: 400;
```

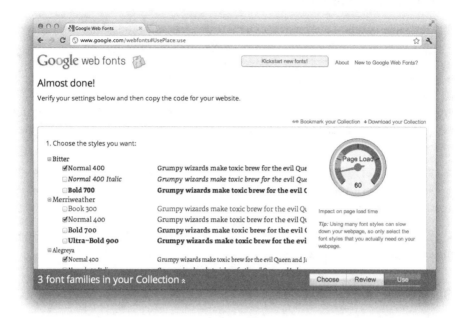

Figure 2-3.
Google Web Fonts collection showing page performance impact of utilizing three fonts

```
    src: local('Alegreya'), local('Alegreya-Regular'),
url('http://themes.googleusercontent.com/static/fonts/alegreya/v3/MYF
QxfgoxFvFirdbdLj3M_esZW2xOQ-xsNqO47m55DA.woff') format('woff');
}
@font-face {
    font-family: 'Bitter';
    font-style: normal;
    font-weight: 400;
    src: local('Bitter-Regular'),
url('http://themes.googleusercontent.com/static/fonts/bitter/v4/SHIcXh
dd5RknatSgOzyEkA.woff') format('woff');
}
@font-face {
    font-family: 'Merriweather';
    font-style: normal;
    font-weight: normal;
    src: local('Merriweather'),
url('http://themes.googleusercontent.com/static/fonts/merriweather/v4/
RFda8w1V0eDZheqfcyQ4EHhCUOGz7vYGh680lGh-uXM.woff') format('woff');
}
```

Nontraditional Font Access

Although Google offers a number of options for loading web fonts, there may be some scenarios that just don't fit into the provided options. Don't lose hope. There is a hack for this situation, too! Google Web Fonts allows you to take your fonts with you. Nestled in the corner of each Use page is a link to download all the fonts in your current collection. This gives you the ability to package those fonts locally, or even use them locally through another application such as Adobe Photoshop. This is essential for designers who do mockups in Photoshop, and want to use the same font in their mockup as they do in their final project.

For even greater flexibility, Google gives developers full API access to the Web Fonts service. The team provides additional guidance on its website (*https://developers.google.com/webfonts/docs/developer_api*).

API access is essential for any developer who wants to build functionality on top of the existing Google services.

Optimizing Your Font Usage

As if all this isn't enough, here's where Google Web Fonts gets really good! Loading fonts can be a drag in terms of page load time, but Google Web Fonts has another trick up its sleeve to make implementation a little lighter. Many times, special fonts are used in more static portions of your page where the content is predictable. For these circumstances, Google has built a font request optimization feature (note that this feature is in beta at the time of this writing).

Each implementation loads a CSS file that contains the `@font-face` declaration. The URL of the file looks something like this:

```
http://fonts.googleapis.com/css?family=Inconsolata
```

To specify a limited character set in your font file, add a *query string parameter* to the end of the called text, by adding **&text=** to the end of the URL. Then specify your character set after the text parameter as follows:

```
http://fonts.googleapis.com/css?family=Inconsolata&text=Hello
```

This will return an optimized font file that can reduce the download size by up to 90%. This is a smart way to utilize your favorite fonts while keeping the file sizes manageable for your users.

Common Mistakes

Utilizing fonts can require a lot of work, and doing it well can require even more work. A lot of effort went into making Google Web Fonts easy to use, but there are a few easy-to-make mistakes to bring to your attention.

In some cases it can be too easy to load web fonts on your page—so easy that you can be prone to load more fonts than you need. Many Google web fonts offer more than your standard weight (400) and style. Let's go back to one of my favorite fonts, Bitter. Let's search for "Bitter" and view the Use page (see Figure 2-4).

Figure 2-4.
Google Web Fonts Use page for the Bitter font

You'll notice that on this page you can access multiple versions of the Bitter font. Whether you download all weights and styles so that you have access to them or you load some of the additional versions unintentionally, keep in mind that web fonts can have an adverse effect on the performance of your page. The more font versions you load, the longer it will take to render your page. It's highly recommended that you use the Collection Builder in Google Web Fonts to specify the exact fonts and styles you need to load for your web application.

A second common problem has more to do with the proper use of fonts. It's quite common to use custom web fonts in the headers on your pages. Headers also have a little-known "feature" called auto-bolding. Browsers provide base styles for each of their HTML tags. A common example is an indentation of each list item (li) nested inside an unordered list (ul). Another common style is to make headers larger and heavier than all other text. Typical text has a font weight of 400; most browsers set a default font weight for headers at 700.

Let's look back at that Use page for the Bitter font. This particular font provides a version in a font weight of 700 so that the font will render properly. Not all fonts provide a version in a font weight of 700; in fact, many only provide a standard version in a font weight of 400.

Let's look at a font that only provides the standard font weight of 400. The font Inconsolata is a great example (see Figure 2-5).

Figure 2-5.
Google Web Fonts Use page for the Inconsolata font

Here is the CSS:

```
p{
font-family: Inconsolata, Arial, Sans Serif;
}
```

It's a great-looking font. Now let's apply that same font to a header (see Figure 2-6).

Here is the CSS:

```
h1{
font-family: Inconsolata, Arial, Sans Serif;
}
```

Figure 2-6.

Inconsolata font on an h1 header allowing its default font weight of 700 to be utilized

Since a version of Inconsolata in a font weight of 700 isn't available, the browser kicks in and tries to compensate by applying its own version of bold to the font. This usually ends in a noticeably ugly product.

Luckily, the solution is fairly simple. You need to reset the font weight to 400 for your font that would be affected by auto-bolding. Many CSS resets (an additional CSS file you add to your page to wipe out all the default styles set by the browser) will remove the font weight for you with code that looks something like this:

```
h1, h2, h3, h4, h5 {
    font-weight: 400;
    }
```

I prefer this method, as it gives a predictable baseline for all browsers, but it might make more sense for you to reset your font weight when you implement your **font-family** reference to your problematic font. The code might look something like this:

```
h1{
font-family: Inconsolata, Arial, Sans Serif;
font-weight: 400;
}
```

Either option will guarantee a pristine implementation of your web font. For more information about Google Web Fonts, visit the product home page (*http://www.google.com/webfonts*).

HACK 14 Use CSS3 Text Effects to Make Your Text Not Suck

CSS3 text effects finally give you control over your text. Explore some of the newest and greatest text control features with CSS3 text effects.

CSS has always been spectacular to developers and designers. We love the power of controlling look and feel with a simple declaration. Unfortunately, as we learned the inner workings of the style language we started to realize its shortcomings. For a language designed to style HTML (remember the "T" stands for "Text"), we have never had a lot of control over text. I've often seen the limitations of CSS text control, as illustrated with the simple phrase shown in Figure 2-7.

Figure 2-7.
Popular CSS example that shows the limitation of text flow control

Figure 2-7 was created from this CSS:

```
p.test{
    width: 45px;
    padding:5px;
    border: 1px solid black;
    text-transform: uppercase;
}
```

and from this markup:

```
<p class="test"> CSS is awesome!</p>
```

This "bug" occurs because CSS cannot wrap text that doesn't contain spaces. In the past, we've had to employ JavaScript solutions or manually enter break tags, neither of which was elegant. Finally, CSS3 solves the problem. Let's take the same markup we had before, a simple line of text inside a paragraph, and apply a new CSS attribute to it (see Figure 2-8).

Figure 2-8.
New and improved CSS example with word-wrap feature

Here is the CSS that was used to create Figure 2-8:

```
p.test{
    width: 45px;
    padding:5px;
    border: 1px solid black;
    word-wrap:break-word;
    text-transform: uppercase;
}
```

And here is the markup:

```
<p class="test"> CSS3 is awesome!</p>
```

Now, CSS3 is truly awesome! The **word-wrap** attribute allows your text to break within a word to the next line. CSS will add a hyphen at the word break by adding an additional attribute of **word-break: hyphen**. Now your HTML can lay out text just like your word processor.

The Text Shadow Property

Sometimes what makes type so impactful isn't just the font, but the way it's presented. That's why text shadows are getting web designers so excited. In the past, shadow text required the use of images or Flash objects. With CSS3, shadow text can be controlled through a few attributes:

```
h2{
text-shadow: 2px 2px 4px #ccc;
}
```

The resultant text appears as shown in Figure 2-9.

Text Shadow is Awesome!
No Text Shadow is NOT Awesome!

Figure 2-9.
An h1 header with a text shadow contrasted against an h1 header without a shadow

Let's break down the different properties we are using with this attribute:

h-value
> Distance of horizontal shadow, negative or positive

v-value
> Distance of vertical shadow, negative or positive

blur size
> Size of blur of text, optional

color
> Color of shadow

It's as simple as that—a drop shadow test without the weight of Flash or images!

Other Text Controls

CSS3 adds a list of additional text controls that give you more control over your text and expand the usefulness of HTML as a language. Some of these new controls are geared primarily toward publishing in non-Latin-based languages. A full list of these controls is available in the W3C Level 3 text specification (*http://www.w3.org/TR/css3-text/*).

HACK 15 Make Elements Appear Transparent Without Altering the Opacity

Opacity enables you to make items appear to be transparent, but it often comes with unexpected side effects, especially with nested items. CSS3's introduction of alpha transparency gives you the freedom to use transparency without the side effects.

You can use transparency to give the illusion of depth in your design. Most commonly you would use transparency to mute the screen with an overlay, or add a drop shadow to a menu. Transparency gives the eye the impression of three-dimensional space within your application.

For many years, opacity was the primary mechanism used to provide transparency. This widely supported feature is present in virtually all browsers released in the past six years. You can add opacity to any element with the following attribute:

```
.opacity {
    opacity: .5;
}
```

The best thing about opacity is also the worst thing about it: opacity is an inherited characteristic. In CSS, some properties apply to the element the declaration is written for (such as **background-color**), whereas others pass on those values to their children (such as **font-family**). Opacity does neither. Opacity passes on the characteristic. In the preceding example, every child element inside an element with a class of **opacity** will also have opacity of 50%. This isn't an inherited property that can be changed or reset. Let's look at an example of nested opacity:

```
<div class="opacity">
    <p class="opacity">this is text</p>
</div>
```

In the preceding example, the text will render with opacity of .25 or 25%, since it has inherited the characteristic of opacity twice. Sometimes the inherited characteristic can be useful, but other times it can cause problems that require that you circumvent the property altogether.

Introducing Alpha Transparency

CSS3 introduced two new color options with an additional parameter for alpha transparency: RGBA and HSLA.

RGB and HSL are color formats you can use to generate millions of colors. The A channel is added to each format to provide an option for setting the alpha transparency to your color. This enables you to alter the percentage of "light" that passes through your color to allow objects behind it to be seen.

This concept is best understood through illustration. Figures 2-10, 2-11, and 2-12 show a set of RGB (red, green, blue) color circles in different states of opacity and transparency.

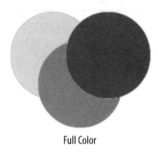

Full Color

Figure 2-10.
Overlapping circles with no transparency set and no opacity set

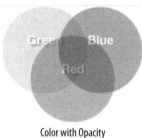

Color with Opacity

Figure 2-11.
Overlapping circles with opacity set to 50%

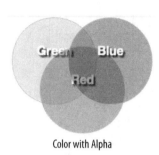

Color with Alpha

Figure 2-12.
Overlapping circles with alpha transparency set to 50%

Figure 2-10 has no opacity settings and no alpha channel, which renders it with full visibility. Figure 2-11 has 50% opacity set on each circle and Figure 2-12 has the transparency channel set to 50%.

As you can see, the color circles look nearly identical in Figures 2-11 and 2-12, but the text inside the circles looks very different. In Figure 2-11, the text inside the circles also took on the opacity characteristic; in Figure 2-12, the text remains unchanged. Let's take a look at the CSS for both of these solutions:

```
.one.opacity {
    background-color: rgb(0, 255, 0);
    opacity: .5;
}

 .two.opacity {
    background-color: rgb(255, 0, 0);
     opacity: .5;
}

 .three.opacity {
```

```
        background-color: rgb(0, 0, 255 );
        opacity: .5;
    }
    caption: css for circles with alpha transparancy

    .alpha.one {
        background-color: rgba(0, 255, 0, .5);
    }

    .alpha.two {

        background-color: rgba(255, 0, 0, .5);
    }

    .alpha.three {
        background-color: rgba(0, 0, 255, .5 );
    }
```

The new alpha transparency allows us to set the transparency where we set the color. This could be to a background color, a gradient, a drop shadow, or any other property that takes a color value. It inherits with the color value only, and doesn't affect the presentation of child elements. There may be times when opacity and all its inherited characteristics are what your design calls for. For all other situations, CSS3 provides the ability to set transparency without opacity.

A Word About Color Formats

You may have noticed that we have two different color formats to choose from when setting alpha transparency. RGBA (red, green, blue, alpha) and HSLA (hue, saturation, lightness, alpha) are both introduced with CSS3, and for all practical purposes they provide the same results. Don't be confused about which pattern to utilize. Choose the format you're most comfortable with. Some developers prefer RGBA because it can generally be copied directly out of the Photoshop palette; others prefer HSLA because it gives more predictable values. In HSLA, when you raise the L value the color gets lighter, and when you lower the S value the saturation decreases. Base your color format choice on the look you're seeking to achieve.

HACK 16 Use Media Queries to Build Responsive Design

Your web page can look just as great on a mobile phone as it does on the desktop. The secret to achieving this feat is called responsive design, and media queries are the key to making your pages responsive.

Mobile is all the rage these days. And with HTML5, the mobile web is even hotter. The industry decided pretty early on that it wasn't a good idea to design different websites for different types of visitors. You don't want to have one website for your mobile phone users, another for your desktop users, and a third for your tablet users. Instead, it makes sense to develop one website that can "respond" to the type of interface you're using and provide an experience suitable for that device. This is what we call *responsive design*.

There are a few techniques that make responsive design work, but the heart of a responsive page starts with the use of media queries. Before we get into the details of how to use media queries, let's take a look at what we want to accomplish. Figure 2-13 shows our responsive website as viewed through a desktop browser.

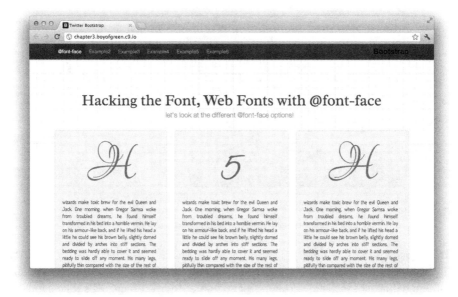

Figure 2-13.
Our example site as viewed through the desktop version of Google Chrome

Figure 2-14 shows the same website on an iPhone without any responsive characteristics.

Figure 2-14.
Our example website as viewed through mobile Safari on an iPhone 4s

The website is hard to utilize in its current state. The iPhone does give us the ability to "pinch and zoom" the page so that we can read it, but it's not a great experience. Although it is accessible, it certainly doesn't cater to my device. Let's take a look at the markup that makes up this center column section:

```
<div class="row">
    <div class="span4">...</div>
    <div class="span4">...</div>
    <div class="span4">...</div>
</div>
```

Here's the CSS that handles the layout:

```
.row {
    width: 100%;
    }

.span4 {
```

```
    width: 300px;
    float: left;
    margin-left: 30px;
}
```

In order to make the website respond to our device, we want to lose the multicolumn layout and stack all our content into one column—in essence, we want to move from a horizontal layout to a linear one. Currently, our page splits our window space into three columns and places content into each column. Our new layout will convert those columns into one linear flow. Now that we don't have three fixed-width columns next to one another, our page will have a smaller width, and our text and content will wrap within the iPhone viewport. With our new CSS, our page will look significantly improved on an iPhone, as shown in Figure 2-15.

Figure 2-15.
Our example page with a linear view on mobile Safari on an iPhone 4s

The markup stays the same for this new layout, but we have changed our CSS a bit:

```
.row {
    width: 100%;
    }

.span4 {
    width: auto;
    float: none;
    margin: 0;
    }
```

In Come the Media Queries

Congratulations! You have a responsive design! Now you need to program the browser to know when to use one design over the other. In come the media queries. Media queries allow you to place conditions around your CSS to tell it whether it should apply the CSS declarations inside the condition or not. There are a number of characteristics you can use to determine whether the rules should be applied. Here are some of the highlights:

- Width
- Height
- Device width
- Device height
- Resolution
- Orientation
- Aspect ratio

For this hack we'll focus on the device width to determine our rule. Here's a sneak peek at our rule:

```
@media (max-width: 767px)
```

We've determined that if the screen width is less than 767 px, we apply the CSS rules. The rule will be applied if the statement within the parentheses evaluates to **true** (in this case, it will evaluate to **true** when the window cannot get any bigger than 767 px). We can apply this rule to our CSS in a number of ways. Remember, we are going to wrap our CSS for the new linear layout with the media query condition so that it only gets applied when the rule is **true**.

There are three different ways to apply the conditional rule:

<link> *tag*

The media query can be set in the <link> tag. Then the declarations within that file are only applied to the page if the media query is satisfied:

```
<link rel="stylesheet" type="text/css"
    media="screen and (max-width: 767px)" href="test.css" />
```

@media *condition*

> A block of CSS can be wrapped within curly brackets in the CSS document, and
> the CSS declarations are only applied to the document if the media query is
> satisfied:

```
@media screen and (max-width: 767px) {
.row {
    width: 100%;
    }

.span4 {
    width: auto;
    float: none;
    margin: 0;
    }
}
```

@import *condition*

> An import will bring in the external CSS file only if the media query conditions are
> met. The CSS declarations in the external file will not be applied to the document
> until the conditions are met.

```
@import url("test.css") screen and (max-width: 787px);
```

We've used media queries to change the layout of the page, but it's also possible to
use them to condition CSS declarations of any kind. Many times, it will be advantageous to change font size, image quality, spacing, and other qualities to better suit
different types of devices.

HACK 17 Make Your Web App Respond to Device Orientation Changes

Your native apps are smart enough to know how you're holding your device. Now your
web apps can be, too. Use orientation-based media queries to make your site
responsive.

Mobile devices have brought a new paradigm to web development. Unlike desktops
and laptops that have a fixed orientation (I rarely see people flip their PowerBook on
its side), mobile devices can be viewed in either landscape or portrait mode. Most
mobile phones and tablets have an accelerometer inside that recognizes the change

in orientation and adjusts the screen accordingly. This allows you to view content on these devices in either aspect ratio. For example, the iPad has a screen aspect ratio of 3:4 where the device is taller than it is wide. When you turn it on its side, it has an aspect ratio of 4:3 (wider than it is tall). That's an orientation change.

Using media queries, you can natively identify which orientation the device is being held in, and utilize different CSS for each orientation. Let's go back to our example page and see what it would look like in landscape mode (see Figure 2-16) and portrait mode (see Figure 2-17).

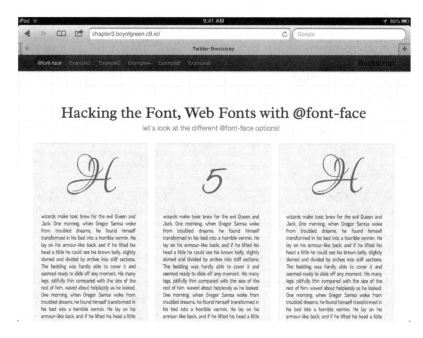

Figure 2-16.
Our sample page in landscape mode on an iPad, with three columns of content

Here is the markup that makes each view work:

```
<div class="row">
    <div class="span4">...</div>
    <div class="span4">...</div>
    <div class="span4">...</div>
</div>
```

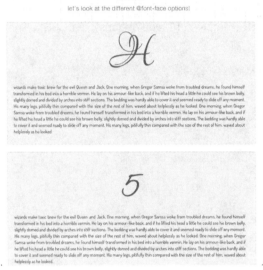

Figure 2-17.
Our sample page in portrait mode on an iPad, with one column of linear content

Here is the CSS for the three-column view:

```
.row {
    width: 100%;
    }

.span4 {
    width: 300px;
    float: left;
    margin-left: 30px;
    }
```

and the CSS for the single-column view:

```
.row {
    width: 100%;
    }

.span4 {
```

```
        width: auto;
        float: none;
        margin: 0;
        }
```

Now we'll wrap each CSS option in media queries so that they only apply in their proper orientation. Remember, the media queries wrap the CSS in conditions that only apply the declarations when the media query resolves to **true**. Using inline media queries (see Hack #16 for an explanation of other implementation options), our CSS will now look something like this:

```
@media screen and (orientation:landscape) {
.row {
    width: 100%;
    }

.span4 {
    width: 300px;
    float: left;
    margin-left: 30px;
    }

}
@media screen and (orientation:portrait) {
.row {
    width: 100%;
    }

.span4 {
    width: auto;
    float: none;
    margin: 0;
    }
}
```

With the CSS and media queries in place, our page will have three columns of content in landscape mode, and only one in portrait mode.

Why Not Width?

If you compare device orientation to max-width pixel media queries, you may realize you can accomplish this hack with max- and min-width queries, since the width will change when the device changes orientation. However, there are pros and cons to doing this.

Media queries based on orientation can often be simpler. You don't need to know what screen size to expect for landscape versus portrait view. You simply rely on the orientation published by the device. You also gain consistency between devices in terms of how the pages appear in each orientation.

The argument against orientation media queries is pretty much the same. You really shouldn't care if your orientation is portrait or landscape. If your screen width is 700 px, it shouldn't matter which way the device is being held: the layout should cater to a 700 px screen. When you design for the available space, the actual orientation becomes inconsequential.

`HACK 18` Take Full Control of Your DOM with Pseudoclasses

You've been working with pseudoclasses for years with the few options available in CSS 2.1. Now, CSS3 allows you to use those implied classes on just about any element on the page.

Pseudoclasses are some of the more exciting parts of CSS. A *pseudoclass* is a class that is implied on an element based on its ability to satisfy generic criteria, such as the fact that a button is in the disabled state or that it is the first child of your parent element. The pseudoclass is written by preceding the class with a colon.

A few extremely popular pseudoclasses were introduced in CSS 2.1. One of the most common was the link **hover** class. It looked like this:

```
a:hover {
    color: green;
}
```

The anchor pseudoclass would apply the CSS declaration when you "hovered" your mouse over a **<link>** tag. It would be common to switch colors with the hover event.

CSS3 has introduced a large number of new pseudoclasses. Specifically, it has introduced a lot of classes that can be based on DOM (Document Object Model) position. Let's look at a few:

```
div:first-child {
    color: blue;
    }
span:nth-child(5){ /*chooses the fifth child element */
    color: red;
    }
p:empty {
    display: none;
    }
```

Each CSS declaration applies to elements not through class names, IDs, or tag names, but through other characteristics that meet the pseudoclass criteria.

The CSS Zebra Stripe Data Table

Let's look at an example that focuses on DOM relations (how an element relates to its parent element). A nice feature to have on tables with a large amount of data is a shade that is applied to every other row. This practice, commonly called *zebra striping*, helps your eyes follow a row all the way across a table. In the past, there was a JavaScript function that would run against the table rows and would determine which were odd-numbered rows and which were even-numbered rows. Even-numbered rows would then have a class added to them that would shade the row, thus "striping" the table.

Using CSS pseudoclasses, we can do the same thing, but using DOM relations instead of JavaScript. Let's start by looking at our table markup:

```
<table class="zebraStripe">
    <tr>
        <th>Name</th>
        <th>Town</th>
    </tr>
    <tr>
        <td>Jeff</td>
        <td>Dayton, OH</td>
    </tr>
    <tr>
        <td>Carla</td>
        <td>Rochester, NY</td>
    </tr>
    <tr>
        <td>Chloe</td>
        <td>San Juan, PR</td>
    </tr>
    <tr>
        <td>Maddy</td>
        <td>San Juan, PR</td>
    </tr>
    <tr>
        <td>Jude</td>
        <td>San Antonio, TX</td>
    </tr>
</table>
```

Without any CSS, every row of this table will be the same color. Now let's use an **nth-of-type** pseudoclass to color our rows. This pseudoclass takes a keyword (such as **odd** or **even**), a number, or an expression. For our example we will use the **odd** keyword, but we could have easily used an expression such as **2n-1**. Let's look at our table CSS:

```
.zebraStripe {
    width: 100%;
    text-align: left;
    }
.zebraStripe td, .zebraStripe th {
    padding: 10px;
}

.zebraStripe tr th {
    color: white;
    background-color: #858385;
    }

.zebraStripe tr:nth-of-type(odd) td{
    background-color: #a6caf5;
    }
```

Our table will now appear with every other row shaded, as shown in Figure 2-18.

Shaded rows only scratch the surface of the control you have with pseudoclasses and DOM position. There are many new ways to identify the element on the page you want to control: first-of-type, last-of-type, only, empty, root; the list goes on. Pull out those pseudoclasses and start hacking!

HACK 19 Hack Up Your Sprite and Put Your Images Inline with Image Data URIs

Forget the hassle of ever constructing an image sprite again. You can use image data URIs to "inline" your image directly in your HTML or CSS.

Like butter goes with bread, sprites go with CSS. An *image sprite* combines a number of images together into one image. Then, instead of using image tags to display these images, you use CSS background images to display them. In CSS, you then alter the background position on your elements to display different portions of the sprite. Figure 2-19 shows a common sprite.

Figure 2-18.
Sample table with our zebra stripe CSS using the nth-of-type pseudoclass to apply a light blue shade to every other row

Figure 2-19.
Image sprite pulled from Google Gmail application (*http://bit.ly/TvBhMV*)

This sprite has just about every icon used within the Gmail application. Now let's look at the code that turns this big image into each small icon.

Here is the markup:

```
<div class="uF">
    <div id=":99" class="uE dk dh"></div>
    <div class="uD">
        <span id=":98" class="uC">Jeffrey Burtoft</span>
    </div>
</div>
```

And here is the CSS:

```
.dh {
    background: url(images/2/icons_ns10.png) no-repeat -40px -100px;
}
.dk {
    width: 16px;
    height: 16px;
}
```

This code renders an icon next to my name in Gmail. You can see that the background position defines what part of the image is shown. The height and width of the icon stop the rest of the background image from showing. The end result looks like Figure 2-20.

Figure 2-20.
Contact list from Google Gmail with icon from sprite

Why Do a Sprite?

Sprites were introduced as a performance technique. Web Performance 101 tells us that the first step to improving your page performance is to reduce the number of connections you are making to the server. Generally, the fewer connections you make, the better the page will perform. This sprite reduces the number of connections significantly. Without this sprite, each icon would require a small but separate connection to the server. In a nutshell, sprites make your page load faster.

An additional common performance gain is the reduction in total file size. This reduction wouldn't be apparent, since you generally need to add additional whitespace to the sprite that you may not need in each image, but sprites do often reduce the total size of the image payload. Since images on a page often look similar, a shared color palette between the images reduces the file size. The more you group similar images together, the more you save.

The Problem with Image Sprites

Although sprites solve the problem of reducing image requests, they're not a perfect solution. The biggest problem with using sprites is that they're difficult to maintain. Every time one of your icons changes you need to rework the whole sprite. If your icon size has changed you may need to tweak the layout of the sprite, which may mean going back and altering a lot of CSS to reposition your background images correctly. Some automation systems are available, such as the CSS Sprites Generator (*http:// csssprites.com/*), but generating sprites automatically tends to be not as effective as assembling them by hand, since the assembly tool can never know all the use cases of your sprite image. Additionally, total file reduction usually only happens when you sprite like images together (e.g., images with a similar color palette). This may add to the maintenance time, as you may need to rearrange your sprites when you change colors in an icon.

Another side effect of CSS sprites is increased memory usage in the browser. CSS sprites generally use additional whitespace to make CSS positioning possible without unintentionally showing another part of the image. The whitespace will download quite well, as whitespace is generally compressed out of images. The problem has to do with rendering those images. The browser does not render images in compressed form, so it has to render out the full, uncompressed version of the sprite. Depending on the amount of whitespace, an image that requires 25 KB to download can render more than 10 MB in memory usage. This is especially a problem in mobile browsers that have limited memory available.

Hacking Up the Sprite

So, how can we solve the problems inherent in image sprites? We can use the image data URI (Uniform Resource Identifier). This URI works in browsers as early as IE 8, and it lets you "inline" your image right in your CSS, or even your image tag. Instead of using a URL, which would call out to retrieve the image, the data URI includes the Base64-encoded version of the image inline with your document. The format of the data URI is fairly simple:

```
data:[<mime type>][;base64],<encoded data>
```

In this case, **data** is your protocol, `<mime type>` is the type of image you are using, **base64** is the type of encoding you will use for your images, and `<encoded data>` is your string of encoded data. The code for a realistic inline image would look something like this:

```
data:image/png;base64,iVBORw0KGgoAAAANSUhEUgAAACAAAAAgCAYAAABzenr0AA
AAGXRFWHRTb2Z0d2FyZQBBZG9iZSBJbWFnZVJlYWR5ccllPAAAAs1JREFUeNq8VztvE0
EQnnsFxbJxlCAEIiAoiC0q0xJpkCAoHRIKLR0VFRJdWugQBRX8EBASDUIkSGlC4XTEps
DiIVEAcsA6x77Hsrs5+24ft7d+6FY6rc8+z8x+M983cwbg9f32yjre3k0+6+by69a2Gd
3sQ/6L+jSGdxgFNImVwqKp/WwwAOh3Q/oZn576tqc9hjVnjBGAeEaThyRP+HkEOkJ01b
rSimGYYJ+ey/TmN/fojhASfClT4Gy9UBp2HAcK5XJmAH/vXzlOgQfKFOzwP6Kvn6fGOm
h9lH29IwtAWKjXnWniUSAWobIGhNPsvgH49TM2aJnQX5pX/if8/SP+HICyBgQWoIMGQC
UuxBAHEJLvEqt/xpqKBWZevAt9uc4lA2gLCLj/2Icrq5PnP2RuR74YGePlmOiAioqEhu
UMGrrP7lEdICro/mFlONcUkD6QlQKhEJE7PQ2Db59A5YNXwg4vRGGzkW7csiFYLLInWq
6CUSgJdSSTYa1u6D19kP4bMcDRsPjkLRPAKFhPbsOWwLPOPHD3IRgXLmsFRBFYOpeA/0
CpAbIADoWOh52blfpkBdCLaRxngPUxNguMU2fTh5Pz1XQh8pBWCrbx9UjoiAkEnK3ntD
CJTAeNDzjfNti1DbBX1sCqXJXOARIf+kUIHBUJAhZB4dotmHceQ0ljHkg0oUwd6MxSfE
YUZNSw40OYKGXTMZFks36dFmOSETIpJpXv77+jg8gwBWkyrD0VkxY8asOFIlg4GIP0ib
UN3OW6EDSxs9Yedcw3MBqAryhqCQJf8HZRF+aSxjww6KLh+0AbI3Api4btmfR/XHheD8
HRYQgDN0y1bc+y6Eiu/T6+Bum8z0xB4mV1M5LlmsrAiZPmseMjpBq/CPdfkZdRrQC4YB
bwdgdfN6J9IeMv7cghGb1fYqedsRHICKgWIbOZaFz0hGTHDsd6xfsvwAB8ABqbrMgqHw
AAAABJRU5ErkJggg==
```

The preceding code would produce a 32 × 32 image that looks like Figure 2-21.

Figure 2-21.
HTML5 logo icon

To implement this in your CSS, just replace your normal URL with the Base64 version of the image:

```
.backgroundImageClass {
  background-image:
url(data:image/png;base64,iVBORw0KGgoAAAANSUhEUgAAACAAAAAgCAYAAABzen
r0AAAAGXRFWHRTb2Z0d2FyZQBBZG9iZSBJbWFnZVJlYWR5ccllPAAAAs1JREFUeNq8Vz
tvE0EQnnsFxbJxlCAEIiAoi. . . );
}
```

To implement the data URI in an image tag, set the **src** to the preceding string:

```
<img src="url(data:image/png;base64,iVBORw0KGgoAAAANSUhEUgAAACAAAAgC
AYAAABzenr0AAAAGXRFWHRTb2Z0d2FyZQBBZG9iZSBJbWFnZVJlYWR5ccllPAAAAs1JRE
FUeNq8VztvE0EQnnsFxbJxlCAEIiAoi. . . " />
```

It's that simple. But I'm sure you're wondering how you can convert these images (that were previously sprited as one image) into data URIs. Luckily many tools are already available on the Web for this very task. My favorite is Data URL Maker (*http://data-url.net/#dataurlmaker*). With this tool you can quickly upload an image and convert it into Base64-encoded characters.

The Downsides of Data URIs

There are a few downsides to using data URIs in place of images or sprites. Looking first at maintenance, it's generally not as difficult to maintain data URIs as it is to maintain sprites, but it is still difficult, as every time you change the image you need to reconvert it. There are a few libraries out there that will help you with this aspect by converting your images at runtime so that you get all the advantages of data URIs without the maintenance headache.

A second downside is the fact that you lose your compression. When an image is transported, a compressed version of the image is sent back and forth. When you "explode" the image into a data URI, it loses its compression and appears as a very large image, thus increasing the payload. The good news is that most HTTP servers *Gzip* all requests, which is a type of compression done over HTTP. This makes up for any loss of compression you had by converting to the base URI.

The third downside is that a data URI is not as cacheable. With traditional images, if you use the same image more than once on a page the browser will cache the image so that it doesn't need to download it more than once. Many times browsers will even cache images from page to page, when the image is used again. Since data URIs are inline, they can't be cached unless the parent document is cached.

So, there are pros and cons to both image sprites and inline images (data URIs). Every application has specific characteristics. Look at the details of your app, do some testing, and determine which solution is better for you.

HACK 20 Build Gradients the Easy Way

CSS3 gives you the ability to apply color gradients to the background of your HTML elements. Getting the right shading from your gradient properties can be quite difficult, but the folks at ColorZilla have built a tool to make it easy!

This hack was contributed by Alex Sirota, the mind and talent behind colorZilla.com (http://colorzilla.com) and the ColorZilla Ultimate Gradient Generator.

Gradients are images that contain smooth color transitions between two or more colors. They are widely used in graphic and web design to create classy-looking backgrounds, slick buttons, and interesting visual effects for your pages.

Historically, you needed to use an image editor such as Photoshop or GIMP to create an image containing your gradient, save it in a file, and then apply it as a repeating background to your page or panel. Figure 2-22 shows an example.

Figure 2-22.
A simple gradient that is common across the Web

This gradient can easily be applied to a design as a background image:

```
#my-panel {
    background: url(http://www.example.com/my-gradient.png);
    background-repeat: repeat-x;
}
```

The preceding CSS will result in an element that looks like Figure 2-23.

Figure 2-23.
An element with my-gradient.png applied as a repeated background image

Although this was a relatively straightforward process, it did have some major disadvantages. First, if you wanted to tweak your gradient you needed to go back to your image editor and change your background image. Also, using an image required the browser to make another HTTP request to load it, which made pages load a bit more slowly.

Pure CSS Gradients

The good news is that CSS3 introduced pure CSS gradients, among many other great features. These enable you to specify all your gradient settings—colors, orientation, and so on—as pure CSS, allowing for much better flexibility and improved performance.

In a perfect world, the previous example would simply become:

```
#my-panel {
    background-image: linear-gradient(rgb(0, 0, 88), rgb(0, 0, 255));
}
```

Another benefit of using CSS gradients is that, because we're no longer using a statically sized image for our gradient, we can apply our gradient to a panel of any size and have the gradient effect stretch correctly. Figure 2-24 shows an example. On the lefthand side of the figure the panel is higher than the original gradient image, and the gradient cannot stretch to cover the whole panel height. On the righthand side the CSS gradient is correctly stretching to cover the whole height of the panel.

Figure 2-24.
A gradient that is unable to cover the whole panel height (left) and a gradient that correctly stretches to cover the whole panel height (right)

The ColorZilla Ultimate Gradient Generator

As you might have noticed, with many different browsers, each having its own quirks and syntaxes, things are rarely simple when it comes to web development, and gradients are no exception. Because there's still no standard and finalized syntax for CSS gradients, each browser has implemented a vendor-specific prefix for gradient declaration. So, in order to support various browsers, our simple one-line pure-CSS declaration becomes:

```
#my-panel {
  background-image: -moz-linear-gradient(rgb(0,0,88), rgb(0,0,255));
  background-image: -webkit-linear-gradient(rgb(0,0,88), rgb(0,0,255));
  background-image: -ms-linear-gradient(rgb(0,0,88), rgb(0,0,255));
  background-image: -o-linear-gradient(rgb(0,0,88), rgb(0,0,255));
}
```

If you want to add support for older IE versions and additional browsers, things become even crazier with additional CSS declarations, each having its own syntax.

Tools such as the ColorZilla Ultimate Gradient Generator were created in order to save
you from this multibrowser syntax mess, and make pure-CSS gradients simple. With
this tool, you can use a familiar UI similar to Photoshop's to design your gradient, and
it handles the syntax complexities, automatically producing the needed CSS declarations for cross-browser gradients. Figure 2-25 shows the ColorZilla Ultimate Gradient Generator interface.

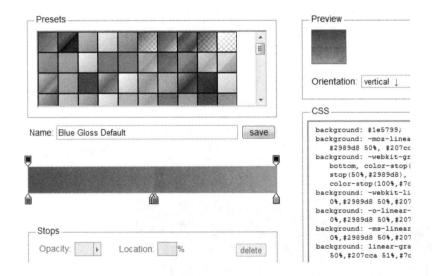

Figure 2-25.
The ColorZilla Ultimate Gradient Generator interface

To create the gradient in the previous example, specify the beginning and end colors
of your gradient by clicking on the color handles (see Figure 2-26), grabbing the resultant CSS output, and adding it to your stylesheet.

Figure 2-26.
Using the color handles to specify the beginning and end colors of the gradient

Now copy your CSS directly out of the tool (see Figure 2-27).

```
background: rgb(0,0,88); /* Old browsers */
background: -moz-linear-gradient(top,  rgb(0,0,88) 0%, rgb(0
background: -webkit-gradient(linear, left top, left bottom, 
Chrome, Safari 4+ */
background: -webkit-linear-gradient(top,  rgb(0,0,88) 0%,rgb
background: -o-linear-gradient(top,  rgb(0,0,88) 0%,rgb(0,0,
background: -ms-linear-gradient(top,  rgb(0,0,88) 0%,rgb(0,0
background: linear-gradient(top,  rgb(0,0,88) 0%,rgb(0,0,255
filter: progid:DXImageTransform.Microsoft.gradient( startCol
```

Figure 2-27.
The CSS generated from the ColorZilla Ultimate Gradient Generator

Designing and customizing gradients

The ColorZilla Ultimate Gradient Generator has options for designing and customizing your gradients. For example, you can create vertical, horizontal, or diagonal gradients, as shown in Figure 2-28.

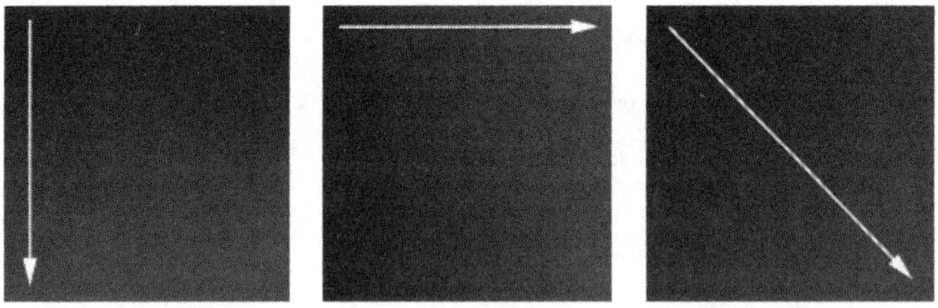

Figure 2-28.
Vertical, horizontal, and diagonal gradients

As noted earlier, simple gradients are typically smooth transitions between two colors: a beginning color and an end color. You can also create more elaborate gradients with multiple *color stops*, in which color transitions occur between more than two colors. In this case, the color transition starts with the first color, smoothly goes to the "first stop" color, then the "second stop" color, and so on, until it smoothly transitions to the final color. Figure 2-29 shows an example.

HTML5 HACKS

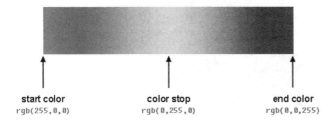

start color
rgb(255,0,0)

color stop
rgb(0,255,0)

end color
rgb(0,0,255)

Figure 2-29.
Gradient color stops

You can also create gradients with varying opacities, which is great for seamlessly blending your gradient with other visual elements. For example, you can create a gradient that goes from being opaque to being transparent, and then you can position it above an image. The varying opacity of the gradient will gradually reveal or adjust the underlying image content. Figures 2-30, 2-31, and 2-32 show how this works.

Figure 2-30.
The original image

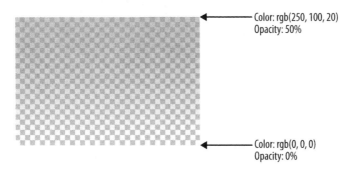

Color: rgb(250, 100, 20)
Opacity: 50%

Color: rgb(0, 0, 0)
Opacity: 0%

Figure 2-31.
The gradient

Figure 2-32.
The final result, with the gradient overlaying the image

Additionally, the tool includes a number of presets if you prefer not to start your gradient designs from scratch, and you can also save your favorite designs in the tool.

Modernizing your old gradients

The ColorZilla Ultimate Gradient Generator allows you to import your existing gradients either from an image or from browser-specific CSS, which is a simple way to edit your existing gradients and convert them to cross-browser CSS.

CSS gradients offer great benefits in terms of performance and flexibility, and tools such as the ColorZilla Ultimate Gradient Generator hide the complexities of cross-browser support behind a convenient UI. With some experimentation and imagination you can now easily add a great deal of visual appeal to your pages.

HACK 21　Make Borders Interesting Again, with Border Treatments

CSS3 makes boring borders exciting. Forget corner images and shadow "shivs." CSS3 provides a number of new treatments that bring your borders back to life.

The border is one of the most frequently used properties in CSS. It's applicable to any visual HTML element and has been used in various ways to draw your eye to content on a page. Borders have traditionally been limited in their presentation. With CSS 2.1, we were limited to the use of solid colors, straight corners, and limited styles (solids, dots, and dashes only).

CSS3 brings a number of new features to modernize borders. The border radius, box shadow, and border image are the main enhancements.

The Border Radius

The border radius has been a sought-after feature for years, as it's a design pattern that has been mimicked with background images or pixel size elements in countless applications. The border radius is fairly straightforward to implement:

```
.borderRadiusClass {
border: 1px solid #777;
border-radius: 15px 15px 15px 15px
}
```

The border radius implies having a border, so first you must state a border property in your declaration. You need to start with a border for the radius to be visible. Then you set the radius for each corner (top-left, top-right, bottom-right, and bottom-left) with a numeric value. The image resulting from the preceding code would look like Figure 2-33.

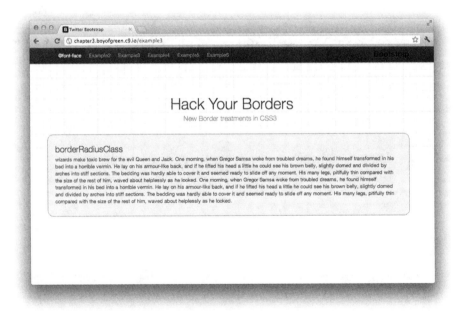

Figure 2-33.
Div with a class of borderRadiusClass which gives each corner a 15 px radius

The Box Shadow

Web designers have long used drop shadows to give elements a sense of depth on a web page. CSS has finally formalized this capability with the native box-shadow feature. The box-shadow feature adds true drop shadows to your elements. Implementation requires you to declare the horizontal and vertical offsets (both numeric values), the optional blur radius, the optional spread radius, and the color of the drop shadow (any supported color format is fine). You would define your property as follows:

```
.myShadowClass {
    box-shadow: 3px 3px 5px 5px #ddd;
}
```

Applying this to an element will produce the effect shown in Figure 2-34.

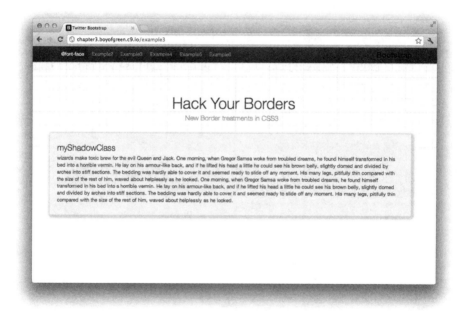

Figure 2-34.
Div with the myShadowClass applied, giving it a 3 × 3 px drop shadow

The Border Image

One of the most powerful new features in CSS3 is the border image. In essence, this feature lets you utilize an image file as your border, as opposed to solid colors. Border images can be difficult to utilize at times, as the property patterns may not follow other border attribute conventions. The `border-image` attribute is stated as follows:

```
border-image: source slice width outset repeat;
```

Let's look at the function of each property:

source
> Defines the path of the image you are using for the `border-image`

slice
> Defines the inward offset, or the percent of inset to use, of the image from each of the four corners

width
> Defines the width of the image borders

outset
> Defines the optional amount by which the border image extends beyond the border box

repeat
> Defines whether the image should repeat, be rounded, or stretch

Let's take a look at this attribute in action. First we will utilize this CSS class on a button element:

```
.borderImageClass {
    border-image:url(../img/borderImage.png) 29 30 stretch;
    border-width: 25px;
    color: white;
    background: transparent;
    font-weight: 800;
}
```

Now let's see what our `borderImageClass` class looks like applied to our button (see Figure 2-35).

Figure 2-35.
Button with borderImageClass applied

Figure 2-36 shows the image we are using to create the button.

Figure 2-36.
Image used to render the button

The inward offset of this image essentially divides the image into nine parts. Figure 2-37 shows the image again with our inward offset drawn in.

Figure 2-37.
Image used to render the button with an inward offset of 25% overlaid

Here we are placing our inward offset corners on each of the four corners of the button. Since we have the `repeat` attribute set to `stretch`, we are going to stretch out the center region of the image to fill the remainder of the borders. Our button will then appear as it does in Figure 2-38.

Figure 2-38.
Final button with image border

New border features have given us a lot of design flexibility. Gone are the days of using fixed images for each visual treatment. Border radius and box shadow meet a lot of our design needs, and most of the remainder can be addressed with border images.

HACK 22 Set Multiple Background Images to the Same Element

The CSS3 version of the **background** attribute allows you to set layers of images as the background of your elements. Each layer can have its own background properties for designs that are more intricate than were previously possible.

Background images have always been an extremely useful feature in CSS. Prior to CSS3, if you wanted to have multiple background images (say, a background pattern and a logo) you had to hack up a solution that included nested elements and separate CSS declarations. It was both tedious to write and difficult to troubleshoot. When it was all said and done, you were left with a slew of extra markup that only existed to facilitate the needs of the design. CSS3 now supports the long-awaited feature of multiple background images. Any one element can have multiple background images set to different "layers" of the background.

Multiple background images are particularly useful in a design that requires a fluid layout, such as responsive design. If you have a text box that has an undetermined amount of content in it, you can use CSS3 to provide "bookend" style treatments around it. In our example we have a mountain scene that provides a panoramic view regardless of the page size. Figure 2-39 shows our element in a small screen, and Figure 2-40 shows the element in a larger screen.

Figure 2-39.
Example of our panoramic view requiring multiple background images shown on a small screen

The syntax for multiple background images is simple and intuitive. The properties are written just as they were in previous versions, with comma-separated lists for the different "layers" of backgrounds:

```
.mybackgroundClass{
    background-image: url(../img/tree.png),url(../img/
mountains.png),url(../img/sky.png);
    background-color: #f2f7fb;
    background-position: right bottom, left bottom, top left;
    background-repeat: no-repeat, no-repeat, repeat-x;
    height: 300px;
}
```

Our image required three background images: the trees are in one corner, the mountain and hills are in another, and our sky is repeated on the very bottom layer.

Figure 2-40.
Example of our panoramic view requiring multiple background images shown on a larger screen

How It Works

Here's how it works. Each **background-image** declaration creates a background "layer" on your element. If you have four **background-image** declarations, you will have four layers (note that we have three in our class). Each property can have a comma-delimited list as well. The first **background-position** will be associated with the first **background-image** layer, and so on and so forth. If any given background property has more declarations than there are **background-image** declarations (e.g., five **background-repeat** declarations but only four **background-image** declarations), the remaining declarations will be ignored. If there are too few property declarations (e.g., three **background-repeat** declarations and four **background-image** declarations), the property list will cycle—the first property will be used over again and it will cycle through the whole property list until the list of **background-image**s is exhausted. If a **background-color** is declared, it will only apply to the final (and bottom) "layer."

Shorthand syntax can also be used in a similar manner. With the shorthand style, the whole property is declared as a comma-delimited list:

```
.mybackgroundClass{
  background: url(../img/tree.png) right bottom no-repeat,
```

```
     url(../img/mountains.png) left bottom no-repeat,
     #f2f7fb url(../img/sky.png) top left repeat-x;
    height: 300px;
  }
```

Notice that a background color can only be defined on the final "layer" which renders as the bottom layer.

This easy-to-implement feature shows the power and simplicity you will find all across the HTML5 family of technologies.

HACK 23 Free Your Page Elements from Their Traditional Space with CSS3 Transforms

CSS3 transforms give you the ability to add perspective to your HTML elements. Use CSS3 transforms to arrange your elements in the 2D or 3D space.

HTML generally is a linear presentation, as all the elements are essentially rectangles. Transforms allow you to take advantage of the different planes to give your design perspective. There are two types of transforms: 2D and 3D. Let's look at the options provided in the 2D transforms:

Skew
 Defines a 2D skew along the x- and y-axes

Scale
 Provides a 2D scale on the x- and y-axes

Rotate
 Provides a 2D rotation at a defined degree

Translate
 Translates (or displaces) the element at a 2D defined location

Let's apply each transform to a single class and then roll them up into a shorthand class as well:

```
.elementSkew {
    transform:skew(30deg);
}
.elementScale {
    transform:scale(1,0.5);
}
.elementRotate {
    transform:rotate(30deg);
}
```

```
.elementTranslate {
  transform:translate(25px, 25px);
}
.elementRotate-skew-scale-translate {
  transform:skew(30deg) scale(1,.5) rotate(30deg) translate(25px,25px);
}
```

Each element shown in Figure 2-41 has its corresponding class assigned to it. Notice the use of the x- and y-axes to transform each element. Our traditional square can take on many different perspectives with transforms.

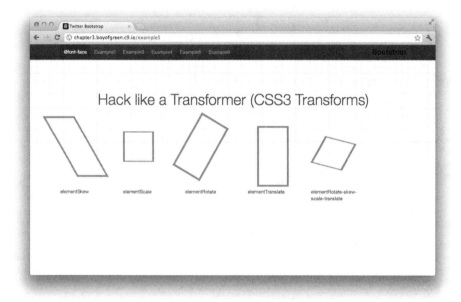

Figure 2-41.
Repeated rectangle with corresponding class names added to demonstrate the transform effect

CSS3 Transforms in 3D

Three-dimensional transforms are implemented in a similar manner to 2D transforms, but you are given access to the third plane. Here are the options provided in 3D transforms:

translate3d
: Translates (or displaces) the element at a 3D defined location on the x-, y-, and z-axes

scale3d
: Specifies a 3D scale operation on the x-, y-, and z-axes

rotateX
    Specifies a clockwise rotation by the given angle about the x-axis

rotateY
    Specifies a clockwise rotation by the given angle about the y-axis

rotateZ
    Specifies a clockwise rotation by the given angle about the z-axis

perspective
    Value that determines the perceived distance of the 3D object (smaller numbers make objects appear closer)

Once again, we will create a class for each property. This is how the CSS will appear:

```
.elementTranslate3d{
    transform: translate3d(75%, -25%, 0);
}
.elementScale3d{
    transform: scale3d(.5, 1.25,1);
}
.elementRotateX {
    transform:rotateX(100deg);
}
.elementRotateY {
-webkit-transform:rotateY(10deg);
}
.elementRotateZ {
    transform:rotateZ(10deg);
}
.elementPerspective{
    perspective: 800px;
}
```

Let's take the same boring boxes from our first example, and apply our new 3D classes to them (see Figure 2-42).

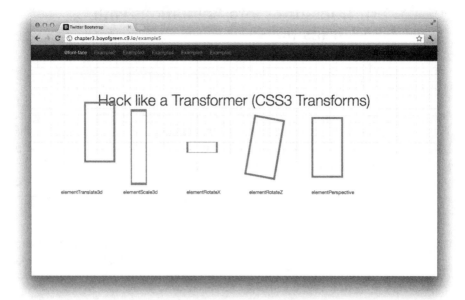

Figure 2-42.
Repeated rectangle with corresponding class names added to demonstrate the transform effect

You may not see a lot of value in 3D transforms right off the bat. When you move an element on the z-axis (or the 3D plane) it tends to just look like a different effect (such as 2D skew or a line), but hold on for the next hack where 3D meets transitions for some amazing effects.

Even More Advanced Effects

Transforms give you enormous control over your page elements. Bringing in the third dimension has additional benefits on many of today's modern mobile devices. Utilizing 3D transforms engages the GPU of your device and gives you the benefit of hardware acceleration. For more information on the pros and cons of 3D transforms, see this great description from HTML5Rocks.com (*http://www.html5rocks.com/en/tutorials/speed/html5/*):

> There may be some very rare cases when you want to be incredibly precise with your transformations. For advanced users, CSS3 transforms give access to both the matrix (for 2D) and 3Dmatrix (for 3D), which give users the ability to specify the transform in 6 different values and 16 different values, respectively. All I can say is good luck with that! High school geometry was a long time ago!

HACK 24 Turn Transforms into Animations with CSS3 Transitions

You can turn 2D and 3D transforms into custom animations with the simple-to-use `transition` attribute.

Animations have always been fascinating for web developers. The only animation mechanism available to us in the past has been JavaScript, but it has always been so laborious to constantly redraw our elements on the page—like creating those old flip-book animations my parents use to make back before there were televisions. A number of JavaScript libraries, including jQuery and YUI, have simplified the process of animating elements, but in the end it was still JavaScript moving elements. The results have always been disappointing.

Then along came this ray of light called *transitions*. Transitions aren't animations per se, but they do allow us to add a property to a CSS declaration that changes another property over a specified duration, and wow, is it smooth!

Transitions are pretty darn easy to use as well. Let's break down the process and look at the attribute syntax. Your transitions could look as simple as this:

```
.elementTransition {
    transition: width 2s;
    width: 100%;
}
```

It doesn't get much easier than that, right? For this class, we are stating two properties:

`transition-property`
> Defines which property will be transitioned

`transition-duration`
> Defines how long it will take to complete the transition

While we are at it, let's look at our other two definable properties:

`transition-timing-function`
> Describes a few predefined transition styles; the default is **ease**

`transition-delay`
> Defines when the transition will start

In the sample class shown earlier we are stating our timing and what value we are transitioning "to." The most obvious follow-up question is what are we transitioning "from." The simple answer is whatever that value was defined as before we added the class. Let's look at the full example. We'll start with our simple markup:

```
<div class="elementStart">
    <button id="myAction">Hello world!</button>
</div>
```

And here is the CSS class that defines the original view of our markup:

```
.elementStart {
    width: 50%;
    border: 1px solid green:
    height: 300px;
}
```

Notice that first we defined the width of our element to be set to 50%. This is the starting value we will be transitioning from. To start the transition, we need to add the new class (named **elementTransition**) to our element via some timer or user action. In this case, we will add a simple **onclick** to the button inside our **div** that will add our new class and start the transition. It's one simple line of JavaScript:

```
document.getElementById('myAction').onclick = function(e){var a =
e.target.parentNode;a.className = a.className += ' elementTransition';};
```

Put these together in your document and see what happens (see Figures 2-43 and 2-44).

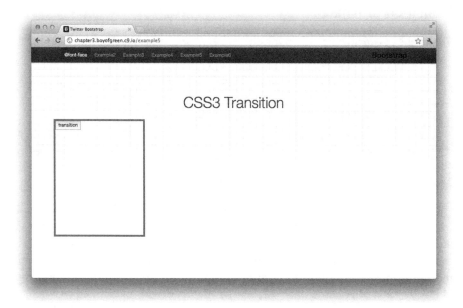

Figure 2-43.
Illustration of the div before adding the button class name that starts the transition

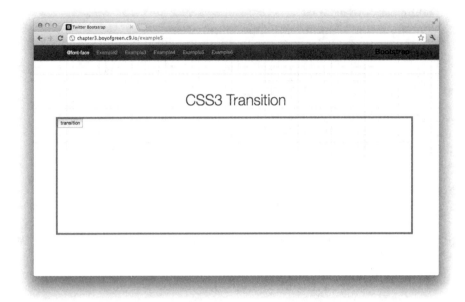

Figure 2-44.
Illustration of the div after adding the button class name that starts the transition

Transition to What?

The `transition` attribute is not the only attribute that can take a transition. Here are some additional attributes that can be transitioned, according to the W3C spec:

background	bottom	color	font-size	height	left
margin	opacity	outline	padding	right	transforms
text-shadow	visibility	width	z-index		

Make 3D Transitions with Transforms

CSS3 transitions really shine when they are coupled with CSS3 3D transforms. A 3D transform on its own may seem to lack a clear purpose. Setting a 3D rotate, for example, to (90, 90, 90) will make your object appear as a line on your page, but pair that value with the `transition` attribute and you now have what looks like a 3D animation as your box appears to turn on its side. The CSS should be very similar to that of the 2D transform. Remember, we have two definitions for the transform. The first definition is the starting point of the `div`. The second is added later and tells the transition where to end.

Transition Events

In many cases you may want to trigger an event at the end of one of your transitions. Your browser will publish an event when each event completes. The syntax follows the same structure as user events. In JavaScript, you simply add an event listener to the element that is receiving the transition:

```
document.getElementById('myAction').addEventListener("transitionend",
  myFunction, true);
```

Once any transition completes on that event, the event will be fired and the `myFunction` function will be called. Make sure you explore the experience on each browser, as there is no way to tell whether each browser will have the same meaning of "complete" to determine when the event is fired.

HACK 25 Make iOS-Style Card Flips with CSS Transforms and Transitions

Wow your users with custom animations they are used to seeing in native applications. This hack shows you how to re-create a common iOS animation in CSS.

Mobile applications have increased our expectations when it comes to user experience, and Apple has led the way with its iconic and realistic applications. Apple has built a number of user patterns that work so well and make so much sense that we have come to expect them in all applications. One of those iconic patterns is the card flip. One of the most memorable uses of the card flip is in the iOS weather application, where it presents your weather on the screen, which has an "i" icon in the corner. When you tap on the "i", the card flips over and allows you to configure it with the settings on the reverse (see Figure 2-45).

Figure 2-45.
iOS weather application, transitioning from the information to the settings side

We can re-create this animation using some simple markup and CSS. Let's start by creating the markup:

```
<div class="viewPort">
    <div id="card" class="card">
        <div class="frontView">HTML5 Hacks</div>
        <div class="backView">Rocks!</div>
    </div>
</div>
```

We've built out a few simple structural elements for our component. Let's review them:

viewPort

In our example, this is the parent container for our component, but on a mobile device where this "card" will take up the whole screen, it's important to understand your viewing area. On a mobile device, any transitions that would cause part of our elements to be outside this div would be cut off by the window.

card

This parent container is key for this transition, as it gives us a common parent for the two sides for the card.

frontView *and* backView

The markup in each of these divs will become the content for the two sides of the card.

Styling the Elements

The viewPort, which is the parent container in this component, plays a key role in the cards' behavior. Let's take a look at the CSS:

```
.viewPort {
    width: 200px;
    height: 260px;
    position: relative;
    margin: 0 auto 40px;
    border: 1px solid #CCC;
    perspective: 800px;
}
```

In the preceding code, the viewPort is actually the container that sets the size of the two-sided card. In our example we have a pixel width set, but in an example for a device such as an iPhone, where this would be a full-screen treatment, the height and width would simply be 100%. One additional key attribute in this declaration is the per spective. The perspective is a property that sets the "apparent" distance of the 3D rendering. Technically, it is stating how many pixels the 3D image is away from the view. We use the perspective to set the depth of our flip to match that of Apple's native card flip.

The **card** element is the **div** that actually gets flipped with a transition, so our original **transaction** property is assigned to this element in our CSS:

```
.card {
        width: 100%;
        height: 100%;
        position: absolute;
         transition: transform 1s;
          transform-style: preserve-3d;
          transform-origin: right center;
}
```

Take special note of the transforms within this declaration. We set the transform style to 3D in order to have access to the x-, y-, and z-axes. Our transform origin sets the distance our element is from the "origin" or nucleus of the transform. In this case, we want our rotation to stay to the right and centered. Last but not least, on this element we set the **transition** attribute. We specify the property that gets transitioned (in this case, the transform) and the time duration, which is one second.

Since the card is the element that's getting the transition, we need to specify the value we are transitioning to. In this case, we start at right center, and we set an additional class name on the card element to define the new **transform** property, which is where we are transitioning:

```
.card.flipped {
        transform: translateX( -100% ) rotateY( -180deg );
}
```

Our transform started at right center, and transitioned to our end point of −100% on the x-axis and rotated −180 degrees on the y-axis. The transition happens when we add the new class to our **card** element, which will leave us with markup that looks like this:

```
<div class="viewPort">
    <div id="card" class="card flipped">
        <div class="frontView">HTML5 Hacks</div>
        <div class="backView">Rocks!</div>
    </div>
</div>
```

This simple transition is what gives us the appearance of the card flip.

The last two elements in our component are the front and back of the cards. Surprisingly enough, there isn't a whole lot of CSS to each card:

```
.card .frontView, .card .backView {
        height: 100%;
        width: 100%;
```

```
    background: black;
    line-height: 260px;
    color: white;
    text-align: center;
    font-weight: bold;
    font-size: 5em;
    position: absolute;
    backface-visibility: hidden;
}

.card .backView {
  -webkit-transform: rotateY( 180deg );
   transform: rotateY( 180deg );
}
```

There are really only two "functional" CSS attributes on these elements to call attention to here. The first applies to both elements, and is the attribute **backface-visibility**. The **backface-visibility** defines whether you can see the element inverted when you turn it around, or whether the element disappears. The default is **visible**, so in order to not have our **div**s bleed through when the card is flipped, we will set this attribute to **false**.

The second attribute applies to the back of the card only. We set a simple **rotateY** transform of **180deg**. This turns the back around completely, and our positioning allows the two cards to occupy the same space, thus appearing as the front and back of the same card. You may be wondering whether we need to switch up the transform when we flip the card. Well, we don't. This is a great example of how to build a complex context with transforms. We have a nested transform where the card has a transform, and then the back face of the card inside it also has a transform. In this scenario, the back face of the card will always have a 180-degree rotation from the front of the card, and only the parent card is flipped back and forth to control which of the card faces is shown.

Putting It All Together

We have all the ingredients of a traditional iOS card flip. All we are missing are a few lines of JavaScript that we can call to tell the card when to flip. For this scenario, I've added a button to the bottom of the page with the **controls** class, and this JavaScript:

```
document.querySelector('.controls').addEventListener('click',
  function(){
    var elem = document.querySelector('.card');
    elem.className = (elem.className == 'card')?'card flipped':'card';
});
```

This simple listener will add the **flipped** class to the **card** element if it doesn't have the class, and will take it away if it does. Figure 2-46 shows how our pure CSS card flip looks now.

Figure 2-46.
iOS-style card flip re-created in CSS using CSS3 transforms and CSS3 transitions

Now we have a good, old-fashioned iOS card flip.

HACK 26 Use Respond.js to Polyfill CSS3 Media Queries in IE

Media queries are key to developing a responsive design, which can be problematic for browsers and phones that don't yet support the feature. Respond.js was developed to fill that need. Now you can build a responsive website from which everyone can benefit.

Responsive design can be an efficient way to build websites. Instead of writing one website, one mobile website, and one tablet website, you just write one website that works well on all devices. One of the foundational tools of responsive design is CSS media queries, but unfortunately media queries don't work in Internet Explorer versions earlier than IE 8. That's a problem for us web standards folks. The basic principle of modern web standards is to write an application once, and have it function on all standards-based web browsers. The lack of web standards could severely hinder the adoption of HTML5 features, as functional features such as media queries would have no backward-compatible support in older browsers.

Luckily, God created polyfills. In the HTML5 community we talk a lot about these wonderful things. A polyfill is a traditional web component, such as JavaScript or Flash, which is used in place of an HTML5 feature when that feature is not supported by the browser. This allows us to adopt HTML5 features as they arrive on the market, and still hold true to our web standards principles.

Media queries now have a first-class polyfill as well, and it's called Respond.js. Developed by Scott Jehl, Respond.js is a JavaScript polyfill that recognizes when media queries are not supported, and runs a script that loops through the content of your CSS file and identifies the media queries being implemented. The script actually uses Ajax to load a version of the CSS file as text so that it can parse it and interprets the CSS inside the conditional media query rules. The script then listens for the appropriate width and height changes on your window and applies the CSS according to the rules you defined in your media queries. It's that easy!

Just Add JavaScript

The implementation couldn't be simpler. Use the media-query-based CSS that you would normally use for your responsive website, and after you have added your CSS `<link>` tags, add this small JavaScript file into your `<head>` tag:

```
<head>
    <meta charset="utf-8">
    <title>Respond JS Test Page</title>
    <link href="test.css" rel="stylesheet">
    <link href="test2.css" media="screen and (min-width: 37.5em)"
    rel="stylesheet"> <!-- 37.5em = 600px @ 16px -->
    <script src="../respond.src.js"></script>
</head>
```

Let's take a look at the results. In Hack #16 we built a rad responsive website with media queries, and if you have an HTML5 browser, the website will work great (see Figure 2-47).

Now let's look at the same site in IE 8 (see Figure 2-48).

The problem with our website is that it doesn't service all our visitors, because many of them surf the Web with a browser that doesn't support media queries. So let's add our script tag to the head of our page, and load the page again (see Figure 2-49).

Figure 2-47.
Our responsive website as viewed in the Google Chrome browser, version 15

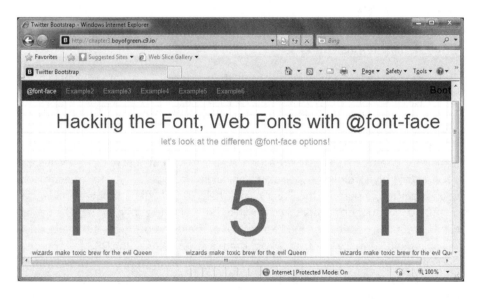

Figure 2-48.
Our responsive website as viewed in Microsoft Internet Explorer version 8

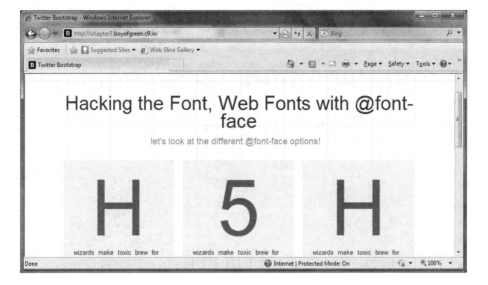

Figure 2-49.
Our responsive website as viewed in Microsoft Internet Explorer version 8 after adding Respond.js to the page

I told you it was easy!

Caveats and Quid Pro Quo

There are a few keys to achieving success with Respond.js. First, you will want to place the *respond.js* file directly after your last CSS `<link>` tag. If you give your browser time to load content before loading the *respond.js* script, your non-HTML5 users will likely see a flash of improperly styled content. This isn't a functionality issue, as the site will fix itself once the *respond.js* file is run, but it could be a negative or confusing loading experience for your users. Second, keep in mind that Respond.js is specifically designed to polyfill media queries based on height and width. If you have your media queries set to orientation, this library won't help. The media attributes on link elements are fully supported, but only if the linked stylesheet contains no media queries. If it does contain queries, the media attribute will be ignored and the internal queries will be parsed normally. In other words, `@media` statements in the CSS take priority. Additionally, Respond.js works by requesting a pristine copy of your CSS via Ajax, so if you host your stylesheets on a CDN (or a subdomain), you'll need to upload a proxy page to enable cross-domain communication.

A full list of implementation details and instructions for setting up a proxy page for CDNs is available on the Respond.js GitHub page (*https://github.com/scottjehl/Respond*).

HTML5 HACKS

Control Mobile Layout with the viewport <meta> Tag

Browser makers have conformed to the use of a `<meta>` tag that helps your mobile and small-screen devices load a page as the author desired. This one tag can be the difference between a viewable website and one that is "made for mobile."

When smartphones with fancy HTML5 browsers hit the market, they opened up the Web at a whole new level. After years of being limited to a WAP (Wireless Application Protocol)-based Web of limited markup on alternate versions of sites, we now had the entire Web accessible from the palm of our hand. Smartphones generally adopted a technique of scaling the entire page down so that it would fit on a small screen (with limited pixels). Basically, the average 920 px website would be scaled down to 320 px (or whatever the device's pixel width happened to be).

Browser makers wanted to encourage developers to build interfaces with appropriate screen sizes, so they introduced a few new tags that aren't sanctioned by any standards group, but are generally agreed upon by browser makers. One of the most common, and generally most useful, tags is the `viewport` `<meta>` tag.

The `viewport` `<meta>` tag addresses the problem of avoiding the auto-scale feature on smartphones for websites that are designed for viewing at a specific scale. Let's take a look at the tag:

```
<meta name="viewport" content="width=device-width,initial-scale=1.0">
</meta>
```

This `<meta>` tag, like all `<meta>` tags, should be a child of the `<head>` tag. It follows the pattern of other HTML `<meta>` tags by having a **name** and a **content** attribute. The **content** attribute holds some or all of the following properties:

`width`
> The width of the viewport in pixels

`height`
> The height of the viewport in pixels

`initial-scale`
> The viewport's initial scale as a multiplier

`minimum-scale`
> The minimum amount that the viewport can be scaled

`maximum-scale`
> The maximum amount that the viewport can be scaled

```
user-scalable
```
Defines whether the user can scale the page (through pinch and zoom)

This tag also allows you to specify characteristics of your site and control the presentation for your visitors. A picture is worth a thousand words, so let's take a look at an example. Figure 2-50 shows a responsive web page with the `<meta>` tag, and Figure 2-51 shows the same page without the `<meta>` tag.

Figure 2-50.
Sample web page designed for a mobile phone and using the viewport <meta> tag as viewed on an iPhone 4s Safari browser

We're aiming to control a few key aspects of our design. First and most noticeably is the `initial-scale` property. This property is set to `1.0`, which means there is no scale on the page, and one pixel is equal to one pixel. The second property is `width`, which we set to `device-width` (note that some devices, such as Windows Phone 7, override `device-width` to a standard width for that phone). This tells our page that the viewport will be set to the width of our device's screen. This is particularly helpful in designs that are set to 100% width. The width can be set to clearly constrain the page.

One property I did not include in this tag is the `user-scalable` property, set to `no`. Many websites use this parameter to disable pinch and zoom. Although the text is significantly larger, it may not be large enough for some users. I want to leave the

HTML5 HACKS

Figure 2-51.
Sample web page designed for a mobile phone without the use of the viewport <meta> tag as viewed on an iPhone 4s Safari browser

option for them to zoom in further if necessary. Generally, I leave the pinch and zoom feature on, unless I am using pinch and zoom for something else on the page (such as zooming into a map). You'll find this property set to **no** quite often, but for my users' sake, I try to leave it on whenever possible.

Will the Real HTML5 Spec Please Stand Up?

If you caught it earlier, I mentioned that this particular feature wasn't originally a specification, but more a convention agreed upon by browser makers. Due to the lack of standardization, there is a deviation in how some of these features are supported among different devices. Luckily, browser makers are on our side and they like to see conventions become standards. Fortunately, along came the W3C standard for viewport properties.

The big surprise was that instead of using a **<meta>** tag, the W3C decided to make the feature part of the CSS3 specification and call it *CSS device adaptation*. The good news is that it's still just as easy to implement. The W3C even walks you through an easy conversion from **<meta>** tag to CSS declaration on its spec (*http://dev.w3.org/csswg/css-device-adapt/*).

From a high level, device adaptation is fairly simple. Let's look at how we would declare the same `<meta>` tag we've been using for this hack:

```
@viewport {
    width: device-width;
    initial-scale=1.0"
}
```

The `viewport` property can be placed inside a style block on the page, or on any stylesheet. It can even be wrapped in a media query. I encourage you to review the specification before implementing it, as some of the property names have changed slightly. At the time of this writing, the specification is so new that I hesitate to print the specific properties, as they are subject to change.

3

Multimedia Hacking

HTML5 introduces new native multimedia functionality that upgrades audio and video elements into first-class elements. Because they are native elements (as opposed to plug-ins), they can be styled with CSS, can be accessed via JavaScript, and will utilize the GPU.

In addition to being flexible, this functionality is also easy to use—in most cases it's as easy as embedding an image in the page. HTML5 audio and HTML5 video have very similar implementation methods and very similar JavaScript APIs. Although most of this chapter presents hacks that utilize HTML5 video, take note that many of the same hacks can be performed with the audio element as well. The API for "play" on a video element is the same as the API for "play" on an audio element.

If there is anything to get excited about in HTML5, it's how web developers have been freed from using "browser plug-ins" to deliver multimedia. Gone are the days of users having to download and install a different plug-in for every website just to view a video clip.

HACK 28   Embed Video Directly in Your Application with HTML5 Video

Video is now mainstream in HTML5. Forget plug-ins, forget supporting video players, and welcome to the world of native video through HTML5. See why it's such a big deal to have video as its own page element.

What's the big deal with HTML5 video? We've been playing video on the Web for years. The answer is that the Web is changing. In years past it was pretty easy to predict what technologies your users would support when they came to your website: the site could use Flash, or Silverlight, or any other technology website developers could find to make it work.

In today's world of desktop cell phones, tablets, and e-readers all sharing the same Web, it's important to standardize on a format for video and audio that all players can consume. This need has really come to a head with Apple directly excluding plug-ins such as Flash and Silverlight in order to better control battery and power consumption on iOS devices. This in turn has thrust HTML5 video into the mainstream. On today's Web, if you want to support all your users HTML5 video is essential.

Writing the Code

HTML5 video isn't just flexible; it's also easier for developers to implement. You can place HTML5 video on your page with a simple tag. Let's look at a sample implementation:

```
<video width="320" height="240" autoplay="autoplay"
  poster="examples/sanfran.jpg" source="examples/sanfran.m4v">
</video>
```

The preceding code will cause your video to appear on the screen as shown in Figure 3-1.

Figure 3-1.
Google Chrome rendering a page with the HTML5 <video> tag

You've got quite a bit of control built directly into the tag itself. Let's look at the most common attributes:

width *and* height

With these attributes you can set the size of the video directly in the tag itself. These attributes will determine what size the embedded video is on the page, not the size of the file you are loading. The height and width do not necessarily need to match the original source. These attribute values are represented in pixels, which equates to stating "340" and not "340 px." You can set height and width with CSS to return the same results.

controls

Setting the **controls** attribute allows you to hide or show the native controls for your video. The default is set to **show**. You may want to hide the controls if you're going to build your own controls with JavaScript.

autoplay

This attribute sets your video to start playing as soon as the source is ready. It defaults to **off** (thank God). I beg you to not use this parameter on your website's home page.

autobuffer

This is similar to **autoplay** but without actually playing the video. This attribute defaults to **off**. Once the source is located, turning on **autobuffer** causes the video to start downloading, so it can be played as soon as the user initiates it. This is another attribute to use with caution, as it will use the data plan of your mobile users. Only use this attribute when you're fairly confident your users are going to start the video.

poster

This attribute allows you to set a path to an image you want to use as your video poster board. This is the image that represents the video to your users before it starts playing, and it is often a screen capture from the video itself. If you don't have a poster board set, the first frame of the video will be used to represent the image, once that frame is loaded.

loop

This attribute allows you to set your video to start over again once it reaches the end. The default value is **off**.

As you can see, there is a lot of flexibility in the **<video>** tag itself. Video can be a powerful way to get a message across, but be cautious about using some of these attributes as the added flexibility could result in adverse experiences for your users.

Video As a First-Class Element

HTML5 `<video>` tags finally give you native control over your video. Unlike embedded objects such as Flash objects, HTML5 `<video>` tags can be treated just like any other element on your page. One of the greatest advantages of this is the ability to control the element with CSS. Just as with any other element on the page, your `<video>` tag can have borders, text color (for subtitles), opacity, or any other CSS characteristic.

In addition, `<video>` tags provide JavaScript APIs that give you added functionality. You can use JavaScript to start, stop, buffer, skip ahead, or control your video in other ways. This allows you to build your own custom controls for your videos, or even build a more advanced buffering system for loading videos.

As a first-class element, the HTML5 `<video>` tag also gives you access to the data loaded onto your page. Plus, `<video>` tags can interact with other page elements such as the `canvas` element, which would allow you to do frame-by-frame exports from your `<video>` tag onto the `<canvas>` tag, which could in turn be manipulated to perform other functions. Be careful when using the `<video>` tag, though, as security measures are built into the HTML5 `canvas` element which limit you from importing video from a different origin into your canvas file.

HACK 29 Choose the Right Codecs for Your Video Files

Unfortunately for the Web, one video file type still doesn't "rule them all." In this world of different browsers supporting different codecs, be sure your videos can be viewed on all your target browsers.

A *video codec* is basically an algorithm for a video compression format. Raw video would be much too large in terms of file size to transport over the Web, so it must be compressed for delivery. And browsers must support the codec of your encoded file to be able to play the file. Now here comes the sad part. Today's modern HTML5 browsers each support a subset of codecs, so there is no one video codec that can be used to play your video on every browser.

You have to go through the work of encoding your video numerous times for different browsers, but the good news is that you don't have to write your `<video>` tag differently for each browser. Let's start by looking at a traditional `<video>` tag with the source of the video set as the `src` attribute of the tag:

```
<video width="320" height="240" autoplay="autoplay"
 poster="examples/sanfran.jpg" src="examples/sanfran.m4v">
</video>
```

The preceding code is nice and neat, but it only allows you to set one source for your `<video>` tag. Let's rewrite that tag to set the source as its own tag:

```
<video width="320" height="240" autoplay="autoplay"
  poster="examples/sanfran.jpg">
    <source src=examples/sanfran.ogv type=video/ogg>
    <source src=examples/sanfran.mp4 type=video/mp4>
    Your browser does not support the video tag.
</video>
```

This nested tag is the **<source>** tag. This tag is used specifically to set multiple sources for media tags. Your browser will play the first video file in the list of **<source>** tags that it supports. If no supported sources are found, you will have a blank **<video>** tag. The text we included inside the **<video>** tag is for non-HTML5 browsers. If the browser doesn't recognize the **<video>** tag, it will fall back to show the text.

Which Codecs to Support

Now here comes the hard part: figuring out which codec you need to support. Let's look at the most popular codec types on the market, and the pros and cons of each:

H.264 (MP4)

Apple Safari and Microsoft Internet Explorer support this codec. This is not a free codec. At the time of this writing it is released as a royalty-free codec, but since a governing group controls it (of which Apple is a part), the policy could change at any time. This is the basis for reluctance among other browser makers to adopt support for this codec. In version 9, Google Chrome has also started to support this codec, which makes it even more viable as a web codec.

OGG/Theora

This is truly a free, open-standard codec. Its downside is the lack of supporting tools. Since none of the big browser makers support it, there aren't a lot of tools out there to do the encoding for the video files. At the time of this writing, Firefox, Opera, and Google Chrome support this codec.

WebM

This format is based on the VP8 codec that is owned by Google. This is a high-quality form of compression that is free and open source, which makes WebM a good web codec. However, since Google owns the codec, it potentially could change the open source status of the project in the future. Almost every browser maker supports this codec. Apple Safari browsers don't support this codec in any shape or form.

Aren't you glad that the standard supports more than one source file at once? As there is no one codec that is supported by all major browsers, it's necessary to provide at least two different files to cover all major browsers. To be compatible with Apple and Internet Explorer browsers, you must support H.264, and then either OGG or WebM can be used to cover the other browsers.

HACK 30 Create Custom Video Controls with Video APIs

It's great that HTML5 video comes with its own controls, but at times they don't meet the needs of your application. Learn how to use the HTML5 video APIs to create your own controls in JavaScript.

It's fantastic to have built-in controls in every video element. However, in some cases the default controllers just don't meet your needs. For those cases, the HTML5 <video> tag provides a rich set of APIs that you can control through JavaScript. These APIs are flexible enough to allow you to build an entirely new set of controls for your video. Let's look at some of the more relevant controls.

Before building out the JavaScript code, let's start with some basic markup. We'll have a video element and a list of buttons below it:

```
<video id="myVideo" width="400" height="200" autoplay="autoplay"
poster="../sanfran.jpg" src=" examples/sanfran.m4p "></video>
<button class="button skipBack">skip back</button>

<button class="button stop">stop</button>

<button class="button play">play/pause</button>

<button class="button skipAhead">skip ahead</button>


<button class="button volumeUp">volume up</button>

<button class="button VolumeDown">volume down </button>
```

So we've got our basic markup for our video. Now we want to start building out our custom controls. Then, once our custom controls are ready, we'll remove the native controls from the video element. To build out these controls, we'll start by building a JavaScript reference to our video element:

```
var myVideoEl = document.querySelector('#myVideo');
```

It's important that we build a reference to this element so that we can use the reference instead of going back to the DOM (Document Object Model) every time. Now that we have the **video** element identified, we will use it to call out custom controllers. The code should look something like this:

```
myViedoEl.play();
myVideoEl.pause();
myVideoEl. currentTime
```

If we were going to use the same controls we have access to in the HTML5 element, there wouldn't be any point in building custom controls: we would just use the ones provided for us. So we're going to provide some special features. Let's start with the easy ones, the Play and Pause controls:

```
//ref to my video tag
var myVideoEl = document.querySelector('#myVideo');

//add listeners to the play pause button

document.querySelector('.play').addEventListener('click',function(e){
        if(myVideoEl.paused === true){
                        myVideoEl.play();
        }else{
        myVideoEl.pause();
}
)};
```

In the preceding code we added a listener to the button that checks to see if the video is paused. If it is paused we start to play the video, and if it is not paused we pause the video. This provides us with the play and pause functionally through our toggle button.

Next we want to add the Stop button. HTML5 video does not have a true stop capability, so we need to build it. In this case, we are assuming that stop means stop: we will not only stop playing the video (pause it), but also stop loading it. The easy way to do this is to remove the source reference of the **<video>** tag programmatically. Let's add another listener to our JavaScript to perform the stop:

```
document.querySelector('.stop').addEventListener('click',function(e){
        myVideoEl.src = '';
})
```

This will stop the video from playing, as well as stop the data from downloading. But when the user hits Play again the video needs to start again. So, since we removed the source of our **video** element, let's go back into our play/pause function to add a few lines of code to address this:

```
document.querySelector('.play').addEventListener('click',function(e){
        if(myVideoEl.currentTime == 0){ //we know it is stopped
```

```
    myVodelEl.src = 'examples/sanfran.m4p'
    }
            if(myVideoEl.paused === true){
                        myVideoEl.play();
            }else{
            myVideoEl.pause();
    }
    )};
```

Now when the Play and Pause buttons are hit the source will be added back into the video element if it's empty.

The next two buttons in our control bar will be treated similarly. These buttons are the Skip Forward and Skip Back buttons. For our example we will skip five seconds forward in the video or five seconds back. Again, we will control these buttons by adding a few lines of JavaScript to what was previously illustrated:

```
document.querySelector('.skipAhead').addEventListener('click',
    function(e){
        myCurrentTime = myVideoEl. currentTime;

        myVideoEl.currentTime = myCurrentTime+5;
})

document.querySelector('.skipBack').addEventListener('click',
    function(e){
        myCurrentTime = myVideoEl. currentTime;

        myVideoEl.currentTime = myCurrentTime-5;
})
```

For skipping through our video, we simply use the currentTime API to get the current time of the video being played, and then we update the currentTime to be the current value plus or minus five seconds.

Our last two buttons are the volume controls. Volume is represented as a positive numeric value between 0 and 1. Our volume controls will simply increment in fractional numbers. Let's take a look at the code:

```
document.querySelector('.volumeUp').addEventListener('click',
    function(e){
        var myCurrentVolume = myVideoEl. volume;
        if(myCurrentVolume >0){
        myVideoEl. volume = myCurrentVolume -.1;
    }
})
document.querySelector('.volumeUp').addEventListener('click',
```

```
         function(e){
                 var myCurrentVolume = myVideoEl. volume;
                 if(myCurrentVolume <1){
                 myVideoEl. volume = myCurrentVolume +.1;
         }
         })
```

So there we have it. Let's compile all our JavaScript together and review:

```
var myVideoEl = document.getElementById('myVideo');
document.querySelector('.play').addEventListener('click',
     function(e){
             if(myVideoEl.currentTime == 0){//we know it is stopped
myVodelEl.src = 'examples/sanfran.m4p';
}
             if(myVideoEl.paused === true){
                             myVideoEl.play();
             }else{
             myVideoEl.pause();
}
)};


document.querySelector('.stop').addEventListener('click',
     function(e){
             myVideoEl.src = '';
})


document.querySelector('.skipAhead').addEventListener('click',
     function(e){
             myCurrentTime = myVideoEl. currentTime;

             myVideoEl.currentTime = myCurrentTime+5;
})

document.querySelector('.skipBack').addEventListener('click',
     function(e){
             myCurrentTime = myVideoEl. currentTime;

             myVideoEl.currentTime = myCurrentTime-5;
})


 document.querySelector('.volumeUp').addEventListener('click',
```

```
    function(e){
        var myCurrentVolume = myVideoEl. volume;
        if(myCurrentVolume >0){
        myVideoEl. volume = myCurrentVolume -1;
}
})

document.querySelector('.volumeUp').addEventListener('click',
    function(e){
        var myCurrentVolume = myVideoEl. volume;
        if(myCurrentVolume <10){
        myVideoEl. volume = myCurrentVolume -1;
}
})
```

Now that we have run all our JavaScript on the page, one problem still remains. We have two sets of controls: our new controls and the default controls. Since we have our new controls built out, we will add one additional line of JavaScript to turn off the default controls of this **<video>** tag:

```
document.getElementById('myVideo').controls = false;
```

After adding the markup, our JavaScript, and a few lines of CSS to pretty it up, we have new video controls that meet the needs of our application. Figure 3-2 shows the results.

Figure 3-2.
Video element with custom controls built on top of our HTML5 video element APIs

A Word About Audio

We've focused completely on <video> tags for this hack, but we don't want to neglect the fact that HTML5 audio fits into the same specifications as the <video> tag (HTMLMediaElement), so the same APIs exist for audio as they do for video. We can swap out our <video> tag for an <audio> tag, and all the same controls will work.

HACK 31 Replace the Background of Your HTML5 Video with the <canvas> Tag

With HTML5 video, a <canvas> tag, and a little bit of JavaScript you can make Hollywood-style (I'm using the term loosely) effects on your video in real time.

Being able to play video directly on your web application is pretty cool, but being able to manipulate that same video in real time is awesome. We've all see the green screen effects from "making of" videos in which an actor is filmed in front of a green screen, and then a new background is composited into the shot to make it look like the actor is kung-fu fighting at the top of the Golden Gate Bridge, or something cool like that. We're going to accomplish the same thing with a <video> tag, two <canvas> tags, and a few lines of JavaScript.

To get started we'll look at our markup, and then walk through how each component is used:

```
<div class="row">
  <div class="span5">
    <video id="sourceVideo" src="/examples/video.ogv" controls="true">
    </video>
    <canvas id="hiddenCanvas" width="320" height="192"></canvas>
  </div>
  <div class="span5">
    <canvas id="displayCanvas" width="320" height="192"></canvas>
  </div>
</div>
```

We basically have three page elements to work with, and each has a key role in our "production."

Source Video

The source video is the video we start with. It's basically a video of a rascally little boy on a green background. The source video will be played and the pixels from each frame will be pulled out and displayed on our first <canvas> tag for processing. Figure 3-3 shows a frame from our source video to give you an idea of what we will be working with.

Figure 3-3.
Screen capture from our video file showing a young boy in front of a green background

Hidden Canvas

The hidden canvas is where the source video will be dumped frame for frame. Our JavaScript will pull each frame from the video source and write it to this **<canvas>** tag. This gives us a 2D context of data for us to do pixel-level analysis.

Display Canvas

The display canvas is the canvas we actually see. As we play our video and copy the frames to the first **<canvas>** tag, we will pull that pixel-level data from the first canvas and analyze it to find the green screen portion of our video. The identified green pixels will then be removed and replaced with transparent pixels, allowing the background already set on this canvas to shine through. We will initially set our **<canvas>** tag to the background shown in Figure 3-4.

Figure 3-4.
Background image set on the display <canvas> tag before the video data is overlaid

The Nuts and Bolts

We have our markup and we have identified the HTML5 elements we will be using for our application. Now we need to put together the JavaScript that will make all of this work. This JavaScript will reside in the script tag at the bottom of our page.

First we need to make pointers to each element. We also need to create pointers to the 2D content of our <canvas> tags. The 2D content is the "surface" of our <canvas> tag that we will be moving data into and out of.

```
var sourceVideo = document.getElementById("sourceVideo");
var hiddenCanvas = document.getElementById("hiddenCanvas");
var displayCanvas = document.getElementById("displayCanvas");
var hiddenContext = hiddenCanvas.getContext ("2d");
var displayContext = displayCanvas.getContext ("2d");
```

Now we need to set up our listener on the **video** element so that we know when the video starts playing. This will start running the JavaScript we will lay out in a moment, but first let's set that listener:

```
sourceVideo.addEventListener('play', function(){runAnalysis()});
```

With our environment set up, we need to build a function that will make sure the video is playing. We do this by determining that the state of the video is not paused or ended. We will then invoke a new method called `frameConversion`, which will run our video conversions. Finally, we will make this a self-calling method so that it will loop through itself until the video is paused or ended.

```
runAnalysis: function() {
    if (sourceVideo.paused || sourceVideo.ended) {
    return;
    }
    frameConversion();
    setTimeout(function () {
        runAnalysis();
    }, 0);
},
```

The next method is where all the magic happens. This is where we grab the video data, run the analysis, replace the pixels, and write it to our display canvas. We then do it over and over again.

```
var frameConversion = function(){

    hiddenContext.drawImage(sourceVideo,0,0,sourceVideo.videoWidth,
    sourceVideo.videoHeight);

    var frame = hiddenContext.getImageData(0,0,sourceVideo.videoWidth,
```

```
        sourceVideo.videoHeight);

    var length = frame.data.length;
    for (var i =0; i <length; i++){
            var r = frame.data [i * 4 + 0];
            var g = frame.data [i * 4 + 1];
            var b = frame.data [i * 4 + 2];

    if(g>110 && g<200 && r<190 && r>100 && b<200 && b>110){
        frame.data[i * 4 + 3] = 0;
        }
    }
    displayContext.putImageData(frame, 0, 0);
    return
};
```

Our frame conversion method is called repeatedly from the initial setup method. We could streamline and improve the performance of this application in a number of ways, but for the sake of simplicity we will leave it as it is.

The Results

So, we have our video feeding into our `<canvas>` tag, then running analysis on the data in that canvas which we process and display on our display canvas. We started with our rascally little boy video and our background image, and we ended with the wonderful Hollywood-style production shown in Figure 3-5.

Figure 3-5.
Our display canvas with our background image overlaid with our processed video source

HTML5 HACKS

As you can see, putting different HTML5 elements together can result in powerful effects. A green screen tool is just the beginning of what you can create.

HACK 32   Add Subtitles to Your HTML5 Video Element

Video can be a powerful communications tool for the Web, but to fully reach your user base, your `<video>` and `<audio>` tags need to be accessible. HTML5 provides you with easy-to-implement subtitles through the new `<track>` tag, and WebVTT files.

Subtitles can be amazingly beneficial for web-based video files. Primarily, subtitles are important for hearing-impaired users who may be able to watch your video, but without subtitles wouldn't know what was being said. Subtitles can also be used to provide multilingual assistance. If your video is in English, you can provide Spanish, French, and German subtitles to allow non-English speakers the opportunity to enjoy the content as well.

As an auxiliary benefit, you may also be helping the "speaker-impaired." Speaker-impaired users are people like me, who lost the power supply from their desktop computer speakers and refuse to buy a new one because they're going to find it one of these days. If my computer sound doesn't work, subtitles can help me, too!

Easy Implementation

Subtitles are one of the easiest features to implement. You simply add a `<track>` tag as a child of your `<video>` tag, and add a few attributes to it. Let's take a look at the `<track>` tag as it appears in our markup:

```
<video id="myVideo" width="320" height="240" controls="controls"
poster="examples/sanfran.jpg" src="examples/sanfran.m4v">
<track src="/examples/subtitles.srt" default="true" kind="subtitles"
 srclang="en" label="English"></track>
</video>
```

Here's a description of each attribute:

src

> This is the common attribute used in HTML to point to a source file. In this case, it points to a VTT file (more on that in the next section).

default

> One of your **track** elements can have this attribute set for each **video** element. As the name implies, it identifies the default track for that **video** element. If more than one **track** element has this attribute within a video file, the first one in the list will be identified as the default track.

label
> This attribute identifies the title to be used for the track (think "English" instead of "en").

kind
> This identifies the track file type. Its properties can be any of the following:

- Captions
- Chapters
- Descriptions
- Metadata
- Subtitles

srclang
> This specifies the language of the track. The value must be a valid language code and is a required attribute if the track is of type subtitle.

The VTT File

The subtitles are actually stored in the WebVTT file that is referenced in the `<track>` tag. WebVTT stands for Web Video Text Tracks and is a fairly simple file to format. Let's look at our sample file:

```
1
00:00:01.000 --> 00:00:05.000
This is the first line of text, displaying from 1-5 seconds

2
00:00:05.000 --> 00:00:11.000
And the second line of text
on two lines
```

The file contains *cues*. Each cue is numbered and has time settings in the format hh:mm:ss.mmm. The subtitles will follow the time range. The preceding sample will display the first cue from the first second to the fifth second of the video, and the second cue from the fifth second to the eleventh second.

Putting it all together, your video subtitles will appear as shown in Figure 3-6.

Figure 3-6.
Video file with subtitle captions from the VTT file

Karaoke Anyone?

Subtitles can also be presented with inline timing tags. These will present your sub-titles in a "karaoke" or painted-on style. To accomplish this, we put timing tags within each cue text as follows:

```
1
00:00:01.000 --> 00:00:05.000
<00:00:01.000>This is the first line of text, <00:00:03.000>displaying
from 1-5 seconds
```

This cue will present the first half of the cue at second one, and will paint on the second line of the cue on second three (see Figure 3-7).

Figure 3-7.
WebVTT file with timestamps displaying text one segment at a time

Summary

It's recommended that you include `track` elements within all your `<video>` tags that contain audio information. To increase the scope of your audience, it's also good to include multilingual subtitles if possible. The Web has no boundaries, and now your HTML5 video files don't either.

HACK 33 Beautify Your HTML5 Video Cues

Video cues are powerful, but they can be pretty ugly. Luckily, there's a spec for that! Style your HTML5 video cues with formatting, or even CSS.

Video cues are pretty simple out of the box. They appear as basic white text over your video and show up when the timing from your WebVTT file dictates. The WebVTT specification allows you to identify formatting for your cues, which gives you some basic presentation formatting. Additionally, it allows you to utilize CSS for more advanced styling.

Let's take a quick peek at what we are working with before we begin to spice it up (see Figure 3-8).

Figure 3-8.
HTML5 video file with basic WebVTT cues presented on the screen

Basic Formatting from WebVTT

Some basic formatting applies directly to video cues as part of the WebVTT specification. Here are the key attributes:

`D:vertical/D:vertical-lr`

Changes the orientation of the text to be vertical or vertical with text from left to right.

`L:X`

Determines the position from the top of the screen. This can be a value or a percentage. If it's a percentage it will be positioned from the top of the video frame; if it's a value it will be placed on that line.

`T:X%`

Determines the position of the text horizontally. This is displayed as a percentage only.

`A:start/A:middle/A:end`

Determines the alignment of the text within the frame.

`S:X%`

Determines the width of the text box on the video frame.

Each format should be placed beside the time range as follows:

```
1
00:00:01.000 --> 00:00:10.000 A:middle T:50%
```

This provides your basic formatting. For more advanced styling let's turn to CSS.

CSS Styling

For more advanced formatting, we can place format-friendly tags directly within the cues of our WebVTT file. Let's look at a sample:

```
00:00:01.000 --> 00:00:10.000 A:middle T:50%
Hello <b class="name">reader</b>, enjoy your <e>video</e>
```

HTML formatting is added directly into the text of the cue. Without any CSS styling, the cue would be presented as plain text, as shown in Figure 3-9.

Figure 3-9.
HTML formatting of text cue without any CSS styling

As you can see, the text was presented as HTML, where the tag elements are not displayed. To spice up our formatting, let's add some CSS that will make our cues stand out:

```
.name {
    font-weight: 600;


    }
```

With our CSS, the formatted cue will now look like Figure 3-10.

Figure 3-10.
WebVTT HTML-formatted cue with our CSS included which shows the word "reader" in boldface

Pseudoclasses Within a Track Cue

To easily identify the cue, you can use a CSS pseudoclass. Three pseudoclasses are available:

```
::cue
::future
::past
```

The cue identifies the entire cue; the future and past are used to identify those states of the cue text when an inline timing tag is used within the cue.

A set of attributes can be used within this pure text environment. The set is limited to the following:

- `'color'`
- `'text-decoration'`
- `'text-outline'`
- `'text-shadow'`
- `'background'`
- `'outline'`
- `'font'`
- `'line-height'`
- `'white-space'`

All other attributes will be ignored when applied to text inside a cue.

`HACK 34` Use the Cuepoint.js Polyfill for Subtitles

At the time of this writing, IE 10 is the only HTML5 browser that supports subtitles. This hack presents a great little polyfill that will bridge the gap on video tracks until browsers catch up with our needs.

If you have read any of the past few hacks, you probably realize how powerful the **track** element can be. Having a track of cues that accompany your video or audio files helps you to comply with the Americans with Disabilities Act (ADA), translate your files into multiple languages, and even simply enhance the message of your video.

From my perspective, track files are almost essential for audio and video within web applications. That being said, we have a problem because, at the time of this writing, all modern browsers support the HTML5 **<video>** and **<audio>** tags, but none support the use of subtitles with a **track** element. When an HTML5 feature isn't natively available within our browser, we as developers rely on HTML5 polyfills (the use of JavaScript to backfill missing HTML5 functionality) to make the feature usable to all our users.

Using Cuepoint.js

In comes Cuepoint.js. This is a neat little JavaScript polyfill that allows you to overlay subtitles or other cues on top of your native HTML5 video files. It then uses the HTML5 video APIs to align the proper cues with the proper time markings on the video or audio file. Cuepoint.js doesn't rely on `track` elements pointing to WebVTT files like our native subtitles do, but rather is controlled through a simple JavaScript declaration.

Cuepoint.js relies on a systematic markup structure to identify the video file along with the other necessary HTML elements. Let's start our example by looking at our necessary markup:

```
<div id="cuePlayer" class="row">
  <video id="video" width="680" controls="controls"
   poster="examples/sanfran.jpg" src="examples/sanfran.m4v">
  </video>
  <div id="subtitles">An Easy polyfill</div>
</div>
```

We start with a wrapper `div` identifying our player with an `id` of `cuePlayer`. Inside that are the two necessary elements: `video` with an `id` of `video` and an empty `div` with an `id` of `subtitles`. From here there is only one more step to get it going. We need to add a few lines of JavaScript. We'll start by adding the *cuepoint.js* JavaScript file to the page:

```
<script src="/assets/js/cuepoint.js" type="text/javascript"></script>
```

We'll simply put this at the bottom of our page so that we can be sure our necessary markup has already been loaded. Next we will write our configuration object in a script tag directly below this file:

```
//Slides object with a time (integer) and a html string
var slides = {
0: "This is the first subtitle. You can put html in here if you like",
4: "Easy Cues for HTML5 Video.",
7: "An Easy polyfill",

}
//Start cuepoint and pass in our the subtitles we want
cuepoint.init(slides);
```

The configuration file consists of two components. The first is an array of paired values that consists of a time marker and a string of text. That string can be plain text or HTML markup. The second component is the initial method call in which you pass in the reference to your array. For this example, I added a few lines of CSS that make the subtitles overlay the video and provide a bit of smooth styling. Here's the CSS for this example:

```
#subtitles{
    position:absolute;
    bottom:40px;
    width:100%;
    height:40px;
    color:#FFF;
    line-height:40px;
    padding:0 20px;
}

#cuePlayer {
    overflow: hidden;
    position: relative;
}

#video {
        margin: 0 auto 10px auto;
        background: #555;
}
```

Once you add these components to your page, the results will look like Figure 3-11.

Figure 3-11.
Video using the Cuepoint.js polyfill to support HTML5 video subtitles

Remember, it's always important to use subtitles when your video has an audio track, and Cuepoint.js allows you to provide that essential functionality to all your users, regardless of the functionality of their browser.

HACK 35 Easily Build Audio-Rich Applications with Buzz

The term *sound effects* is traditionally ostracized in the web app world and passed off as cheesy and uncharacteristic. With the onset of highly metaphorical applications and HTML5 gaming, being able to tastefully use audio on a website is becoming increasingly necessary. Buzz is an HTML5 audio library that is designed to make that implementation simple and lightweight.

Audio tags make a lot of sense if you're embedding an audio sample into your web application. If you're building something like a library of podcasts, you may have a page full of tags that appear as follows:

```
<div class="clipName">My new Pod Cast</div>
<div class="audio player">
  <audio controls src="mysoundFile.ogg" />
</div>
```

This is great because HTML5 provides all the necessary features, such as buffering and controls. Gone are the days of building your own audio player in Flash or Java. HTML5 provides this capability out of the box.

Now, if you want to use your audio files in a less traditional manner, the `<audio>` tag may not meet all your needs out of the box. For example, if you wanted to have a sound effect for page turns, or a buzzer go off in a game when the user chooses the wrong answer, suddenly you need to start building a JavaScript framework for loading, managing, and controlling your audio files. Luckily, Jay Salvat has provided a solution.

The Buzz Library

Buzz is a library that provides a set of APIs to help you manage all the creative uses of audio in your applications. Best of all, it has a built-in polyfill to provide backward compatibility for browsers that don't yet support the HTML5 standard. To get an idea of how impactful this can be to your application, visit Jay's website (*http://buzz.jaysalvat.com/demo*) to see his Buzz demo. Figure 3-12 shows a screen grab from the demo.

Figure 3-12.
Screen grab from the Buzz demo, which builds a simple game that tastefully utilizes audio files that perform natively in almost all browsers

Using the Audio APIs

Jay allows you to simply call a JavaScript method that uses the HTML5 audio APIs to manage your sound. Here is some sample code that shows how easy it is to implement your sound files:

```
var mySound = new buzz.sound( "/sounds/myfile", {
    formats: [ "ogg", "mp3", "acc" ]
});

mySound.play()
    .fadeIn()
    .loop()
    .bind( "timeupdate", function() {
        var timer = buzz.toTimer( this.getTime() );
        document.getElementById( "timer" ).innerHTML = timer;
    });
```

In this example we are simply starting a new sound and letting Buzz determine what version of the file it should load. We then play the file, which will dynamically load the sound if it hasn't done so already, fade it in, set it to loop, and start it on a simple timer. You can easily use this code in any of your JavaScript applications.

Using the Buzz APIs

Buzz has a lot to offer—in fact, too much to cover in this hack—so we will only look at some of the highlights of the library. I encourage you to visit the online documentation for a detailed list of all available APIs (*http://buzz.jaysalvat.com/documentation/buzz/*).

The documentation is divided into four sections. Let's look at some of the highlights of each.

Buzz

This is the nuts and bolts of the library. Buzz handles loading the library, the methods that determine what file type to utilize for each browser, and preparing the audio files. This code example shows how easy it is to create a single new audio file, or a whole group at once:

```
//a single file
var mySound = new buzz.sound("/sounds/mysound.ogg");
//a group of files
var myGroup = new buzz.group([
    new sound("/sounds/mysound1.ogg"),
    new sound("/sounds/mysound2.ogg"),
    new sound("/sounds/mysound3.ogg")
)}
```

Sound

Sound provides the APIs for utilizing the sounds. It provides some nice options on top of what we get from HTML, such as fade and stop (as opposed to just pause). Each method from this group is preceded with the **sound.** prefix. Here are some common API calls:

```
mySound.load();
mySound.pause();
sound.loop/sound.unloop();
sound.increaseVolume( [volume] )
```

This library of easy-to-implement methods can be embedded directly into your HTML5 applications.

Group

Group provides the APIs for managing groups of data files. The methods in this section all have the prefix **group.**. Here are some popular sample calls from the API:

```
//playing all loaded sound files
var mySound1 = new sound("/sounds/mysound1.ogg"),
    mySound2 = new sound("/sounds/mysound2.ogg"),
    mySound3 = new sound("/sounds/mysound3.ogg");
buzz.all().play();

yGroup.play();
yGroup.pause();
```

Events

The inclusion of events is a big boost in the usefulness of this library. Events are integrated into the core of JavaScript, so being able to use them with your audio files becomes a very natural thing. These events are helpful when you are attaching visual features or other audio features to the implementation of audio. Let's look at a few events from Buzz:

- `abort`
- `canplay`
- `canplaythrough`
- `dataunavailable`
- `emptied`
- `empty`
- `ended`
- `error`
- `loadstart`
- `end`

You can attach a listener to each of those events with a line of JavaScript:

```
mySound.bind("loadeddata", function(e) {
    document.getElementById('loading').style.display = "none";
});
```

Implementing Buzz

To implement Buzz in your web application, simply call the JavaScript file and make a few API calls. Your script tag should look something like this on your page:

```
<script src="/js/buzz.js"></script>
```

Audio has gotten a bad rap over the years, but what's old is new again. Users have new expectations as to what they get from HTML5 apps. Don't be afraid to pull Buzz into your app, and play sounds when the app calls for it. Be creative again!

HACK 36 Simplify Your HTML5 Media with MediaElement.js

HTML5 media is generally easy to implement, but with flexibility comes complexity. MediaElement.js was made to bring simplicity back to even the most complex of multimedia environments.

This hack was provided by John Dyer, creator of MediaElement.js. John is a long-time web developer and is currently the director of Web Development at Dallas Theological Seminary.

In my own situation, I had a backlog of several thousand older H.264-encoded MP4s that couldn't easily be re-encoded to WebM. I wanted to use the HTML5 API, but to do so, I needed a cross-browser way to support H.264 playback with a consistent API. To make this happen, I created MediaElement.js, a JavaScript library that helps all browsers from IE 6 and later think they support HTML5 and H.264 playback.

To get started, go to MediaElementJS.com (*http://mediaelementjs.com*) and download the library, then add jQuery and the two files shown here to your page:

```
<script src="jquery.js"></script>
<script src="mediaelement-and-player.min.js"></script>
<link rel="stylesheet" href="mediaelementplayer.css" />
```

To make the player work, the easiest way to get started is to just add the **mejs-player** class to your **<audio>** and **<video>** tags and they will automatically be converted to a fully functioning player with an identical set of controls in all browsers.

For video:

```
<video class="mejs-player" src="video.mp4" width="320" height="180">
</video>
```

For audio:

```
<audio class="mejs-player" src="music.mp3"></audio>
```

If you want more control over how the player works, you can manually instantiate the player in JavaScript and set several options:

```
<video src="video.mp4" width="320" height="180"></video>

<script>
$('video').mediaelementplayer({
    // an array of controls for the player
features:['playpause', 'progress', 'current', 'duration', 'tracks',
'volume', 'fullscreen'],
    // the volume when the player launches
    startVolume: 0.8,
    // event that fires when the player has been created
    success: function(mediaElement, domNode, player) {
        // do more stuff here
    }
});
</script>
```

This allows you to use H.264-encoded MP4 files across all browsers and mobile devices. You can also use older FLV files you might still need to support (using the Flash shim) or even Windows Media files (using the built-in Silverlight plug-in).

Responsive Video

If you are working with a responsive layout and need your video content to resize accordingly, MediaElement.js will automatically adjust the size of the player and controls to fill the surrounding element. To enable the responsive adjustment, make sure to set a width and height that correspond to the video's aspect ratio, and also include **100%** in the **style** attribute (according to the HTML5 spec, percentage values are not allowed in the **width** and **height** attributes, so you must use **style**).

```
<div id="container">
<video src="video.mp4" width="320" height="180"
style="width: 100%; height: 100%;"></video>
</div>
```

Event Listeners

MediaElement.js supports all the events in the HTML5 Media API (*http://www.w3.org/TR/html5/the-video-element.html#mediaevents*). For example, if you want to play another video when the current one ends, you can listen for the **ended** event on the **mediaElement** object. This works best if you add all your code inside the **success** event so that the Flash fallback has time to load.

```
<script>
$('video').mediaelementplayer({
    success: function(mediaElement, domNode, player) {
```

```
        mediaElement.addEventListener('ended', function() {
            mediaElement.setSrc('nextvideo.mp4');
            mediaElement.load();
            mediaElement.play();
        }, true);
    }
});
</script>
```

Captions and Subtitles

The HTML5 spec also includes a `<track>` tag that is used to load external text files that contain captions, subtitles, or chapter breaks. The proposed format is WebVTT, or Web Video Text Tracks (*http://dev.w3.org/html5/webvtt/*), a simple text-based format that begins with a single-line declaration (`WEBVTT FILE`) and then lists start and end times separated by `-->` characters, followed by the text to display between the two times. Here's a simple WebVTT file that will display two lines of text at two different time intervals:

```
WEBVTT FILE

00:00:02.5 --> 00:00:05.1
This is the first line of text to display.

00:00:09.1 --> 00:00:12.7
This line will appear later in the video.
```

At the time of this writing, few browsers automatically support WebVTT, but MediaElement.js has a built-in WebVTT parser that will display the text in all browsers. To add a track, save your WebVTT file as *subtitles.vtt* (make sure you add text/vtt to your server's MIME types) and add the file using the `<track>` tag:

```
<video width="320" height="180">
    <source src="video.mp4" type="video/mp4" />
<track src="subtitles.webm" srclang="en" kind="subtitles"
 label="English" />
</video>
```

Wrapping It Up

MediaElement.js offers a bunch of other features, including the ability to play back YouTube videos through the YouTube API, pre- and post-roll ads, custom skins, and more, so check it out (*http://mediaelementjs.com/*).

4

Hacking Your Graphics with Canvas and SVG

Over the past decade Adobe Flash became very popular because it allowed us to create and manipulate imagery directly within our web pages. This demand resulted in development of the Canvas specification.

The `<canvas>` tag is one of the most flexible of the new HTML5 tags. This has made the `<canvas>` tag the new foundation for web-based gaming and other interactive components. The `<canvas>` tag itself, much like the name, is a blank slate. It's a "drawing" surface that gives developers the freedom and flexibility to create imagery that can blend with and complement the rest of the DOM (Document Object Model).

The "underdog" HTML5 illustration tool presented in this chapter is Scalable Vector Graphics (SVG). SVG is probably the oldest technology discussed in this book—it has been supported in some browsers for the past 12 years as it was first supported by Microsoft's Internet Explorer version 6. Rarely does anyone have anything nice to say about IE 6, but in terms of its support of SVG it was ahead of its time.

SVG is an XML markup language that is very similar to HTML, and will probably be pretty easy for those of you who are experienced with HTML. SVG basically does for graphics what HTML did for text. SVG is lightweight and flexible, and can scale to any size with the same lightweight file.

Although there may seem to be a lot of overlap between these two languages, you will quickly see where each technology shines. It's clear why the HTML5 family encompasses both of these powerhouse visual tools.

HACK 37 Draw Shapes on Your HTML5 <canvas> Tag

Flash became insanely popular because of the flexibility it brought to the browser. With Flash the Web was free from decorating DOM elements and became a platform for real drawing and animation. HTML5 brings this same type of flexibility and power directly to the DOM with the HTML5 <canvas> tag. This hack starts us off slow by walking through the creation of basic shapes on a canvas.

The <canvas> tag provides you with a blank slate to create your imagery. In order to do this you first need to create a <canvas> tag in the DOM, and then identify the context. The <canvas> tag is created as a DOM element:

```
<canvas id="myCanvas" width="200" height="200"></canvas>
```

This basic <canvas> tag will be presented as a 200 × 200-px empty block on the page. To add to it, we need to identify the context:

```
var myCanvas = document.getElementById('myCanvas')
var myCtx = myCanvas.getContext('2d');
```

Notice that we identify the '2d' context which may seem to imply that there would also be a '3d' context, but don't be fooled: "3d" isn't really addressed by the <can vas> tag; it has only an x- and y-axis. Now that we have the context identified, we have a host of APIs at our fingertips.

Drawing to a <canvas> tag is all about the '2d' context and finding the appropriate coordinates on the grid. Generally, one pixel on the screen correlates to one point in the canvas (this value can vary when you zoom in or out on a small screen such as on a mobile browser, or when your element is resized with CSS). The key point on our grid is (0,0) or the *origin*, which is the top-lefthand corner of our canvas. Our canvas is 200 × 200, which means it contains 200 points on the x-axis and 200 points on the y-axis. Figure 4-1 shows how our canvas would appear with grid lines on the x- and y-axes over 10 points.

Figure 4-1.
The 200 × 200 <canvas> tag with grid markers every tenth point on both the x- and y-axes

Drawing Rectangles

We'll start with one of the simplest shapes: the rectangle. These are easy to draw into the context of our **<canvas>** tag. The **'2d'** context gives us access to the API to draw three basic types of rectangles:

fillRect
Draws a rectangle with a solid color fill

strokeRect
Draws a rectangle that has a border but no fill

clearRect
Clears a rectangle-shaped transparency that removes any imagery or fills in the defined area

Taking our sample canvas from before, let's combine these three shapes onto our **<canvas>** tag:

```
var myCanvas = document.getElementById('myCanvas')
var myCtx = myCanvas.getContext('2d');
myCtx.strokeRect(10,10, 180, 180);
myCtx.clearRect(50,50, 100, 100);
```

The preceding code laid on top of our **<canvas>** tag looks like Figure 4-2.

Figure 4-2.
The 200 × 200 canvas demonstrating the different rectangle APIs in the <canvas> tag

Each of the three APIs follows the same pattern. They are passed four parameters: the *x* and *y* coordinates, along with the width and height of the rectangle.

Drawing Paths

Rectangles are just the tip of the iceberg when it comes to drawing on a canvas. Most imagery is produced by combining a series of lines. Like all methods in the **<can vas>** tag, these drawing APIs are available on the **'2d'** context. Paths require a few steps to start and complete a drawing. To start a drawing (a single path or series of paths), we use this method:

```
myContext.beginPath();
```

This method takes no arguments; it simply initiates a drawing. Once the path has begun, we need to determine where we are going to start and end the path. To start the path, we will use the **moveTo** method. This is similar to determining where you would move your pencil on a piece of drawing paper. Think of it as picking up a pencil and putting it down directly on your starting point. From there, we will use the **line To** method to determine where our line will end. Here is the first line of our grid:

```
myContext.beginPath();
myContext.moveTo(0,0);
myContext.lineTo(200,0);
```

At this point our canvas will still be blank, as we have not yet closed our path. To close the path we use the following method:

```
myContext.closePath();
```

Now we have one line on our canvas. To create our grid, we want to draw multiple lines within our path. To accomplish this, we will begin the path, and then create a series of **moveTo** and **lineTo** methods. Once we have all our grid lines, we will write them to the canvas with our **stroke** method. Our code will look something like this:

```
var myCanvas = document.getElementById('myCanvas')
var myContext = myCanvas.getContext('2d');
var ctx = myContext;

myContext.beginPath();
for(i=0; i<201; i++){

myContext.moveTo(0,i);
myContext.lineTo(200,i);
i+=10;
}

for(i=0; i<201; i++){

myContext.moveTo(i,0);
myContext.lineTo(i, 200);
i+=10;
}
myContext.stroke();
```

Paths have a number of different JavaScript APIs that create different line effects. In many cases we may have a few lines that we want to connect and consequently fill the area. To accomplish this we can simply call the following method:

```
myContent.fill();
```

Smile, the Canvas Loves You!

We can get pretty far with straight lines in our drawings, but we can use the canvas to draw arcs as well. Remember, the <canvas> tag will always be a square, but we can draw any shape inside the square. To draw an arc on the canvas, call the following method off the canvas context:

```
arc(x, y, radius, startAngle, endAngle, anticlockwise);
```

As illustrated in the preceding code, a number of arguments are passed into the **arc** method. The first two are the coordinates for the arc's center, followed by the arc radius. The startAngle and endAngle parameters declare the start and end points of the arc in radians, which are measured from the x-axis. The final optional anti clockwise parameter, when set to true, draws the arc in a counterclockwise direction. The default is false, which would draw the arc in a clockwise direction.

Looking back at the radius argument, we want to make a special note. In CSS, we are comfortable with declaring values in degrees, but in this case the arc radius is measured in radians. It's quite common to see an inline conversion from radians to degrees using the JavaScript math equation for pi:

```
myRadians = (Math.PI/180)*degrees
```

Let's put this to good use by creating something recognizable on the <canvas> tag. When I think of circles I think of two things: smiley faces and bombs. To keep the violence level down, we'll work on the smiley face in this chapter. Using a similar 200 × 200 <canvas> tag let's center our outer circle directly in the middle of our tag, and then draw our head:

```
smileCtx.beginPath();
smileCtx.arc(100,100,99,0,Math.PI*2);
```

We now have a canvas with a circle on it, as shown in Figure 4-3.

Figure 4-3.
The <canvas> tag with a circle centered on the element

This isn't very exciting. So next we will add the mouth. For this we will use the **move To** method, and then draw a half circle (notice that the **radius** will be **PI** instead of **PI*2** as it was for the full circle):

```
smileCtx.moveTo(170,100);
smileCtx.arc(100,100,70,0,Math.PI);    // Mouth
```

The last two components are the eyes. Since we want our eyes to be solid fills, we need to make separate strokes for each of them so that we can apply the fill. The first step to accomplish this is to close the current stroke. We will then start a new stroke, move to a new start point, draw a new circle, and call our **fill** parameter for each eye:

```
smileCtx.stroke();
smileCtx.beginPath();
smileCtx.moveTo(60, 65);
smileCtx.arc(60,65,12,0,Math.PI*2);   // Left eye
smileCtx.fill();
```

Let's put all this code together, and see our masterpiece:

```
var mySmile = document.getElementById('mySmile')
var smileCtx = mySmile.getContext('2d');

smileCtx.beginPath();
smileCtx.arc(100,100,99,0,Math.PI*2); // head
smileCtx.moveTo(170,100);
smileCtx.arc(100,100,70,0,Math.PI);    // Mouth
smileCtx.stroke();

smileCtx.beginPath();
smileCtx.moveTo(60, 65);
smileCtx.arc(60,65,12,0,Math.PI*2);   // Left eye
smileCtx.fill();

smileCtx.beginPath();
smileCtx.moveTo(140,65);
smileCtx.arc(140,65,12,0,Math.PI*2);   // Right eye
smileCtx.fill();
```

Our canvas now holds all three strokes to form the face, as shown in Figure 4-4.

Figure 4-4.
The 200 × 200 <canvas> tag with the smiley face

Advanced Drawing

We've plowed right through lines and arcs, but many illustrations call for lines that can't be accomplished by either of these shapes. The Canvas specification includes two additional tools for creating custom shapes:

```
quadraticCurveTo(cp1x, cp1y, x, y);
bezierCurveTo(cp1x, cp1y, cp2x, cp2y, x, y);
```

Each of these methods has control points and an ending x,y point. The control points determine the curvature of the path. The `bezierCurveTo` method has a second control point for an uneven curvature. Additional information about the implementation of each method is available in the W3C spec (*http://www.w3.org/TR/2dcontext/#building-paths*).

HACK 38 Apply Styles to Your Canvas Elements

We don't live in a black-and-white Web, which makes it essential to be able to apply colors and styles to your <canvas> tag elements. Style your canvas elements with this familiar CSS syntax.

If you need to catch up on how to create shapes, strokes, or fills on your <can vas> *tag, read* Hack #37.

Shapes and strokes have little effect on our applications if we can't apply color and styles to them. The specification for canvas styles borrows heavily from CSS, so a lot of the syntax should be familiar to you.

Color

Canvas elements can be colored with any CSS color value style, and they even support transparency with RGBA and HSPA colors. Also, canvas strokes and shapes have a default color value of black.

Let's look at a code example for drawing a grid of lines across a 200 × 200 <can vas> tag:

```
var myCanvas = document.getElementById('myCanvas')
var myContext = myCanvas.getContext('2d');
myContext.beginPath();
for(i=0; i<201; i++){
    myContext.moveTo(0,i);
    myContext.lineTo(200,i);
    i+=10;
}

for(i=0; i<201; i++){
    myContext.moveTo(i,0);
    myContext.lineTo(i, 200);
    i+=10;
}
myContext.stroke();
```

This example draws vertical lines every 10 points, and then loops around again to draw horizontal lines every 10 points. As stated previously, the default color for each line is black. To give the look of graph paper we want to make the lines a light blue color. We can accomplish this by adding a single line of code:

```
myContext.strokeStyle = '#99C4E5';
```

Since the whole grid is accomplished through one stroke, we only need to declare the style once. To add a bit of depth to our grid we will make the horizontal lines slightly darker than the vertical lines. Since we are going to style the lines in two different ways, we need to add a few lines of JavaScript to our code to separate our illustration into two different strokes. To accomplish this, we will end the stroke after the first for loop and then start a new stroke for the second for loop:

```
var myCanvas = document.getElementById('myCanvas2')
var myContext = myCanvas.getContext('2d');
myContext.strokeStyle = '#1487E0';

myContext.beginPath();
for(i=0; i<201; i++){
    myContext.moveTo(0,i);
    myContext.lineTo(200,i);
    i+=10;
}
myContext.stroke();
myContext.beginPath();
myContext.strokeStyle = '#B1CADD';

for(i=0; i<201; i++){
    myContext.moveTo(i,0);
    myContext.lineTo(i, 200);
    i+=10;
}
```

As soon as we started the second stroke with the **beginPath** method, we set a new, darker stroke style for the horizontal lines.

There are two different methods for adding color to your shapes. **strokeStyle** applies to lines and the outline of shapes, and **fillStyle** applies to shapes or strokes that have a fill applied to them. It's important to note that once you set a stroke or fill style, the setting will persist in the context until it is changed back to the original value, or until it is set to a new value.

Gradients

Just as with other HTML5 elements, adding gradients can provide for deep visual depth, and can be quite useful. Let's take a look at our example of a simple black-and-white smiley face, before applying a few gradients to spice it up:

```
var mySmile = document.getElementById('mySmile')
var smileCtx = mySmile.getContext('2d');

smileCtx.beginPath();
smileCtx.arc(100,100,99,0,Math.PI*2); // head
smileCtx.moveTo(170,100);
smileCtx.arc(100,100,70,0,Math.PI);   // Mouth
smileCtx.stroke();

smileCtx.beginPath();
```

```
smileCtx.moveTo(60, 65);
smileCtx.arc(60,65,12,0,Math.PI*2);   // Left eye
smileCtx.fill();

smileCtx.beginPath();
smileCtx.moveTo(140,65);
smileCtx.arc(140,65,12,0,Math.PI*2);  // Right eye
smileCtx.fill();
```

The preceding code provides us with the basic smiley face shown in Figure 4-5.

Figure 4-5.
The <canvas> tag with the smiley face illustration

As every child who wasn't raised by wolves knows, smiley faces are supposed to be yellow. Let's redraw our smiley face with a yellow background:

```
var mySmile = document.getElementById('mySmile')
var smileCtx = mySmile.getContext('2d');

smileCtx.beginPath();

smileCtx.fillStyle = '#F1F42E';
smileCtx.arc(100,100,99,0,Math.PI*2); // head

smileCtx.stroke();
```

```
smileCtx.fill();

smileCtx.beginPath();
smileCtx.moveTo(170,100);
smileCtx.arc(100,100,70,0,Math.PI);    // Mouth
smileCtx.stroke();

smileCtx.beginPath();
smileCtx.fillStyle = 'black';
smileCtx.moveTo(60, 65);
smileCtx.arc(60,65,12,0,Math.PI*2);    // Left eye
smileCtx.fill();

smileCtx.beginPath();
smileCtx.moveTo(140,65);
smileCtx.arc(140,65,12,0,Math.PI*2);   // Right eye
smileCtx.fill();
```

This gives us a more iconic version of our smiley face, as shown in Figure 4-6.

Figure 4-6.
The same canvas smiley face with a yellow fill on the head circle

In order to accommodate the introduction of color, we had to make a few changes to our code. First, we extracted the mouth from the same stroke that made the head so that the fill would not overwrite the line used for the mouth. Then we added a fill method to the end of the head circle to color it yellow. The last change we made was to reset the fill color back to black for the eyes. Again, once we set the style, we needed to reset it to black to return to the default value.

Now, to prove that we have some artistic talent, we will change our yellow color to a yellow gradient. We can apply two types of gradients:

```
createLinearGradient(x1,y1,x2,y2)
createRadialGradient(x1,y1,r1,x2,y2,r2)
```

The createLinearGradient method is passed four different arguments: the start point (x1,y1) and the end point (x2,y2) of the gradient.

The createRadialGradient method is passed six arguments. The first three define an inner circle with coordinates (x1,y1) and one radius (r1) and an outer circle with coordinates and a second radius.

Our example will use a radial gradient to give our smiley face three-dimensional depth. First we will set our gradient to a variable, and then we will add a series of color stops to the gradient. In our code example, we'll replace the fillStyle with our gradient:

```
var mySmile = document.getElementById('mySmile')
var smileCtx = mySmile.getContext('2d');

var radgrad = smileCtx.createRadialGradient(100,100,10,100,100,100);
radgrad.addColorStop(.5, 'rgba(247,241,192,1)');
radgrad.addColorStop(1, 'rgba(244,225,56,1)');
smileCtx.beginPath();

smileCtx.fillStyle = radgrad;
smileCtx.arc(100,100,99,0,Math.PI*2); // head

smileCtx.stroke();
smileCtx.fill();

smileCtx.beginPath();
smileCtx.moveTo(170,100);
smileCtx.arc(100,100,70,0,Math.PI);    // Mouth
smileCtx.stroke();

smileCtx.beginPath();
smileCtx.fillStyle = 'black';
smileCtx.moveTo(60, 65);
smileCtx.arc(60,65,12,0,Math.PI*2);  // Left eye
smileCtx.fill();
```

```
smileCtx.beginPath();
smileCtx.moveTo(140,65);
smileCtx.arc(140,65,12,0,Math.PI*2);   // Right eye
smileCtx.fill();
```

We have simply replaced our fill color with the gradient as a fill. This gives us the added depth we want to make our smiley face stick out from the crowd (see Figure 4-7).

Figure 4-7.
The smiley face canvas drawing with a gradient in place of a solid fill color

Additional Styles

You can accomplish a transparency effect with a color of your choosing, or you can apply the transparency globally to a stroke. To adjust the transparency level, use the `globalAlpha` method:

```
globalAlpha = .2;
```

Unlike the color styles, the `globalAlpha` method only applies to the current stroke. Once a new stroke is started, the `globalAlpha` method resets to **1**.

Because they play such a large role in illustrations, lines are given additional control values in your `<canvas>` tag. You can set the following values for a stroke on your `<canvas>` tag:

lineWidth

A numerical value that represents the width in points

lineCap

The shape of the end of a line, which can be declared as butt, round, or square

lineJoin

The shape of a line joint, which can be declared as round, bevel, or miter

miterLimit

Determines how far the outside connection point can be placed from the inside connection point, when the lineJoin type of miter is selected

Patterns and shadows can also be applied to canvas elements, and they follow similar syntax to CSS implementations. For details on these features and more, see the W3C specification on the <canvas> tag (*http://www.w3.org/TR/2dcontext/*).

HACK 39   Style Canvas Elements with Image Files

Shapes in a <canvas> tag have some of the same controls as other page elements. In this hack, you'll learn how to take your canvas illustrations one step further by utilizing images as fills.

The Canvas specification gives you a lot of flexibility to create your HTML5 illustrations. Other hacks have covered basic shapes, colors, gradients, and other styles, so this hack will focus on importing another object for use on your canvas element.

The Basic Fill

For details on fills and other styles, see Hack #38.

To illustrate the use of an image as a fill, we'll start by looking at a smiley face example with a basic yellow color fill for the head (see Figure 4-8).

Figure 4-8.
The 200 × 200 <canvas> tag with a drawing of a smiley face

We set the background color by adding a color fill to the circle that makes up the head. Once the stroke is started, it's a simple line of code:

```
smileCtx.fillStyle = '#F1F42E';
```

Our end result will have a simple image used as a repeating background (see Figure 4-9).

Figure 4-9.
The 200 × 200 <canvas> tag with a drawing of a smiley face and a repeating heart background image

To change that solid color to an image, we will use a very similar API:

```
smileCtx.fillStyle = myPattern;
```

You can see in the preceding code that we are using the same API for an image background as we are for a fill color (similar to the background attribute in a CSS declaration). However, a bit of additional overhead is required when using an image.

Using an Image as a Fill

In JavaScript, to use an image you first must have a reference to it. In our case, we will start by creating the image dynamically, and then setting its **src** attribute:

```
var img = new Image();
img.src = '/assets/img/heart.png';
```

The image we are using is the small icon-size image shown in Figure 4-10.

Figure 4-10.
The small image used as a repeating background

That was easy enough; we now have a variable called **img** that references our image file. The second step is to set that image as a pattern to be utilized by the **<canvas>** tag:

```
var myPattern = smileCtx.createPattern(img,'repeat');
smileCtx.fillStyle = myPattern;
```

To accomplish this, we used a canvas method called **createPattern**. This requires two parameters: the first is the reference to the image file, and the second is our **DOMstring** repetition. Similar to a CSS implementation, we can set the **DOMstring** repetition to **repeat**, **repeat-x**, **repeat-y**, or **no-repeat**. If no value is specified, it defaults to **repeat**.

Now let's put all of this together and see what it looks like. Here is a view of the code used to generate our smiley face with the image as a background:

```
var mySmile = document.getElementById('mySmile4')
var smileCtx = mySmile.getContext('2d');

// create new image object to use as pattern
var img = new Image();
img.src = '/assets/img/heart.png';
// create pattern
var myPattern = smileCtx.createPattern(img,'repeat');
```

```
smileCtx.fillStyle = myPattern;
smileCtx.arc(100,100,99,0,Math.PI*2); // head
smileCtx.stroke();
smileCtx.fill();

smileCtx.beginPath();
smileCtx.moveTo(170,100);
smileCtx.arc(100,100,70,0,Math.PI);    // Mouth
smileCtx.stroke();
smileCtx.beginPath();
smileCtx.fillStyle = 'black';
smileCtx.moveTo(60, 65);
smileCtx.arc(60,65,12,0,Math.PI*2);    // Left eye
smileCtx.fill();

smileCtx.beginPath();
smileCtx.moveTo(140,65);
smileCtx.arc(140,65,12,0,Math.PI*2);   // Right eye
smileCtx.fill();
```

If we were to run this code, we would probably be disappointed with the results. In most cases, our smiley face would look like Figure 4-11.

Figure 4-11.
The smiley face canvas rendering with the background image set as in the previous code sample

Can you identify the problem? Think about the load time. The canvas is taking advantage of real-time data. In the preceding sample, we created the image and then set it as a background immediately. Since the pattern failed, the canvas fill reverted back to its default state of black for the fill color. The problem has to do with the availability of the image data, which in our case hasn't been loaded yet.

To solve this problem we will add a few lines of JavaScript that wait for the image to load before we execute the necessary canvas code. Browsers have supported the image **onload** event for years. In this example we'll use the image **onload** event to know when we have the necessary data loaded:

```
var mySmile = document.getElementById('mySmile4')
    var smileCtx = mySmile.getContext('2d');

    // create new image object to use as pattern
    var img = new Image();
    img.src = '/assets/img/heart.png';
    img.onload = function(){

    // create pattern
    var myPattern = smileCtx.createPattern(img,'repeat');
    smileCtx.fillStyle = myPattern;
    smileCtx.arc(100,100,99,0,Math.PI*2); // head
    smileCtx.stroke();
    smileCtx.fill();

    smileCtx.beginPath();
    smileCtx.moveTo(170,100);
    smileCtx.arc(100,100,70,0,Math.PI);    // Mouth
    smileCtx.stroke();

    smileCtx.beginPath();
    smileCtx.fillStyle = 'black';
    smileCtx.moveTo(60, 65);
    smileCtx.arc(60,65,12,0,Math.PI*2);   // Left eye
    smileCtx.fill();

    smileCtx.beginPath();
    smileCtx.moveTo(140,65);
    smileCtx.arc(140,65,12,0,Math.PI*2);  // Right eye
    smileCtx.fill();
    }
```

Now we're sure that our image data has loaded, and the **<canvas>** tag can take full advantage of the image for use in its pattern background.

Easy Image Data

Adding image **onload**s around whole segments of code can sometimes be cumbersome. A nice shortcut available in HTML5 browsers is the use of inline image data. We can easily remove the **onload** event from the preceding example and simply reference the image data. Since the image data was loaded when the page was loaded, there is no need to wait for the **onload** event to fire before we attempt to use the image. Our new code would look like this:

```
var mySmile = document.getElementById('mySmile5')
var smileCtx = mySmile.getContext('2d');

// create new image object to use as pattern
var img2 = new Image();
img2.src = 'data:image/png;base64,iVBORw0K... image data here
...f5v038BfQ3g/3mcvqgAAAAASUVORK5CYII=';

// create pattern
var myPattern = smileCtx.createPattern(img2,'repeat');
smileCtx.fillStyle = myPattern;
smileCtx.arc(100,100,99,0,Math.PI*2); // head
smileCtx.stroke();
smileCtx.fill();

smileCtx.beginPath();
smileCtx.moveTo(170,100);
smileCtx.arc(100,100,70,0,Math.PI);    // Mouth
smileCtx.stroke();

smileCtx.beginPath();
smileCtx.fillStyle = 'black';
smileCtx.moveTo(60, 65);
smileCtx.arc(60,65,12,0,Math.PI*2);    // Left eye
smileCtx.fill();

smileCtx.beginPath();
smileCtx.moveTo(140,65);
smileCtx.arc(140,65,12,0,Math.PI*2);   // Right eye
smileCtx.fill();
```

It may not make sense to utilize the Base64 version of your image in all cases, since it results in added weight in the initial page load, but sometimes it may be appropriate in order to utilize and simplify your code. It's a good practice to have multiple implementation methods to choose from.

HACK 40 Use the HTML5 <canvas> Tag to Create High-Res, Retina-Display-Ready Media

When Apple first introduced the Retina display on the iPhone 4, parts of the Web started to look pretty shabby. The display's higher resolution made your quick-loading "web-ready" images look pixelated. In general, higher-resolution images mean longer load times. This hack uses the HTML5 <canvas> tag to provide Retina-ready imagery without the added weight.

There is a problem with our Retina screens. They look great (few people will debate that), but the way in which they accomplish this has caused a lot of problems for web developers. Apple first introduced the Retina display with the iPhone 4, in an attempt to solve two problems: create a display in which the pixels were indistinguishable to the naked eye, and not make iOS and Apple apps look like crap. To do this, Apple marked the pixel density much higher than was necessary, and in fact gave the display a density that was evenly divisible by the previous iPhone screen density. This enabled Apple to update all the visual assets of the iOS SDK and the iOS operating system to a higher resolution, and simply downsize it for older, less dense screens. For all the other assets in the Apple apps, the company used a method called *pixel doubling* to help the assets remain at the proper size.

Assets such as images and media on the Web fall prey to pixel doubling. This makes our web pages look pixelated and jagged. The common solution to this problem is to utilize images with twice the pixel resolution, which leaves us with images that are larger and web pages that take significantly longer to load.

In Comes the <canvas> Tag

The <canvas> tag is a drawing space for vector illustrations. Since the <canvas> tag is created using a set of definitions, the size of the illustration is inconsequential to the amount of data that is necessary to create it (unlike images that required the transfer of additional data to accommodate more pixels). This being the case, we can make our <canvas> tag Retina-ready without any additional page weight.

Let's start by loading a simple example of a smiley face drawn out on a 200 × 200-point <canvas> tag. Here is the code for creating our example:

```
var mySmile = document.getElementById('mySmile2')
    var smileCtx = mySmile.getContext('2d');

    smileCtx.beginPath();

    smileCtx.fillStyle = '#F1F42E';
    smileCtx.arc(100,100,99,0,Math.PI*2); // head
```

```
smileCtx.stroke();
smileCtx.fill();

smileCtx.beginPath();
smileCtx.moveTo(170,100);
smileCtx.arc(100,100,70,0,Math.PI);    // Mouth
smileCtx.stroke();

smileCtx.beginPath();
smileCtx.fillStyle = 'black';
smileCtx.moveTo(60, 65);
smileCtx.arc(60,65,12,0,Math.PI*2);   // Left eye
smileCtx.fill();

smileCtx.beginPath();
smileCtx.moveTo(140,65);
smileCtx.arc(140,65,12,0,Math.PI*2);  // Right eye
smileCtx.fill();
```

Our smiley face looks great on a standard display, but it's pretty jagged on the Retina display. Figure 4-12 shows how our canvas image looks on the iPhone 3Gs and the iPhone 4.

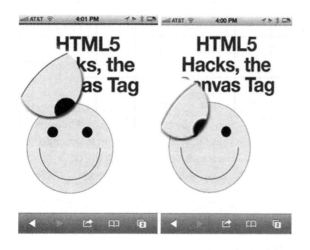

Figure 4-12.
The canvas image displayed on the iPhone 3GS (left), and on the iPhone 4 with a Retina display (right)

In order to have the illustration be smooth for the Retina display, we need to counteract the pixel doubling that is taking place. To accomplish this, we will add a few simple lines of code to our JavaScript:

HTML5 HACKS

```
if(window.devicePixelRatio == 2) {
    mySmile.setAttribute('width', 400);
    mySmile.setAttribute('height', 400);
    smileCtx6.scale(2, 2);
    }
```

We will insert this into our code right after we declare our context, but before we start to apply our elements to the `<canvas>` tag. In essence, we have detected when pixel doubling is being applied (by checking the device pixel ratio) and then doubled the size of our `<canvas>` tag. These lines of code will result in the big, fat smiley face shown in Figure 4-13.

Figure 4-13.
The smiley face twice the size it was before, thanks to the new JavaScript code

Now we need to rescale our `<canvas>` tag to fit our original page space. In order to have the page render all the pixels in half the size, we will set our canvas to 400 and then use CSS to shrink it back down to 200 px. Let's add this CSS to the top of our page:

```
#mySmile{
    height: 200px;
    width: 200px;
}
```

With just a few lines of code we have essentially Retina-enabled our <canvas> tag without having to increase the page weight significantly. Let's go back to our iPhone 3GS–iPhone 4 comparison to see our results (see Figure 4-14).

Figure 4-14.
The canvas image displayed on the iPhone 3GS (left), and on the iPhone 4 with a Retina display after the addition of the new JavaScript code

We've improved the experience for our Retina-display users without affecting the rest of our user base. You can apply this technique to any <canvas> tag, whether it is a page illustration or a canvas element used as a CSS background image. The only time you will not benefit from using this technique is when you import an image into your <canvas> tag that doesn't support the Retina display's higher resolution.

HACK 41 Accelerate Animation with Canvas Drawings

Use of the <canvas> tag is often one of the most efficient ways to create animations in your web applications. This hack digs into the nitty-gritty of creating animations while using the <canvas> tag.

Clean animation can make or break your web applications. Native applications on desktop and mobile devices have raised users' expectations: if your web application fails to include clean, concise animations, users will often write it off as being a poorly performing app.

Canvas animation can be a powerful tool for web animations. As more and more browser makers enable the GPU for canvas animations, it becomes even more beneficial to perform your animations with a canvas element.

Write and Clean

Animation on a `<canvas>` tag is reminiscent of early cartoon animations where each frame is drawn out and then displayed in the correct order and at the determined frame rate. Canvas animation basically consists of these three steps:

1. Draw on the canvas.
2. Erase what you just drew.
3. Repeat steps 1 and 2 until the animation is complete.

In JavaScript, when things need to be called over and over again we often use methods such as `setTimeout` and `setInterval` to call our drawing methods. The problem with each of these methods is they need to be set to a specific amount of time. If we set that time to, say, 100 milliseconds, we would never be able to achieve a frame rate higher than 10 frames per second.

A powerful new standard has been introduced to address this issue with the `<canvas>` tag: the `requestAnimationFrame` method. With this method, you are asking the browser to render the next frame as soon as it is available for rendering, as opposed to attempting to render at a fixed interval. The goal of `requestAnimationFrame` is 60 frames per second, but it doesn't fail if it can't render that quickly; it simply renders as soon as it can. Note that this method isn't limited to use in canvas animations; it's available for any web drawing technology, including WebGL.

Smile, You're Being Animated!

Let's take a good look at an example of a canvas animation. If you've worked your way through the previous hacks in this chapter you have seen the smiley face examples. Each example drew the smiley face on a 200 × 200 canvas element. For this illustration we will draw it on a much larger canvas to give us room to move. Let's start by dropping our `<canvas>` tag onto the page:

```
<canvas id="moveSmile" width="800" height="200"></canvas>
```

Now that we have a big, fat, blank canvas, we will draw the smiley face on top of it. To do this, we'll pull in a few lines of JavaScript to build our page elements:

```
var canvas  = document.getElementById("moveSmile");
var smileCtx = canvas.getContext("2d");

smileCtx.beginPath();

smileCtx.fillStyle = '#F1F42E';
smileCtx.arc(100,100,99,0,Math.PI*2); // head

smileCtx.stroke();
smileCtx.fill();

smileCtx.beginPath();
smileCtx.moveTo(170,100);
smileCtx.arc(100,100,70,0,Math.PI);   // Mouth
smileCtx.stroke();

smileCtx.beginPath();
smileCtx6.fillStyle = 'black';
smileCtx6.moveTo(60, 65);
smileCtx6.arc(60,65,12,0,Math.PI*2);  // Left eye
smileCtx6.fill();

smileCtx6.beginPath();
smileCtx6.moveTo(140,65);
smileCtx6.arc(140,65,12,0,Math.PI*2); // Right eye
smileCtx6.fill();
```

Our code simply draws out this smiley face on the lefthand side of the <canvas> tag. For illustration purposes, a 1 px border has been added to the <canvas> tag so that we can see the boundaries (see Figure 4-15).

Going back to our three-step process, once we draw our illustration we need to erase what we've drawn:

```
smileCtx.clearRect(0, 0, 800, 200); //smileCtx is the 2d context
```

For simplicity I'm erasing the whole canvas, but to optimize performance you should focus on erasing what is changing for the next frame. In the preceding method I am clearing the whole canvas by setting the **clearRect** coordinates from the top-lefthand corner of the canvas to the bottom-righthand corner. This erases a rectangular shape the size of the canvas.

Our canvas should now be void of illustration, as shown in Figure 4-16.

Figure 4-15.
The smiley face illustration on the lefthand side of an 800-point canvas

Figure 4-16.
The 800 × 200 <canvas> tag after the clearRect method has cleared the entire canvas context

Now, for step 3 we will redraw our smiley face, but we will move it slightly to the right. In order to do this, we will move the x position of both our **moveTo** methods and our element start position (**arc** in this case).

To accomplish this, we will replace each number with a simple equation to generate the proper *x* coordinate each time the element is drawing:

```
x+startingposition
```

Our code will now look like this:

```
var x = 0;
smileCtx6.beginPath();

smileCtx6.fillStyle = '#F1F42E';
smileCtx6.arc(x+100,100,99,0,Math.PI*2); // head

smileCtx6.stroke();
smileCtx6.fill();

smileCtx6.beginPath();
smileCtx6.moveTo(x+170,100);
smileCtx6.arc(x+100,100,70,0,Math.PI);    // Mouth
smileCtx6.stroke();

smileCtx6.beginPath();
smileCtx6.fillStyle = 'black';
smileCtx6.moveTo(x+60, 65);
smileCtx6.arc(x+60,65,12,0,Math.PI*2);    // Left eye
smileCtx6.fill();

smileCtx6.beginPath();
smileCtx6.moveTo(x+140,65);
smileCtx6.arc(x+140,65,12,0,Math.PI*2);   // Right eye
smileCtx6.fill();
```

For the preceding code x is set to 0, but in order to move the smiley face across the screen we need to change the x position. We'll do this with a simple statement that increases or decreases the x value appropriately (this will move it across the screen and then back again).

There is one additional value we need to determine: the speed of the animation. If we simply increment the value by 1, the smiley face will only move one pixel per iteration. We want to put a little bit of pep in this animation, so we will create a new variable called **speed** and set it to 6. When this number is added to the current x position, it will move the smiley face forward or back six pixels, thus increasing the speed. Let's look at the code:

```
var speed = 6; //px it moves on each loop determines how fast it moves

 x += speed;

if(x <= 0 || x >= 600){ //as far as we can go without cutting off
    speed = -speed;  //determines if it moves forwards or backwards;
}
```

Implementing requestAnimationFrame

As mentioned earlier, `requestAnimationFrame` is a new specification in the HTML5 family. It's so new that most browsers only support a prefixed version of it. In order to utilize it in modern browsers, we need to do a quick check to see which version of the method we need to use, and then build a reference to it.

We will use the `requestAnimationFrame` method in our example to iterate through our animation. To accomplish this, we will use it to call the same **draw** method cyclically. Remember, the frame rate will be determined by `requestAnimationFrame`, as it will call the **draw** method as soon as the browser is ready to draw another screen.

Putting It All Together

The `requestAnimationFrame` method is really the glue that holds this example together. To get everything working properly, we will set our variables at the top of our page and then break our code into two methods. The first will determine the new **x** value and then call the **draw** method.

The **draw** method will first clear the canvas from the previous frame and then draw out the new frame. This method gets called over and over again. Our final code assembles into this:

```
var x =  0;
var speed = 6; //px it moves on loop determines how fast it moves
var canvas  = document.getElementById("moveSmile");
var smileCtx = canvas.getContext("2d");

function animate(){

   reqAnimFrame = window.mozRequestAnimationFrame||window.webkitRequestAnima
tionFrame
 ||window.msRequestAnimationFrame||window.oRequestAnimationFrame
       reqAnimFrame(animate);

    x += speed;
```

```
    if(x <= 0 || x >= 600){
       speed = -speed;   //see if it moves forwards or backwards;
    }

    draw();
}


function draw() {

    smileCtx6.clearRect(0, 0, 800, 200);

    smileCtx6.beginPath();

    smileCtx6.fillStyle = '#F1F42E';
    smileCtx6.arc(x+100,100,99,0,Math.PI*2); // head

    smileCtx6.stroke();
    smileCtx6.fill();

    smileCtx6.beginPath();
    smileCtx6.moveTo(x+170,100);
    smileCtx6.arc(x+100,100,70,0,Math.PI);    // Mouth
    smileCtx6.stroke();

    smileCtx6.beginPath();
    smileCtx6.fillStyle = 'black';
    smileCtx6.moveTo(x+60, 65);
    smileCtx6.arc(x+60,65,12,0,Math.PI*2);  // Left eye
    smileCtx6.fill();

    smileCtx6.beginPath();
    smileCtx6.moveTo(x+140,65);
    smileCtx6.arc(x+140,65,12,0,Math.PI*2);  // Right eye
    smileCtx6.fill();
}

    animate();
```

Figure 4-17 shows a snapshot from our example. Our smiley face starts at the far-left side of the canvas element, and then animates to the far-right side. It will then repeat this step over and over again.

Figure 4-17.
A frame from the smiley face animation showing the smiley face moving from one side of the canvas element to the other and back again

HACK 42 Build "Native" Illustrations with Scalable Vector Graphics

Scalable Vector Graphics (SVG) is usually the most "familiar" graphics format in the HTML5 family of technologies. This hack will quickly get you working with the SVG format as though it were part of the DOM (hint: it really is part of the DOM!).

Scalable Vector Graphics is the W3C's recommendation for web illustrations. Similar to Flash, SVG is a markup language for describing two-dimensional vector graphics, but it's an open XML-based language as opposed to being proprietary. Think of SVG as being the graphical equivalent to HTML, and like HTML, SVG works seamlessly with other browser technologies such as JavaScript, CSS, and the DOM.

Why SVG?

Compared to all the other graphics and media-based technologies introduced in HTML5, SVG has some major advantages. The primary advantage is the technology itself. Being an XML-based language, SVG doesn't require an editing program like Flash, Photoshop, or even Paint. You can create and edit SVG images with any simple text editor, or with your favorite web editor. The *S* in SVG stands for Scalable, and scalable it is! SVG is resolution-independent. Your SVG images can be zoomed in or out, and even printed at any size, and they will still maintain their quality, which is the primary benefit of the technology.

Being pure XML, SVG is natively searchable, indexable, and easily compressible. It's also quite natural to embed text within your SVG files and then style them with CSS. It's also easy to make SVG graphics compliant with the Americans with Disabilities Act (ADA), by embedding descriptions of the images within the SVG file itself.

Creating Your SVG Image

In most cases SVG is managed in its own file. This is a text-based file ending with *.svg*. You would then embed that file into the DOM in a manner similar to how you would work with an image. In our example, we'll start with a new SVG file named *smiley.svg* and embed it into our sample page with the following code:

```
<object data="smiley.svg" type="image/svg+xml" />
```

Technically, our SVG file is an object on the page, not an image, and therefore is embedded with an object file. At this point we will see our object in the DOM, but it will not display anything, as the SVG file is blank. But we will fix that.

Now, to really impress our friends and enemies we'll build an SVG object that demonstrates the cross-cultural symbol for love, peace, and hope: the smiley face.

Drawing with XML

Unlike a JPEG or PNG image, where the image is transmitted in Unicode, an SVG image is drawn out by a series of rules that follow the XML schema. This tends to make the images lightweight and ultra-scalable. In the preceding code example, we created an `object` element that has a `data` attribute pointing to an SVG file. This SVG file contains a few lines of code that draw out our smiley face. Before we start, let's see how our end product will look (see Figure 4-18).

This cheeky smiley face is truly simple. The SVG file consists of only five elements, and each element becomes a discrete DOM element once it's imported into the page. As DOM elements, they follow all the same rules and have access to the same APIs as all other page elements. Let's take a quick look at each element comprising our smiley face:

```
<circle cx="300" cy="164" r="160" fill="yellow" stroke="black"
stroke-width="2" />
```

This first element is the yellow circle that represents the head of the smiley face. As you can glean from the preceding code, the element is actually a `circle` element that has attributes representing the following:

Figure 4-18.
The smiley face SVG image represented in our sample web page template

cx, cy

> These are the x and y positions of the circle as it relates to the SVG object in the page.

r

> This is the radius of the circle represented in points (a numeric value).

fill

> This refers to how the inside of the object is painted. An element can be filled with a color, a gradient, or a pattern (such as an imported image).

stroke

> This represents the actual shape of the object or line (including the text). The stroke can be colored with the same options as the fill.

stroke-width

> This is only necessary when you have a stroke declared. As is obvious in the attribute name, this declares the width of the stroke in points. The default is 1.

The next two elements are the eyes of the smiley face. They contain many of the same attributes as the previous circle. The two circles are identical to each other except for the x positions that draw them on different sides of the head.

```
<circle cx="210" cy="100" r="20" fill="black" />

<circle cx="380" cy="100" r="20" fill="black" />
```

The clip path may be an unexpected element for this illustration. Not to give away the ending, but the final element will be another circle that represents the smiling mouth in the illustration.

```
<clipPath id="MyClip">
  <rect x="30" y="200" width="600" height="100" />
</clipPath>
```

The clip path is a parent element to other SVG elements that have a clipping effect instead of a painting effect. The clip path has a single attribute:

id

> The id looks a lot like a DOM id because it is a DOM id, and it's necessary in this case for us to reference the clip path by another SVG element.

The clip path contains another element:

```
<rect x="30" y="200" width="600" height="100" />
```

This is exactly what it looks like. You were already introduced to the `circle` element; well, this is a rectangle element. If the `rect` element wasn't contained by a clip path, it would draw a 600 × 100 rectangle on the SVG object.

```
<circle cx="300" cy="160" r="120" fill-opacity="0" stroke="black"
stroke-width="5" clip-path="url(#MyClip)" />
```

This final object is the mouth. This circle has two new attributes that we want to look at:

fill-opacity

> This is a value between 0 and 1 that declares how opaque our fill should be. Since we want the circle to appear empty, we have it set to 0.

clip-path

> This references the DOM id for the clip path within our SGV file. When we reference the clip path, the shape gets applied to this element, in a manner that clips off anything (fill or stroke) within the image.

We could have drawn a line for the mouth of the smiley face, but it would have been a lot more work to draw out that shape in XML than it would be to just declare a whole circle, and then clip half of it off.

When we take all those SVG elements and wrap them in an **<svg>** tag, we can see how simple the code really is:

```
<svg version="1.1"
    baseProfile="full"
    xmlns="http://www.w3.org/2000/svg">
  <circle cx="300" cy="164" r="160" fill="yellow" stroke="black"
   stroke-width="2" />
  <circle cx="210" cy="100" r="20" fill="black" />
  <circle cx="380" cy="100" r="20" fill="black" />
  <clipPath id="MyClip">
    <rect x="30" y="200" width="600" height="100" />
  </clipPath>
  <circle cx="300" cy="160" r="120" fill-opacity="0" stroke="black"
   stroke-width="5" clip-path="url(#MyClip)" />
</svg>
```

These 11 lines of code are all we need to draw out our friendly smiley face. The code is significantly lighter than a JPEG or even a GIF that would represent the same image. Additionally, you inherit all the benefits of first-class DOM objects, as we previously discussed.

HACK 43 Style SVG Elements with CSS

SVG has the same privileges as all other DOM elements, including the ability to be styled with CSS. This hack demonstrates how easy it is to create elements with SVG, and then turn them into illustrations with CSS.

The most powerful part of SVG is its standing in the DOM. SVG elements are first-class elements in HTML5, and they have every privilege that other DOM elements have. That being said, it's simple to control the presentation of these elements with CSS.

For a refresher on how to implement SGV, see Hack #42, *which discusses how to create SVG elements.*

SVG has the ability to control the presentation of its elements by setting attributes on the elements themselves. Here are some of the more popular presentation attributes in SVG:

- `fill`
- `stroke`
- `stroke-width`
- `fill-opacity`

- height
- width
- x, y
- cx, cy
- orientation
- color
- cursor
- clipPath

Many times it makes sense to embed these attributes within the SVG itself where it can be downloaded as one file. Other times it may be more flexible to create our base SVG elements within the SVG file, and style them with a language we are very familiar with: CSS.

Starting with SVG

To get started we will illustrate a simple smiley face with SVG elements. This is a basic illustration that consists of five elements, and nine lines of code:

```
<svg version="1.1"
    baseProfile="full"
    xmlns="http://www.w3.org/2000/svg">
  <circle cx="300" cy="164" r="160" fill="yellow" stroke="black"
   stroke-width="2" />
  <circle cx="210" cy="100" r="20" fill="black" />
  <circle cx="380" cy="100" r="20" fill="black" />
  <clipPath id="MyClip">
    <rect x="30" y="200" width="600" height="100" />
  </clipPath>
  <circle cx="300" cy="160" r="120" fill-opacity="0" stroke="black"
   stroke-width="5" clip-path="url(#MyClip)" />
</svg>
```

This simple code snippet gets stored in a file called *smiley.svg* and embedded into our page with an **<object>** tag as follows:

```
<object data="smiley.svg" type="image/svg+xml" />
```

Once the object is on the page, we see the SVG image as it should appear (see Figure 4-19).

Figure 4-19.
SVG representation of a smiley face

Stripping Away the Noise

In order to move our visual aspects of the illustration to CSS, we need to strip all the visual aspects out of our SVG. We basically want to leave ourselves with some raw shapes that we can manipulate. We will do this by removing most of the attributes from the SVG file. The one attribute we will not remove is the circle radius, as there is no CSS equivalent to this. Here is what our plain Jane SVG will look like:

```
<svg version="1.1"
    baseProfile="full"
    xmlns="http://www.w3.org/2000/svg">
  <circle r="160" class="head"  />
  <circle r="20" class="eye leftEye" />
  <circle r="20" class="eye rightEye" />
  <clipPath id="MyClip">
    <rect class="clipBox" width="100%" height="100%" />
  </clipPath>
  <circle r="120" class="mouth"  />
```

I want to point out a few things about the preceding SVG code. First, note the `rect` element with the class of `clipBox`. We have inserted a `width` and `height` of 100%. At the time of this writing, current implementations of clip boxes require some `height` and **width** attributes set in the element to take effect. Second, I have added a **class** attribute to each element and assigned at least one class name to each element. Although I could have assigned all the CSS via pseudotags based on DOM position, I prefer to use class names, as they're more flexible if the DOM should change.

Since our elements have no look and feel to them, we end up with an SVG element that looks like Figure 4-20.

Figure 4-20.
Our SVG components as they appear unstyled

Our SVG elements have no visual characteristics or positioning, so we're starting with a series of circles stacked on top of the SVG object. Think of your SVG object as being like an *iframe* (an HTML element that loads a new page inside your current page), having its own separate DOM. As an aside, if you don't want to use an **<object>** tag to create your element on the page, you can use an iframe to create SVG elements on the page as well.

In the preceding example we have a few simple class names, such as **head** and **eye**. If we write CSS declarations based on these class names and put them in our master stylesheet, they won't actually affect our SVG elements, as the CSS will not cascade down to the SVG elements. To resolve this issue we need to load our CSS in one of three ways. The first way is with inline CSS where we put a **style** attribute on the element itself and set our styles directly in the element:

```
<circle class="head"  r="160"  style= fill: yellow; stroke: black;
stroke-width: 2px; "/>
```

The second way is by attaching a class name to the element (as we have) and then referencing it in an embedded style block. It's important to remember that the style block needs to be directly in the SVG file, not in the page DOM:

```
<circle class="head"  r="160" />
<style>
.head {fill: yellow; stroke: black; stroke-width: 2px;}
</style>
```

The third method, and our choice for this hack, is to attach a class name to the element and then reference an external stylesheet. Again, it's important to reference the stylesheet from the SVG file and not from the HTML page file. There is also a bit of a twist on this stylesheet. SVG is XML-based but it isn't HTML, so our traditional link reference will not work properly within the SVG file. For external CSS, the SVG specification references an ancient specification on referencing a stylesheet within an XML document. My only assumption was that this specification was part of the Dead Sea Scrolls discovery or something. You can find the old specification at w3.org (*http:// www.w3.org/1999/06/REC-xml-stylesheet-19990629/*).

According to this specification, the stylesheet is loaded with a tag at the top of the SVG file, like so:

```
<?xml-stylesheet type="text/css" href="/assets/css/svg.css"?>
```

This, of course, will have an **href** that will point to the location of your stylesheet on the server, so yours may look different from this example.

Building the CSS

Now that our structure is in place, let's dig into the CSS that we will use to return our little smiley face to its full glory. We basically have two factors to deal with for each element. The first is the visual attributes, and the second is the position. The visual attributes are quite simple: you will see in our CSS that we have basically taken our old inline attributes of stroke, fill, stroke size, and the like and set them in CSS. Here is a sample from our CSS:

```
.head{
     fill: yellow;
     stroke: black;
     stroke-width: 2px;
     }

.mouth {
```

```
      stroke: black;
      fill-opacity: 0;
      stroke-width: 5px;
   }
```

That was simple enough. The second factor to address is positioning. In order to not have all our elements stacked up on top of one another, we need to tell them where to go. For this, we will pull out one of our new CSS3 attributes called **transform**, which we will use to move our elements into place. Here is a sample of our CSS3 transforms within our CSS:

```
.eye {
   transform:translate(210px, 100px);
   }

.rightEye {
   transform:translate(380px, 100px);
   }
```

The **transform** specifies the **translate** (or repositioning) of each element from its current position, which again is with the radius centered at (0,0) or the top-left corner of the SVG element.

Each element has CSS specified to provide the visual attributes and the positioning. When we put it all together, our CSS file contains the following declarations:

```
.head{
   fill: yellow;
   stroke: black;
   stroke-width: 2px;
  transform:translate(300px, 164px);
   }
.eye {
   fill: black;
  transform:translate(210px, 100px);
   }

.rightEye {
   transform:translate(380px, 100px);
   }

.mouth {
   stroke: black;
   fill-opacity: 0;
   stroke-width: 5px;
   clip-path: url(#MyClip);
```

```
        transform:translate(0px, 0px);


}
.clipBox {
    width: 600px;
    height: 100px;
  transform:translate(30px, 200px);


}
```

For more information on how the clip path works, see Hack #42 *where we clarify how and why we use clip paths.*

With this CSS, our finished product looks identical to the one we started with where all our attributes were directly within the SVG elements. Figure 4-21 shows our finished product.

Figure 4-21.
The SVG element using CSS for styling

HACK 44 Animate Illustrations with SVG

Easily turn your SVG illustrations into SVG animations by adding a few lines of HTML or CSS. That's right, no JavaScript is necessary for this easy animation.

Before HTML5, animation was cumbersome. It was never intended to be done on the Web, which might be why developers worked so hard to make it happen. Before HTML5, all animation had to be done with JavaScript. It took us back to the days of stop-frame animation where we had to move the object being animated one frame at a time. With JavaScript, we would slowly change the attribute we were trying to animate one or two pixels at a time. Whether it was height (to make a window slide open) or position (to animate something across the screen), JavaScript would repetitively alter the style attributes until the "animation" was complete. As you can imagine, it wasn't only code-heavy, but processor-heavy as well.

Along comes SVG, bringing with it some easy-to-perform, hardware-accelerated animations. In this hack we'll look at two animation options in our SVG tool belt.

The SVG <animateMotion> Tag

SVG is completely XML-based. So it only makes sense that it has a tag for animation. Let's start with a simple box and bouncing ball. This requires only a few lines of SVG:

```
<svg version="1.1"
    baseProfile="full"
    xmlns="http://www.w3.org/2000/svg">

    <rect x="100" y="0" width="400" height="100"  fill="pink"
    stroke="black" stroke-width="1" />
    <circle cx="120" cy="50" r="20" fill="blue" stroke="black"
    stroke-width="1" />
</svg>
```

From this code we end up with a rectangle with a circle inside it (see Figure 4-22).

In order to animate this ball moving from one side of the rectangle to the other, we will add a new tag and nest it inside the **circle** element, as a child element (think of it as a command associated with the **circle** element). Let's look at our new SVG and then we will walk through the details of the new tag:

Figure 4-22.
SVG elements without any animation

```
<svg version="1.1"
     baseProfile="full"
     xmlns="http://www.w3.org/2000/svg">

    <rect x="100" y="0" width="400" height="100"  fill="pink"
    stroke="black" stroke-width="1" />
    <circle cx="120" cy="50" r="20" fill="blue" stroke="black"
    stroke-width="1">
      <animateMotion path="M 0 0 H 380 Z" dur="3s"
      repeatCount="indefinite" />
    </circle>
  </svg>
```

This new **animateMotion** tag allows us to animate the **circle** element while all other elements stay fixed. In this tag we are utilizing three attributes:

path

The path is the hardest part of this tag. It appears to be a random list of numbers and letters that somehow give us a perfect path from one end of the rectangle to the other. This path is actually a wrap-up of our motion command. Breaking it down, the M represents the command to "move to" a new location, the 0 0 is the x,y start position, and **H** tells it to move horizontally. From there, **380** is the distance it should move measured in points, and the **Z** command closes the path and tells it to start back at the beginning. This notation is all part of the SMIL (Synchronized Multimedia Integration Language) Specification, the details of which you can access on the W3C website (*http://www.w3.org/TR/REC-smil/*).

dur *(duration)*

This attribute defines how long it will take to complete a full path. Values are represented in seconds with the format of **3s**.

repeatCount

This attribute defines how many times the path will "repeat." Don't be fooled by the word *repeat*; a value of **1** will run the path only once, and a value of **5** will run the path five times. In our case, we set it to **indefinite**, so it will run until the page is closed or the value is changed.

Our ball will now bounce back and forth within the rectangle. With SVG, animation is at the root of the language. Just as any other component becomes a value in the DOM, so does our **<animation>** tag, and it can be accessed and altered with JavaScript. Figure 4-23 shows a view of our end product.

Figure 4-23.
SVG animating the ball back and forth inside the box with only one line of code

Flexibility in Structure

In our first example, we made the `<animation>` tag a child tag to the element that was being animated. In many cases you may have a group of tags that you want to animate. To address such situations we will pull out some code from a previous hack of our smiley face created in SVG. If we want to animate this smiley face back and forth on the screen, we certainly don't want to have to animate each element separately. This would be both time-consuming to code and intensive on our processor, as the engine would be calculating each element separately. Let's look at two different code samples showing how to animate a group of SVG tags together.

Here is our first sample:

```
<svg version="1.1"
     baseProfile="full"
     xmlns="http://www.w3.org/2000/svg">
  <g>
  <circle cx="300" cy="164" r="160" fill="yellow" stroke="black"
  stroke-width="2" />
  <circle cx="210" cy="100" r="20" fill="black" />
  <circle cx="380" cy="100" r="20" fill="black" />
  <clipPath id="MyClip">
    <rect x="30" y="200" width="600" height="100" />
  </clipPath>
  <circle cx="300" cy="160" r="120" fill-opacity="0" stroke="black"
  stroke-width="5" clip-path="url(#MyClip)" />
  <animateMotion path="M 0 0 H 300 Z" dur="3s"
  repeatCount="indefinite"></animateMotion>
  </g>
</svg>
```

Here is our second sample:

```
<svg version="1.1"
     baseProfile="full"
     xmlns="http://www.w3.org/2000/svg">
  <animateMotion path="M 0 0 H 300 Z" dur="3s" repeatCount="indefinite">
  <circle cx="300" cy="164" r="160" fill="yellow" stroke="black"
  stroke-width="2" />
  <circle cx="210" cy="100" r="20" fill="black" />
  <circle cx="380" cy="100" r="20" fill="black" />
  <clipPath id="MyClip">
    <rect x="30" y="200" width="600" height="100" />
  </clipPath>
  <circle cx="300" cy="160" r="120" fill-opacity="0" stroke="black"
```

```
      stroke-width="5" clip-path="url(#MyClip)" />
    </animateMotion>

  </svg>
```

In the first sample we had a parent element to our code, named **g**, which is code for "group". Once we group our code together, it's treated as one element (on that level) and our **<animateMotion>** tag simply becomes another child tag to the **g** element whose job is to animate the group of elements.

In the second sample, instead of introducing the new tag we simply use the **<anima teMotion>** tag as a parent to enclose the tags that produce the smiley face. The **<animateMotion>** parent tag animates the tags nested inside it as a group, and the process is streamlined significantly as compared to animating each element individually.

One Last Option

Don't you just love SVG? Just like HTML, there is always more than one way to accomplish everything. This flexibility allows you to pick the method that works best in your particular situation. With SVG animation, there is no shortage of options.

Keeping in mind that SVG elements become DOM elements just like any other HTML page elements, we can animate our SVG just as we would HTML, by using CSS. In the preceding sample that introduced the **g** element, we can remove the **<animate Motion>** tag completely, and set an **id** on the **g** element. From here, we can use a CSS3 transform to create the same animation. For more on applying CSS to SVG elements, see Hack #43.

HACK 45 Embed SVG Directly in Your HTML

You can embed SVG directly within your HTML file, negating the need for an external *.svg* file. With HTML5, your SVG elements can live in the same DOM as your HTML, and you'll be removing some of the barriers of managing the two code bases separately.

SVG is powerful and can be quite complex, creating limitless illustrations and animations with a simple XML-based language. But in some cases you may only have a simple illustration that doesn't require the rigor of an external file to manage the code. Just as HTML5 provides the ability to inline images directly in your markup, SVG can be embedded directly within your HTML as well.

Looking at the code that is involved, you can see that it's exactly what you'd expect it to be. We have our HTML page, and instead of using an **\<object>** tag that points to an external SVG file, we see the entire content of the previously external SVG file directly within our HTML. In our example, we will use our trusty old smiley face SVG illustration embedded directly within our HTML:

```
<doctype !html>
<html>
<head>
<meta charset="utf-8">
    <title>SVG Sample</title>
<link href="assets/css/bootstrap.css" rel="stylesheet" />
<link href="assets/css/bootstrap-responsive.css" rel="stylesheet" />
<head>
<body>
<div class="navbar...  ...</div>
<h1> My Inline SVG Sample</h1>
<div id="svgWrapper" class="row">
<svg version="1.1"
     baseProfile="full"
     xmlns="http://www.w3.org/2000/svg">
  <circle cx="300" cy="164" r="160" fill="yellow" stroke="black"
  stroke-width="2" />
  <circle cx="210" cy="100" r="20" fill="black" />
  <circle cx="380" cy="100" r="20" fill="black" />
  <clipPath id="MyClip">
    <rect x="30" y="200" width="600" height="100" />
  </clipPath>
  <circle cx="300" cy="160" r="120" fill-opacity="0" stroke="black"
  stroke-width="5" clip-path="url(#MyClip)" />

</svg>

</div>

</body>
</html>
```

In the preceding example, once the renderer sees the SVG declaration tag it switches parsers from HTML to SVG. When the tag closes it goes back from SVG to HTML. Our results look exactly as they did when the SVG was in an external file (see Figure 4-24).

Figure 4-24.
The SVG smiley face illustration where the SVG is inline with the HTML

Why Inline?

Aside from the obvious "ease of use" argument, there are additional benefits to putting your SVG inline. Above all, inline SVG can be used as a performance enhancement. In some scenarios, you may benefit from not having to load the external file (as it will require an additional call to your server) and can put the SVG code directly in the page. Keep in mind that this is not always a performance enhancement, especially when you have a large amount of SVG code, which your browser may be able to load in parallel with your elements to save time. In cases like ours, when your illustration consists of only a few lines of code, it will generally be better in terms of performance to inline it and remove the additional call.

An additional benefit of inline SVG can be for DOM reference. In general, your SVG file is a separate DOM from your page when it's loaded in an external SVG file (think of it as an iframe, an HTML element that loads a separate page inside the element). That being the case, any CSS that affects your SGV must be placed in or linked from your SVG file, and therefore can't be applied to the HTML or the page. JavaScript similarly needs to access the SVG elements through the SVG object and falls prey to the same limitations as accessing items in an iframe. Moving the SVG into the DOM directly removes those barriers and allows you to truly treat your SVG elements just as any other DOM element.

Let's look at a quick and quirky example of how inline SVG is affected by CSS declarations. In our example, we have a simple CSS declaration:

```
<style>
circle {
stroke: red;
 stroke-width: 12px;
}
 </style>
```

This style block is embedded directly into our HTML page, and in our page we have two SVG smiley faces. The first face is loaded as an external SVG image (Figure 4-25), and the second is loaded as an inline SVG image (Figure 4-26).

Figure 4-25.
An SVG smiley face, loaded as an external .svg file

Figure 4-26.
An SVG smiley face, loaded inline in the HTML document

As you can see, the CSS applies to none of the circles within our embedded SVG and to every circle within our inline SVG. Embedded SVG may not always be the best choice for your documents, but it's always nice to have options.

5

User Interactions

It may seem like HTML5 has a lot to do with how things work under the covers. We discussed a new way to draw, a new way to present imagery, a new way to perform animation, new ways to store data, and new ways to talk to the server. This chapter focuses on a different aspect of HTML5: the new way you interact with the page.

Drag-and-drop might not be a new idea. We've had drag-and-drop in apps for years, where we as developers built some slick JavaScript engine that helped us drag things from one spot on the page to another. Drag-and-drop was really an industry-changing idea when it was introduced, but HTML5 has taken this capability one step further. HTML5 drag-and-drop is not just about what you can drag around the page, although it does that; it's also about dragging things between your browser and your computer. HTML5 drag-and-drop lets you bring data into a web app simply by dragging it. It also lets you take data out with the same drag-and-drop interface you've grown used to over the years. Drag-and-drop takes your web applications one step closer to being integrated into your operating system.

Editable content takes data entry to a new level as well. In the past, we've been able to edit data within a form field. HTML5 takes this capability to the next level by allowing us to edit content in any element of the page, whether it is in a paragraph, a list of items, or a page header. Editable content has the potential to bring new levels of customization to our web applications. Imagine if you allowed your user to determine what he named every selection in a drop-down menu, or if you could enable your users to update any information that was presented to them right in the application, without having to go to a separate form. The implications of these capabilities point to a much richer, more interactive web application. Editable content doesn't have to stop at a single paragraph either: HTML5 allows you to make the entire page editable. Basically, it can turn any browser into a WYSIWYG editor.

Every version of a browser seems to have fewer and fewer buttons on the screen to interact with. I think this is a good trend. The fewer buttons there are on the page, the less confusion there is for the user. HTML5 allows us to take full control of the buttons that are left, namely, the history buttons. In one form or another, there will always be a way to go backward and forward on the Web—after all, hyperlinks are what make the World Wide Web the "web" that it is today. With HTML5 history, you can make your own history just within the page you are on. No longer do you need to rely on hash map tricks. HTML5 also gives you full control of those buttons. As an application developer, you decide what happens when users click the history button while they are on your page. It's awesome. Now, let's get started!

HACK 46 Make Any Content Draggable Within Your Application

Just a few lines of code can turn any item on your page into a draggable item. HTML5 makes drag-and-drop a first-class citizen with easy implementation and brand-new features that help you know exactly what's going on with your web application.

Gone are the days of writing hundreds of lines of code to allow your users to drag an item from one part of the page to another. HTML5 has capitalized on that idea and brings us a modern version of that age-old interaction. With HTML5 the implementation is easy, and the data around it is rich. Let's start by looking at how easy it is to make any item on your page draggable:

```
<div id="myDraggableItem" draggable="true">
   this is content I want to drag around the screen
</div>
```

And there you have it! Didn't I say it was easy?

OK, if that was all you needed to do with drag-and-drop, this hack would be finished and the book would be much thinner. Keep reading, and you'll see that this hack provides a ton of information that will make it easy for you to implement this feature in your applications today.

Turning On the Drag

Drag-and-drop might not be that foreign to your users. Many browsers have drag-and-drop turned on by default for certain page elements—mainly, anchor tags and image tags. These two items have clear pointers to the assets they are associated with. The anchor tag has an **href** that can easily become a bookmark when dragged over the bookmark bar, or a shortcut when dragged to your operating system. The shortcut that is formed when you drag a link to the desktop may look something like Figure 5-1.

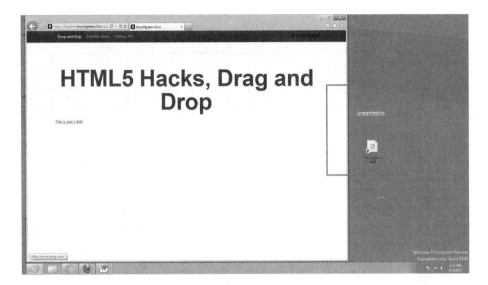

Figure 5-1.
Shortcut formed when dragging a link to the desktop

Images have a similar behavior. Since an image tag is tied directly to a file, it can be dragged as well. Keep in mind that not every image in a web application is an image tag. Many images are embedded in CSS with background images, or are created through SVG or canvas tags. This inherent **draggable** attribute refers specifically to an image tag.

Adding this behavior to any item is easy, as you can see in Figure 5-2. You simply add the **draggable** attribute to your page element, and it suddenly has "dragability"!

Let's take this capability to the next level and look at all the events that are published when we grab onto that element. Then we'll do something with those events. Let's start with some standard markup. We will have a few circles on the page that are created by adding some fancy CSS to some **div**s, and a "garbage can" made out of another fancy styled **div**. Here's the markup we are using:

```
<div class="row">
<div class="span-6 dragTarg"></div>
</div>
<div class="row">
<div class="span-6 dragItems">
<div draggable="true" class="red"></div>
<div draggable="true" class="green"></div>
<div draggable="true" class="blue"></div>
</div>
</div>
```

It's pretty simple, and when we add the CSS, we get what's shown in Figure 5-3.

Figure 5-2.
Copy of the image dragged to the desktop

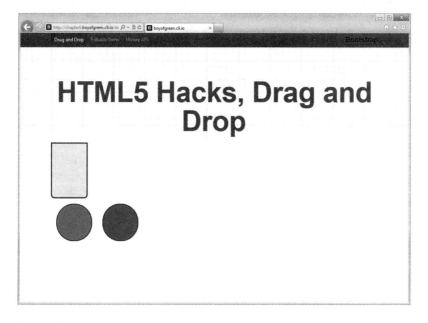

Figure 5-3.
Two draggable components and one target div

At this point we can pick up the targets and drag them around the page, but as soon as we drop them they skulk back to their original positions. Without any listeners to catch what's going on, there isn't much to hack about. Now let's look at our events.

Listening for All Those Great Events

HTML5 really does take DOM (Document Object Model) events to the next level by providing in-depth events on all interactions. Drag-and-drop alone has the following events associated with it:

- `dragstart`
- `drag`
- `dragenter`
- `dragleave`
- `dragover`
- `drop`
- `dragend`

Let's act on a few of these events by applying listeners. To accomplish this, we will add a few lines of JavaScript to a script tag on our page. We'll start by adding a few listeners to the elements that will be draggable:

```
var circles = document.querySelectorAll('.dragItems div');

for(var i=0;i<circles.length;i++){
    circles[i].addEventListener('dragstart', startDrag, false);
    circles[i].addEventListener('dragend', endDrag, false);

}
```

We started with a query selector that creates a collection of our circles, and then we looped through each one to add two different listeners to them: the first listens for the event that is published when we first start to drag the item, and the second listens for the event when we stop dragging the item. Each listener will call its respective function:

```
function startDrag(event) {
    this.style.border = '5px solid pink';
}

function endDrag(event) {
    this.style.display = 'none';
}
```

Here we have added a little bit of additional context to the elements while they are being dragged, to emphasize which element is being moved. In this case, when we start dragging our circle we change the border to a pink dotted line, and when we finish dragging we add a `display = 'none'` to the `div` to make it look like it vanished from the DOM. Remember, these events are attached to the items that are being dragged.

We also have the additional page element, the garbage can, to deal with. We will set up that `div` as the drag target. Here is the JavaScript we'll need for that:

```
var dragTarg = document.querySelector('.dragTarg');
dragTarg.addEventListener('dragenter', function(e){
    this.style.border = '3px #aaa dashed'});

dragTarg.addEventListener('dragleave', function(e){
    this.style.border = 3px solid black''});
```

This interaction is fairly simple. We identify our element with a query selector, and then we add two listeners to it. The first identifies what happens when we drag an item, any item, over the element, and the second defines what happens when the event is published that says the drag item is no longer over our element. All we are doing during the period in between these events is changing the color and style of the border around the outside of the `div`. This gives the user a visual cue that she is dragging over the element on the page. Remember, the page may contain other draggable items (such as an image or link) that, when dragged over the garbage can, will activate the `dragenter` and `dragleave` events.

When we put this code together we have a few elements on the page that interact with each other when we drag them. For example, we can drag any circle around the page, and when it crosses over the garbage can the can changes its state; then when we release the dragging element it disappears from the page (see Figure 5-4). We did all that with just a few lines of code. Who doesn't love HTML5!

HACK 47 Update the DOM with a Drag-and-Drop Data Transfer Object

HTML5 drag-and-drop imparts a true relationship between the dragged item and the drop zone. This hack shows you how to transfer data between the two using drag data, and then updating the DOM from the information that is transferred.

As you might have guessed, HTML5 drag-and-drop provides a much richer interaction than what was available in the past with just JavaScript. HTML5 publishes a slew of DOM events telling us what is going on all along the way.

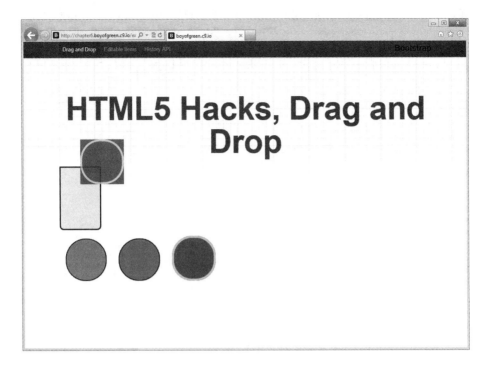

Figure 5-4.
Page while draggable circle is dragged on top of our simple garbage can

Many times you drag an element because you want to move it to another place on the page. This requires that your dragged item and your drop zone be able to communicate the appropriate information. Luckily, HTML5 has an API for that!

For this hack we will start with four elements on the page: the drop zone (where we want to drop the elements to), which is styled to look like my garbage can, and three draggable items that are styled to look like colorful balls. Let's look at the markup:

```
<div class="row">
<div class="span-6 dragTarg"></div>
</div>
<div class="row">
<div class="span-6 dragItems">
<div draggable="true" class="red"></div>
<div draggable="true" class="green"></div>
<div draggable="true" class="blue"></div>
</div>
</div>
```

Note that our **divs** styled as colorful balls all have the attribute of **draggable** set to **true**. This enables them to be dragged around the page.

Events play a big part in this interaction (for more information on events that are published while dragging and dropping, read "Make Any Content Draggable Within Your Application"). To grab hold of the events that are being published while the elements are being dragged, we add a few listeners to the page:

```
function startDrag(event) {
    this.style.border = '5px solid pink';

}

function endDrag(event) {
    this.style.border = '';

}

var circles = document.querySelectorAll('.dragItems div');

for(var i=0;i<circles.length;i++){

    circles[i].addEventListener('dragstart', startDrag, false);
    circles[i].addEventListener('dragend', endDrag, false);

}
```

This is a pretty simple script that adds listeners to the drag start and end of each element. The **startDrag** function changes the border of the element while it is being dragged, and the **endDrag** function changes it back when it's done.

Let's keep going and add a few listeners to our garbage can **div** that we have designated as our drop zone:

```
var dragTarg = document.querySelector('.dragTarg');
dragTarg.addEventListener('dragenter', function(e){
    this.style.border = '3px #aaa dashed'});

dragTarg.addEventListener('dragleave', function(e){
    this.style.border = '3px solid black'});
```

These two listeners are added to the drop zone. Again, they only change the appearance of the items (no additional functionality has been added yet). The drop zone changes during the drag-over (in this case, from a solid border to a dashed border), and changes back when the item is no longer over it. When we put all this code together we have a nice, pretty picture of a drag scenario (see Figure 5-5).

Figure 5-5.
Single draggable div element being dragged over the drop zone

Incoming: Data Transfer Object

At this point, you may not be satisfied with this hack: you've probably figured out that you can drag an item just fine, but this capability isn't very impressive if you can't drop the item somewhere. We want the colorful ball divs to change position in the DOM when they are dragged and dropped. For that to happen we need to have the dragging item be able to pass information to the drop zone.

In comes the data transfer object. The HTML5 spec authors thought of everything, even how to transfer data between a drag object and a drop zone. The data transfer object holds the piece of data that is sent in a drag event. The draggable element listener sets the data transfer in the drag start event; the data is read in the drop event. We make a simple call to set the data:

```
e.dataTransfer.setData(format, data)
```

This sets the object's content to the MIME type and data payload passed as its arguments. In our case, we want that data to be identifying information about the drag element itself, so we can move it in the DOM when the actual drop happens. Let's revisit our code sample and see if we can plug this into our dragging event:

```
function startDrag(event) {
    this.style.border = '5px solid pink';
    event.dataTransfer.setData("text", this.className);
}
```

```
function endDrag(event) {
    this.style.border = '';

}

var circles = document.querySelectorAll('.dragItems div');

for(var i=0;i<circles.length;i++){

    circles[i].addEventListener('dragstart', startDrag, false);
    circles[i].addEventListener('dragend', endDrag, false);

}
```

All we really did here was add a single line of code. We set the MIME type to text (since we are passing a string), and then we have the item pass data about itself—in this case, its class name. We will use the class name to identify the object in the DOM.

Publishing data isn't very useful if there isn't anything reading it. So our next step is to move the content once the drop is performed. For this, we will set up a listener for the drop event. This listener goes on the drop zone. We already have a **dragenter** and a **dragleave** event on our drop zone, but we need a listener to attach to the drop event. Here is our additional code:

```
function dropit(event){
 event.preventDefault()
   var myElement = document.querySelector('.dragItemsB .'
   +event.dataTransfer.getData('text');
   this.appendChild(myElement), false);

};

dragTarg.addEventListener('dragover', function(e){
   e.preventDefault();
   });

    dragTarg.addEventListener('drop', dropit, false);
```

You might have noticed that we handled two different listeners. First, we added a **dragover** listener, whose only purpose is to prevent the default action of **dragover**. This is necessary to expose the drop event, which again is the only place you can have access to your data transfer object that you published in your **dragstart**.

The functionality is fairly simple. We use the class name we pulled from the data transfer object to find our dragging element in the DOM. We then do a simple **append Child** to put that element inside the drop zone. Once it's in the drop zone, our CSS kicks in to turn that colorful ball into a colorful flat line. After the drop, the drop zone looks like Figure 5-6.

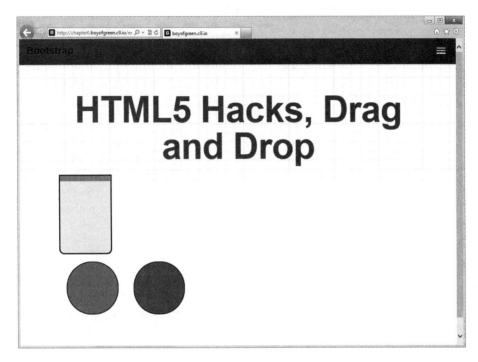

Figure 5-6.
Drop zone after one colorful ball element has been dropped into the drop zone

The Drop Zone Attribute

Here's an additional tidbit about drag-and-drop. Although it can be a fun and intuitive way for users to work with your application, many users may be accessing your site in a different manner, such as via a screen reader. HTML5 has added an attribute that will give some additional clarity to those users. The **dropzone** attribute was added to identify areas of the document where items can be dropped. This helps nontraditional interfaces understand where things can be dropped on the page. Let's update our drop zone to take advantage of this:

```
<div class="row">
<div class="span-6 dragTarg" dropzone="true"></div>
</div>
```

Don't get too excited—by no means does adding this attribute make this `div` any more of a drop zone than it already was. We still need our listeners for that. Rather, this attribute provides additional information and makes our page that much more accessible.

HACK 48 Drag Files In and Out of Your Web Application

No longer are you constrained by the limits of your browser window. HTML5 drag-and-drop can move files from the cloud to your computer, and files from your computer to the cloud—all with just a few lines of JavaScript.

HTML5 has the power to process data right within the browser, without going to the server. From text to images to video, HTML5 has the horsepower. Along with that, HTML5 drag-and-drop gives us an easy interface for getting data into and out of the browser. We simply grab the data from our operating system and drop it into our browser. In this hack we will transfer files to the OS from our browser, and then back into our browser from the OS. Let's start by dragging data to our OS from the browser.

Bringing Files Home

Being able to drag content from the browser to our OS starts with a single element in our app. Every file we want to bring down from the cloud needs to be tied to an element in some form or another. For this hack we will start with three `div`s on our page, all styled as colorful balls. Each element will be tied to a text file in the cloud. Let's look at our markup:

```
<div class="span-6 dragItemsC">
 <div class="red" draggable="true"
 data-downloadurl="application/octet-stream:colorRed.txt:
this is the color red">
 </div>
 <div class="green" draggable="true"
 data-downloadurl="application/octet-stream:colorGreen.txt:
http://chapter6.boyofgreen.c9.io/assets/test.txt">
 </div>
 <div class="blue" draggable="true" data-downloadurl="application/oc
tet-stream:test.txt:http://thecssninja.com/gmail_dragout/Eadui.ttf">
 </div>
</div>
```

The markup is fairly simple, and when rendered in our browser it looks like Figure 5-7.

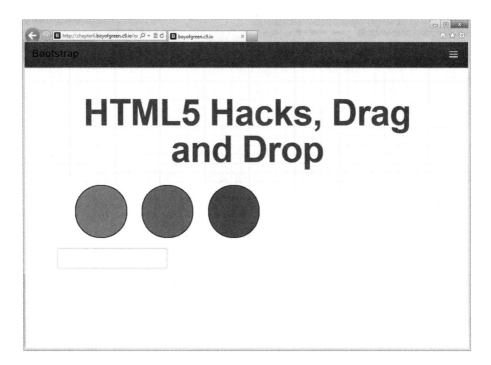

Figure 5-7.
Three divs rendered as colorful balls, all tied to files in the cloud

Let's dig into our attributes here a bit. The first attribute we have on each `div` is the `draggable` attribute, set to `true`. This is a foundational attribute for drag-and-drop because it allows us to be able to pick the element out of the page and drag it around. Some elements, such as images and `href`s, are draggable by default. In fact, if we drag an image or an `href` to the OS a file will appear. For an image it would copy the image out of the cloud, and for an `href` it would make a shortcut to the web page that the link tag was pointing to. In our case, we are using `div`s, so the attribute is necessary.

The second attribute we see is `data-downloadurl`, and each of these attributes is pointing to a URL of a file we want to pull down from the cloud. If you read some of the earlier hacks in this book, you may recognize the "data-" format as being a custom data attribute. This is another HTML5 feature that allows us to add additional data to any element within our DOM. In this case we are using it to store our URL. If you loaded this page right now you would be able to drag these `div`s around the page, but if you tried to drag them to the desktop nothing would happen. To make that data file transfer take place, we need to add a few drag-and-drop listeners.

We will add a few lines of JavaScript to our page that adds listeners to each `div`. The listeners will fire some simple functionality to help our drop know what to drop.

```
function startDrag(event){
    event.dataTransfer.setData("DownloadURL",
      this.getAttribute("data-downloadurl"))
};

var circles = document.querySelectorAll('.dragItems div');

for(var i=0;i<circles.length;i++){

    circles[i].addEventListener('dragstart', startDrag, false);

};
```

Let's walk through what is going on here. The listeners are attaching to the **drag start** event. The **dragstart** event is important in this process because it is the only point in a drag-and-drop when you can add data to the **dataTransfer** object. (For more about the data transfer object, see Hack #47.) In this case, we attach a listener that fires the **startDrag** function. This function has only one line of code in it that pulls the **data-downloadurl** string from each element and adds it to an attribute of the **dataTransfer** object called **DownloadURL**. To accomplish this, we are using a simple **setData** method.

Once we have this value in place on the **dataTransfer** object, our HTML5-enabled browser takes over. Let's see what happens when we drag one of these elements outside our browser window now (see Figure 5-8).

Figure 5-8.
Dragging and dropping one of our divs after the dataTransfer object is updated by our listener

Instead of getting a "not allowed" symbol when we drag, we get a pointer symbol telling us all is well in the drag-and-drop world. Even better, once we drop the element outside the browser window, we see that text file from the cloud appear in our OS filesystem (in this case, the desktop). It's drag-and-drop magic!

Bringing Files Back to the Browser

Wow, now that we have the ability to bring files from the cloud to our OS, let's use some of that HTML5 power to bring into the browser the files we have saved locally. It's important to note that the next step isn't actually transferring files to the cloud; that would require a different hack. What we are doing here is bringing files from the OS into the browser, so we can manipulate that data.

We'll start with a text file named *coolKid.txt* that resides on the desktop. In that text file is a simple line that says, "Jeff really is a cool kid"; at this point we want to put that text inside a text area in our app so that we can work with the text in the browser. This time around, the markup we will start with is very simple. It's a text area:

```
<div class="row">
<textarea id="showDrop"></textarea>
</div>
```

The only attribute on this text area is the **id**, and you guessed it, we will add listeners to it. Let's jump right into the JavaScript where we add the listeners:

```
var showDrop = document.getElementById('showDrop');

showDrop.addEventListener('dragover', function(e){
    e.preventDefault()
  });

showDrop.addEventListener('drop', readData, false);
```

If we didn't add JavaScript to this page and we dragged our text file over our text area, the browser would treat the dragged file as a hyperlink and try to load it in the browser window. In our case we would have left the app, and loaded up our line of text that says, "Jeff really is a cool kid" (I'm Jeff, by the way, and I am a cool kid).

As you can see in the preceding code, we are adding two listeners to this element. The first is a **dragover** listener, which exists for only one reason: to prevent the default action from occurring. Without the listener, the drop event will never be fired. The next listener calls out to a function that will handle bringing the data into our HTML5 application:

```
var readData = function(e){

e.stopPropagation(); // Stops some browsers from redirecting.
e.preventDefault();
var filelist = e.dataTransfer.files;
if(!filelist){ return}

var filelist = event.dataTransfer.files;

if(filelist.length > 0){

    var file = filelist[0];

        var filereader = new FileReader();

        filereader.myTarg = document.getElementById('showDrop');

        var myData = function(event){
          this.myTarg.value = this.result
        };

        filereader.onloadend = myData;


        filereader.readAsText(file);

    };
};
```

This function seems relatively complex compared to the one line of code that it took to bring the file down to our desktop, so let's walk through what is going on. The first thing we have to do is to stop the browser from trying to load the file in the browser window. We have two methods that we call for that, as some browsers require both:

```
e.stopPropagation(); // Stops some browsers from redirecting.
e.preventDefault();
```

Next we will build a pointer (we will use this reference a few times) to our **dataTrans fer** object, which you will probably remember from when you brought the file down to the OS. In this object should be an array called **files**, which will list all the files (yes, we can have more than one) that are being dragged into this element:

```
var filelist = e.dataTransfer.files;
```

Not everything that is dragged and dropped in the window is a file, so the next step is to check to see if we are uploading a file; if we are, the length of this array will be at least 1. We will wrap the rest of our code in this `if` condition, because if there isn't a file in the drag, there is nothing else to do:

```
if(filelist.length > 0)
.....
}
```

For the next step we will invoke a method that will help us read the file and get the data we want out of it. It's called the **FileReader** method, so we will invoke it as a variable named **filereader**:

```
var filereader = new FileReader();
```

The next few lines of code have to do with the file reader. The first thing we will do is to build a reference to where we want the text to appear—in this case, our text area—into the **filereader** object. This will make it easy to reference later.

```
filereader.myTarg = document.getElementById('showDrop');
```

This is probably the trickiest part: we are going to set up a *closure*, which is basically a partially executed function that we will use once the file is fully loaded in the browser. This method takes another value we will add to the **filereader** object, called **re sults**. The **results** value will actually be the text from our file that we will pull on in just a moment.

```
var myData = function(event){this.myTarg.value = this.result};
```

The last two lines of code fire the closure called **myData** on the **loadEnd** event and then fire a **readAsText** method that has a reference to the actual file inside it:

```
filereader.onloadend = myData;

filereader.readAsText(filelist[0]);
```

The order of events here is very important. If you try to call the **readAsText** *method before the file is fully loaded in the browser, you will get a blank value.*

When we put all of this together we get a result that looks like Figure 5-9.

Figure 5-9.
Text area after the text file from the desktop is dragged to it

There are endless possibilities as to what you can do with local files once you get them into the browser. In this case, I can upload that data to the server, or I can edit it some more and drag it locally again. HTML5 brings the functionality that used to be limited to the server, right into your browser.

HACK 49 Make Any Element on Your Page User-Customizable with Editable Content

User input used to be limited to form elements such as inputs and text areas, but with HTML5's Editable Content feature, any element of your page can become editable. Use this feature to allow users to customize their pages.

HTML5 opens the door for ultimate customization for our users. One of the new features that make this especially easy is Editable Content. It might also be one of the simplest features to implement.

In this hack we want to allow our users to customize their page content—personalize their page, if you will. To make this possible we will make the main content of the page editable content. Let's look at our markup:

```
<div contenteditable="true" class="row" id="editable">
    <p>
    This is a really great book.
    I am so glad I am reading it because:
    </p>
    <ul>
        <li>it is witty</li>
        <li>i am now well informed about HTML5</li>
        <li>the authors are all around great guys</li>
    </ul>
</div>
```

The preceding markup is the main content for our page and the results should look like Figure 5-10.

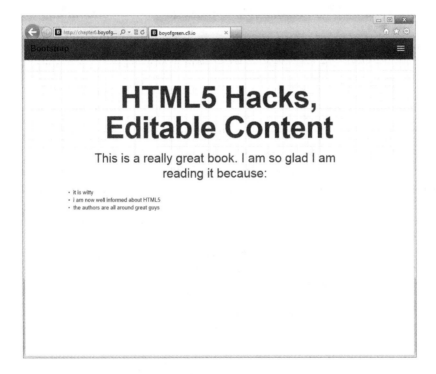

Figure 5-10.
Our content inside an HTML5 page

You may have noticed the new attribute on our container **div** that says **contente ditable="true"**; this attribute is all we need to make our content user-customizable. Just as though they were typing in a text area, our users can now edit this section of the web page right within their browser, without requiring any extra tools. The HTML is smart enough to know what part of the markup they are editing, and matches their new content to the elements they are in. For example, if the user is in an unordered list (`ul`) and presses Return she will add another `li` to the list. Pressing Return inside a paragraph creates a new paragraph, and so on.

Now, at this point, if the user refreshes the page all the content she updated will go away and it will reload from the server. It's important to note that editable content is not a back door to updating content on the server. We don't want to update the data in the cloud, but we do want it to stick for this user, so we will turn to another tool from the HTML5 toolkit, called *local storage*. Local storage allows us to save data right in the browser. Unlike cookies, which eventually get erased over time, local storage sticks around until you (the app developer) or the user intentionally erases it. We'll take the content the user updated in this editable area, and save it off to local storage so that we can use it again. To accomplish this we will pull out a few lines of JavaScript:

```
var myEdit = document.getElementById('editable');

var setEditMemory = function(content){
    localStorage.setItem("myContent", myEdit.innerHTML);

};

myEdit.addEventListener('blur',setEditMemory);
```

We are basically adding a listener to the `blur` event of our editable `div`. Usually, `div`s don't have `blur` events (as they can't naturally take focus), but since we have made our `div` editable, it automatically takes focus, and therefore has a `blur` event fired when we exit the editable content. That listener is simply taking the content from the `div` and storing it as a string in local storage under a value name of `myContent`.

We've successfully saved the content; now we just need to use it to update the page content when the user revisits our page. For this we will add a few additional lines of JavaScript when the page loads:

```
if(localStorage.getItem("myContent")){
    myEdit.innerHTML = localStorage.getItem("myContent");
}
```

We are simply checking to see if our `myContent` value has been created. If it has, we know the user has visited the page before, and may have updated this content. So we pull the `myContent` value from local storage and update our editable `div` with the content. Now, the user will see the updated content every time she returns to this page. Magical!

Spellcial!

Another nice feature that comes with editable content is spellcheck. That's right, built-in spellcheck. Much like you are used to in your desktop word processor, if you misspell a word in HTML5, a squiggly line appears underneath it, and if you right-click on that word you can choose a replacement word from the browser's built-in dictionary. If for some reason you decide you don't want this feature in your document, you can simply turn it off by setting the `spellcheck` attribute to `false`:

```
<div class="row" id="editable" contentEditable="true"
spellcheck="false">...</div>
```

HTML5 has given us the bulk of a word processor right in our browser! Just think about the possibilities.

HACK 50 Turn Your Web Page into a WYSIWYG Editor

Make it easy to update your web page content without ever leaving your browser. A few simple lines of code can turn your web page into a web page editor.

Back in the day, WYSIWYG editors were all the rage. Unfortunately, it was always difficult to transition from what you saw in your editor to what you saw in the browser. HTML5 provides the key to make it all work.

Make the Page Editable

The first step to turning your web page into a web page editor is to make all the content on your web page editable. In previous hacks we talked about what it takes to make a section of our page editable, and it's just as easy to make our whole page editable. It takes only one line of code:

```
document.designMode = "on"
```

So, to put a bit of control around this feature we will start with a web page with some fabulous content on it (see Figure 5-11).

Figure 5-11.
Page before any content is edited, and with design mode off

We will use the controls we added to turn our document's design mode off and on, and to export the code. Let's look at the markup for our page controls:

```
<div class="row">
  <p>
   use this button to make your entire document
   editable or turn it off:
  </p>
  <p><button class="btn" id="makeEdit">toggle design mode</button></p>
  <p>use this button to show the markup</p>
  <p><button class="btn" id="showMarkup">show my markup</button></p>
  <p><textarea id="exportContent"></textarea></p>
</div>
```

We basically have text, two buttons, and a text area. The buttons will need listeners to have functionality. Let's look at the JavaScript we have for this app:

```
var button = document.getElementById('makeEdit');
  button.addEventListener('click', function(e){
        if(document.designMode === "off"){
            document.designMode = "on"
        }else{
```

```
            document.designMode = "off"
        }
    });

    var showMarkup = document.getElementById('showMarkup');
    showMarkup.addEventListener('click', function(e){
        var str = '<HTML>'+document.documentElement.innerHTML+'</HTML>'
        document.getElementById('exportContent').value = str;
    });
```

The first button is used to toggle the design view. We have a listener attached to the click event on the button that executes some simple JavaScript. It checks to see if design mode is off, and if it is, it turns it on. If design mode is on, it turns it off.

The second button also has a listener that fires functionality for the export of the page content. The logic is fairly simple. At any given point this button can be clicked, and we will run some JavaScript that will copy all the content (HTML, any inline scripts, etc.) from the **documentElement**. This gives us all the content inside the HTML tags as a string. The string of content is taken, the HTML tags and **<doctype>** tag (since it is outside the body) are added back into the string, and then the string is set as the value of the text area. We use a text area so that the string remains as text, and the browser does not try to execute any of it.

At this point we have the entire page markup in a location where it can be copied and reused again (see Figure 5-12).

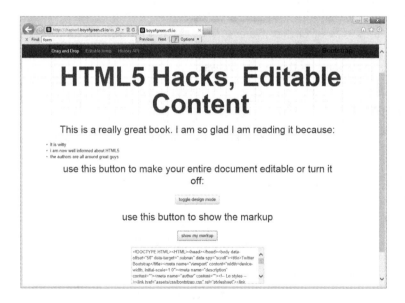

Figure 5-12.
Page with entire page markup inside the text area

We can now make our edits directly in our web page. Keep in mind that we are editing text on the page; we cannot resize or reposition elements. But we don't have to worry that our page will not render the same way it appears in our editor, since our rendered page has become our editor!

HACK 51 Take Control of the Browser History Buttons with HTML5 Session History

HTML5 provides an elegant way to programmatically control the history stack while in your web application.

How many times have you been inside a great web app, only to click the browser back button thinking it will undo your last navigation, but instead it takes you back to the last website? HTML5 session history gives you an easy interface for managing the history within your application.

In the past, developers have done tricky things to applications to enable them to "fool" the behavior of the browser history by using hash tags within the URL. Usually, the developer would add something like "#mynewurl" to the end of his page URL, and it would add a new position in the history stack. Anytime you add a "#" to a URL, it considers it a position within the page, and doesn't leave the page when the back button is clicked.

Session history allows you to program that behavior directly into your application. You can even update the URL of your page without refreshing the page (be careful, though; you don't want to make up URLs that your server can't resolve, in case the user bookmarks them or tries to come back at a later time). For this hack we have a `<canvas>` tag onto which we will build a smiley face. We will execute each step of the build process by clicking the back button on the browser.

Smile, It's History!

We'll begin with a page that has no header and only a bit of content (see Figure 5-13).

Normally, if you click the back button at this point it will take you back to the page you were on before you came to this site. So we'll add a few new entries to our history stack to get us started:

```
window.history.pushState('leftEye', 'makeLeftEye');
window.history.pushState('rightEye', 'makeRightEye');
window.history.pushState('mouth', 'makeMouth');
window.history.pushState('face', 'makeface');
window.history.pushState('ready', 'letsgo');
```

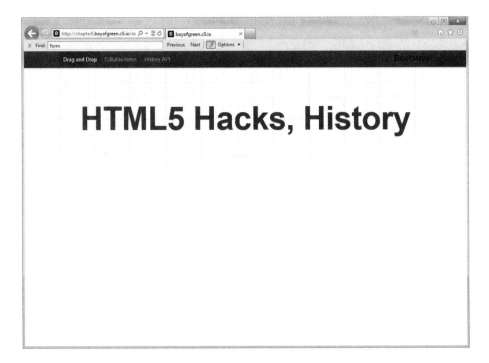

Figure 5-13.
Page with missing content

Here we have entered five new entries into our history stack. At this point, if we refreshed our page we could click the back button five times before it would take us back to the previous website. However, nothing would change about the page when we click the back button. For that we need to set up a listener:

```
window.addEventListener("popstate", drawStack, false);
```

This listener will fire the **drawStack** function every time the back button is clicked. Since it's an event, it will automatically pass an event object along, just as a click event would:

```
var drawStack = function(){
  switch(window.history.state)
      {
      case 'leftEye':
        makeLeftEye();
        break;
      case 'rightEye':
        makeRightEye();
        break;
      case 'mouth':
```

```
      makeMouth();
      break;
    case 'face':
      makeFace();
      break;
    default: break


  }

};
```

Inside this method we actually see a **switch** statement. This **switch** statement is used to determine which step of our process is being called on each time the back button is clicked, and what method will be fired to handle the functionality. If you look back at when we added the entries to the history stack, you will see each of them went in with a value name and a value. This **switch** statement is looking at the value name to determine which position of the stack we are in. Each case in this statement fires one of these functions:

```
var mySmile = document.getElementById('mySmile2')
var smileCtx = mySmile.getContext('2d');



var makeFace = function(){
        smileCtx.beginPath();

        smileCtx.fillStyle = '#F1F42E';
        smileCtx.arc(100,100,99,0,Math.PI*2); // head

        smileCtx.stroke();
        smileCtx.fill();
};

var makeMouth = function(){
    smileCtx.beginPath();
    smileCtx.moveTo(170,100);
    smileCtx.arc(100,100,70,0,Math.PI);    // Mouth
    smileCtx.stroke();
};

var makeLeftEye = function(){

    smileCtx.beginPath();
    smileCtx.fillStyle = 'black';
    smileCtx.moveTo(60, 65);
```

```
        smileCtx.arc(60,65,12,0,Math.PI*2);  // Left eye
        smileCtx.fill();
    };

    var makeRightEye = function (){
        smileCtx.beginPath();
        smileCtx.fillStyle = 'black';
        smileCtx.moveTo(140,65);
        smileCtx.arc(140,65,12,0,Math.PI*2);  // Right eye
        smileCtx.fill();
    };
```

Each phase draws something new. If we again refresh the page and click the back button, we will now see a yellow circle on the page (see Figure 5-14).

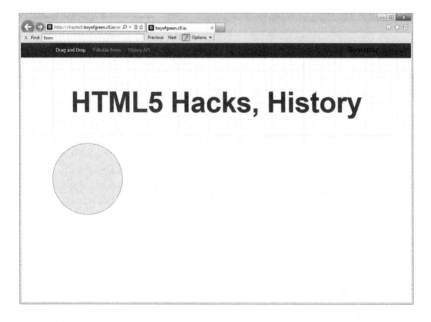

Figure 5-14.
Our web page after the back button is clicked one time

If we continue to click the back button, the smile will be drawn, then the right eye, and then the left eye. After clicking the back button four times we will have a full smiley face (see Figure 5-15).

Figure 5-15.
Our web page after the back button is clicked four times

If you have a keen eye, you may have noticed that we clicked the back button four times but we put five entries in the history stack. You may think you still have one additional back button click on this page before you would go back to the previous page. You would be wrong. The extra entry actually handles the initial page load. The event that is fired for the **popstate** happens on history change, not on back button clicks, so it actually fires when you load the page, as a page load adds to the history.

Other History Features

The session history has a lot more to offer than just a single pop event. Here are some basic methods that can be called on the page history stack:

`window.history.length`
>   Number of entries in the session history.

`window.history.state`
>   Current state of the object.

`window.history.go(n)`
>   Goes backward or forward by the specified number of steps. If the value you specify is 0, it will reload the current page.

`window.history.back()`
>   Goes backward by one step.

`window.history.forward()`

Goes forward by one step.

`window.history.pushState(data, title [, url])`

Pushes the data specified in the arguments onto the session history.

`window.history.replaceState(data, title [, url])`

Updates the current entry in the session history.

6

Client-Side Data
Storage Hacks

As the modern web browser continues to evolve into a capable application platform, another area of exciting advancements is occurring in client-side data storage, most notably in the AppCache, WebStorage, IndexedDB, and FileSystem API standards. The need for offline capabilities and performance improvements for reading and writing large amounts of data is driving browser manufacturers to build tools that allow client-side applications to define quotas on storage capacity, retrieve sandbox data to defined origins, and perform asynchronous reads/writes from local databases.

As we explore the storage APIs, we will continue our trend of exploring the pros and cons of each solution, introduce third-party libraries that offer polyfill support, and provide contextual examples for client-centric applications and the mobile web.

HACK 52 Embed Binary Data in an Inline URL

Data URLs offer an alternative to referencing external resources with image and link tags. The most common scenario involves images that you can reference directly from within an HTML document or an individual stylesheet.

In Hack #19 we explored the performance trade-offs between CSS sprites and using data URIs within external stylesheets. In this hack we will focus on inlining image data within our HTML markup, and even see some of the different ways to do so using different server-side templating implementations.

Data URLs are a subtype of the Uniform Resource Identifier (URI) scheme that embeds resource data within the URL as a Base64-encoded string. Unlike with traditional URLs that point to external resources such as images, stylesheets, and JavaScript code, the browser does not make an HTTP request for remote content.

Sometimes we can improve web application performance by leveraging a technique—for example, in an environment where connectivity bandwidth may be constrained, such as an Internet connection aboard a U.S. naval ship. Within mobile web applications, it is also often advantageous to reduce the number of HTTP requests by embedding smaller images within a page. Furthermore, instances where you may want to dynamically generate server-side images based on a unique profile, time of day, or location of a site visitor may also warrant an embedded image.

Data URLs utilize the following syntax:

```
data:[mimetype][;base64],[data]
```

Within an Image Tag

For this hack, first we will make use of an online service by manually uploading an image to dataurl.net (*http://dataurl.net/#dataurlmaker*) (see Figure 6-1).

Figure 6-1.
Uploading an image to http://dataurl.net

Once we have copied the Base64-encoded string of data from the text area on the left, we can paste it within our document (the following code is abbreviated for brevity, but note that the larger the image is, the longer the string of data will be):

```
<img src="data:image/jpeg;base64,/9j/4AAQSkZJRgABAgAAAQABAAD//gA ...  />
```

Within an External Stylesheet

Now we'll use the `url()` syntax within a CSS selector, much like we would when calling an external background image:

```
#backg {
        height: 326px;
        background-image:
url("data:image/jpeg;base64,/9j/4SJnRXhpZgAATU0AKgAAAgADAEAAAMA ...
}
```

Don't forget your respective markup tag:

```
<div id="backg"></div>
```

Figure 6-2 shows the results.

Figure 6-2.
Inline image in the document, and a repeated background image within the stylesheet

See Hack #19 for more information on using data URIs within external stylesheets.

Getting Help from Your Web Application Framework

It is often not feasible to manually upload our images to dataurl.net (*http://data-url.net/#dataurlmaker*), so in production environments we can do this programmatically within our server-side web application framework. Here are a few of the most popular tools for doing this:

Grails

Via the Grails Rendering Plugin (*http://gpc.github.com/grails-rendering/docs/manual/guide/single.html#7*):

```
class SomeController {
    def generate = {
        def file = new File("path/to/image.png")
        renderPng(template: "thing", model: [imageBytes: file.bytes])
    }

}
```

In the view:

```
<html>
  <head></head>
  <body>
   <p>Below is an inline image</p>
   <rendering:inlinePng bytes="${imageBytes}" class="some-class" />
  </body>
</html>
```

Node.js

By setting up a route and creating a buffer, with the second argument as `bina ry` followed by a Base64-encoded string conversion:

```
express = require("express")
request = require("request")
BufferList = require("bufferlist").BufferList
app = express.createServer(express.logger(), express.bodyParser())
app.get "/", (req, res) ->
  if req.param("url")
    url = unescape(req.param("url"))
    request
      uri: url
      encoding: 'binary'
    , (error, response, body) ->
      if not error and response.statusCode is 200
        data_uri_prefix = "data:" + response.headers["content-type"]
  + ";base64,"
```

```
image = new Buffer(body.toString(),
"binary").toString("base64")
image = data_uri_prefix + image
res.send "<img src=\"" + image + "\"/>"
```

```
app.listen 3000
```

Ruby On Rails (via the Asset Pipeline)

By using the **asset_data_uri** helper:

```
#logo { background: url(<%= asset_data_uri 'logo.png' %>) }
```

Django

By using a simple Django filter, such as the one mentioned at djangosnip-pets.org (*http://djangosnippets.org/snippets/2516/*):

```
from django import template
from base64 import b64encode

register = template.Library()

@register.filter
def dataURI(filename, mime = None):
    """

    This filter will return data URI for given file, for more
    info go to:
    http://en.wikipedia.org/wiki/Data_URI_scheme
    Sample Usage:
    <img src="{{ "/home/visgean/index.png"|dataURI }}">
    will be filtered into:
    <img src="data:image/png;base64,iVBORw0...">
    """

    with open(filename, "rb") as file:
        data = file.read()

    encoded = b64encode(data)
    mime = mime + ";" if mime else ";"
    return "data:%sbase64,%s" % (mime, encoded)
```

Disadvantages to Using Data URLs

There are some disadvantages to using data URLs, namely the following:

Caching

The browser will not cache inline images that use data URLs to store their Base64-encoded data. If an image is used more than once in an application, it may not be optimal to use a data URL. You will need to base the optimal balance on user behavior and traffic to the pages where the image is repeated.

File size

A Base64-encoded image is one-third larger than an equivalent binary image. Again, you will need to decide on this balance based on given user behavior and traffic patterns.

HACK 53 Convert a Data URI to a Blob and Append It to Form Data with XHR2

HTML5 has turned the web browser into a full-fledged runtime. With all that new functionality in the client, you need ways to transmit data back to the server in a safe and programmatic manner. This hack shows you just how to do that.

At the time of this writing, the `FormData` *object only accepts* `File` *or* `Blob` *objects from the File API for uploading images from within a form. Firefox offers the proprietary* `canvas.mozGetAsFile()`, *and the W3C-recommended* `canvas.toBlob()` *is yet to be implemented.*

Imagine you are building an interface within a social media site that allows users to theme their profile page from a form that generates styles dynamically. You want to persist these styles in a database on the server by uploading the images in the background via an `XMLHttpRequest`, and load them on additional page requests. To do so you can make use of XHR2 and the new feature that allows you to upload `Blob`s and `File`s by attaching them to the `FormData` object.

Before we get into the details of `FormData` and XHR2, let's create a simple `Blob`. First, we'll call **new** on a `Blob` class and then pass data to the `Blob`. How about a simple style that declares our text as red?

```
var stylesblob = new Blob(['body{color:red;}'], {type:'text/css'});
```

Now we'll create a new `link`, set a few attributes, and append it somewhere in the document:

```
var link = document.createElement('link');

link.rel = 'stylesheet';
link.href = window.URL.createObjectURL(stylesblob);
document.body.appendChild(link);
```

This is a simple demonstration of the **Blob** utility, but what if we need to append this data to a form and upload the data to a remote server? First, we need to deal with the form:

```
<form enctype="multipart/form-data" method="post" name="profileStyle">

    <label>username:</label>
    <input type="email" autocomplete="on" autofocus name="userid"
      placeholder="email" required/>

    <label>Styles to save!</label>
    <input type="file" name="file" required />

</form>
```

There are a few important items to notice here. The **enctype** attribute indicates that the data will need to be chunked into a multipart data item. Also notice that we are making use of a few new attributes: **autofocus** and **required**, mentioned in Chapter 1.

```
function sendForm() {

    var data = new FormData(document.forms.namedItem("profileStyle "));

    data.append("myfile", stylesblob);

    var req = new XMLHttpRequest();
    req.open("POST", "/styleStore", true);
    req.onload = function(oEvent) {
      if (req.status == 200) {
        console.log("Styles Saved!");
      } else {
        console.log("Error "+req.status+" occurred uploading your file")
    };

    req.send(data);
  }
```

The requirements for our application also include uploading an image to a separate remote web service. The image is available as a data URL and we would like to append it to **FormData** and send the request in the background.

```
var durl = $("#carter_small").attr("src")
var blob = dataURItoBlob(durl);
```

So, to further demonstrate, let's first convert our **dataURI** to a **Blob** so that we can attach it to the **FormData**. Let's take a closer look at **dataURItoBlob()**:

```
function dataURItoBlob(dataURI) {

  var byteString;

    if (dataURI.split(',')[0].indexOf('base64') >= 0){
        byteString = atob(dataURI.split(',')[1]);
    }else{
        byteString = unescape(dataURI.split(',')[1]);
    }

    var mimeString = dataURI.split(',')[0].split(':')[1].split(';')[0]

    var ab = new ArrayBuffer(byteString.length);
    var ia = new Uint8Array(ab);

    for (var i = 0; i < byteString.length; i++) {
        ia[i] = byteString.charCodeAt(i);
    }

    var bb = new Blob([ab], {type: mimeString});
    return bb;

  }
```

Once we pass the reference into our **dataURItoBlob()** function we check to see if it is **URLEncoded**, and unescape it if necessary.

Then we set a reference to the MIME type, write the bytes of the string to an **Array Buffer**, and pass the **ArrayBuffer** to a new **Blob**, along with the MIME value set to the **type** property.

Now, we generate the new **FormData** and append the **blob** as a **canvasImage**:

```
var fd = new FormData(document.forms[0]);
fd.append("canvasImage", blob);
```

HACK 54 Use the WebStorage API to Persist User Data

Web applications often need a way to store data. With HTML5's LocalStorage and SessionStorage APIs you have a simple way to store data in an easy-to-use API.

This hack was contributed by Raymond Camden, a senior developer evangelist for Adobe Systems Inc.

Data persistence in the early days of web applications relied on one basic technology: cookies. Although cookies were serviceable, they were burdened by privacy concerns and limitations (in terms of storage size and their impact on network performance). Luckily, HTML5 provides a much-improved way to handle persistent data storage: LocalStorage. Technically called the WebStorage API (*http://dev.w3.org/html5/webstorage/*), most people refer to it as LocalStorage. There is also a corresponding API called SessionStorage that we will discuss later.

The Basics

LocalStorage, at a basic level, is a set of name–value pairs. So, for example, I may have a name called "FavoriteBeer" with a value called "Abita Amber." In this way, they are much like cookies. Unlike cookies, the data itself is not sent to the server on every request. Instead, the JavaScript has access to get, set, or delete these values when it needs to.

LocalStorage values are stored per domain. That means if foo.com sets a LocalStorage value with the name "FavoriteBeer" and goo.com tries to read that value, it will not be able to. Goo.com (*http://goo.com*) can set its *own* value called "FavoriteBeer," but it will exist in its own collection of data and not interfere, or overwrite, LocalStorage values set in other sites.

Finally, you should know that LocalStorage is saved to a physical file on the user's machine. This has two implications. First, there is a limit to the total amount of data you can store in LocalStorage. This limit varies per browser, but most enable 5 MB (IE 8 allows 10 MB of user data). Second, reading and writing to LocalStorage is a single-threaded file I/O operation. Basically, "sensible" use of LocalStorage should be perfectly fine. Much like how cookies were useful for storing settings and basic sets of data, LocalStorage can fit the same role as well. Note that you do not want to store large blocks of data. For that, you may want to consider the Native File System API instead.

Probably the best thing about LocalStorage is how well supported it is across browsers, both desktop and mobile. According to caniuse.com, support is currently at 88.73%.

The API

You have two main options for working with LocalStorage. You can write and set values using direct access to the **window.localStorage** object. Here are some examples:

```
window.localStorage.favoriteBeer = "Abita";
```

```
window.localStorage["favoriteBeer"] = "Abita";
```

Or you can use one of the following methods:

- setItem(key, value);
- getItem(key);
- removeItem(key);
- clear();

I'd be willing to bet you can figure out what the first two do. The third, removeItem, allows you to completely remove a value from LocalStorage. And lastly, clear will remove all values. Again, though, remember that operations on LocalStorage are domain-specific. Calling window.localStorage.clear() while visiting foo.com will not clear the items that had been set at goo.com.

Let's look at a simple example.

```html
<!doctype html>
<html>
<head>
<script>

function init() {
 //Do we have a value yet?
 if(!localStorage.getItem("visits")) localStorage.setItem("visits",0);

 //Get and increment the value
 var visits = Number(localStorage.getItem("visits")) + 1;

 //Display it
 document.querySelector("#resultDiv").innerHTML = "You have been here"
+visits + " time(s).";

 //And store it back
 localStorage.setItem("visits", visits);
}

</script>
</head>

<body onload="init()">

<div id="resultDiv"></div>

</body>
</html>
```

This template fires off a simple function, `init`, when the page has loaded. We begin by seeing if the `visits` key exists in `localStorage`. If it doesn't, we default it to `0`.

Next we get and increment the value. Since everything is stored as a string, we wrap the call in the `Number()` constructor to ensure that the math operation works.

We then update the DOM and display the number of visits.

Finally, we store the value back into `localStorage`. The net result is a simple web page that can track how many times you've visited it. If you open it in your browser and reload it multiple times you will see the counter increase one by one. If you close your browser and open the HTML file again, it will continue from where it left off.

Believe it or not, that's really all there is to the API.

LocalStorage and Complex Data

One thing you may be wondering about is how to store complex data such as arrays and objects. The value passed to `setItem` must be a string. So how do you store more complex values? It's simple: you serialize the object first. *Serialization* refers to converting a complex object into a simpler form, in our case, a string. Of course, that means you have to deserialize the string back into its original form later on. How you serialize data is up to you. You can build your own code to take complex data and turn it into strings. For example, arrays have a native method, `toString`, which will convert the data into a string. I prefer to use JSON to handle these operations. It works with pretty much any form of data, and like `localStorage`, it has decent browser support. (And for those of you who are worried about nonsupported browsers, plenty of JSON libraries exist.)

In the next example, a form with multiple values is converted into one simple object that is stored into `localStorage`. Let's take a look at the code and then we'll walk through the parts.

```
<!doctype html>
<html>
<head>
<script>

function init() {

    //If we have old data, load it
    var oldData = localStorage.getItem("formdata");
    if(oldData) {
        var realData = JSON.parse(oldData);
        document.querySelector("#yourname").value = realData.name;
        document.querySelector("#yourage").value = realData.age;
```

```
            document.querySelector("#youremail").value = realData.email;
            document.querySelector("#yourphone").value = realData.telephone;
        }

        //listen for changes in our form fields
        document.querySelector("#myForm").addEventListener("input",
         function() {
            //get all the fields

            var data = {name:document.querySelector("#yourname").value,
                        age:document.querySelector("#yourage").value,
                        email:document.querySelector("#youremail").value,
                        telephone:document.querySelector("#yourphone").value
                        };
            console.dir(data);
            localStorage.setItem("formdata", JSON.stringify(data));
        },false);
    }

</script>
</head>

<body onload="init()">

<form id="myForm">

    <p>
    <label for="yourname">Your Name</label>
    <input type="text" id="yourname">
    </p>

    <p>
    <label for="yourage">Your Age</label>
    <input type="number" id="yourage" min="0">
    </p>

    <p>
    <label for="youremail">Your Email</label>
    <input type="email" id="youremail">
    </p>

    <p>
    <label for="yourphone">Your Phone Number</label>
    <input type="tel" id="yourphone">
```

```
    </p>

  </form>

  </body>
  </html>
```

Starting from the bottom, you can see a simple form with four unique fields: name, age, email, and telephone. The interesting part is up on top in the JavaScript. The `init` function has two main parts to it now.

In the first section, we look for the existence of a LocalStorage value called `formda ta`. If it exists, it is assumed to be a JSON version of our data. We use the JSON API to parse this back into "real" data that we can then assign to our form fields.

The second half handles storing the form data. We use the `input` event for forms, which is fired whenever any change is made. We take all the fields, one by one, and assign them into a new object called `data`. This is then serialized using `JSON.stringify` and stored into LocalStorage.

With about 10 lines of code, we've created a form that will automatically store, and restore, values. If the user's browser crashes, or he accidentally closes his browser, none of his changes are lost. (In case you're curious, you could use `removeItem` in the submit handler to clear out the form fields.)

Using SessionStorage

So far we've focused on LocalStorage, a persistent storage API for data in your Java-Script applications. You also have available a semipersistent storage system called SessionStorage. It works exactly like LocalStorage except that it is session-based, which is simply a way of saying it works with "one typical use" of a web application. When the user closes her browser or has not interacted with the site in a certain time frame, it is safe to assume the value will be closed. As I just stated, the API is *exactly* the same. You simply replace any call to `localStorage` with `sessionStorage`:

```
window.sessionStorage["favoriteBeer"] = "Abita";
```

Security Concerns

It should go without saying that any client-side data should not be trusted, LocalStorage included. Much like you wouldn't implicitly trust data sent via XHR to your server, you should assume that any LocalStorage value can be seen and manip-ulated by users in their browsers.

Polyfill LocalStorage with YepNope.js and Storage.js

Although the WebStorage API is widely supported across major browsers, there is still a need for polyfill support in IE 7. One of the most popular and easy-to-use polyfill script loaders is YepNope.js.

Remy Sharp defines polyfills as follows:

> A polyfill, or polyfiller, is a piece of code (or plugin) that provides the technology that you, the developer, expect the browser to provide natively. Flattening the API landscape if you will.

Shim, *polyfill*, and *fallback* are terms used to describe the scripts used to patch a missing API within a particular browser so that a developer can write future-friendly code that works across all major browsers.

In this hack we will use two fantastic libraries that will allow us to achieve 100% support for local storage across all of the major browsers: YepNope.js, as mentioned in the hack synopsis, and Modernizr, a JavaScript library that works with YepNope.js for feature detection.

For more details on the WebStorage API, see Hack #54.

Including Modernizr

To get started we first need a way to detect whether LocalStorage is supported. Modernizr is a JavaScript library that detects HTML5 and CSS3 features in the user's browser. Let's start by adding Modernizr to the page:

```
<script src="/i/js/modernizr.com-custom-2.6.1-01.js"></script>
```

It runs a series of object detections on page load, returns a Boolean value for each test, and stores the data in a JavaScript **object ()** (see Figure 6-3).

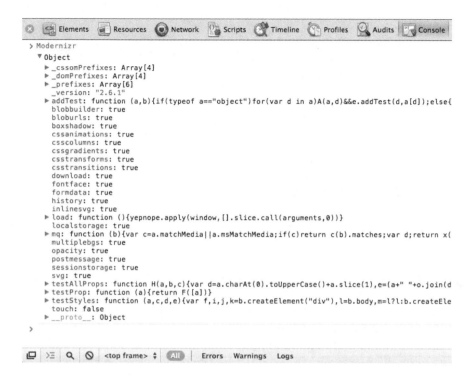

Figure 6-3.
Modernizr object in Chrome console

Modernizr includes YepNope.js as an option for conditionally loading external *.js* and *.css* resources. This is quite handy for managing the support of polyfills within your application.

Using YepNope

YepNope is described as "an asynchronous conditional resource loader that's super-fast, and allows you to load only the scripts that your users need."[1] Well, as I stated before, the only script we need is a polyfill for local storage in IE 6 and 7 and Firefox versions 2 and 3. So first we will call **yepnope**, which holds a reference to a Modernizr property for **localstorage**. We'll set the value of this property to **test**. If the test passes we'll move on to **complete**, which will execute our application code. If it fails it will call **yepnope**'s built-in script loader to download *storage.js*. The callback function referenced by **complete** will also be called.

[1] *http://yepnopejs.com/*

```
yepnope({

    test: Modernizr.localstorage,
    nope: ['../../js/storage.js'],
    complete: function (url, result, key) {

      if (url === '../../js/storage.js') {
        console.log('polyfill loaded');
      }

    // applications code

    }
});
```

Using Storage.js

Storage.js is a library written by Brett Wejrowski. The script uses **userData** for IE 6 and 7 and **globalStorage** for Firefox versions 2 and 3 to implement a polyfill for **localStorage** when it is not supported.

You can view the contents of the storage.js file on GitHub (https://github.com/ wojodesign/local-storage-js/blob/master/storage.js).

To demonstrate the effectiveness of our polyfill loader, we will implement a simple counter that stores an incremented value in **localStorage**. We will attach a click event listener to a button that fires the counter:

```
<button id="counter" type="button">Click me!</button>
```

Now we will add the counter logic within the complete callback of our YepNope script:

```
yepnope({

    test: Modernizr.localstorage,
    nope: ['../../js/storage.js'],
    complete: function (url, result, key) {

      if (url === '../../js/storage.js') {
        console.log('polyfill loaded');
      }

      function counter(){
        var c = (localStorage.clickcount) ? localStorage.clickco
```

```
unt++ : localStorage.clickcount=1;

            var str = "clicked " + c + " times"
            $("#clicks").html(str);
        }
        $("#counter").on("click", function(){counter()});


    }
});
```

Figure 6-4 shows the results.

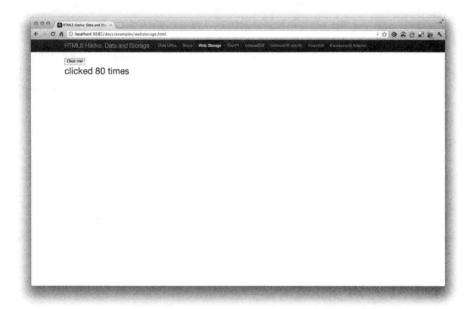

Figure 6-4.
Clicks counter stored in LocalStorage

HACK 56 Cache Media Resources Locally with the FileSystem API

With the FileSystem API, you can provide your browser with a sandbox where data (both textual and binary) can be read and written.

This hack was contributed by Raymond Camden, a senior developer evangelist for Adobe Systems Inc.

One of the more powerful features coming soon to a browser near you is the ability to read and write to the local filesystem. You can find the "File API: Directories and System" working draft on the W3C website (*http://dev.w3.org/2009/dap/file-system/pub/FileSystem/*).

Dubbed the FileSystem API, it provides the browser a safe little sandbox where data (both textual and binary) can be read and written. Many excellent articles out there detail the API. This hack assumes you have at least a familiarity with the basics. With that assumption, we're going to look at a real-world scenario where browser filesystem access can be useful: the local caching of media resources.

Imagine for a moment that you are creating a hip, new web property. You want to make use of several high-quality images or sound files. Now imagine you can package up all these resources into one ZIP file, send it to the browser, and have it store a copy locally. This is not necessarily for offline access, but as a way to minimize remote network calls and simply offload some of the "weight" to the client. To be even more efficient, you also want to track the date the ZIP file was last updated. You can then use a light-weight network request to see if it has been updated before you go through the work of processing it again. Let's get started!

Initializing and Preparing the Filesystem

One of the first things the demo code does is determine if it can even use the FileSystem API feature.

Right now the API is fraught with vendor prefixes (see Chapter 1). In the future, the API needs to be generalized, but here, we start off caring only about Chrome. Notice a variety of vendor prefixes in the code, as in the following example:

```
function init() {
        if(!window.webkitStorageInfo) return;
}
```

(In case you're curious, the `init()` function is being run via a body/onload call. The full template appears shortly.) The initialization routine begins by checking for the existence of `webkitStorageInfo`. Because this demo is only concerned with demonstrating the FileSystem API, we can immediately quit if it isn't supported.

The FileSystem API differentiates between a temporary and persistent filesystem. Their very names indicate when you would use one over the other. For this application, we will choose a persistent filesystem so that we can store our resources until they have to be updated. To work with the persistent filesystem, we request access from the user. This is done via a JavaScript function, but the actual prompt is handled by the browser, much like with geolocation. The following code block demonstrates how to request the storage and what will be done after it has been approved (or denied):

```
window.webkitStorageInfo.requestQuota(window.PERSISTENT,
        20*1024*1024,
        function(grantedBytes) {
            console.log("I was granted "+grantedBytes+" bytes.");
            window.webkitRequestFileSystem(window.PERSISTENT,
            grantedBytes, onInitFs, errorHandler);
}, errorHandler);
```

Note that you have requested a size, but it's possible the size given may be smaller. Don't even worry about what you're given for now. In the future, you may want to record this (localStorage) and ensure you stay within your quota. But the important thing to note here is that once you've been approved a bucket of space you can request the actual filesystem.

Figure 6-5 shows what the user sees using the latest version of Chrome at the time of this writing. This UI may change in the future.

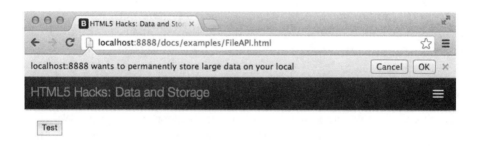

Figure 6-5.
Browser prompt to store large data locally

The call to webkitRequestFileSystem returns a pointer for all future read/write file and directory options. Its success handler, in this case onInitFs, is run once we're good to go. Finally, our errorHandler is run if anything goes wrong. Let's take a quick look at that before moving on:

```
function errorHandler(e) {
  var msg = '';
  console.dir(e);
  switch (e.code) {
    case FileError.QUOTA_EXCEEDED_ERR:
      msg = 'QUOTA_EXCEEDED_ERR';
      break;
    case FileError.NOT_FOUND_ERR:
      msg = 'NOT_FOUND_ERR';
      break;
    case FileError.SECURITY_ERR:
```

```
    msg = 'SECURITY_ERR';
    break;
  case FileError.INVALID_MODIFICATION_ERR:
    msg = 'INVALID_MODIFICATION_ERR';
    break;
  case FileError.INVALID_STATE_ERR:
    msg = 'INVALID_STATE_ERR';
    break;
  default:
    msg = 'Unknown Error';
    break;
};

  console.log('Error: ' + msg);
}
```

The preceding code was taken (and slightly modified) from the HTML5 Rocks article (*http://www.html5rocks.com/en/tutorials/file/filesystem/*). It's just for testing and doesn't actually present any nice response to the user. It only uses the console to report errors. Be sure you do your testing with the console open.

Working with the Filesystem

So, at this point we've established that our browser supports a filesystem. We've requested storage from the user. And we've asked for a pointer to the filesystem. After all of that, `onInitFs` is finally run.

It's probably a good idea to refresh to clarify the goal at this point. The goal is to download a ZIP file, extract the contents, and store it on the local filesystem. To enable that, we'll begin by defining a folder where our files are stored. We'll call this variable `re sourceDIRLOC`:

```
var resourceDIRLOC = "resources";
```

There isn't anything special about this name, but you want a subdirectory to add more stuff in the future, and not have to worry about organization. Even though this is a sandbox separated from the rest of the filesystem, it's important to think of this as any other filesystem. You don't want to make a mess—both for your users' sake and for your own sanity.

First, let's open this directory. The API allows us to open a directory that doesn't exist. We do this by passing a **create** flag. We can only do this for one level of directory at a time. So, for example, we can't try to open */resources/images/highres* and have the API simply create all those nested folders. In a case like that, we need to create each subdirectory one at a time. Luckily, this example has a simpler target:

```
function onInitFs(fs) {
    fileSystem = fs;

    fileSystem.root.getDirectory(fs.root.fullPath + '/' +
resourceDIRLOC, {create:true}, function(dir) {
        resourceDIR = dir;
}
```

Let's copy the filesystem handle, **fs**, to a globally scoped variable. We need **fs** later, so it's best to copy it right away. Next, we'll call to get the directory. Notice the path is based on one of the properties of the filesystem handle: **root.fullPath**. The root object is a directory pointer to the path of our sandbox. The **fullPath** is simply that: the actual directory path. Combining that with a separator (and note, you can use **/** whether or not you are on Windows) and the resource directory name, we then have a complete path to the folder to use. The **create** flag handles the first-time creation. All calls to the FileSystem API are asynchronous, so we'll begin a callback function in the last argument. Finally, the very first thing we'll do in the callback is cache a pointer to the new directory. **resourceDIR** is a global variable to use again later.

Now for the interesting part: the ZIP file we've downloaded is pretty large. We only want to download it the first time, and after that, only if it's been modified. To remember the modification date, we'll use **localStorage** to cache it. Consider the next block:

```
if(localStorage["resourceLastModified"]) {
    var xhr = new XMLHttpRequest();
    xhr.open("HEAD", resourceURL );
    xhr.onload = function(e) {
      if(this.status == 200) {
        var lastMod = this.getResponseHeader("Last-Modified");
        if(lastMod != localStorage["resourceLastModified"]) {
            fetchResource();
        } else {
          console.log("Not fetching the zip, my copy is kosher.");
        }
      }
    }
    xhr.send();
} else {
    fetchResource();
}
```

The first portion of the preceding code block executes if we have a value for when the ZIP file was last modified. (Soon we will see where to set that.) If **resourceLast Modified** exists, we create a **HEAD**-only Ajax request. This is a lightweight network call that just returns the headers of the remote resource. We check the **Last-Modified** header. If it is different in any way, we need to re**get** our ZIP file. That's done in the **fetchResource()** call. Finally, we see the **else** block simply runs **fetchRe source()**.

Getting and Processing the ZIP File

Let's take a look at the **fetchResource()** method. It's responsible for getting the remote ZIP file, unzipping it, and saving it to the filesystem. JavaScript doesn't have native support for working with ZIP files. I used the simple, yet powerful, zip.js library written by Gildas Lormeau (*http://gildas-lormeau.github.com/zip.js/*). You can find the zip.js library on GitHub. Note that you only need the files *zip.js* and *deflate.js*.

Let's begin by looking at **fetchResource**:

```
function fetchResource() {
    var xhr = new XMLHttpRequest();
    xhr.responseType="arraybuffer";
    xhr.open("GET", resourceURL,true);
    xhr.onload = function(e) {
        if(this.status == 200) {
        }
    }
    xhr.send();
}
```

The preceding code shows the portions of the function that handle the Ajax request. For now, the **onload** is empty, because it's a bit complex. Note a few things. First, the response type is **arraybuffer**. We need this to process the binary data from the ZIP. Second, the **resourceURL** is simply a static URL defined earlier in our code:

```
var resourceURL = "resources.zip";
```

Now let's dig into the code that is run when the request is done:

```
var lastMod = this.getResponseHeader("Last-Modified");
localStorage["resourceLastModified"] = lastMod;
```

The very first thing we do is cache the date the ZIP file was modified. LocalStorage makes this incredibly easy to do. Make note of the **resourceLastModified** key. We can test the code multiple times. We can either build new ZIP files and update their last modified value via the command line, or simply use our browser's console to delete the value.

```
var bb = new WebKitBlobBuilder();
bb.append(this.response);
var blob = bb.getBlob("application/zip");
```

Next, we'll prepare the binary data before handing it off to the ZIP library. This is a multistep process that involves a `Builder` sourced by the raw response and then the actual `Blob` object created by specifying our particular MIME type for our data. The end result, though, is ZIP binary data. Now, let's parse the ZIP file:

```
zip.createReader(new zip.BlobReader(blob), function(reader) {
    reader.getEntries(function(entries) {
        entries.forEach(function(entry) {
            resourceDIR.getFile(entry.filename,
                                {create:true},
                                function(file) {
                entry.getData(new zip.FileWriter(file), function(e) {
                }, function(current, total) {
                // onprogress callback
                });
            });
        });
    });
}, function(err) {
    console.log("zip reader error!");
    console.dir(err);
})
```

The preceding code is probably a bit confusing, as we have callbacks calling callbacks. In a nutshell we begin by creating an instance of a ZIP reader. This is based on the zip.js API. One of the many ways to initialize the ZIP reader instance is by passing in our **blob** object. We then provide a callback to handle the reader. Within that, we call **getEntries()** on the reader. This allows us to enumerate over each item in the ZIP file.

This is the point where we begin writing data to the filesystem. Remember **resource DIR**? It's just a pointer to our directory. We'll use it to create files within it by calling **getFile()**. We'll pass in a name, based on the ZIP file entry name. So, if the first entry in our ZIP is *foo.jpg*, **entry.filename** is **foo.jpg**.

Then, **getFile()** opens the file on the filesystem. Within the success handler, we can use *entry*, which is the file in the ZIP file, and pull the data out with **getData()**.

Essentially, we open a file on the filesystem and siphon out the bits from the ZIP file entry into the file we opened. The first argument to **getData** is a file writer. That handles the actual bits. Two empty callbacks in there could optionally monitor the progress. But since this is a relatively simple process (again, sucking the bits from one thing to another), we can leave them alone for now.

And that's it. To test, I used the excellent Chrome plug-in HTML5 FileSystem Explorer (https://chrome.google.com/webstore/detail/nhnjmpbdkieehidddbaeajffijock-aea), an extension that lets you browse the filesystem associated with a website (see Figures 6-6 and 6-7).

Figure 6-6.
HTML5 FileSystem Explorer Chrome extension

The files listed in Figure 6-7 are all images from the ZIP file. I also built a simple function that renders a few of these images:

```
document.querySelector("#testButton").addEventListener("click",
    function() {

        //Attempt to draw our images that exist in the file system
        //If they exist, we draw from there, if not, we do not display them.
                var images = ["bobapony.jpg",
                    "buy bacon.jpg",
                    "cool boba.jpg",
                    "chuck-norris.jpg"
                    ];

                for(var i=0, len=images.length; i<len; i++) {
                    var thisImage = images[i];
                    resourceDIR.getFile(thisImage, {create:false},
                        function(file) {
                        document.querySelector("#images").innerHTML +=
```

Figure 6-7.
HTML5 FileSystem Explorer (seen in the top-righthand corner), which browses the filesystem associated with a website

```
"<img src='"+file.toURL() + "'><br/>";
            });
        }
    }, false);
```

After the user clicks on a button, the code loops over an array of filenames to see if they exist in the filesystem. If so, the code simply adds an image to the DOM. Note the use of `file.toURL()`. I used this call to get a reference to the image that I can then reference from HTML.

Where to Go from Here

I hope this hack gave you an idea of what you can do with the filesystem. While support is still somewhat limited, the benefits of being able to store resources locally make it more than worthwhile, even if the API is a work in progress. Keep your eye on the File API W3C working draft (*http://dev.w3.org/2009/dap/file-system/pub/FileSystem/*) for updates.

Build a Milestone Calendar with IndexedDB and FullCalendar.js

IndexedDB is a persistent object data store in the browser. Although it is not a full SQL implementation and it is more complex than the unstructured key–value pairs in `localStorage`, you can use it to define an API that provides the ability to read and write key–value objects as structured JavaScript objects, and an indexing system that facilitates filtering and lookup.

For this hack we will use IndexedDB to store milestone objects for a calendar application. The UI will provide a simple means to create a new milestone and provide a title, start date, and end date. The calendar will then update to show the contents of the local data store. Figure 6-8 shows the result.

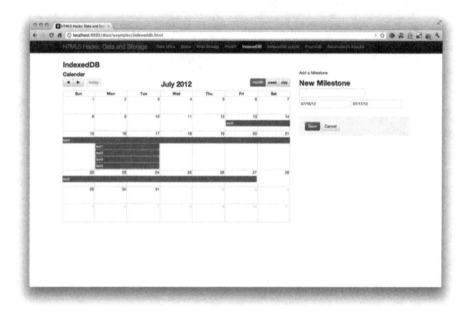

Figure 6-8.
FullCalendar.js and IndexedDB

We need to start by including the markup for the two pieces of the UI: the calendar and the form.

We'll begin with the form. You may notice that the input fields for the dates include data-date-format attributes. We will use these later for the JavaScript date pickers.

```
<form>
    <fieldset>

        <div class="control-group">
          <label class="control-label">Add a Milestone</label>
          <div class="controls">
            <h2>New Milestone</h2>
            <input type="text" name="title" value="">
            <input type="text" class="span2" name="start"
              value="07/16/12" data-date-format="mm/dd/yy" id="dp1" >
            <input type="text" class="span2" name="end"
              value="07/17/12"  data-date-format="mm/dd/yy" id="dp2" >
          </div>
        </div>

        <div class="form-actions">
            <button type="submit" class="btn btn-primary">Save</button>
            <button class="btn">Cancel</button>
        </div>

    </fieldset>
</form>
```

The calendar is provided by FullCalendar.js, a fantastic jQuery plug-in for generating robust calendars from event sources. The library will generate a calendar from a configuration object and a simple div.

```
<div id='calendar'></div>
```

And we can't forget to include a few dependencies:

```
<link href="../assets/css/datepicker.css" rel="stylesheet">
<link href="../assets/css/fullcalendar.css" rel="stylesheet">

<script src="http://code.jquery.com/jquery-1.7.1.min.js"></script>
<script src="../assets/js/bootstrap-datepicker.js"></script>
<script src="../assets/js/fullcalendar.min.js"></script>
```

To improve the user experience, we will also include date pickers for choosing the dates within the form fields for start and end dates (see Figure 6-9).

Figure 6-9.
Date pickers

To instantiate the date pickers we will include the following toward the beginning of our script:

```
$(function(){
    $('#dp1').datepicker();
    $('#dp2').datepicker();
});
```

The Milestone IndexedDB

Now we will set up a global namespace to hold our code, and set up a public `milestones` array (within the namespace) to hold our milestones temporarily while we pass them between our database and the FullCalendar API. This should make more sense as you continue to read. While we are at it we will need to normalize our `indexedDB` variable across all of the vendor-specific properties.

```
var html5hacks = {};

html5hacks.msArray = [];

var indexedDB = window.indexedDB || window.webkitIndexedDB ||
                window.mozIndexedDB;
```

```
if ('webkitIndexedDB' in window) {
  window.IDBTransaction = window.webkitIDBTransaction;
  window.IDBKeyRange = window.webkitIDBKeyRange;
}
```

Now we can begin to set up our database:

```
html5hacks.indexedDB = {};
html5hacks.indexedDB.db = null;

function init() {
  html5hacks.indexedDB.open();
}


init();
```

This will obviously fail for now, but as you can see the initialization begins by calling the **open()** method on an **html5hacks.indexedDB**. So let's take a closer look at **open()**:

```
html5hacks.indexedDB.open = function() {

  var request = indexedDB.open("milestones");

  request.onsuccess = function(e) {
    var v = "1";
    html5hacks.indexedDB.db = e.target.result;

    var db = html5hacks.indexedDB.db;

    if (v!= db.version) {
      var setVrequest = db.setVersion(v);
      setVrequest.onerror = html5hacks.indexedDB.onerror;

      setVrequest.onsuccess = function(e) {
        if(db.objectStoreNames.contains("milestone")) {
          db.deleteObjectStore("milestone");
        }

        var store = db.createObjectStore("milestone",
          {keyPath: "timeStamp"});

        html5hacks.indexedDB.init();
      };
    }
    else {
```

```
        html5hacks.indexedDB.init();
    }
};
    request.onerror = html5hacks.indexedDB.onerror;
}
```

First, we need to open the database and pass a name. If the database successfully opens and a connection is made, the **onsuccess()** callback will be fired.

Within the **onsuccess**, we then check for a version and call **setVersion()** if one does not exist. Then we will call **createObjectStore()** and pass a unique timestamp within the **keypath** property.

Finally, we call **init()** to build the calendar and attach the events present in the database.

```
html5hacks.indexedDB.init = function() {

    var db = html5hacks.indexedDB.db;
    var trans = db.transaction(["milestone"], IDBTransaction.READ_WRITE);
    var store = trans.objectStore("milestone");

    var keyRange = IDBKeyRange.lowerBound(0);
    var cursorRequest = store.openCursor(keyRange);

    cursorRequest.onsuccess = function(e) {
        var result = e.target.result;

      if(!result == false){

            $('#calendar').fullCalendar({
              header: {
                left: 'prev,next today',
                center: 'title',
                right: 'month,agendaWeek,agendaDay'
              },
              weekmode: 'variable',
              height: 400,
              editable: true,
              events: html5hacks.msArray
            });

        return;

      }else{
```

```
    console.log("result.value" , result.value);
    buildMilestoneArray(result.value);
    result.continue();
  }
};
cursorRequest.onerror = html5hacks.indexedDB.onerror;
};
```

At this point we are poised to retrieve all the data from the database and populate our calendar with milestones.

First, we declare the type of transaction to be a `READ_WRITE`, set a reference to the `datastore`, set a `keyrange`, and define a `cursorRequest` by calling `openCursor` and passing in the `keyrange`. By passing in a `0`, we ensure that we retrieve all the values greater than zero. Since our key was a timestamp, this will ensure we retrieve all the records.

Once the **onsuccess** event is fired, we begin to iterate through the records and push the milestone objects to `buildMilestoneArray`:

```
function buildMilestoneArray(ms) {
  html5hacks.msArray.push(ms);
}
```

When we reach the last record, we build the calendar by passing a configuration object to `fullCalendar()` and returning:

```
$('#calendar').fullCalendar({
  header: {
    left: 'prev,next today',
    center: 'title',
    right: 'month,agendaWeek,agendaDay'
  },
  weekmode: 'variable',
  height: 400,
  editable: true,
  events: html5hacks.msArray
});

return;
```

Adding Milestones

Now that we are initializing and building our calendar, we need to begin adding milestones to the database via the form. First let's use jQuery to set up our form to pass a serialized data object to `addMilestone()` on each submission:

```
$('form').submit(function() {

  var data = $(this).serializeArray();

  html5hacks.indexedDB.addMilestone(data);
  return false;
});
```

Now let's submit a few events and then view them in the Chrome Inspector to ensure they are there (see Figure 6-10).

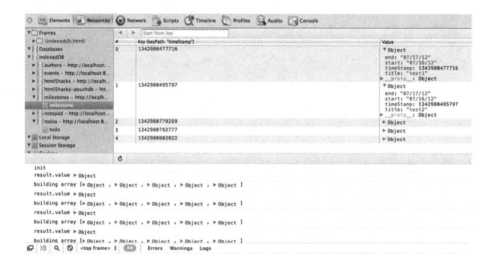

Figure 6-10.
Viewing milestone objects in the Chrome Inspector

Let's take a closer look at our **addMilestone** method:

```
html5hacks.indexedDB.addMilestone = function(d) {
  var db = html5hacks.indexedDB.db;
  var trans = db.transaction(["milestone"], IDBTransaction.READ_WRITE);
  var store = trans.objectStore("milestone");

  var data = {
    "title": d[0].value,
    "start": d[1].value,
    "end": d[2].value,
    "timeStamp": new Date().getTime()
  };

  var request = store.put(data);
```

```
    var dataArr = [data]
    request.onsuccess = function(e) {
      $('#calendar').fullCalendar('addEventSource', dataArr);
    };

    request.onerror = function(e) {
      console.log("Error Adding: ", e);
    };
  };
```

We established our read/write connection in much the same way as our
html5hacks.indexedDB.init(), but now, instead of only reading data, we write a
data object to the data store each time by calling store.put() and passing it data.
On the onsuccess we then can call fullcalendar's addEventSource() and pass it
the data wrapped in an array object. Note that it is necessary to transform the data
object into an array since that is what the FullCalendar API expects.

7

Geolocation Hacks

An exploration of the future of web technologies and browser capabilities would not be complete without covering the tools and techniques available to enable location awareness.

Location-aware web applications provide content, functionality, and services based on the cooperative detection of the user's physical location. These applications can then provide the user with real-time filtering of online information relevant to his current location, such as place markers indicating the user's location within a map, local consumer reviews, local coupons and offers, and even relevant traffic and public transportation notices.

These applications also enable users to provide their location to friends in a social network and vice versa, creating possibilities for meetups and blended online and physical interaction.

As you might imagine, the opportunities are not just limited to enhancing the life of the consumer. Given real-time location data of potential consumers and their friends, retailers can also create highly targeted, location-specific marketing campaigns for both digital and physical products.

How Does Geolocation Work?

The web browser employs various technologies to pass parameters via a background HTTP request to a Location Information Server that returns a data set that includes an estimated longitude and latitude.

The technologies used to gather location data depend on the device and on the operating system running on the device. The most common sources are:

- Public IP address
- WiFi access points
- Bluetooth MAC IDs

- GPS
- GSM/CDMA cell tower IDs

Geolocation libraries for the Web are not new. In fact, today's W3C Geolocation specification is largely reflective of the original Google Gears API introduced by Google in 2008. The API has been standardized and is one of the most widely adopted of the HTML5 specifications covered in this book.

Fortunately, the API is also easy to use—a benefit we will explore in Hack #58 and Hack #60.

In addition, a number of third-party services are available for creating really interesting hacks, and they explore concepts such as reverse geocoding and geofencing. In Hack #59 and Hack #61 we will pass our location data to a service that will provide an enhanced API for working with location data.

In Hack #62 we will blend the power of the WebSocket API with location awareness to make our application update in real time.

For browsers that don't provide this functionality natively, Google's IP geocoding service can serve as a polyfill, as we will explore in Hack #63.

The main drawback to this functionality is related to privacy and security, and for good reason. After all, as responsible application developers we should be doing what we can to protect the sensitive data of our users. In Hack #58 we will take an in-depth look at how the browser employs cooperative detection, allowing the user to opt-in to only sharing location data with trusted web applications.

HACK 58 Use the Geolocation APIs to Display Longitude and Latitude in a Mobile Web Application

The Geolocation API exposes an easy-to-use API. With only a couple of lines of code, you can obtain the user's current position. What's more, jQuery Mobile provides a simple framework for building a cross-browser mobile web application.

In this hack we will utilize the jQuery Mobile framework to provide a relatively simple means of authoring a cross-browser mobile application. Since this hack is focused on displaying our current longitude and latitude and exercising the API across the mobile web, we will only need a simple UI.

A Simple jQuery Mobile App

As always, we'll start by building a basic page utilizing the HTML5 **<doctype>** and including our dependencies:

```
<!DOCTYPE html>
<html lang="en">
  <head>
    <title>jQuery Mobile GeoLocation demo</title>
    <meta name="viewport" content="width=device-width,
initial-scale=1">

    <link rel="stylesheet"
href="http://code.jquery.com/mobile/1.1.1/jquery.mobile-1.1.1.min.css"
 />

    <script src="http://code.jquery.com/jquery-1.7.1.min.js"></script>

    <script src="http://code.jquery.com/mobile/1.1.1/jquery.mobile-
1.1.1.min.js"></script>

  </head>
<body>

    // jQuery mobile declarative markup here

</body>
</html>
```

As you can see, we have declared a dependency on one stylesheet, and three Java-Scripts. We will build the remainder of the application using declarative HTML markup and **data-** attributes that the jQuery Mobile framework will interpret.

Within the **<body>** tag, we can now place the following:

```
<div data-role="page" data-theme="a">

  <div data-role="header">
      <h1>Geo Location</h1>
  </div><!-- /header -->

  <div data-role="content">
      <ul data-role="listview" data-inset="true">
      <li>
        <a href="./longlat-embed.html" data-ajax="false">LongLat</a>
      </li>
```

```
    </ul>
  </div><!-- /content -->

</div><!-- /page -->
```

At this point you should see what's shown in Figure 7-1, if you access this page from a smaller screen or shrink your desktop browser window to the size of a mobile browser.

Figure 7-1.
jQuery Mobile simple button

As you might expect, the UI wasn't created through magic. jQuery Mobile uses JavaScript to consume the **data-** attributes present in your HTML markup to dynamically generate more HTML and CSS. The end result is what you see in your browser.

Now we will create a separate page to link to. You many have noticed a link to *longlat-embed.html* within the main page.

```
<ul data-role="listview" data-inset="true">
  <li>
    <a href="./longlat-embed.html" data-ajax="false">LongLat</a>
  </li>
</ul>
```

This will take us to a page that will run our JavaScript that contains our geolocation code. Notice that we designated for this to not be a jQuery Mobile Ajax page. This ensures that upon the click of the link we navigate to the new page. It is important that the linked page is loaded so that its JavaScript will execute.

This page is structured similarly to the other page, with the same dependencies. I intentionally kept the jQuery Mobile code as simple as possible. You can find more information on working with jQuery Mobile in the excellent set of documentation available on their website (*http://jquerymobile.com/demos/1.1.1/*).

```
<div data-role="page" data-theme="a">

  <div data-role="header">
      <h1>LongLat</h1>
  </div><!-- /header -->

      <div data-role="content">

      </div><!-- /content -->

</div><!-- /page -->
```

In the content, we will create a **div** element that will contain our longitude and latitude data once it is returned from the remote service. We will also include a back capability to return to the previous page.

```
<div class="geo-coords">
    GeoLocation: <span id="Lat">lat: ...</span>°,
          <span id="Long">long: ...</span>°
</div>

<a href="./jqueryMobile-embed.html"
    data-role="button"
    data-inline="true">
    Back
</a>
```

Now we will address our geolocation JavaScript. If you are familiar with jQuery the initial $ variable will look familiar in the code that follows. If not, you can learn more about jQuery online (*http://docs.jquery.com/Main_Page*).

Simply put, the jQuery function wrapper ensures that our page is ready before we execute the following script. Then we will set up a global namespace object that we will use to store our data. This type of organization will be important as our script gets more complex moving forward.

Next, we will check to make sure the current browser supports geolocation by checking the **navigator** object for the presence of the **geolocation** property. If it is available, we will call the **getCurrentPosition** method and pass a **success** and **error** object.

Then we will construct both a **success** and **error** object. Within our **success** object we can accept a position as a parameter and query the object for its nested **coords** object which contains both latitude and longitude properties.

We will then call **populateHeader()**, which uses jQuery to append the returned values to the **span** tags that contain the IDs **Lat** and **Long**.

```
$(function() {

    var Geo={};

    if (navigator.geolocation) {
        navigator.geolocation.getCurrentPosition(success, error);
    }

    //Get the latitude and the longitude;
    function success(position) {
        Geo.lat = position.coords.latitude;
        Geo.lng = position.coords.longitude;
        populateHeader(Geo.lat, Geo.lng);
    }

    function error(){
        console.log("Geocoder failed");
    }

    function populateHeader(lat, lng){
        $('#Lat').html(lat);
        $('#Long').html(lng);
    }

});
```

Now let's return to our browser and navigate to the new page. When a user accesses a web page that includes a call to `navigator.geolocation.getCurrentPosi tion()`, a security notification bar will be presented at the top of the page. Browsers that support the Geolocation API have their own security notification, which asks the user to allow or deny the browser access to the device's current location (see Figure 7-2).

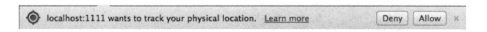

Figure 7-2.
Google Chrome geolocation security notification

If the user allows the web application to track her physical location, the script will continue to execute and make a request to the Location Information Server. The re-mote server returns a data set that includes longitude and latitude. Once we have the information and the `success()` callback has been called, we update the page (see Figure 7-3).

Security and Privacy Concerns

The ability for web application developers to collect location data about end users raises quite a bit of concern in regard to security and privacy. The W3C specification clearly indicates that client applications should notify users and provide an interface to authorize the use of location data, allowing them to determine which web applications they trust:

> User agents must not send location information to Web sites without the express permission of the user. User agents must acquire permission through a user interface, unless they have prearranged trust relationships with users, as described below. The user interface must include the host component of the document's URI [URI]. Those permissions that are ac-quired through the user interface and that are preserved beyond the current browsing session (i.e. beyond the time when the browsing context [BROWS-INGCONTEXT] is navigated to another URL) must be revocable and user agents must respect revoked permissions.[1]

[1] http://dev.w3.org/geo/api/spec-source.html

Figure 7-3.
Latitude and longitude

HACK 59 Use Google's Geocoding API to Reverse-Geocode a User's Location

Longitude and latitude data is only beneficial to the application if it can do something more interesting than just display it. One common use case is to reverse-geocode, or find a human-readable location based on longitude and latitude.

In Hack #58 we hacked together a simple mobile web application that displayed the user's current longitude and latitude. In this hack we will use the same jQuery Mobile application and add an additional button to the home screen. This button will take us to a separate page that displays the nearest city and state based on our current location.

First, let's add the additional button:

```
<ul data-role="listview" data-inset="true">
    <li>
        <a href="./longlat-embed.html" data-ajax="false">
            LongLat
        </a>
    </li>
    <li>
        <a href="./location-name-embed.html" data-ajax="false">
            Location By Name
        </a>
    </li>
</ul>
```

We also have to remember to include Google's Maps APIs to support our geocoding service call (more on that later):

```
<script src="http://maps.googleapis.com/maps/api/js?sensor=false">
</script>
```

We now have two buttons on our jQuery Mobile home screen (see Figure 7-4).

This takes us to a new page that will run some JavaScript that makes a call to a remote Google service. The script is structured similarly to the longitude and latitude script in Hack #58, so I won't repeat those details here.

After checking for the existence of the **navigator** objects' **geolocation** property, we create a **geocoder** variable and instantiate a new **google.maps.Geocoder()**:

```
if (navigator.geolocation) {
    geocoder = new google.maps.Geocoder();
    navigator.geolocation.getCurrentPosition(success, error);
}
```

In our **success** object we designate the callback that will execute. There we can add our future **reverseGeo()** method.

Figure 7-4.
Adding a Location By Name button

```
function success(position) {
    Geo.lat = position.coords.latitude;
    Geo.lng = position.coords.longitude;
    reverseGeo(Geo.lat, Geo.lng);
}
```

Now we will create a `reverseGeo()` method that accepts the longitude and latitude that was returned by `getCurrentPosition()`. First we'll take our latitude and longitude data and pass it to the `google.maps.LatLng` helper function. Then we'll set that value to the `latLng` property of an empty object.

```
function reverseGeo(lat, lng) {
    var latlng = new google.maps.LatLng(lat, lng);

        // make the call to a geocode service
}
```

The **geocode()** method will make a call to Google's Geocoding API and return a large result set that contains more information than we need. Therefore, we will need to parse out the city and state from the result set. Our **city** value is stored in a property named **locality** and the **state** is stored in **administrative_area_level_1**. The code for doing this follows; Figure 7-5 shows the result.

```
geocoder.geocode({'latLng': latlng}, function(results, status) {
    if (status == google.maps.GeocoderStatus.OK) {
     if (results[1]) {
        var addressComponents = results[0].address_components;
        for (var i = 0; i < addressComponents.length; i++) {
        for (var b = 0; b < addressComponents[i].types.length; b++){
         if (addressComponents[i].types[b] == "locality") {
           city = addressComponents[i];
           break;
        }
         var adminString = "administrative_area_level_1";
         if (addressComponents[i].types[b] == adminString) {
           state = results[0].address_components[i];
           break;
         }
        }
       }

     Geo.location_name = city.long_name + ", " + state.short_name;
     $('#storeLocation').html(Geo.location_name);
     } else {
        console.log("No results found");
     }
    }else {
        console.log("Geocoder failed due to: " + status);
    }
});
```

Figure 7-5.
Showing the location name

Here is the final script:

```
$(function() {

    var Geo={};
    var geocoder;

    if (navigator.geolocation) {
        geocoder = new google.maps.Geocoder();
        navigator.geolocation.getCurrentPosition(success, error);
    }
```

```
//Get the latitude and the longitude;
function success(position) {
    Geo.lat = position.coords.latitude;
    Geo.lng = position.coords.longitude;
    populateHeader(Geo.lat, Geo.lng);
    reverseGeo(Geo.lat, Geo.lng);
}

function error(){
    console.log("Geocoder failed");
}

function populateHeader(lat, lng){
    $('#Lat').html(lat);
    $('#Long').html(lng);
}

function reverseGeo(lat, lng) {

  var latlng = new google.maps.LatLng(lat, lng);

    geocoder.geocode({'latLng': latlng},
      function(results, status) {
        if (status == google.maps.GeocoderStatus.OK) {
          if (results[1]) {
            var addressComponents = addressComponents;
              for (var i = 0; i < addressComponents.length; i++) {
                for (var b=0;b< addressComponents.length;b++){

                  if (addressComponents[i].types[b] == "locality") {
                        city = addressComponents[i];
                          break;
                        }
                  var adminString = "administrative_area_level_1";
                  if (addressComponents[i].types[b] == adminString){
                      state = results[0].address_components[i];
                      break;
                    }
                  }
                }
              }

            Geo.location_name = city.long_name+", "+state.short_name;
            $('#storeLocation').html(Geo.location_name);
```

```
        } else {
          console.log("No results found");
        }
      } else {
        console.log("Geocoder failed due to: " + status);
      }
    });
  }

});
```

HACK 60 Update a User's Current Location in a Google Map

Sometimes the user of your application is moving and a location needs to be updated at a regular interval. You can use a Google map to display a moving pin of the user's locations.

Using the Google Maps API

In this hack we will start by including the necessary dependencies for displaying Google maps within our application. Fortunately, the Google Maps API makes this very simple. Just be sure to include the dependency in the head of your application's document.

```
<script type="text/javascript" src="http://maps.google.com/maps/api
/js?libraries=geometry,places&amp;sensor=false"></script>
```

We also need an empty div element to populate with our map:

```
<div id="map"></div>
```

Including the map is as simple as setting a reference to the HTML element we want to populate, creating a configuration object called configObj, and passing both to an instantiation of a new Google map:

```
var configObj = {
        zoom: 15,
        center: latlng,
        mapTypeControl: false,
        navigationControlOptions: {
            style: google.maps.NavigationControlStyle.SMALL},
            mapTypeId: google.maps.MapTypeId.ROADMAP
```

```
        };

        var map = new google.maps.Map(document.getElementById("map"),
          configObj);
```

Figure 7-6 shows the result.

In case this type of programming is new to you, the properties within `configObj`
are optional and configurable. The complete API reference is available online
(https://developers.google.com/maps/).

Figure 7-6.
Reverse-geocoding a location with Google's Geocoding API

Now that we have a working Google map, let's start updating our map with a map pin. To do so, we will use **getCurrentPosition()** to determine our location.

```
if (navigator.geolocation) {
  navigator.geolocation.getCurrentPosition(success, error)
} else {
  error('not supported');
}
```

Updating the Current Location with a Timer

An application that can auto-update would obviously make our users' lives easier, by not asking them to update their location as they move.

To enable an auto-update, we will create a timer that uses the **navigator.geoloca tion.watchPosition()** method. This method will execute the **success** callback when the location changes or when the device improves the accuracy.

```
var positionTimer = navigator.geolocation.watchPosition(
    function(position){

        updateMarker(
            marker,
            position.coords.latitude,
            position.coords.longitude
        );
    }
);
```

Finally, we will call **updateMarker()**, which internally calls the Google Maps API's **setPosition()** method:

```
function updateMarker(pin, lat, long){
    pin.setPosition(
        new google.maps.LatLng(
            lat,
            long
        )
    );
}
```

Improving the Map

Everything else, including the code for our Google map, will reside in the **success** callback that is called once the user has allowed her location to be determined, and the service has returned a longitude and latitude.

The **position** property is available within the **success** callback object, so we will pull the latitude and longitude from there and pass it to the Google Maps API's **LatLng()** method:

```
var latlng = new google.maps.LatLng(position.coords.latitude,
  position.coords.longitude);
```

Now we will set up our simple marker. The **map** property is a reference to the HTML local variable we used to store the **Map** object earlier.

```
marker = new google.maps.Marker({
  position: latlng,
  map: map,
  title:"Html5 Hacks!"
});
```

The following code allows us to place a circle around our map pin to emphasize the location visually. (Be sure to try different values with the **radius** property.) While we are at it, we will also center the map to the current location.

```
var circle = new google.maps.Circle({
  map:map,
  radius:300
});

circle.bindTo('center', marker, 'position');

map.setCenter(
 new google.maps.LatLng(
  position.coords.latitude,
  position.coords.longitude
  )
);
```

Figure 7-7 shows what we end up with.

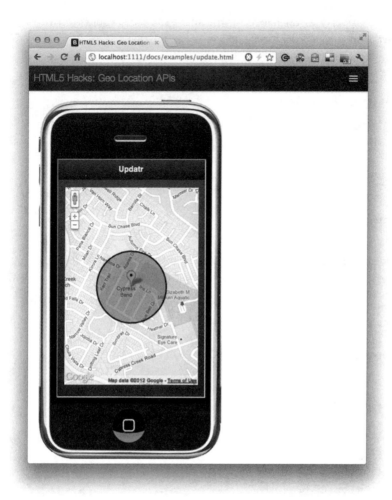

Figure 7-7.
Placing a radius around the pin

Improving Accuracy

In the introduction to this chapter I listed a number of technologies (public IP address location, cell tower triangulation, GPS, WiFi/Bluetooth MAC addresses, and signal strengths) that a particular device can use to pass parameters to a Location Information Server to estimate a user's location.

The `getCurrentPosition()` method, if used with the default configuration, typically uses the first and quickest service that is available on the device, which isn't necessarily the most accurate. The most common example is a smartphone handset using an IP address location before GPS. Determining location by IP address is known to be very inaccurate.

The **enableHighAccuracy** attribute provides a hint that the application would like to receive the best possible results. This may result in slower response times or increased power consumption. The user might also deny this capability, or the device might not be able to provide more accurate results than if the flag wasn't specified.

Saving Power and/or Bandwidth

One of the original intentions of **enableHighAccuracy** was to provide mobile handset application developers with the option to avoid the use of GPS, which typically consumes a significant amount of power. So, while it may improve accuracy, there is also another side to the story. Oftentimes, it is necessary to strike a balance between accuracy and resource consumption.

A few attributes are available that can aid in these decisions within your application design:

maximumAge
> The maximum age (ms) of the last location response (the device may cache location responses to save power and/or bandwidth)

timeout
> The maximum time (ms) until the device retries a location lookup

`HACK 61` Use the Geoloqi Service to Build a Geofence

With Geoloqi, you can push messages and execute events to a single end user at the moment he crosses into a geofence, dwells within it, or departs the zone. And with the Geoloqi JavaScript SDK you can build a location-aware app that gives the user the ability to build a geofence.

In this hack we will build a simple *geofence*, a virtual perimeter for a real-world geographic area.[2] We will do this by traveling to our favorite establishments in downtown Austin, Texas. (After all, we needed a good excuse to get out.)

Building a Geofence

As we move from one establishment to the next, we will tag and push the new location up to the Geoloqi service to store the data in a remote datastore.

---

[2] *http://en.wikipedia.org/wiki/Geo-fence*

To demonstrate the fence we will then retrace our steps, and make a call to request the nearest tagged location. As we move back through the tagged locations, Geoloqi's service will perform the necessary logic to determine which stored location is nearest to our current location.

This is only a small portion of the Geoloqi API, as a complete exploration would be beyond the scope of this book. Hopefully, this sparks your interest enough to get you started hacking with this service on your own. You can find the complete API online (*https://developers.geoloqi.com/api*).

Getting Started

First, we need to create an account at geoloqi.com. Once we have an account, we will create a new application (see Figure 7-8).

We will be redirected to a screen that contains the Client ID, Client Secret, and Application Access Token (see Figure 7-9).

Once we have this information we can begin building our app.

Building the Geofencing Application

We will begin by building a jQuery Mobile form. (For more information on setting up and including jQuery Mobile's dependencies see Hack #58.)

Once we have all the jQuery Mobile dependencies we will include the following form:

```
<form>
  <fieldset>
    <h2>New Location</h2>

    <input type="text" name="name" value="">

    <button type="submit" class="btn btn-primary">Save</button>
    <button onclick="getLastLocation(); return false" class="btn">
     Get Last Location
    </button>
    <button onclick="getNearbyLocation();return false" class="btn">
      Get Nearby Location
    </button>

  </fieldset>
</form>
```

Figure 7-8.
Creating a new application

The form has three main purposes. The button with `type="submit"` submits a new location to the Geoloqi service by making a call to `addLocation()`. The second button returns the last location that was added. The third button returns the location nearest to our current location.

To finish the necessary HTML markup for our interface we will also include the following placeholders for any dynamic updates to the UI:

Figure 7-9.
Viewing the application

```
<span id="lastLocation">...</span>

<span id="nearbyLocation">...</span>
```

Calling the Geoloqi API

To call the Geoloqi API, first we need to include the Geoloqi JavaScript APIs within our application's document:

```
<script type="text/javascript"
src="http://api.geoloqi.com/js/geoloqi.min.js"></script>
```

We also need to initialize the Geoloqi library and pass in the **access_token** we received when we created our application at geoloqi.com:

```
geoloqi.init();
geoloqi.auth = {
  'access_token': '142b6-cfb41aaca58aed5f73b58085e1ff21cf6ae0c9a7'};
```

Next, as we have done in the other hacks in this chapter, we will use **navigator.geo location.getCurrentPosition()**. Review those hacks if you want more detail, but here is the gist of it:

```
Geo = {};
if (navigator.geolocation) {
    navigator.geolocation.getCurrentPosition(success, error);
}

//Get the latitude and the longitude;
function success(position) {
    Geo.lat = position.coords.latitude;
    Geo.lng = position.coords.longitude;
}

function error(){
    console.log("GeoLocation failed");
}
```

Now let's begin building our event handlers.

First we need to create a function that will accept the coordinates returned from our call to **navigator.geolocation.getCurrentPosition()**, and persist them at Geoloqi:

```
function addLocation() {
  geoloqi.post("place/create", {
    latitude: Geo.lat,
    longitude: Geo.lng,
    radius: 100,
    name: "Lavaca Street Bar"
  }, function(response, error){
      console.log(response, error)
  });
}
```

To receive the last location we entered, we create the **getLastLocation()** method:

```
function getLastLocation() {
    geoloqi.get('place/list', function(result, error) {
      $('#lastLocation').html(result.places[0].name);
    });
}
```

To get our nearest location within our geofence we use the following:

```
function getNearbyLocation() {
    geoloqi.get('place/nearby', {
      latitude: Geo.lat,
      longitude: Geo.lng,
      radius: 100
    }, function(result, error){
        $('#nearbyLocation').html(result.nearby[0].name);
    });
}
```

Finally, to set up both a *trigger* (an event such as an SMS message or push notification) and a place in one call, we will create an object called a *geonote* that will be called when we get within 100 yards of a location. So, within our **addLocation()** method we will change the **post** from **place** to **geonote**:

```
function addLocation() {
   geoloqi.post("geonote/create", {
     latitude: Geo.lat,
     longitude: Geo.lng,
     radius: 100,
     name: "You are getting close to Lavaca Street Bar"
   }, function(response, error){
       console.log(response, error)
   });

}
```

Now we will receive a message when we get close to our favorite establishments in downtown Austin, Texas.

The finished product looks like this:

```
geoloqi.init();
geoloqi.auth={'access_token':'142b6-... ae0c9a7'};
Geo = {};

if (navigator.geolocation) {
    navigator.geolocation.getCurrentPosition(success, error);
}
```

```
//Get the latitude and the longitude;
function success(position) {
    Geo.lat = position.coords.latitude;
    Geo.lng = position.coords.longitude;
}

function error(){
    console.log("GeoLocation failed");
}

function getLastLocation() {
  geoloqi.get('place/list', function(result, error) {
    $('#lastLocation').html(result.places[0].name);
  });
}

function addLocation() {
    geoloqi.post("geonote/create", {
    latitude: Geo.lat,
    longitude: Geo.lng,
    radius: 100,
    name: "You are getting close to Lavaca Street Bar"
  }, function(response, error){
      console.log(response, error)
  });
}

function getNearbyLocation() {
  geoloqi.get('place/nearby', {
    latitude: Geo.lat,
    longitude: Geo.lng,
    radius: 100
  }, function(result, error){
      $('#nearbyLocation').html(result.nearby[0].name);
  });
}
```

This is just the beginning of what you can do with the Geolocation API and the Geoloqi service. Now, take this as inspiration and build a more ambitious hack!

Use the Geoloqi Real-Time Streaming Service to Broadcast a Remote User's Movement

The combination of the Geolocation API and the Geoloqi Websockets server creates a world of opportunity for innovative hacks. The WebSocket Protocol's full-duplex, bidirectional transport enables you to provide real-time updates of the remote user's location on a map.

The WebSocket Protocol creates a single, persistent TCP socket connection between a client and server, allowing for bidirectional, full-duplex messages to be distributed without the overhead of HTTP headers and cookies. In this hack we will use this light-weight protocol to message our user location back to the server.

> For more on the WebSocket Protocol refer to Chapter 9, which is dedicated to next-generation connectivity protocols and advancements in HTTP.

The Geoloqi Real-Time Streaming Service

Geoloqi real-time streaming is provided through Node.js and Socket.IO. Socket.IO normalizes different transport mechanisms for real-time support. If a browser does not support the WebSocket Protocol, it will fall back to polyfill support from one of the following alternative transport mechanisms:

- Adobe Flash Socket
- Ajax long polling
- Ajax multipart streaming
- Forever iFrame
- JSON polling

> More details on Socket.IO are available in Hack #76.

Adding the Geoloqi JavaScript SDK is as simple as including a few script tags in the head of your document:

```
<script type="text/javascript"
src="https://subscribe.geoloqi.com/socket.io/socket.io.js"></script>

<script type="text/javascript"
src="http://api.geoloqi.com/js/geoloqi.min.js"></script>
```

Now we need to make sure we have the Geoloqi test account share token. We would obviously replace this with a real share token once we are ready to implement it with real users.

```
window.onload = function () {
  var trip = new geoloqi.Socket('trip', 'TQ4ew3Z');

  trip.events.location = function(location) {
    console.log(location);
  }

  trip.events.disconnect = function() {
    console.log('trip socket disconnected');
  }

  trip.start();
}
```

If we open the console, we will see objects being logged in the console (as shown in Figure 7-10).

Figure 7-10.
Google Chrome Developer Console viewing Geoloqi trip event objects

These objects contain information related to the location of the user with a shared token each time our application polls for a location.

First we will include the `div` element with `id="map"`:

```
<div id="map"></div>
```

Now let's add a Google map to display the user's location. In Hack #60 we discuss using the Google Maps API in more detail. For this hack we will keep the map simple. Create a new map and pass it to the `setDefault()` method of the Geoloqi Maps API:

```
window.onload = function () {

    map = new google.maps.Map(document.getElementById('map'), {
      zoom: 10,
      center: new google.maps.LatLng(0, 0),
      mapTypeId: google.maps.MapTypeId.ROADMAP
    });

    geoloqi.maps.setDefault(map);

}
```

Now that we have a map, we need to set up a new socket as we did in the first example. We will again use the test account to instantiate a new `geoloqi.Socket`. It accepts a `Socket` type, which can be either `trip` or `group`. The `group` type allows the developer to subscribe to location updates for all users in a group using a group token.

For now, we will use a `trip` token to see only one user:

```
var remoteUser = null;

var sckt = new geoloqi.Socket('trip', 'TQ4ew3Z');

sckt.events.location = function(location) {

 if(remoteUser === null) {
    remoteUser = geoloqi.maps.pins.Basic(
 {position: new google.maps.LatLng(
      location.latitude,
      location.longitude)
  });
 }

    remoteUser.moveTo(new google.maps.LatLng(
      location.latitude,
      location.longitude),
```

```
    true);
    }

    sckt.start();

}
```

Now we should see the pin moving on the map in real time, in sync with the remote user we are tracking. To test it yourself create an account and replace the **trip** token with your own. The result should look like Figure 7-11.

Figure 7-11.
Google map pin of a remote user updating in real time

For more information about Geoloqi socket streaming, visit the fantastic API documentation (*https://developers.geoloqi.com/api*).

HACK 63 Polyfill Geolocation APIs with Webshims

Often, web application developers are tasked with achieving cross-browser compliance with the functionality they are targeting within an application. The Geolocation API is not available natively in IE 8 and earlier, but there are alternative polyfills, such as webshims, that you can use to get the job done.

I have included polyfill hacks throughout this book. For a general overview of the problem that polyfills solve, read the introduction to Hack #55. For this hack I will assume you are familiar with Modernizr and YepNope.js.

To get started we will include our dependencies:

```
<script src="http://code.jquery.com/jquery-1.7.1.min.js"></script>

<script src="js/modernizr.js"></script>

<script src="js/yepnope.js"></script>
```

We will set up some basic markup to populate once we have received our location coordinates:

```
<div class="geo-coords">
    GeoLocation: <span id="Lat">lat: ...</span>°,
                 <span id="Long">long: ...</span>°
</div>
```

Now we will include the **yepnope** script loader that uses the `Modernizr.geoloca`
`tion` property to test the browser for geolocation support. If the **nope** call returns
true, **yepnope** will dynamically load the *polyfiller.js* file from the webshims library, patching the browser with geolocation support.

Once complete, the callback will be fired. For now, we will test these conditions with a simple **alert** of the **url** of the polyfill:

```
yepnope({

    test: Modernizr.geolocation,
    nope: ['../../js/polyfiller.js'],

    callback: function (url, result, key) {
```

```
        // test yepnope loader
        alert(url);
    }
});
```

When we refresh a browser that lacks geolocation support, such as IE 8 and earlier, we should see the alert.

So, now we can remove it and replace it with our webshims script.

First we will set up an option, **confirmText**, to configure the message displayed to the user. Then we will call **polyfill()** and pass in the features we want to add. For this hack, we will only need to add geolocation.

Now we can make a call to **navigator.geolocation.getCurrentPosition()** and pass in the **success** and **error** callback objects:

```
$.webshims.setOptions({
    geolocation: {
        confirmText: 'obtaining your location.
    }
});

//load all polyfill features
$.webshims.polyfill('geolocation');

$.webshims.polyfill();

$(function() {

    var Geo={};

    function populateHeader(lat, lng){
        $('#Lat').html(lat);
        $('#Long').html(lng);
    }

    //Get the latitude and the longitude;
    function success(position) {
        Geo.lat = position.coords.latitude;
            Geo.lng = position.coords.longitude;
            populateHeader(Geo.lat, Geo.lng);
    }

    function error(){
        console.log("Geocoder failed");
```

```
            }
            navigator.geolocation.getCurrentPosition(success, error);

    });
```

And here it is, all together:

```
yepnope({
    test: Modernizr.geolocation,
    nope: ['../../js/polyfiller.js'],

  callback: function (url, result, key) {
    $.webshims.setOptions({
        waitReady: false,
        geolocation: {
            confirmText: '{location} wants to know your position.
        }
    });

    //load all polyfill features
    $.webshims.polyfill('geolocation');

    $.webshims.polyfill();

    $(function() {

        var Geo={};

        function populateHeader(lat, lng){
            $('#Lat').html(lat);
            $('#Long').html(lng);
        }

        //Get the latitude and the longitude;
        function success(position) {
            Geo.lat = position.coords.latitude;
            Geo.lng = position.coords.longitude;
            populateHeader(Geo.lat, Geo.lng);
        }

        function error(){
            console.log("Geocoder failed");
        }

        if (navigator.geolocation) {
```

```
            navigator.geolocation.getCurrentPosition(success, error);
        }
    });
    }
});
```

8

WebWorker API

The WebWorker API provides a simple set of methods for web content to run scripts in background threads. Web workers are executed from a main browser window but run independently and in parallel. Once a script in the main thread spawns a worker, the worker can send messages back by posting them to a defined event handler. Data is serialized, not cloned, as it is passed back and forth. This is important to note because poor design or use of too many workers can actually cause performance issues.

Web workers are beneficial in that they run without impacting the other user interface scripts executed from the main window, but they do have limitations. They have limited access to core JavaScript, and no access to the Document Object Model (DOM).

However, you can perform I/O through the `XMLHttpRequest` object and even import third-party scripts, as you will see in Hack #68.

There are three types of web workers: inline, dedicated, and shared. Browser adoption for shared workers is still very sparse, so most of the following hacks will focus on the simpler, dedicated worker.

In the last hack in this chapter, Hack #69, you will see how shared web workers allow any number of browser window contexts to communicate with a single worker simultaneously.

Why are web workers so important to web application developers today? It has to do with how browsers handle JavaScript.

How Browsers Handle JavaScript

JavaScript runs in the same thread as the rest of the browser UI, and as the interpreter, it pulls event handlers off the event loop as they are queued for execution. This queue is shared with all event handlers to include those initiated by user interaction. In Hack #65 we will compare the perceived performance of array manipulation both within the main thread and within a dedicated worker. If you haven't witnessed the power of offsetting work to a worker, you will get a clear demonstration in the first hack.

JavaScript code bases continue to grow, and as more JavaScript runs, more applications block, waiting for the code to finish. Ultimately, we end up with unresponsive script prompts.

How often have you seen the dialog in Figure 8-1, or something similar, telling you that some scripts on a page are taking too long while your browser has become completely unresponsive?

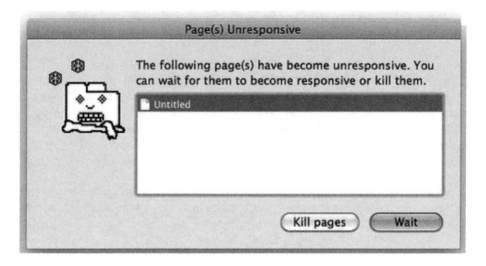

Figure 8-1.
Unresponsive script prompt in Google Chrome

What can create unresponsiveness in the browser? Here are a few of the more common cases, some of which we will explore in the following hacks:

- Processing large arrays or JSON responses
- Prefetching and/or caching data for later use
- Analyzing video or audio data
- Polling web services
- Image filtering in Canvas
- Updating many rows of the local storage database
- Encoding/decoding a large string

HACK 64 Use the BlobBuilder Interface to Create an Inline Worker

Sometimes developers need to keep scripts and markup together in one HTML file. When necessary, you can create an inline worker with the BlobBuilder interface. This hack will teach you how to parse batched Facebook data.

As I mentioned in this chapter's introduction, there are three types of web workers: inline, dedicated, and shared. In this hack we will utilize an inline web worker by leveraging the BlobBuilder interface. We already covered blobs in Chapter 6, in Hack #53.

Unlike dedicated and shared workers, inline workers do not require a worker to be maintained within an external script. Inline workers are useful in that they allow the developer to create a self-contained page. By utilizing the BlobBuilder interface, you can "inline" your worker in the same HTML file as your main logic by creating a **Blob Builder** and appending the worker code as a string.

The best way to think of a **Blob** is as a DOM file. The BlobBuilder interface provides an intuitive way to construct **Blob** objects. If you are familiar with getters and setters, the API should make a lot of sense to you. Just instantiate a new **BlobBuilder** and use the **append()** method to set data to it. You can then use the **getBlob()** method to get the entire **Blob** containing the data.

We will start by setting the **type** to the JavaScript/worker script so that the JavaScript interpreters won't parse it:

```
<script id="worker1" type="JavaScript/worker">
    self.onmessage = function(event) {

        var jsonText = event.data;
        //parse the structure

        var jsonData = JSON.parse(jsonText);


        //send back the results
        // Loop through the data and send back objects with
        // name of the band and the talking_about_count number
        self.postMessage(jsonData);
    }
</script>
```

The Facebook Graph API and Batching Responses

Often it is desirable to reduce an application's HTTP requests to as few as possible, if not a single request. In this hack we want to fetch data from the fan pages of a large number of bands within a particular genre. The data we are interested in is the `talk ing_about_count` property. This property is a metric that is intended to gauge the success of Facebook pages, and in our application we are interested in monitoring the "buzz" of bands within our selected genre.

The `talking_about_count` property tallies the following Facebook user behaviors:

- Page likes
- Number of postings to a page's wall
- Commenting on content within a page
- Sharing a page's status update
- Answering a question posted by a page
- RSVPing to an event hosted by a page
- Mentioning a page
- Tagging a page in a photo
- Liking or sharing a check-in deal
- Checking in at a place

You get the idea. We plan to perform operations on this data. The possibilities for working with data such as this are endless, so for the scope of this hack we will just parse out that particular property, create an unordered list, and update the UI.

Reducing the Batch to a Single Request

We want to be optimized for mobile; we also want to cache the data locally, so we have decided to use the Facebook Graph API's batch support to make one single request for all of our data (see Figure 8-2).

Facebook's batch support allows you to pass instructions for several operations in a single HTTP request. You can also specify dependencies between related operations (described shortly). Facebook will process each independent operation in parallel and will process your dependent operations sequentially. Once all operations have been completed, a consolidated response will be passed back to you and the HTTP connection will be closed.

Figure 8-2.
Facebook Graph API's batch support

Building the Blob

First we will use a fairly common approach to fetch the worker content from our inline worker and append it to a **Blob**. We'll use the following vendor-specific methods:

```
var bb = new (window.BlobBuilder || window.WebKitBlobBuilder ||
window.MozBlobBuilder )();
```

Now we'll grab the content using the **querySelector()** method and the **textCon
tent** property of our selected element:

```
bb.append(document.querySelector('#worker1').textContent);
```

Finally, we need to create a **blobURL** and a **worker**. Our **worker** consumes a parameter that is really a reference to a script. So the parameter uses the **createObjec
tURL()** method to create a URL to our previously created **Blob**.

```
var objUrl = (window.webkitURL || window.URL);
var worker = new Worker(objUrl.createObjectURL(bb.getBlob()));
```

Fetching Data from the Facebook Graph API

Now we can fetch the data we need by calling the public Facebook Graph API. So first we will set our URL, making sure `callback` is set to `?` to overcome the cross-domain problems with JSONP (more on JSONP in Hack #68):

```
var url = "https://graph.facebook.com/?ids=TheFlecktones,
umphreysmcgee,SpearheadRecords&callback=?";
```

Next we will use jQuery's `.getJSON()` method to make our `XMLHttpRequest` object, serialize the response, and pass it into our worker. At this point, we will have achieved our goal of transferring the parsing operations out of the main thread by calling `worker.postMessage()` and passing the data.

```
$.getJSON(url, function(json) {
console.log(json)
data = JSON.stringify(json);
worker.postMessage(data); // Start the worker.
});
```

If you are using Google Chrome or Safari, press Option-Command-I to open the Developer Tools, and then navigate to the console (see Figure 8-3).

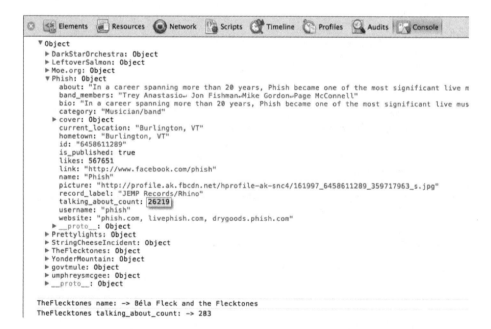

Figure 8-3.
Facebook Graph API's batch support

Now we'll update our worker with some logic to make our data somewhat interesting. We need to manipulate it a bit, so first we will create a new array that holds simple objects with two properties: `name` and `talking_about_count`.

```
var arr = new Array();
for (var key in jsonData) {
  if (jsonData.hasOwnProperty(key)) {
    arr.push({ "name": jsonData[key].name,
            "count": jsonData[key].talking_about_count
  });
  }
}
```

Now that we have this new simple array, let's sort it by creating a basic `compare()` function, which we can pass to JavaScript's native sort method. As a result, our counts are now in descending order.

```
function compare(a,b) {
  if (a.count < b.count)
    return 1;
  if (a.count > b.count)
    return -1;
  return 0;
}


var newarr = arr.sort(compare);
```

All in all, our new inline worker looks like this:

```
<script id="worker1" type="JavaScript/worker">

self.onmessage = function(event) {
  var jsonText = event.data;
  var jsonData = JSON.parse(jsonText);


var arr = new Array();
for (var key in jsonData) {
  if (jsonData.hasOwnProperty(key)) {
    arr.push({ "name": jsonData[key].name, "count":
jsonData[key].talking_about_count});
  }
}

function compare(a,b) {
  if (a.count < b.count)
    return 1;
```

```
      if (a.count > b.count)
        return -1;
      return 0;
    }

    var newarr = arr.sort(compare);

    //send back to the results
    self.postMessage(newarr);
      }
```

```
    </script>
```

Now we can set up our listener to respond to messages that come back from the worker. Once we get the data back from our worker thread we will handle it by updating our UI. First, let's take a look at the data by examining it in the console. We should see that our data is now minimal, with only the **name** and **talking_about_count** properties. Also, the bands should be sorted in descending order by **talking_about_count**.

```
    worker.onmessage = function(event){

    //the JSON structure is passed back
      var jsonData = event.data;
        console.log(jsonData);

    };
```

Let's take another look at our new data in the console (see Figure 8-4).

Figure 8-4.
Facebook JSONP data in the console

Now our **onmessage()** handler in our main thread will update the UI with the fresh data from Facebook. We can use jQuery to append the list to the UI:

```
    var list = $('<ul>').attr('class','list');
        $("#status").append(list);
```

```
    for (var i = 0; i < newarr.length; i++) {
       var listitem = $('<li>').attr('class','listitem')
.text(newarr[i].name + " : " + newarr[i].count)
       $("#status > ul").append(listitem);
    };
```

Figure 8-5 shows the result.

Figure 8-5.
Top 10 list of Jam Bands by talking_about_count

HACK 65 Perform Heavy Array Computations in a Dedicated Web Worker

Dedicated web workers are a great solution for expensive computations such as array manipulation. With this hack you can move such a computation to a worker without impacting the performance of an interactive canvas animation in the main thread.

To begin to understand the power of web workers we need to manufacture an expensive operation, and create a UI that uses some type of animation that we would like the user to be able to interact with seamlessly.

For the expensive operation we can manipulate array data, and for the animation we can create a simple canvas that has balls bouncing as the user interacts with it.

We will then provide a simple UI that provides tools for testing heavy array manipulation inside and outside a web worker. The test will be focused on the user experience. We will not output data to show the performance of our code, but we will rely on the popular concept of perceived performance to determine which solution is higher performing.

An Expensive Computation

First let's create a function that manipulates the array data by taking an input of two large integers and outputting a two-dimensional array of all the combinations of the two numbers. With smaller numbers, performing these operations is handled fairly well outside the web worker, or in the main thread, in all the modern browsers. But as we begin to increase the size of the input integers, our UI and our canvas animation begin to demonstrate sluggishness.

Our computation will be maintained inside a **process()** function. At the end of the script we will access the element in our markup with the **id** of **textarea**, and pass it the string **"PROCESSING COMPLETE"** as well as set the background in red. This gives us a clear indicator as to when the array processing is complete.

```
function process() {

    console.log("WITHOUT WORKER")
    var r = $('select#row').val();
    var c = $('select#col').val();

    var a = new Array(r);

    for (var i = 0; i < r; i++) {
        a[i] = new Array(c);

        for (var j = 0; j < c; j++) {
            a[i][j] = "[" + i + "," + j + "]";
        }
    }

    var complete = "PROCESSING COMPLETE";
    $('#textarea').text(complete);
    $('#textarea').css({'background-color': '#BF3831',
'color': '#fff'});

};
```

We also need to create a simple UI for demonstrating our worker test. So let's create select boxes that contain the values we will pass to our computations. One select box will fire the **process()** function and the other will fire the **processWorker()** function that will perform the same computation inside a worker (more on the **processWork er()** function later in this chapter). We can also add the **textarea** we referenced in our previous processing script.

```
<form class="form-horizontal">
  <fieldset>

<div class="control-group">
        <label class="control-label"
for="select01">Select Row Value</label>
        <div class="controls">
          <select id="row">
            <option>choose a value</option>
            <option>1000</option>
            <option>2000</option>
            <option>3000</option>
            <option>4000</option>
          </select>
        </div>
      </div>

<div class="control-group">
        <label class="control-label" for="select01">
Select Column Value</label>
        <div class="controls">
          <select id="col">
            <option>choose a value</option>
            <option>1000</option>
            <option>2000</option>
            <option>3000</option>
            <option>4000</option>
          </select>
        </div>
      </div>

<div class="control-group">
        <label class="control-label" for="textarea">
Output</label>
        <div class="controls">
          <textarea class="input-xlarge" id="textarea"
rows="1"></textarea>
        </div>
```

```
            </div>

            <div class="control-group">
              <label class="control-label" for="textarea">
Process</label>
              <div class="controls">
                <button id="worker" class="btn-small
btn-danger" href="#">With Web Worker</button>
                <button id="non-worker" class="btn-small
btn-primary" href="#">Without Web Worker</button>
              </div>
            </div>
          </fieldset>
        </form>
```

Figure 8-6 shows the result.

Figure 8-6.
Building the basic UI

We also need to use jQuery to add a few event listeners to listen for click events on the select boxes. Our select boxes' event handlers will be **process()** and **process Worker()**, respectively. And finally, we will add an **init()** function that listens for the window's **onload** event and initializes our scripts.

```
function init() {

    $('#worker').click(function() {
        var complete = "PROCESSING WITH WEB WORKER";
        $('#textarea').text(complete);
        processWorker();
    });

    $('#non-worker').click(function() {
        var complete = "PROCESSING WITHOUT WEB WORKER";
        $('#textarea').text(complete);
        process();
    });
}

window.onload = init;
```

The Bouncing Balls Canvas

Now let's include the canvas animation. We'll use a modified version of an existing canvas demo provided by Eric Rowell (*http://www.html5canvastutorials.com/labs/ html5-canvas-google-bouncing-balls*). For our purposes we just need an animation that we can interact with.

First let's add just a bit of style to our **canvas** element:

```
<style type="text/css">
    #canvas {
        width: 575px;
        height: 300px;
        background-color: #000;
        cursor: pointer;
    }
    #myCanvas {
        border: 1px solid #9C9898;
    }

    .thing {
        position:absolute;
    }
```

```
.dying {
    color:#ff0000;
    font-weight:bold;
}

</style>
```

Now we can add the script. We won't include Eric's long script here, but you can see it in the companion Git repository (*https://github.com/html5hacks/chapter8*).

We should now have a fully functioning demonstration. As we begin to increase the size of the values in the select boxes and press the Without Web Worker button (see Figure 8-7), we should see the interaction among the balls in the canvas become increasingly sluggish.

Figure 8-7.
Adding the canvas animation

```
function processWorker() {

    console.log("WORKER")
    var r = $('select#row').val();
    var c = $('select#col').val();

    var worker = new Worker('assets/js/demojs/twoDarray-worker.js');
    var message = {
        "compfn": "create2Darray",
        "rowValue": r,
        "colValue": c
    }

    worker.postMessage(JSON.stringify(message));
    worker.onmessage = function (event) {
        // print results of array in result div
        // var data = event.data
        // Must stringify before appending to DOM
        // console.log('data has returned as: ' + typeof data
    + ' ...time to stringify and append to DOM');

        var complete = "PROCESSING COMPLETE";
        $('#textarea').text(complete);
        $('#textarea').css({'background-color': '#BF3831',
    'color': '#fff'});
    };
};
```

Spawning a Dedicated Web Worker

The WebWorker API is straightforward and easy to get started with.

First we will obtain the values from our select boxes and store them in the variables **r** and **c**. Then we will instantiate a new web worker by using the **new** operator on the **Worker** class and passing a URI that points to our worker script.

```
function processWorker() {

    console.log("WORKER")
    var r = $('select#row').val();
    var c = $('select#col').val();

    var worker = new Worker('assets/js/demojs/twoDarray-worker.js');

    ...
```

Now we'll craft an object to pass to our worker. As you will see in a moment, our worker will be organized as a library of methods. This object is actually a configuration object that has a **compfn** property that instructs the worker library as to how to parse the data. We'll then pass our data to the worker via **postMessage()**.

```
var message = {
    "compfn": "create2Darray",
    "rowValue": r,
    "colValue": c
}
```

We also need to serialize our data before passing it to the worker. To do this we can use the **JSON.stringify()** method.

```
worker.postMessage(JSON.stringify(message));
```

Before we craft our worker, let's finish our work in the main thread by setting up a listener to handle any messages sent back to the main thread from the worker.

Here, we actually aren't interested in the data that is returned, only that the callback has been fired indicating that the processing is complete.

```
worker.onmessage = function (event) {
    var complete = "PROCESSING COMPLETE";
    $('#textarea').text(complete);
    $('#textarea').css({'background-color': '#BF3831',
'color': '#fff'});
    };
```

Here is the completed processing function utilizing the WebWorker API:

```
function processWorker() {

    console.log("WORKER")
    var r = $('select#row').val();
    var c = $('select#col').val();

    var worker = new Worker('assets/js/demojs/twoDarray-worker.js');
    var message = {
        "compfn": "create2Darray",
        "rowValue": r,
        "colValue": c
    }

    worker.postMessage(JSON.stringify(message));
    worker.onmessage = function (event) {
        var complete = "PROCESSING COMPLETE";
        $('#textarea').text(complete);
```

```
         $('#textarea').css({'background-color': '#BF3831',
    'color': '#fff'});
         };
    };
```

Now we need to craft our worker script. Earlier I described the format of the script as being a library, and being able to handle a compfn() method that allows us to divide functionality into different methods within the library. To match common industry conventions, we capitalize the Computations variable to indicate that we are creating a JavaScript pseudoclass.

The create2darray is just one of many computations that we could include in this worker library. For the scope of this hack we will only craft the one method, but it's important that you understand the power of this pattern moving forward.

```
Computations = {

    create2Darray: function (data) {

        var r = data.rowValue;
        var c = data.colValue;

        var a = new Array(r);

        for (var i = 0; i < r; i++) {
            a[i] = new Array(c);

            for (var j = 0; j < c; j++) {
                a[i][j] = "[" + i + "," + j + "]";
            }
        }

        return a;
    }
};
```

The secret to our worker library pattern is held within the onmessage() listener. We use the bracket syntax to pull the name of the function out of the config object we passed from our main thread. We use this function to match a function by that name within the Computations class, and pass the rest of the data to be processed by that function.

```
self.addEventListener('message', function(e) {

    var message = JSON.parse(e.data)
    computated = Computations[message.compfn](message);
```

```
        self.postMessage(computated);

    }, false);
```

Finally, here is our worker script in its entirety:

```
var Computations = {

  create2Darray: function (data) {

    var r = data.rowValue;
    var c = data.colValue;

    var a = new Array(r);

    for (var i = 0; i < r; i++) {
        a[i] = new Array(c);

        for (var j = 0; j < c; j++) {
            a[i][j] = "[" + i + "," + j + "]";
        }
    }

    return a;
  }
};

self.addEventListener('message', function(e) {

    var message = JSON.parse(e.data)
    computated = Computations[message.compfn](message);

    self.postMessage(computated);

}, false);
```

Figure 8-8 shows the result.

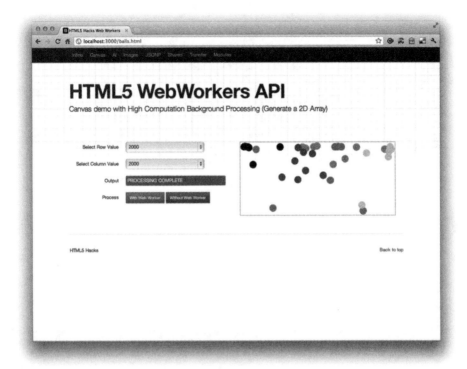

Figure 8-8.
Processing complete

HACK 66 Use a Timer to Send Application State to Workers

The combination of timers and web workers opens new opportunities in the development of client-centric HTML5 applications. It is possible to make your application artificially intelligent (in a very basic way) by giving it a set of functions called at a regular interval. Although these operations can be performed in the main thread, it is often optimal to perform them in a separate worker thread process.

In this hack we will gain inspiration from Angus Croll's post, "web workers vs. the crazy flies" (*http://javascriptweblog.wordpress.com/2010/06/21/web-workers-vs-the-crazy-flies/*).

For the most part, we will use most of Angus's design, where he animates flies that are eliminated over time based on array manipulations being performed within web workers (see Figure 8-9). We will do much the same thing, but add our own flavor to the hack.

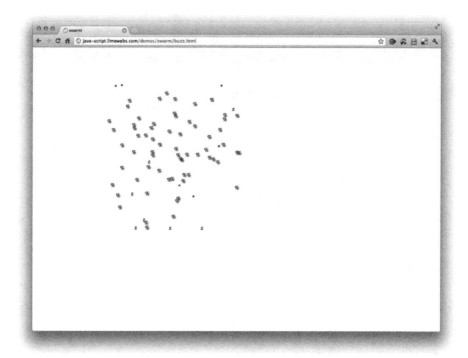

Figure 8-9.
Angus Croll's crazy flies

In the hack we will explore very basic concepts of artificial intelligence by using Java-Script timers and random number generation to create a web-based visualization.

One might argue that this is not artificial intelligence, but it is a basic simulation of intelligence demonstrating two main subproblems: *localization* (knowing where you are or finding out where other things are) and *mapping* (learning what is around you or building a map of the environment); see Figure 8-10.

Each time you run this script it will behave differently. It will take on a life of its own: creating data, consuming the data, and making decisions based on the current state of the data. Eventually, the script will run out of data to process and will stop.

Besides the enormous amount of potential with the core concept of artificial intelligence within the browser, the significance of this hack is twofold. First, we are adding timers to the mix in order to set up `postMessage`s on a regular interval. Second, we are evolving our worker library further than we did in Hack #65. Our library will utilize a few advanced syntactical techniques that you can use to make your own worker library.

Figure 8-10.
Localization and mapping illustrated with icons of users

In doing so, we will also extend JavaScript core to create a curry utility. We will then use it within our `setInterval()` calls, a handy trick that is worth understanding if you haven't seen currying before (more on that later).

Here is a general idea of what we will accomplish in this hack:

1. Spawn the worker and add `EventListener`s.
2. Generate DOM movement (characters).
3. Start snapshot timers and capture the state of the UI.
4. At each interval, send the state of the UI to a worker (AI library).
5. Do heavy processing in the worker (AI library).
6. Pass back updates to the main thread.
7. Make updates to DOM elements.

General Overview

The general idea of this hack is to generate a number of elements and append them to the DOM. These elements will be icon elements that we will refer to as **Thing** objects and we will append them to the **<body>** tag. But first let's set up a few objects to hold our data:

```
var things = [], thingMap = {}, elemMap = {};
```

Now we'll define a **Thing** class that we can instantiate when creating new **Thing**s. Our **Thing** will maintain a number of different properties that we can see in the constructor that follows. Also, when we create a **Thing** object we will call **createThingElem( )**, which will create the actual DOM element, and assign a reference by **id** to the **elemMap** object.

```
var Thing = function(left, top, id) {
    this.id = id;
    this.minDx = -7; this.maxDx = 7;
    this.minDy = -7; this.maxDy = 7;
    this.x = this.xOld = left;
    this.y = this.yOld = top;
    this.pxTravelled = 7;
    elemMap[id] = createThingElem(left, top);
}
```

Here is the **createThingElem( )** function used to create the icons. You can see that we are creating an icon element and appending it to the body of the document.

```
var createThingElem = function(left, top) {
    var elem = document.createElement("i");
    elem.innerHTML = "";
    elem.className = "thing user-big";
    document.body.appendChild(elem);
    elem.style.left = this.x;
    elem.style.top = this.y;
    return elem;
}
```

Initializing the Things

To begin, we will create an HTML form that will enable us to control the hack. We will create the form with one select box allowing the user to choose the number of **Thing**s to create.

Then we will create a button to generate the movement.

```
<form class="form-horizontal">
<fieldset>
  <div class="control-group">
    <label class="control-label" for="select01">Number of
    Characters</label>
    <div class="controls">
      <select id="number">
        <option>choose a value</option>
        <option>10</option>
        <option>15</option>
        <option>20</option>
        <option>25</option>
        <option>30</option>
        <option>35</option>
        <option>40</option>
        <option>45</option>
        <option>50</option>
      </select>
    </div>
  </div>
  <div class="control-group">
    <label class="control-label" for="textarea"></label>
    <div class="controls">
        <button id="go" class="btn-large btn-primary" href="#">
Generate Movement</button>
    </div>
  </div>
</fieldset>
</form>
```

Now that we have set up our UI to give us some controls, let's initiate our script by adding an event listener to the Generate Movement button, and a callback event handler called `init()`. `init()` will accept the value that was selected in the select box.

```
$('#go').click(function(e) {

    e.preventDefault();
    var num = $('select#number').val();
    var approach = "with worker";
    init(num);

});
```

Once `init()` is called, two things will happen. First, we will begin moving our Thing icons around in the viewport, and second, we will set up another click listener on another button that will start the timers. From now on we will call this our AI button. Let's add the additional button:

```
<form class="form-horizontal">
 <fieldset>

    ...

  <div class="control-group">
    <label class="control-label" for="textarea"></label>
    <div class="controls">
      <button id="ai" class="btn-large btn-primary" href="#">
Begin AI</button>
    </div>
  </div>

 </fieldset>
</form>
```

Figure 8-11 shows the basic UI.

Now we can begin moving the Things around by creating a `while` loop based on the number passed in from the select box. On each iteration we will create a new Thing and add it to the `things` array; call `start` on each Thing in the `things` array; and add each Thing to the `thingMap` by setting each `thing` object in the `things` array as a property with its `id` as the key in the `thingMap` (more on `thingMap` later):

```
init = function(num) {

    var i = -1;

    while (i++ < num) {
        things[i] = new Thing(400, 300, i);
        things[i].start();
        thingMap[things[i].id] = things[i];
    };

    ...

};
```

The `start()` method begins the movement of the Thing icons in the DOM:

Figure 8-11.
Building the basic UI

```
Thing.prototype.start = function() {
    var thisElem = elemMap[this.id];
    var thing = this;

    var move = function() {
        thing.x = bounded(thing.x +
scaledRandomInt(thing.minDx,thing.maxDx),200,600);
        thing.y = bounded(thing.y +
scaledRandomInt(thing.minDy,thing.maxDy),100,500);
        if (!thing.dead) {
            setTimeout(move, 1);
        }
        thisElem.style.left = thing.x;
        thisElem.style.top = thing.y;
    };
    move();
}
```

Now we'll add another click event handler to the AI button that will start the timers:

```
init = function(num) {

    ...

    $('#ai').click(function(e) {
    e.preventDefault();
      var intervals = [];
      ...
    });

};
```

At this point we're ready to add the timer calls that invoke workers on regular intervals. For now we will set the timers to 1000 ms or one second. We will set up four actions that will process our data in four different ways.

```
init = function(num) {

    var i = -1;

    while (i++ < num) {
        things[i] = new Thing(400, 300, i);
        things[i].start();
        thingMap[things[i].id] = things[i];
    };

    $('#ai').click(function(e) {
     e.preventDefault();
      var intervals = [];
      intervals[0] = window.setInterval(invokeWorker.curry(
'updatePaths'),1000);
      intervals[1] = window.setInterval(invokeWorker.curry(
'fireToBelow'),1000),
      intervals[2] = window.setInterval(invokeWorker.curry(
'rocketToSky'),1000);
      intervals[3] = window.setInterval(invokeWorker.curry(
'eradicateSlow'),1000);
    });

};
```

You might be asking, "What is the curry function inside our **setInterval**s? What does the curry give us?"

Currying uses a closure to give us the ability to dynamically create functions based on arguments passed in. Here is the very common custom `curry()` function that augments JavaScript core:

```
Function.prototype.curry = function() {
    if (arguments.length<1) {
        return this; //nothing to curry with - return function
    }
    var __method = this;
    var args = toArray(arguments);
    return function() {
        return __method.apply(this, args.concat(
toArray(arguments)));
    }
}
```

Currying provides a handy pattern for writing less code and making your code reusable across your application. We can better understand this by looking at the `invokeWorker()` function:

```
var invokeWorker = function(action) {
    // console.log(things)
    worker.postMessage({
        'action': action,
        'things': things
    });
}
```

By extending JavaScript core, we can call `curry` on an existing function and pass it a string. The string becomes a reference to a method in our worker library (more on that later; for now, just know that the `action` parameter of `invokeWorker` is set to a string variable and then set as the value of the `action` property of our custom object that we send in `postMessage()` to our worker). In this example we don't need to serialize our object, since we are creating it manually through the object literal syntax.

```
{
    'action': action,
    'things': things
}
```

At this point we have icon elements moving around the screen, each having a configuration object associated to it. So, once a user clicks the event handler to begin the artificial intelligence (or start the timers), the script begins to poll for these elements' information, such as their *x* and *y* coordinates, and posts the data to a web worker library for processing. When the library has received the data, it will perform a computation on the data by utilizing the action function that was passed in with our curried function. Figure 8-12 shows the result.

Figure 8-12.
Generating movement

The Worker Library

As we discussed before, the curried function that is being called by our `setInterv`
`al` timers is passing a reference to the action we want to take within our worker library.
It does this by creating the object within `invokeWorker()` and passing it to our worker's `postMessage()` API.

```
var things;
var updates;

// UTILITIES
var scaledRandomInt = function(max, min) {
    return Math.round(min + Math.random()*(max-min));
}

var getDistance = function(x1,x2,y1,y2) {
    return Math.sqrt(Math.pow(Math.abs(x1-x2),2) + Math.pow(
Math.abs(y1-y2),2));
```

```
}


// ACTION Methods
var Actions = {
    fireToBelow: function(){
        var highest = things.sort(function(a, b){
            return a.y - b.y
        });
        updates = {};
        updates.action = 'fireToBelow';
        updates.id = highest[0].id;
        updates.minDy = -2;
        updates.maxDy = 3;
        updates.symbol = '';
        updates.className = 'thing user-fire';
        postMessage(updates);
    },

    rocketToSky: function(){
        var lowest = things.sort(function(a, b){
            return b.y - a.y
        });
        updates = {};
        updates.action = 'rocketToSky';
        updates.id = lowest[0].id;
        updates.minDy = -3;
        updates.maxDy = 2;
        updates.symbol = '';
        updates.className = 'thing user-plane';
        postMessage(updates);
    },

    eradicateSlowest: function(){
        var slowest = things.sort(function(a, b){
            return a.pxTravelled - b.pxTravelled
        });
        updates = {};
        updates.action = 'eradicateSlowest';
        updates.id = slowest[0].id;
        updates.kill = true;
        postMessage(updates);
    },
```

```
    updatePaths: function(){
        for (var i = things.length-1; i; i--) {
            var t = things[i];
            t.pxTravelled += getDistance(t.xOld, t.x, t.yOld, t.y);
            t.xOld = t.x; t.yOld = t.y;
        }
    }
}

onmessage = function(e){
    things = e.data.things;
    Actions[e.data.action]();
}
```

Now that our worker library has done the necessary processing it posts the data back
to the main thread that has been listening for any new messages. Any new messages
will trigger the **onmessage()** event handler, which will make updates to the UI (see
Figure 8-13).

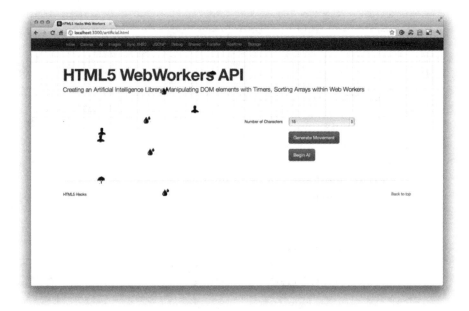

Figure 8-13.
Things being eliminated

As you can see, numerous methods within our worker library are processing the data through array manipulations. These manipulations can be very expensive, especially as we increase the size of the data payload. One of the main points to take away from this hack is that this library is organized to grow in a very clean, maintainable way. Just add an additional method by creating a new property set to a function value.

Finally, the last syntactical sugar that we will use to make this library tidy and well organized takes place within the **onmessage()** listener. Here there is a reference to the **Actions** object, which we could refer to as a JavaScript **Singleton** class. In JavaScript, we can create *singletons*, or classes that are only instantiated once, by making use of a simple associated array of name–value pairs. The pattern looks like this:

```
var Actions = {
    fireToBelow: function(){
        ...
    },

    rocketToSky: function(){
        ...
    },

    eradicateSlowest: function(){
        ...
    },

    updatePaths: function(){
        ...
    }
}
```

It is the same pattern as a simple JSON object.

Now we need to use the array bracket syntax to call the method of choice from within the **Singleton** class. Remember, the name of the function was passed in from the main thread. Now we can manage calls to any method within our library with only one **onmessage()** handler.

```
onmessage = function(e){
    things = e.data.things;
    Actions[e.data.action]();
}
```

Real-World Use

As I mentioned in the introduction to this hack, the core concepts of this simple script bear enormous potential for real-world use. Here are a couple of ideas to get you started:

- Offline analytics
- CoBrowse, user shadowing solutions
- Client-side image processing
- Background XMLHttpRequests
- Background read/write to local storage

We will explore some of these in upcoming hacks. Now go and build your own worker library that can make decisions on its own.

HACK 67 Process Image Data with Pixel Manipulation in a Dedicated Worker

One of the most practical uses of web workers involves processing image data client-side without having to pass data back and forth from a remote server. Pixel manipulation is a common way to add filter-like effects to images. Since you have access to events exposed by the native browser API, you can apply these events based on user input.

In this hack we will apply a grayscale filter to an image of the HTML5 logo. We will apply the filter's configuration based on location data and initiated on a native browser event. The location data we will use will come from the *x* coordinate of the mouse's cursor, and the event we will use will be the **mouseover** event. As we mouse over the HTML5 logo from left to right, the number will be smaller than if we were mousing over the image from right to left. On this event, we will then pass the data to the web worker for image processing. The filter we will create and apply will simply remove all color except for black and white (in essence, it will be a grayscale filter).

As a result the image will become a lighter gray as we enter a mouseover from the lefthand side of the image, and a darker gray as we enter a mouseover from the righthand side (see Figure 8-14).

First, let's use jQuery to apply our event listener to the image, capture the coordinates, and pass the event data to the **process()** function:

```
$(".hover-img").on("mouseover", function(e){
    var x = e.pageX - this.offsetLeft;
```

Figure 8-14.
HTML5 logo

```
        var y = e.pageY - this.offsetTop;
        console.log("X: " + x + " Y: " + y);
        process(this, x, y);
    });
```

Now we'll build our processing function, which will apply our filter to the image data. Our function will accept the image we captured in the **mouseover** event and the x and y coordinates.

```
function process(img, x, y) {

    //process the img based on x,y

}
```

Next, we need to create a canvas in memory that is the same size as the image we passed into the image we are capturing:

```
var canvas = document.createElement("canvas");
canvas.width = img.width;
canvas.height = img.height;
```

Now we'll copy the image into the canvas, and then extract its pixels:

```
var context = canvas.getContext("2d");
context.drawImage(img, 0, 0);

var pixels = context.getImageData(0,0,img.width,img.height);
```

Here we are sending the pixels to a worker thread:

```
var worker = new Worker("javascripts/greyscale.js");

var obj = {
    pixels: pixels,
    x:x,
    y:y
}

worker.postMessage(obj); // Copy and send pixels
```

At this point we need to register a handler to get the worker's response. When we receive the response, we will create a local variable that we will use to put the image back into a context object. We will use the **putImageData()** method to do so and pass an *x* and *y* coordinate to offset the new image data. In this case we want to put the new image in the same place we took the original data from, so we will use **0 0**. Finally, we will use **toDataURL()** to add the data back to the **src** attribute of our image. Canvas has a **toDataURL()** method that will take the data in the canvas and create a string that can be set to the **src** property of an image. Appending that image somewhere on the document will display the data as an image.

```
worker.onmessage = function(e) {

    if (typeof e.data === "string") {
        console.log("Worker: " + e.data);
    return; }

    var new_pixels = e.data.pixels; // Pixels from worker

    context.putImageData(new_pixels, 0, 0);
    img.src = canvas.toDataURL(); // And then to the img

}
```

You may have noticed the debugging technique we can use. Since we cannot use a console API within a worker, we need to check the data type of the returned message in the event handler listening to any messages in the main thread. If the message is of type **string**, we assume an error and log it.

```
if (typeof e.data === "string") {
    console.log("Worker: " + e.data);
return; }
```

Here is the finished product:

```
function process(img, x, y) {

    // Create an offscreen <canvas> the same size as the image
    var canvas = document.createElement("canvas");
    canvas.width = img.width;
    canvas.height = img.height;

    // Copy the image into the canvas, then extract its pixels
    var context = canvas.getContext("2d");
    context.drawImage(img, 0, 0);

    var pixels = context.getImageData(0,0,img.width,img.height);

    var worker = new Worker("javascripts/greyscale.js");

    var obj = {
        pixels: pixels,
        x:x,
        y:y
    }

    worker.postMessage(obj);

    worker.onmessage = function(e) {

        if (typeof e.data === "string") {
            console.log("Worker: " + e.data);
        return; }

        var new_pixels = e.data.pixels;

        context.putImageData(new_pixels, 0, 0);
        img.src = canvas.toDataURL();
    }
}
```

Finally, we need to create our grayscale filter within our worker script. Here, we will make a call to **filter()**, which will process the image data, removing the necessary data to return a gray image. The dynamic magic occurs in the **grayscale** variable, which multiplies the *x* coordinate's position within the formula to return image data that contains nothing more than shades of gray.

```
onmessage = function(e) {postMessage(filter(e.data))};

    function filter(imgd) {

        var pix = imgd.pixels.data;
        var xcord = imgd.x/1000;
        var ycord = imgd.y/1000;

        for (var i = 0, n = pix.length; i < n; i += 4) {
            var grayscale = pix[i] * xcord + pix[i+1] * .59
+ pix[i+2] * .11;

            pix[i] = grayscale;    // red
            pix[i+1] = grayscale;  // green
            pix[i+2] = grayscale;  // blue
        }

        imgd['pixels'].data = pix;
        return imgd;
    }
```

Figures 8-15 and 8-16 show the result.

Figure 8-15.
Left-side mouseover event resulting in darker grayscale

HACK 68 Use Import Scripts to Make Twitter JSONP Requests

The WebWorker API allows you to import third-party or external libraries through the use of the `importScripts()` method. JSONP, or JSON with padding, is a widely used technique for fetching JavaScript from other domains without having to adhere to the browser's same origin policy.

In this hack we will make a call to the Twitter Search API to obtain the last 100 tweets that contain the `html5` keyword within their body. We will leverage the `import Script()` function available to us in the worker context.

As with any dedicated worker, the first thing we will do is to create a new `Worker` and point to an external file:

```
var worker = new Worker("javascripts/jsonp-worker.js");
```

Figure 8-16.
Right-side mouseover event resulting in lighter grayscale

Then we will set up a listener for any messages passed back to our main thread. Within our listener, we will loop through the response and build a `div` for each result. In the process, we will also append the profile image, and the name of the Twitter user that posted the tweet.

```
var worker = new Worker("javascripts/jsonp-worker.js");
worker.onmessage = function(e) {
    console.log(e.data);
    var res = e.data;
    for ( key in res.results){
        var item = res.results[key];
        var img = $('<img>').attr('src',item.profile_image_url);
        var div = $('<div>').append(img);
        var text= $('<div>').html($.trim(item.text));
        div.append(text);
        div.attr('class','tweet');
```

```
            $('#listDiv').append(item.from_user);
            $('#list').append(div);
        }
    }
```

But we are getting ahead of ourselves, so first let's make the request to Twitter from within our worker. Our worker script is fairly straightforward. We need to set up a callback function that we will pass within our request to Twitter. Within our callback, we will simply pass the object back to the main thread to build out the UI. Later, we will explore some of the possibilities for processing the data from Twitter, but for now we will just pass the full object back to the main thread.

```
var callback = function (obj) {
    if (obj.hasOwnProperty("results")) {
        // process the data
        postMessage(obj);

    } else {
        postMessage("No results.");
    }
};
```

Making the request is simple, and involves a combination of JSONP and **import Scripts()**.

JSONP

JSONP or *JSON with padding* is a technique used to work around the browser's same origin policy for fetching JavaScript from another domain. A JSONP API server will read in a callback request parameter and wrap the JSON-formatted response within that function. The technique then takes advantage of the way the browser interprets and executes JavaScript when a script tag is dynamically generated and appended to the DOM.

As I mentioned in other web worker hacks, our worker thread is limited in that we do not have DOM access, but we do have access to the special function **import Scripts()**. So let's make a call to the Twitter API to get the latest 100 tweets with **html5** as a search query. Notice the **callback** parameter and the function reference to **callback**.

```
importScripts("http://search.twitter.com/search.json?
q=html5&rpp=100&since_id=1&callback=callback");
```

Here is the final web worker code:

```
var callback = function (obj) {
    if (obj.hasOwnProperty("results")) {
```

Figure 8-17.
Fetching the latest HTML5-related Twitter data

```
        // process data
        postMessage(obj);

    } else {
        postMessage("No results.");
    }
};

importScripts("http://search.twitter.com/search.json?
q=html5&rpp=100&since_id=1&callback=callback");
```

Figure 8-17 shows the result.

As I mentioned before, this is a very simple example. This approach can be very efficient for processing API data within a web worker. Often, developers will want to alter the format of the data within the worker, and then pass composites or even smaller portions of the original data back to the main thread. Now you can, too.

Connect to Shared Workers
Simultaneously from Multiple
Browser Windows

Dedicated web workers are directly associated with their respective spawning script, but shared web workers allow any number of browser window contexts to communicate with a single worker simultaneously. As you will see in this hack, shared workers implement a slightly different API, but overall the concepts are very much the same.

Just like dedicated workers, to create a shared web worker you pass a JavaScript filename to your **Worker** instance, except this time you use the **SharedWorker** object.

Unlike dedicated web workers, shared workers introduce the concept of a **port** object that must be designated along with the attached message event handler. After that, we call the **port**'s **start( )** method.

And finally, we are set to use our standard **postMessage( )**:

```
var worker = new SharedWorker('javascripts/shared-simple.js');
var log = document.getElementById('log');

worker.port.addEventListener('message', function(e) {
    log.textContent += '\n' + e.data;

    if (e.data.charAt(0) == '#'){
      document.body.style.background = e.data;
    }

}, false);

worker.port.start();
```

Since any of the existing page scripts, or even scripts within other windows, can communicate with a shared web worker, we will create three **iframe**s to demonstrate communication across browser window contexts:

```
<pre id="log">Log:</pre>
<iframe src="/shared-simple-inner.html"></iframe>
<iframe src="/shared-simple-inner2.html"></iframe>
<iframe src="/shared-simple-inner3.html"></iframe>
```

In each document being loaded in the **iframe**s, we will instantiate new **SharedWork er** objects that point to the same external script. The **onmessage** event handler will expect two items as a response: a number that is maintained by a counter with the worker thread, and a randomly generated color that will be set as the background color of the document that spawned the worker.

```
<!DOCTYPE HTML>
<title>HTML5 Hacks: Shared Worker</title>
<pre id=log>Log:</pre>
<script>
  var worker = new SharedWorker('javascripts/shared-simple.js');
  var log = document.getElementById('log');

  worker.port.onmessage = function(e) {
   log.textContent += '\n' + e.data;

   if (e.data.charAt(0) == '#'){
     document.body.style.background = e.data;
   }
  }
}
</script>
```

Figure 8-18 shows the three **iframe**s we included.

Figure 8-18.
Including three additional iframes

Within our worker we will maintain a counter that will increment with each connected client. The number is posted back to the main thread that spawned that particular instance of the worker. We will then generate a random color and post it back to the same context.

```
var count=0;
onconnect = function(e) {
  count++;
  var port = e.ports[0];
  port.postMessage('Established connection: ' + count);

  var randomColor = '#'+(0x1000000+(Math.random())*0xffffff).to
String(16).substr(1,6);
  port.postMessage(randomColor);
}
```

Now, as we refresh the page we will see that the four independent spawning scripts are receiving asynchronous responses from the worker thread. Not only do the backgrounds get randomly generated, but each spawning script connects in a slightly different order each time (see Figure 8-19).

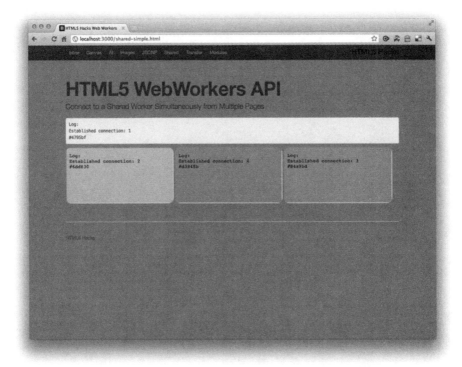

Figure 8-19.
Random background colors for each worker spawned

9

Hacking HTML5 Connectivity

The HTML5 connectivity layer is made up of perhaps the most exciting of the specifications in the HTML5 family. In this group are XHR2, the WebSocket Protocol, the Server-Sent Events feature and EventSource JavaScript API, and SPDY. Many would agree these technologies are already disrupting web application design in much the same way Ajax did in the mid-2000s.

These technologies and protocols make up the next evolution in client/server web technology.

The WebSocket Protocol creates a single, persistent TCP socket connection between a client and a server, allowing for bidirectional, full-duplex messages to be distributed without the overhead of HTTP headers and cookies. This long-awaited technology provides a solution that was formerly created through creative uses of HTTP.

Over the past decade, web application developers have crafted technologies and techniques such as Ajax, Comet, Flash sockets, HTTP streaming, BOSH, and Reverse HTTP to achieve solutions that provided real-time UI updates. In the section "Polyfill WebSocket Support with Socket.IO" (page 423) and in Hack #76, we will rehash some of those techniques as we set up a Node.js socket server that provides fallbacks for browsers that have yet to implement the WebSocket specification. While we are at it, we will also inspect the network and peer deeper into the connectivity layer by exploring the command-line interface of the **ws** module for Node.js in Hack #71, and by using the Chrome Developer Tools to inspect packets sent to and from the browser in Hack #70 and Hack #77.

At the same time, the Server-Sent Events feature and the EventSource JavaScript API are standardizing HTTP streaming. Often overshadowed by web sockets, this standard is making longstanding connections over HTTP nearly trivial. In Hack #74 you will see a Ruby implementation of HTTP streaming as multiple clients connected to an evented web server to subscribe to push notifications.

As we are already seeing in early applications that utilize web sockets today, web sockets do not make HTTP or Ajax techniques such as the **XMLHttpRequest** object obsolete, but they do complement existing technologies by providing another tool for web application developers to use when building solutions that need real-time data updates. In fact, XHR has evolved into the Level 2 specification, which we got a taste of in Hack #53.

In Hack #75 I also will introduce the evolution of cross-domain communication as we configure a server to accept requests from our web application.

In addition to support in modern web browsers such as Google Chrome and Opera, there are also now web socket implementations in Java, .NET, Ruby, PHP, JavaScript (Node.js), Objective-C, and ActionScript. We will explore some of these different implementations for a Java implementation in Hack #73, and for server-side JavaScript in Node.js in Hack #71.

We will also explore a third-party remote socket server at Pusher.com in Hack #72.

And finally, in Hack #78 we will set up a simple SPDY server in Node.js to gain a better understanding of this exciting protocol and what it has to offer.

HACK 70 Use Kaazing's Remote WebSocket Server to Echo Simple Messages from a Browser

The echo server is a web-based socket server created by Kaazing and hosted at websocket.org. It demonstrates the capabilities of the WebSocket Protocol by echoing messages sent from the browser.

> *This example is an extension of the code provided as a test of the Echo Test server on Websocket.org. The code was refactored to follow a more object-oriented approach. You can see the original example at websocket.org (http://www.websocket.org/echo.html).*

Let's open an HTML file and begin by creating a basic `WebSocketDemo` class in JavaScript. Since JavaScript isn't class-based, we will follow a very common pseudoclass pattern to manage our code. I provided the basic structure within our JavaScript tags in the following code:

```
<script language="javascript" type="text/javascript">
  WebSocketDemo = function(){
    return {
      // public methods go here.
    }
  }();
  WebSocketDemo.init("ws://echo.websocket.org/");
</script>
```

We also need to add a **div** tag with **id="output"**. This will be where we log our messages.

```
<h2>WebSocket Test</h2>
<div id="output"></div>
```

The **WebSocketDemo** class has four public methods—**init()**, **onOpen()**, **on Close()**, and **onMessage()**—and one public property, **ws**. The **ws** property will hold the instantiation of our new **WebSocket** object.

Now, let's take a look at the **init()** method.

In **WebSocketDemo.init()** we pass a URL as the only parameter. It is then passed to the instantiation of a new **WebSocket**. Notice that our URL is using the **ws://** prefix.

The WebSocket Protocol defines **ws://** for a basic web socket connection and **wss://** for a web socket secure connection. For this hack, we will stick with the basics and use the **ws://** connection.

```
WebSocketDemo = function(){
  return {
    ws: null,
    init: function(url){
      this.ws = new WebSocket(url);
    }
  }
}();
WebSocketDemo.init("ws://echo.websocket.org/");
```

Now, let's create a method called **onOpen()** to wrap our call to **send()** and to listen for the event that fires once the connection has been established:

```
WebSocketDemo = function(){

  return {
    ws: null,
    init: function(url){
      this.ws = new WebSocket(url);
      this.onOpen();
    },

    onOpen: function(){
      this.ws.onopen = function(evt) {
      console.log('CONNECTED: ' + evt.type);
      WebSocketDemo.ws.send('html5 hacks');
    };
```

```
    }
  }
}();
WebSocketDemo.init("ws://echo.websocket.org/");
```

Within the **onOpen()** method we have also included a **console.log** that will log the event type (see Figure 9-1).

Figure 9-1.
Logging the connection onOpen event

To establish a WebSocket connection, the client and server upgrade from HTTP to the WebSocket Protocol during their initial handshake. There are several handshake mechanisms, but unless you are writing server-side socket implementations, the WebSocket JavaScript API implemented in your browser will abstract these details away from you.

The handshake request is formatted as such (only the basic headers are shown):

```
GET /demo HTTP/1.1
Host: echo.websocket.org
Connection: Upgrade
Upgrade: WebSocket
Origin: null
```

Here is the handshake response (again, only the basic headers are shown):

HTML5 HACKS

```
HTTP/1.1 101 WebSocket Protocol Handshake
Upgrade: WebSocket
Connection: Upgrade
Server: Kaazing Gateway
```

Using the Google Chrome Developer Tools you can inspect this client/server interaction. Click on the Network tab and select "echo.websocket.org" on the left to see the request and response header information (see Figure 9-2).

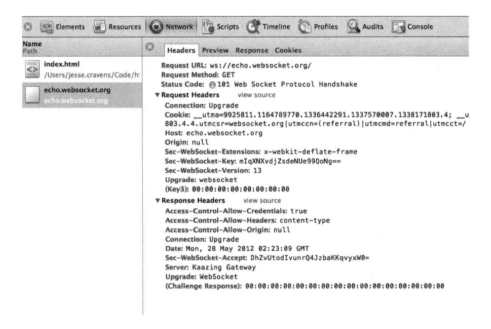

Figure 9-2.
Inspecting web socket request and response headers

You will notice in the request headers that there is a Connection: Upgrade header. You will also see that the type is indicated in the Upgrade header and the receiving host is echo.websocket.org.

HTTP1.1 included a new request header named Upgrade to provide a simple mechanism for transition from HTTP/1.1 to some other, incompatible future protocol. The client sends the Upgrade header in the request, informing the server that it would like to switch protocols. The communication is then dependent on the server to validate the switch between protocols, if it is capable or configured to do so.

In the response, we see that an Upgrade header has been returned, and the corresponding value is WebSocket. This tells the client browser that the requested upgrade type was available and the persistent connection has been opened.

Now, let's evolve our code a bit, and begin to add a few more public methods that will expose more connection events effectively demonstrating the internals of the socket communication: `onClose()` and `onMessage()`.

```
onClose: function(){
    this.ws.onclose = function(evt) {
        console.log('CLOSED: ' + ': ' + evt.type);
    };
},

onMessage: function(msg){
    this.ws.onmessage = function(evt) {
        console.log('RESPONSE: ' + ': ' + evt.data);
        WebSocketDemo.ws.close();
    };
}
}

}();
```

And in our `init()`, let's execute our new methods:

```
init: function(url){
    this.ws = new WebSocket(url);
    this.onOpen();
    this.onMessage();
    this.onClose();
},
```

Now, if we refresh the browser we should see new console logs coming from our new event methods. The send call within **onOpen()** passes the message "html5 hacks" to the remote echo server, and the server echoes a response. The **onMessage()** event logs the message and calls **onClose** (see Figure 9-3).

In the latest version of the Canary build of Chrome, we are also given a new tab in the Dev Tools that allows us to view the traffic being sent back and forth between the browser and the remote server. To take advantage of this capability, first you need to get Canary (*https://tools.google.com/dlpage/chromesxs*). Now, follow these steps:

1. Navigate to the *index.html* we just created.
2. Turn on the Chrome Developer Tools, or press Apple+Shift+I (Mac OS X) or Ctrl-Shift-I (Windows and Linux).
3. Click the Network tab, and click on Web Sockets just like we did in the earlier example.
4. Select "echo.websocket.org."

Figure 9-3.
Console logs from event methods

5. Select the WebSocket Frames tab.

The information given is very beneficial and prevents you from having to install a third-party tool:

Number
> This is a counter, to demonstrate the sequence of the messages.

Arrow
> This is the direction of the message.

Timestamp
> This is the time the message was initiated or received.

Op-code
> Op-codes are split into three categories: continuation, non-control, and control. Continuation and non-control op-codes indicate that user messages and control frames are used to configure the protocol itself: 1 represents a text message, and 8 represents a closed connection.

Length

This is the number of characters in the payload.

Contents

This is the actual data in the WebSocket payload.

Figure 9-4 shows web traffic viewed with the WebSocket Frames tab in Canary.

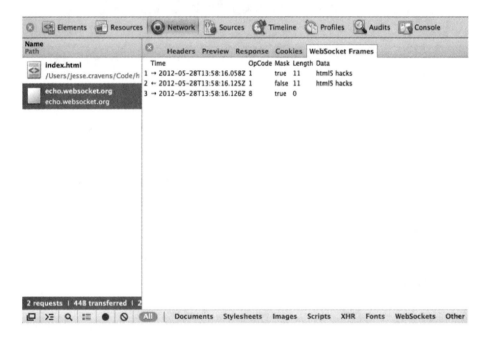

Figure 9-4.
Viewing web traffic with the WebSocket Frames tab in Canary

For clarity, let's recap the interaction:

1. The client browser instantiates a new WebSocket object and passes it a URL using the ws:// protocol.
2. The client browser then makes an HTTP request to the remote server requesting a WebSocket connection upgrade.
3. The server responds with response headers indicating a Connection: Upgrade of type Upgrade: WebSocket.
4. This fires the onopen event.
5. With the onOpen() method the client browser calls send() and passes a payload.
6. The server responds with an echo of the same payload firing the onmessage event.

HTML5 HACKS

7. The onMessage() event method logs the payload to the client console and then calls close().

8. The onClose() event method fires and logs "CLOSED" and the event type to the console.

Here is the final code in its entirety. This is just the beginning of a well-organized Java-Script WebSocket library. Take it and start your own hacks!

```html
<html>
<head>
 <meta charset="utf-8" />

 <title>WebSocket Test</title>
 <script language="javascript" type="text/javascript">

   WebSocketDemo = function(){

     return {
       ws: null,

       init: function(url){
         this.ws = new WebSocket(url);
         this.onOpen();
         this.onMessage();
         this.onClose();
       },

       doSend: function(msg){
         this.ws.send = function(evt) {
           console.log(evt.timeStamp)
         };
       },

       onOpen: function(){
         this.ws.onopen = function(evt) {
           console.log('CONNECTED: ' + evt.type);
           WebSocketDemo.ws.send('html5 hacks');
         };
       },

       onClose: function(){
         this.ws.onclose = function(evt) {
           console.log('CLOSED: ' + ': ' + evt.type);
         };
```

```
      },

      onMessage: function(msg){
        this.ws.onmessage = function(evt) {
          console.log('RESPONSE: ' + ': ' + evt.data);
          WebSocketDemo.ws.close();
        };
      }
    }

  }();

  WebSocketDemo.init("ws://echo.websocket.org/");

  </script>
  </head>

<body>
 <h2>WebSocket Test</h2>
 <div id="output"></div>
</body>
</html>
```

HACK 71   Build a Blazing-Fast WebSocket Server with Node.js and the ws Module

The Node.js ws module is an easy-to-use, blazing-fast and up-to-date web socket implementation that you can use to get web sockets up and running quickly. It also ships with wscat, a command utility that can act as a client or server.

In this hack we will explore the fastest WebSocket Server I could find. I discovered the ws module for Node.js. It just so happens that ws is not only blazing-fast, but also quite simple to set up. The simplicity of its implementation will make this hack the ideal introduction to web sockets.

The ws module is up-to-date against current HyBi protocol drafts, and can send and receive typed arrays (ArrayBuffer, Float32Array, etc.) as binary data. So although it may be simple, it's not a toy.

If you would like to get into the gory details of the WebSocket HyBi protocol, here are a couple of great resources to get you started:

- *http://tools.ietf.org/html/draft-ietf-hybi-thewebsocketprotocol-17*
- *http://updates.html5rocks.com/2011/08/What-s-different-in-the-new-WebSocket-protocol*

ws also ships with a nice command-line client called wscat, which will give us a tool for making and receiving requests without using a browser.

If you are not comfortable with the command line, this section may also help you understand some of the basics. If you have been avoiding the command line because you just haven't seen the value, maybe this will be the turning point. Being able to navigate the command line can be a super-beneficial skill to have in your tool set when troubleshooting and inspecting requests and responses over a network.

Installing Node.js

There are already mounds of great documentation on the Web for installing and running Node.js, so I won't re-create that here. A good starting point can be found on GitHub (*https://github.com/joyent/node/wiki/Installation*).

You can also just click the Install button in the middle of the screen at nodejs.org (*http://nodejs.org/*).

Using the wscat Client to Call the Kaazing Echo Server

After getting Node.js set up and installed, you should be able to open a command prompt and use the Node Package Manager (NPM) to install the ws module:

```
$ npm install -g ws
```

Since this is a socket library and command-line client, we will include the **-g** parameter to install the scripts globally. That way, we can use this library often and for many different applications (see Figure 9-5).

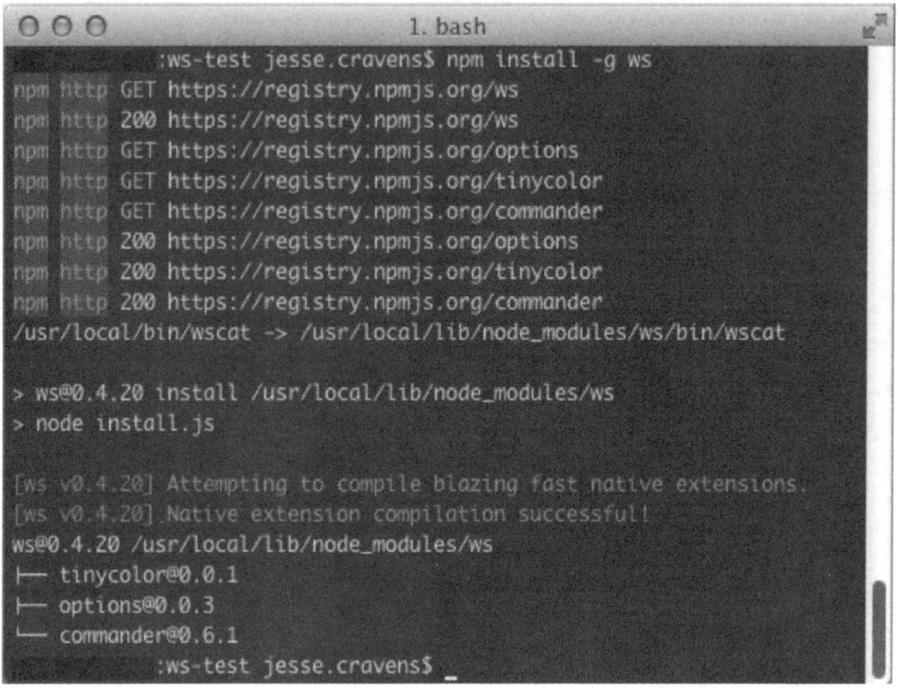

Figure 9-5.
Using the Terminal to install the Node.js ws module

Now, watch as NPM downloads and installs the **ws** module and all the necessary dependencies.

At this point we should be able to immediately use wscat to send a request to the remote echo server hosted by Kaazing (*http://echo.websocket.org*) (see Figure 9-6):

```
$ wscat -c ws://echo.websocket.org
```

There we have it. Our command-line utility is up and running. We can act like a browser and send messages to a remote web socket server.

Creating a Simple Server and Connecting to It with wscat

Now that our tools are in place, let's build our own simple socket server. Navigate to your project directory, open a file, and name it *server.js*:

```
$ cd /your-app-directory
```

```
$ touch server.js
```

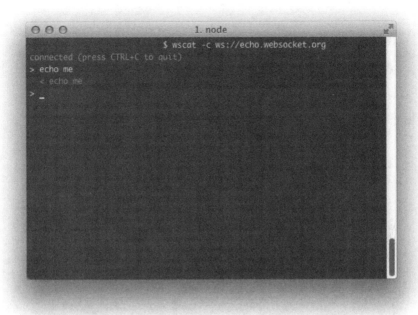

Figure 9-6.
Using the Terminal to make a request to the Kaazing echo server

Now, that was one way to create a file. You could very easily just use your own way of doing it. If you are more comfortable using your OS's GUI to access the filesystem, navigate to your empty directory, open a simple text editor, and create a file named *server.js*.

In your *server.js* file, use `require()` to include the ws library and instantiate a new `WebSocketServer` running on port 8080:

```
var WebSocketServer = require('ws').Server
  , wss = new WebSocketServer({port: 8080});
```

Now we can use the **on()** method to listen for the connection event. Once the connection event fires, the callback function is called that contains another nested function that is listening for the message event from any connected clients. We then fire the **send()** method, passing a payload with the string `'I am a message sent from a ws server'`.

```
wss.on('connection', function(ws) {
    ws.on('message', function(message) {
        console.log('received: %s', message);
```

```
    });

    ws.send('I am a message sent from a ws server');
  });
```

Now we save the file, and start the server:

```
$ node server.js
```

In another Terminal window we can use the wscat client to access our own server
running on port 8080 (see Figure 9-7). And we receive our message.

```
$ wscat -c ws://localhost:8080 -p 8
connected (press CTRL+C to quit)
< I am a message sent from a ws server
>
```

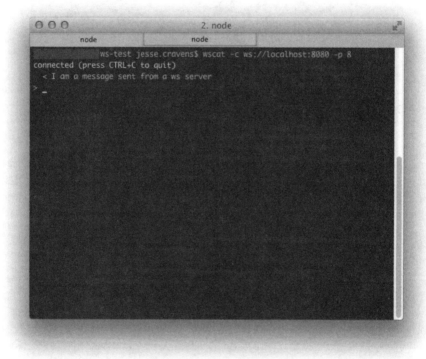

Figure 9-7.
Connecting to the ws server from a separate Terminal

And finally we can send a message back to the server by manually typing **testing** into
the command-line interface (see Figure 9-8).

HTML5 HACKS

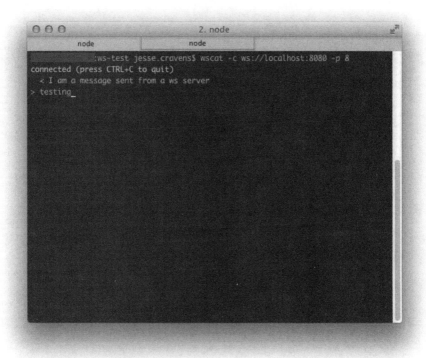

Figure 9-8.
Sending a message back to the server

Now, switch back to the other tab, where the server is running, to see the message from the client (see Figure 9-9).

The socket server is listening and logs **testing**:

```
$ node server.js
Message was received from a ws client: testing
```

Creating a Simple Client

Instead of interacting with our WebSocket Server via the wscat command-line interface, let's write a script that will handle the interaction for us. First, require the ws library and instantiate a new **WebSocket**.

Then, set up two **onevent** handlers: one for listening for the open event for the connection, and one for listening for any incoming messages. We will use the handy echo.websocket.org echo server to mirror the response with our request.

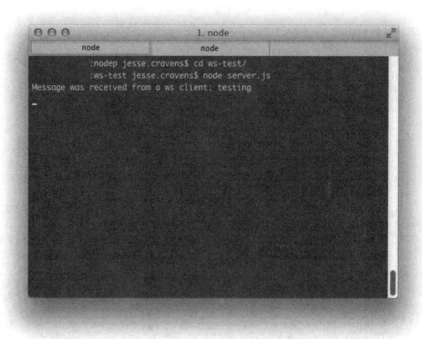

Figure 9-9.
Node.js server logging the message from the client terminal

```
var WebSocket = require('ws')
  , ws = new WebSocket('ws://echo.websocket.org');

ws.on('open', function() {
    ws.send('I am an open Event from ws client');
});

ws.on('message', function(message) {
    console.log('received: %s', message);
});
```

Let's start the client:

```
$ node client.js
received: I am an open EVENT from a ws client
```

On the open event the message `'I am an open EVENT from a ws client'` is sent to the remote echo server. The remote server then returns the message. The client is listening for messages and logs the response with `'received: I am an open EVENT from a ws client'`.

There you have it. You now have a great example of a WebSocket Server running locally, and a command-line interface to create and listen for web socket messages without a browser.

HACK 72 Build a Donation Thermometer with Web Sockets, the Pusher API, and PHP

Donation thermometers are used at a lot of charity events and donation sites, but they tend to only update when you refresh the page. It's now easier than ever to make these thermometers update in real time, the instant somebody makes a donation, by using HTML5 Web Sockets.

This hack was contributed by Phil Leggetter, a Real-Time Web Software and Technology Evangelist.

A number of real-time services and solutions are available today. For the donation thermometer we'll use Pusher, which uses HTML5 Web Sockets, to add real-time functionality to the widget. This real-time functionality will not only ensure that the donation value is instantly correct, but will also add a level of excitement which can result in a "stickiness" that keeps the user's attention.

Progressive Enhancement

Accessibility is always important, but potentially more so for charities, so it's important that the donation thermometer widget at least displays something even if JavaScript isn't enabled. Therefore, we'll progressively enhance a widget.

Applications are progressively enhanced by first defining the structure using static HTML. CSS is then applied to make the user interface more visually appealing. After that JavaScript is used to add interactive features and potentially some visual enhancements. Real-time functionality can be added in exactly the same way. For the widget we are going to do the following:

1. Generate the widget HTML on the server using PHP.
2. Stylize it using CSS.
3. Tweak the UI using JavaScript and jQuery.

4. Use Pusher to make the widget update in real time as new donations come in.

Building the Thermometer HTML

For accessibility it's good to have some textual values, so for the HTML we'll focus on that while adding some elements for the visual display.

```
<div class="thermometer-widget">

  <div class="title">Donation Thermometer</div>
  <div class="cause">A Good Cause</div>

  <div class="figures">
    <div class="goal">
      <span class="label">Our Goal</span>
      <span class="value">&pound;5,000</span>
    </div>
    <div class="current_total">
      <span class="label">Raised so far</span>
      <span class="value">&pound;3,000</span>
    </div>
  </div>

</div>
```

This creates a really simple display, as shown in Figure 9-10.

This isn't very exciting, but it displays the simple values.

Adding a Thermometer to the Widget Using CSS

The next stage in progressive enhancement is to use CSS, so we're going to add a few more elements to the HTML (in an ideal world you wouldn't add markup for styling, but we're not in that world just yet). This doesn't affect the look of the widget if CSS isn't available; it just lets us add our thermometer visualization to the display.

```
<div class="thermometer-widget">

  <div class="title">Donation Thermometer</div>
  <div class="cause">A Good Cause</div>

  <div class="figures">
    <div class="goal">
      <span class="label">Our Goal</span>
      <span class="value">&pound;5,000</span>
```

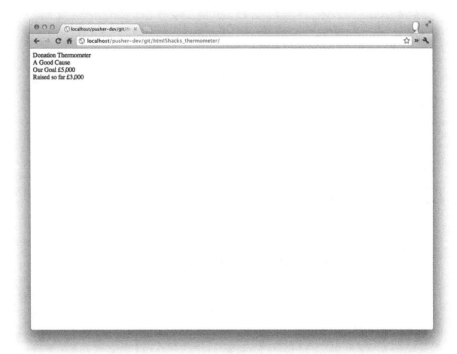

Figure 9-10.
Basic display

```
        </div>
        <div class="current_total">
          <span class="label">Raised so far</span>
          <span class="value">&pound;3,000</span>
        </div>
      </div>

      <div class="display">
        <div class="thermometer">
          <div class="top"></div>
          <div class="middle">
              <div class="value"></div>
          </div>
          <div class="base current_total">
            <div class="value">&pound;3,000</div>
          </div>
```

```
        </div>
      </div>

      </div>
```

It's worth providing a bit of information regarding the structure of the HTML:

.figures

> We saw this previously. It contains the key values for the widget.

.display

> This is the visual thermometer display.

.display .thermometer

> This has the following values:

> .base

> > This is the round bulb at the bottom of the thermometer.

> .base .value

> > This can be used to show the textual value of the funds that have been raised.

> .middle

> > This is the outer part of the thermometer neck.

> .middle .value

> > This will fill depending on the amount raised. *For the moment it has no height.*

> .top

> > This is just a curved top for the thermometer.

There's quite a lot of CSS for this, so I'm not going to include it here. You can view the raw CSS file on GitHub (*https://github.com/pusher/html5-hacks-thermometer/blob/master/styles.css*).

With the additional HTML elements and the CSS applied the widget now looks like Figure 9-11.

You may have noticed in our discussion of the HTML structure that no height has been applied to the thermometer visualization's .middle .value, so it doesn't correctly communicate the amount raised. Since we're not allowed to use JavaScript *yet*, we need to generate the height value on the server and apply the height to the element. To do this we need to work out the percentage of the goal that has been raised and then work out the height in pixels to apply to the value.

Here's an example of doing this in PHP:

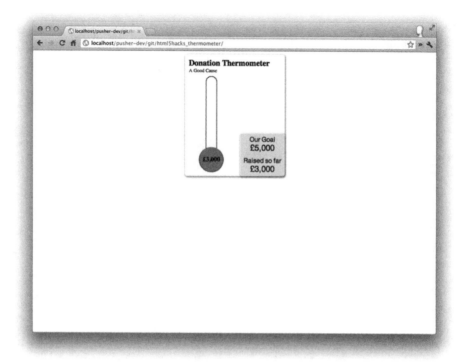

Figure 9-11.
Basic display with CSS

```php
<?php
$goal = 5000;
$current_total = 3000;
$current_percent_fraction = $current_total/$goal; // 0.6 = 60% full
$middle_height = 165;
$middle_height_value = $middle_height * $current_percent_fraction;
?>
```

When we generate the HTML we can then put an inline style on the element. The HTML will look as follows:

```
<div class="middle">
    <div class="value" style="height: 99px"></div>
</div>
```

This results in the thermometer visualization actually indicating a value, as shown in Figure 9-12.

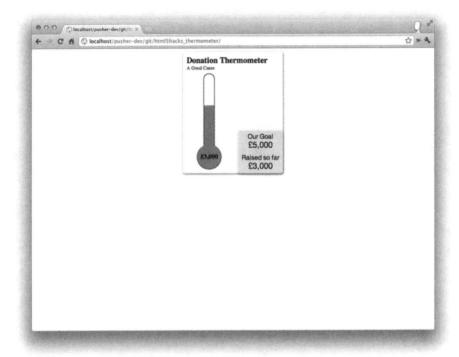

Figure 9-12.
Basic display indicating a value

Tweaking the UI with JavaScript

JavaScript was made available in web browsers so that we can enrich a web page or application. In this case we want to apply some visual effects that would otherwise result in a very large amount of HTML markup. We'll do this with the help of jQuery, so remember to include the jQuery library:

```
<script src="http://code.jquery.com/jquery-1.7.2.min.js"></script>
```

Measurement Markers

We can use JavaScript to improve the widget in a few ways. First we can improve the general look of the thermometer by adding measurement markers to the `.middle` of the thermometer. If we were to do this using HTML the markup would get very ugly, very quickly.

In the following code we reference the `.middle` and `.middle .value` and get their height. We access the charity goal amount and current total from the UI and parse out the values using the `getNumericVal` function. Using all this information, we know how many marks we are going to add to the `.middle` element. Then we add the elements that represent the marks.

There is a bit of setup here to access the elements and values and work out how many marks we need to draw. Because of this, and because we want to reuse this in the following examples, I've wrapped this up in a **setUp** function. Now we can concentrate on just improving the UI.

```
function getNumericVal(el, selector) {
  var el = el.find(selector);
  var val = el.text();
  val = parseInt(val.replace(/\D/g, ''), 10);
  return val;
}

function setUp(thermometerSelector) {
  var config = {};
  config.el = $(thermometerSelector);
  config.middleEl = config.el.find('.display .middle');
  config.middleValueEl = config.middleEl.find('.value');
  config.currentTotalEl = config.el.find('.current_total .value');
  config.numberOfMarks = parseInt(config.middleEl.height()/10, 10);
  config.goalValue = getNumericVal(config.el,
      '.figures .goal .value');
  config.currentTotalValue = getNumericVal(config.el,
      '.figures .current_total .value');
  config.pixelsPerValue = config.middleValueEl.height()/config.current
TotalValue;
  config.valuePerMark = config.goalValue/config.numberOfMarks;

  return config;
}
```

Now that we have all the elements referenced and values set up we can add the markers to the thermometer:

```
function addThermometerMarks(middleEl, numberOfMarks,
    valuePerMark) {
  for(var i = 1; i <= numberOfMarks; ++i) {
    var amount = parseInt(valuePerMark * i);
    var markEl = $('<div class="mark"></div>');
    markEl.css({'position': 'absolute', 'bottom': (i*10) + "px"});
    markEl.attr('title', '£' + amount);
```

```
            var tooltip = $('<div class="tooltip">&pound;' +
                amount + '</div>');
            markEl.append(tooltip);
            middleEl.append(markEl);
        }
    }

    $(function() {
        var config = setUp('.thermometer-widget');
        addThermometerMarks(config.middleEl, config.numberOfMarks,
    config.valuePerMark);
        });
```

It would be nicer if the markers were at more rounded values, but I'm not trying to build a real product, just show what's possible.

This results in the thermometer display shown in Figure 9-13.

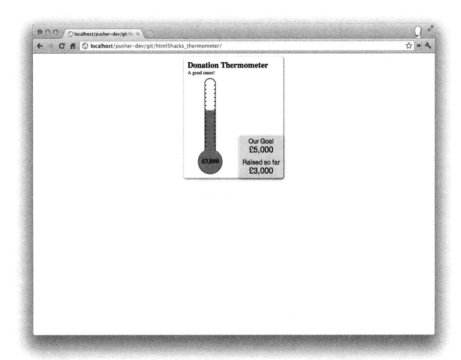

Figure 9-13.
Adding markers

HTML5 HACKS

Marker Values, Hover Highlights, and Tool Tips

The thermometer markings aren't of much use if we don't know what values they represent, so let's display the values when the user hovers over the marker elements by displaying a tool tip. We'll also add a small highlight effect. You'll see from the preceding piece of code that we already got **tooltip** elements, so now we just need to show them on hover. We do this by adding a class to the marker that changes the **display:none** style to **display:block** when the user hovers over the element with his mouse.

```
function addMarkHighlights(middleEl) {
  middleEl.find('.mark').hover(function() {
    var el = $(this);
    el.addClass('mark-selected');
  },
  function() {
    var el = $(this);
    el.removeClass('mark-selected');
  });
}

$(function() {
  var config = setUp('.thermometer-widget');
  addThermometerMarks(config.middleEl, config.numberOfMarks,
config.valuePerMark);
  addMarkHighlights(config.middleEl);
});
```

This results in the donation thermometer widget shown in Figure 9-14. [Again, check out the raw CSS (*https://github.com/pusher/html5-hacks-thermometer/blob/master/styles.css*) for full details.]

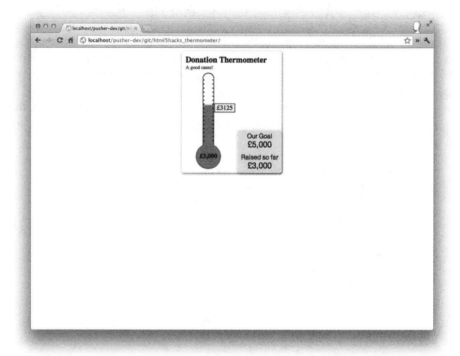

Figure 9-14.
Marker values, hover highlights, and tool tips

Animating Value Changes

The final effect that we can add is to animate the thermometer's `.middle .value` height and the textual values by increasing them from 0 to the current total.

Let's get a utility function out of the way. The following adds commas to values:

```
function addCommas(number) {
  var number = number+''; var l = number.length; var out = '';

  var n = 0;

  for (var i=(l-1);i>=0;i--) {
    out = '<span class="l">'+number.charAt(i)+'</span>'+out;
    if ((l-i)%3 == 0 && i != 0) {
        out = '<span class="lcom">,</span>'+out;
    }
    n++;
```

```
        }

        return out;
    }
```

Next, let's animate the text. This is really just a visual thing. It doesn't need to be too clever, so we'll just increment the value every 50 ms by a calculated amount. We're also going to return the `setInterval` identifier so that it can be cleared elsewhere if required.

See mozilla.org (https://developer.mozilla.org/en/DOM/window.requestAnimationFrame) for information on `requestAnimationFrame` *as an alternative to* `setInterval` *for animations.*

```
    function animateText(el, fromValue, toValue) {
        var total = fromValue;

        var interval = setInterval(function() {

            if(total < toValue) {
                // 2000ms for the animation, we update every 50ms
                total += parseInt((toValue-fromValue) / (2000/50));
                total = Math.min(total, toValue);
                el.html('&pound;' + addCommas(total));
            }
            else {
                clearInterval(interval);
            }
        }, 50);
        return interval;
    }
```

Now let's animate the thermometer visualization. This is very easy, thanks to the `jQuery.animate` function (*http://api.jquery.com/animate/*):

```
    function animateThermometer(valueEl, fromHeight, toHeight,
totalEl, totalValue, callback) {

        // animate down really quickly. If a users sees it then it
        // won't look too bad.
        valueEl.animate({'height': fromHeight + 'px'}, 'fast',
        function() {

            // animate back up slowly. Cool!
```

```
            valueEl.animate({'height': toHeight}, '2000', function() {

                totalEl.html('&pound;' + addCommas(totalValue));

                callback();
            });
        });
    }
```

Finally, let's link up all these functions and fully stylize and animate the thermometer. We'll also shift some of the comment setup calls into an **addBehaviours** function.

```
    function animateValues(valueEl, totalEl, fromValue, toValue,
goalValue, pixelsPerValue) {

        var fromHeight = pixelsPerValue*fromValue;

        var toHeight = Math.min(pixelsPerValue*toValue,
pixelsPerValue*goalValue);
        var interval = animateText(totalEl, fromValue, toValue);

        animateThermometer(valueEl, fromHeight, toHeight,
totalEl, toValue,
            function() {
                clearInterval(interval);
            });
        return interval;
    };

    function addBehaviours(config, setInitialValues) {

        setInitialValues = (setInitialValues === undefined?
true: setInitialValues);
        addThermometerMarks(config.middleEl, config.numberOfMarks,
config.valuePerMark);

        addMarkHighlights(config.middleEl);

        if(setInitialValues) {
            animateValues(config.middleValueEl, config.currentTotalEl, 0,
                    config.currentTotalValue, config.goalValue,
config.pixelsPerValue);
        }
    }
```

```
$(function() {
  var config = setUp('.thermometer-widget');
  addBehaviours(config);
});
```

If you view the widget now you'll see the values and thermometer bar animate, which is a nice little effect.

Adding Real-Time Updates

It feels like we've had to work quite hard to get this far. But the *awesome* news is that adding real-time updates to the charity thermometer widget is super-easy.

First, let's add the Pusher JavaScript library to the page:

```
<script src="http://js.pusher.com/1.12/pusher.min.js"></script>
```

We connect to Pusher by creating a new **Pusher** instance and passing in an application key (to get this you'll need to sign up for a free Pusher account). We'll also subscribe to a public **donations-channel** to which a **new_donation** event will be bound. This event will be triggered any time a new donation is made to the cause. The event itself will tell us who has donated, how much he donated, and what the new total is. The JSON for this will look as follows:

```
{
  "who": "Phil Leggetter",
  "howMuch": "20",
  "newTotal": "3020"
}
```

Now that we know this we can also create a function called **animateDonation** that calls our **animateValues** function with the updated values to display our real-time update. The code for all of this is as follows:

```
    function animateDonation( middleValueEl, currentTotalEl,
  currentTotal, newTotal, pixelsPerValue, goalValue ) {

      var newHeightPixels = parseInt(pixelsPerValue * newTotal, 10);

      return animateValues(middleValueEl, currentTotalEl,
  currentTotal, newTotal, goalValue, pixelsPerValue);
    };

    $(function() {
      var config = setUp('.thermometer-widget');
```

```
      addBehaviours(config, false);

      var pusher = new Pusher("006c79b1fe1700c6c10d");

      var channel = pusher.subscribe('donations-channel');

      var animateInterval = null;
      channel.bind('new_donation', function(data) {
        if(animateInterval) {
          clearInterval(animateInterval);
        }
        var newTotal = data.newTotal;

        var currentTotalValue = getNumericVal(config.el,
'.figures .current_total .value');

        animateInterval = animateDonation(config.middleValueEl,
config.currentTotalEl, currentTotalValue, newTotal,
config.pixelsPerValue, config.goalValue);

      });
    });
```

The `animateDonation` function returns the animation interval, which gives us the opportunity to cancel an ongoing animation if a new update comes in. This stops two animations running at the same time, where we can see some really crazy things.

We're now ready to create the code that triggers the update. We're going to use PHP, and the Pusher PHP library by Squeeks (*https://github.com/squeeks/Pusher-PHP*) for this, but it's really simple to achieve the same thing in other languages using one of the Pusher Server libraries (*http://pusher.com/docs/rest_libraries*). We're going to create a web service that allows donations to be made. It'll just consist of **who** and **how_much** parameters. We'll store this data in a MySQL database (but we won't cover the details of setting that up here) and update the running total. Here's the code for that, before we add the Pusher code:

```
<?php
  require('config.php');

  $con = mysql_connect("localhost", $db_username, $db_password);
  if (!$con)
  {
    die('Could not connect: ' . mysql_error());
  }
  mysql_select_db($db_name, $con);
```

```
$who = mysql_real_escape_string($_GET['who']);
$how_much = mysql_real_escape_string($_GET['how_much']);

if( !$who || !how_much || !is_numeric($how_much) ) {
  die('unsupported who and how_much values');
}

$running_total = 0;
$last_update = "SELECT *
FROM $db_tablename ORDER BY id DESC LIMIT 1";
$result = mysql_query($last_update);
if($result) {
  $row = mysql_fetch_array($result);
  $running_total = $row['running_total'];
}

$running_total = $running_total + $how_much;

$insert_query = "INSERT INTO $db_tablename (who, how_much,
running_total) ";
$insert_query .= sprintf( "VALUES('%s', %f, %f)", $who,
$how_much, $running_total );

$insert_result = mysql_query($insert_query);
if(!$insert_result) {
  die('insert query failed' . mysql_error());
}

mysql_close($con);
?>
```

The config.php `include` *contains the database details.*

Now let's add the real-time magic. All we have to do is to include the Pusher PHP library, create a **Pusher** instance, put the data we want to send into an array, and trigger the event by calling **$pusher->trigger()**. The variables passed into the Pusher constructor are defined in *config.php*.

```
require('Pusher.php');

$pusher = new Pusher($pusher_key, $pusher_secret, $pusher_app_id);
$channel_name = 'donations-channel';
```

```
$values = array('who' => $who, 'howMuch' => $how_much, 'newTotal' =>
$running_total);
```

```
$pusher->trigger($channel_name, 'new_donation', $values);
```

That's it! It's really that easy to trigger a real-time event. And since we've done all the hard work on the client, the real-time charity thermometer updates in real time. Because the PHP is taking values from a GET request, we can test the functionality by navigating to our PHP file, which we'll call *donate.php*, passing the required GET query string parameters:

```
donate.php?who=Phil&how_much=100
```

Here's an example of a form that would submit to the PHP file we just created. There's also some JavaScript supplied which means the form is submitted using Ajax.

```html
<form id="donate_form" action="donate.php">

  <label for="who">Name</label><input type="text" value="Anon"
name="who" /><br />

  <label for="how_much">How Much</label><input type="number"
value="100.00" name="how_much" /><br />

  <label for="reset_total">Reset?</label><input name="reset_total"
type="checkbox" value="1" />

  <input type="submit" value="Donate!" />

</form>

<script>

$(function() {
  $( '#donate_form' ).submit(function() {
    var form = $(this);
    var values = form.serialize();
    $.ajax({
      url: 'donate.php',
      data: values
    });
    return false;
  });
});

</script>
```

Summary

So, what have we achieved?

- Progressively enhanced a widget that starts its life as static, boring HTML
- Added CSS and a few extra HTML elements to turn the widget into something more visually appealing
- Used JavaScript to update the UI further by adding markers which would turn the HTML into a mess, and added animations
- Used Pusher to add real-time updates to the widget so that whenever a new donation comes in the values update

The really interesting thing is that adding the real-time components to the widget took a fraction of the time that everything else required. So, if you've already got a dynamic application, it's really simple to add a sprinkling of real-time magic to enhance that application even further and make it much more engaging.

HACK 73 Build Plug-Ins for jWebSocket

jWebSocket is a cross-platform, real-time communication framework consisting of a server and clients for stationary and mobile, web-based and native. With it you can create HTML5-based streaming and communication applications on the Web. jWeb-Socket comes with its own server implementations but also seamlessly integrates existing servers such as Tomcat, Glassfish, and Jetty.

This hack was contributed by Alexander Schulze, founder of the jWebSocket project.

In addition to the JavaScript client for browser-based real-time web applications, clients for mobile devices based on Android, iOS, Windows Phone, BlackBerry, and Java ME are available. For stationary devices jWebSocket comes with support for Java SE, C#, and Python.

jWebSocket is free and open source. One of its major benefits is that it comes with a powerful core that you can easily extend via plug-ins and web socket applications for up to hundreds of thousands of concurrent connections. SSL encryption and a message filter system provide a high level of security.

Due to the standardization of the IETF and the W3C, web sockets provide a high level of protection for your investments, and code maintainability across all modern platforms. Their use of permanent, full-duplex TCP connections instead of half-duplex HTTP connections ensures a significant increase in speed for your applications, as well as improved responsibility and higher user satisfaction.

jWebSocket is designed to build innovative HTML5-based streaming and communication applications on the Web. HTML5 Web Sockets will replace existing XHR approaches as well as Comet services with a new, flexible, and ultra-high-speed bidirectional TCP socket communication technology. Fallbacks for backward compatibility ensure that your application still works transparently, even in older environments.

jWebSocket is dedicated to applications such as online gaming, online collaboration, and real-time streaming and messaging services. It is a perfect basis for complex computation clusters, service-oriented architectures, and any kind of interface between new and already established communication technologies.

Thanks to the large number of plug-ins provided with the installation packages, jWebSocket is appropriate for covering everything from simple communication needs to complex heterogeneous real-time messaging and data synchronization solutions. The plug-ins are ready to use but also can be extended to match individual requirements.

In this hack I will show how to set up the server, use the client libraries to establish communication, and extend jWebSocket with both client-side and server-side plug-ins.

Running the jWebSocket Server

The jWebSocket Server is written entirely in Java, so it runs on almost all operating systems, including Windows, Mac OS X, and Linux. It is open source and free for download (*http://jwebsocket.org*). To get it, simply download the jWebSocket Server Package, *jWebSocketServer-<version>.zip*, from the download area of the jWebSocket website. It includes the *jWebSocketServer-<version>.jar* file, all required libraries, and *jWebSocketServer-<version>.bat* and *.sh* scripts to start the server.

Unpack the archive into a folder of your choice (e.g., */etc* for Unix/Linux, */Applica tions* for Mac OS X environments, or *c:\program files* for Windows environments). The archive contains a *jWebSocket-<version>* folder, which is the root folder for the jWebSocket Server.

The *jWebSocketServer-<version>.jar* file in the */bin* folder includes all required libraries and provides the ready-to-use folder structure. It can easily be started from the shell or command-line window without any installation or special configuration.

- For Windows: *jWebSocketServer.bat*

- For Linux: *jWebSocketServer.sh*
- For Mac OS X: *jWebSocketServer.command*

Like normal desktop applications the server is terminated when you log off the system. Thus, for production systems it is recommended that you use either the jWebSocket Service (for Windows) or the jWebSocket Web Application (for all operating systems). Appropriate scripts to install and uninstall the service are included in the installation package.

Prerequisites on the server

Since the jWebSocket Server is based on pure Java technology, please ensure that your server has the Java Runtime Environment (JRE) 1.6 or later installed and that the **JAVA_HOME** environment variable refers to the root folder of this Java installation. You should add to your **PATH** environment variable the path to the Java executable. Otherwise, you may need to adjust the provided start batch or script.

jWebSocket "Hello World" for Browsers

Creating your first jWebSocket "Hello World" client from scratch is simple. Even if your jWebSocket Server is not yet running, for your first tests you can use the jWebSocket live server at ws://jwebsocket.org:8787.

Basically, the client initiates web socket communication between it and the server. Once the connection is established the client sends messages either to the server or to other clients via the server. In the opposite direction the server sends messages to the client by using the same connection. Unless the connection is terminated either by the server or by the client, both partners can bidirectionally exchange arbitrary messages. That's almost everything you need to start your first jWebSocket project.

Embedding the jWebSocket script

The only thing you need to do to use jWebSocket in your web pages and open your site to the world of bidirectional real-time applications is to put a single script tag into the head section of your HTML code:

```
<script type="text/javascript"
src="<path_to_jWebSocket.js>/jwebsocket.js">
</script>
```

This makes jWebSocket available to your page. You can use either the full inline documented source code in *jWebSocket.js*, which is the best choice for learning jWebSocket, or the minified version in *jWebSocket_min.js* recommended for your production system.

Creating the jWebSocketClient instance

jWebSocket provides the **jWebSocketJSONClient** class within the jWebSocket-specific namespace **jws**. This class provides the methods to connect and disconnect as well as to exchange messages with the server by using the JSON protocol. The namespace avoids naming conflicts with other frameworks.

```
// jws.browserSupportsWebSockets checks if web sockets are available
// either natively, by the FlashBridge or by the ChromeFrame.
if( jws.browserSupportsWebSockets() ) {
  jWebSocketClient = new jws.jWebSocketJSONClient();
  // Optionally enable GUI controls here
} else {
  // Optionally disable GUI controls here
  var lMsg = jws.MSG_WS_NOT_SUPPORTED;
  alert( lMsg );
}
```

Connecting and Logging On

To initiate the connection from the client to the server you can use the **logon** method of the **jWebSocketClient**. This method connects to the server and passes the username and password for the authentication in one go.

```
log( "Connecting to " + lURL + " and logging in as '" + gUsername +
"'..." );
var lRes = jWebSocketClient.logon( lURL, gUsername, lPassword, {
  // OnOpen callback
  OnOpen: function( aEvent ) {
    log( "<font style='color:#888'>jWebSocket connection established.
</font>" );
  },
  // OnMessage callback
  OnMessage: function( aEvent, aToken ) {
    log( "<font style='color:#888'>jWebSocket '" + aToken.type
         + "' token received, full message: '" + aEvent.data +
"'</font>" );
  },
  // OnClose callback
  OnClose: function( aEvent ) {
    log( "<font style='color:#888'>jWebSocket connection closed.
</font>" );
  }
});
```

The server assigns a unique ID to the client so that a certain client can always be uniquely addressed even if the same user logs in at multiple browser instances.

Sending and Broadcasting Tokens

If the connection was successfully established the client sends its messages via the **send** method to another client, or broadcasts it to all connected clients by using the **broadcast** method of the **jWebSocketClient**.

```
// lMsg is a string
if( lMsg.length > 0 ) {
    var lRes = jWebSocketClient.broadcastText(
        "",    // broadcast to all clients (not limited to a certain pool)
        lMsg   // broadcast this message
    );
    if( lRes.code != 0 ) {
        // display error
    }
}
```

Sending messages is always nonblocking—that is, both the send and the broadcast do not wait until a potential result is returned. An optional result is returned asynchronously, as described next.

Processing Incoming Messages

Messages from the server to the client are pushed asynchronously. Therefore, the **jWebSocketClient** class provides the **OnMessage** event. As already shown in the **logon** method, your application simply adds a listener to this event and processes the message as desired.

```
// OnMessage callback
OnMessage: function( aEvent, aToken ) {
    log( "<font style='color:#888'>jWebSocket '" +
        aToken.type + "' token received, full message: '" +
        aEvent.data + "'</font>"
    );
}
```

You will find the full reference to the **jWebSocket** token set in the online developer guide.

Logging Off and Disconnecting

On demand, both the server and the client can terminate an existing connection. On the client side this is done by the `close` method of the `jWebSocketClient`.

```
if( jWebSocketClient ) {
  jWebSocketClient.close();
}
```

The server automatically terminates the connection after a certain period of inactivity on the line. In this case the `OnClose` event is fired, which can be handled by the corresponding callback as shown in the `logon` method earlier. The timeout can be configured and you can optionally run a keepalive or a reconnect watchdog.

Extending jWebSocket with Plug-Ins

One of the most powerful features of jWebSocket is its extensibility with plug-ins. Plug-ins extend jWebSocket Server functionality by providing methods to process incoming messages from clients, as well as other events such as client connected or client disconnected. Incoming messages are filtered by the jWebSocket filter chain and thus come with a high level of security.

Plug-ins can be loaded either programmatically by your code—especially for development purposes—or dynamically at runtime by simply referencing it in the *jWeb Socket.xml* configuration file, which is recommended for production environments or if you want to distribute your plug-ins.

Unlike WebSocket apps, plug-ins are supposed to implement general services rather than application-specific logic. The main benefit of plug-ins is that they are treated as separate, self-sufficient pieces of software which can even be distributed separately —open source or closed source—or shared across multiple applications.

Creating your first plug-in and providing its functions to your website is a simple process:

1. Create a server-side plug-in.
2. Add your plug-in to the jWebSocket Server.
3. Create a client-side plug-in (recommended to keep modules and namespaces clean).
4. Use the features of your plug-ins in your web pages.

Create a server-side plug-in

The first step to extend the functionality of the jWebSocket Server is to create a server-side plug-in. A plug-in usually is implemented as a descendant of the `TokenPlugIn` class, which is included in jWebSocket. To develop your own plug-ins it is recommended that you create them in separate packages. This will make it easier to distribute them later as single *.jar* files that can be added to each jWebSocket Server instance.

The following listing shows a simple plug-in with a single `requestServerTime` "command":

```
public class SamplePlugIn extends TokenPlugIn {

    private static Logger log = Logging.getLogger(SamplePlugIn.class);
    // if namespace changed update client plug-in accordingly!
    private static String NS_SAMPLE = JWebSocketConstants.NS_BASE +
".plugins.sample";
    private static String SAMPLE_VAR = NS_SAMPLE + ".started";

    public SamplePlugIn() {
      if (log.isDebugEnabled()) {
        log.debug("Instantiating sample plug-in...");
      }
      // specify default name space for sample plugin
      this.setNamespace(NS_SAMPLE);
    }

    @Override
    public void connectorStarted(WebSocketConnector aConnector) {
      // this method is called every time when a client
      // connected to the server
      aConnector.setVar(SAMPLE_VAR, new Date().toString());
    }

    @Override
    public void connectorStopped(WebSocketConnector aConnector,
CloseReason aCloseReason) {
      // this method is called every time when a client
      // disconnected from the server
    }

    @Override
    public void engineStarted(WebSocketEngine aEngine) {
      // this method is called when the engine has started
```

```java
        super.engineStarted(aEngine);
    }

    @Override
    public void engineStopped(WebSocketEngine aEngine) {
        // this method is called when the engine has stopped
        super.engineStopped(aEngine);
    }

    @Override
    public void processToken(PlugInResponse aResponse,
WebSocketConnector aConnector, Token aToken) {
        // get the type of the token
        // the type can be associated with a "command"
        String lType = aToken.getType();

        // get the namespace of the token
        // each plug-in should have its own unique namespace
        String lNS = aToken.getNS();

        // check if token has a type and a matching namespace
        if (lType != null && lNS != null && lNS.equals(getNamespace())) {

            // get the server time
            if (lType.equals("requestServerTime")) {
                // create the response token
                // this includes the unique token-id
                Token lResponse = createResponse(aToken);

                // add the "time" and "started" field
                lResponse.put("time", new Date().toString());
                lResponse.put("started", aConnector.getVar(SAMPLE_VAR));

                // send the response token back to the client
                sendToken(aConnector, lResponse);
            }
        }
    }

}
```

Add your plug-in to the jWebSocket Server

The following listing demonstrates how to add your new plug-in to the plug-in chain of the jWebSocket Server:

```
// start the jWebSocket server sub system
JWebSocketFactory.start( ... );

// add your plug-in to the plug-in chain of the jWebSocket Server
TokenServer lTS = (TokenServer)JWebSocketFactory.getServer("ts0");
SamplePlugIn lSP = new SamplePlugIn();
lTS.getPlugInChain().addPlugIn(lSP);
```

The JWebSocketFactory class loads and starts the jWebSocket Server, including all its required libraries, default plug-ins, and filters. First the TokenServer is obtained by its id, which is configured in the *jWebSocket.xml* configuration file. Next, the new plug-in is instantiated and added to the plug-in chain of the TokenServer. That's it; all the functions of the new plug-in are now available to clients.

Creating a Client-Side Plug-In

In general there are two ways to access the server-side plug-in. First, you can simply use the sendToken method of the *jWebSocket.js* JavaScript library and implement a listener to its OnMessage method. However, I would encourage you to provide a separate JavaScript file as a client-side plug-in to keep the module and API clean and make it easier to distribute your package later in two files (a server-side and a client-side plug-in).

The following listing shows how you can create a client jWebSocket plug-in. It provides the method requestServerTime to the JavaScript jWebSocketTokenClient—and thus to the descending jWebSocketJSONClient class as well by inheritance.

```
jws.SamplesPlugIn = {

  // namespace for shared objects plugin
  // if namespace is changed update server plug-in accordingly!
  NS: jws.NS_BASE + ".plugins.samples",

  processToken: function( aToken ) {
    // check if namespace matches
    if( aToken.ns == jws.SamplesPlugIn.NS ) {
      // here you can handle incoming tokens from the server
      // directy in the plug-in if desired.
      if( aToken.reqType == "requestServerTime" ) {
        // this is just for demo purposes
        // don't use blocking call here!
```

```
          alert( "jWebSocket Server returned: " + aToken.time );
        }
      }
    },

    requestServerTime: function( aOptions ) {
      var lRes = this.createDefaultResult();
      if( this.isConnected() ) {
        var lToken = {
          ns: jws.SamplesPlugIn.NS,
          type: "requestServerTime"
        };
        this.sendToken( lToken,  aOptions );
      } else {
        lRes.code = -1;
        lRes.localeKey = "jws.jsc.res.notConnected";
        lRes.msg = "Not connected.";
      }
      return lRes;
    }

  }

  // add the jWebSocket Samples PlugIn into the TokenClient class
  jws.oop.addPlugIn( jws.jWebSocketTokenClient, jws.SamplesPlugIn );
```

Use the plug-ins in your web pages

The final action to make the plug-in capabilities available to your application is to add
a link to your new client plug-in to your web page(s):

```
<script type="text/javascript" src="<url>/res/js/jWebSocket.js">
</script>
<script type="text/javascript" src="<url>/res/js/jwsSamplesPlugIn.js">
</script>
```

Included jWebSocket Plug-Ins

jWebSocket already comes with a huge and continuously growing set of ready-to-use
plug-ins. Table 9-1 gives a quick overview.

Table 9-1. Plug-ins included with jWebSocket

PLUG-IN	PURPOSE
API-Plug-in	Publishing WebSocket APIs, such as WSDL for Web Services
Arduino-Plug-in	Hardware remote control and monitoring with Arduino
Benchmark-Plug-in	Speed measurement and communication profiling support
Channel-Plug-in	Implementation of the Channel-based communication model
Chat-Plug-In	Support for chat rooms, group and private real-time chats
Events-Plug-in	Implementation of the Event-based communication model
Filesystem-Plug-in	Public and private folders with real-time update notifications
JCaptcha-Plug-in	Captcha support
JDBC-Plug-in	Database access, cache, synchronization and update notifications
JMX-Plug-in	WebSocket interface to the Java EE Management Extensions
JMS-Plug-in	WebSocket interface to the Java EE Messaging Services
jQuery-Plug-in	Real-time data exchange support for jQuery and jQuery Mobile
Logging-Plug-in	Debugging, server and client logging with web sockets
Mail-Plug-in	Mail support for SMTP, POP3, and IMAP via web sockets
Monitoring-Plug-in	Remote server monitoring with the Sigar Library
Reporting-Plug-in	Support for Jasper Report via web sockets
RPC-Plug-in	Remote Procedure Calls, Client-to-Server, Server-to-Client, Client-to-Client
Sencha-Plug-in	Real-time data exchange support for Sencha/Sencha Touch/ExtJS
Shared-Canvas-Plug-in	Demo for sharing an HTML5 canvas in real time; a virtual whiteboard
Shared-Objects-Plug-in	Support for real-time data synchronization between clients
SMS-Plug-in	Support for various providers to distribute SMS messages
Statistics-Plug-in	Access and user statics for WebSocket-based services
Streaming-Plug-in	Demo for realizing streaming services via web sockets
Test-Plug-in	Developer support for token, response, and error processing
Twitter-Plug-in	WebSocket interface to the Twitter streaming services
XMPP-Plug-in	WebSocket interface to the Jabber/XMPP communication services

If Java is your programming language of choice, you should now be ready to begin integrating web sockets into your applications—and if you really get excited, maybe even roll your own plug-in for jWebSocket.

Push Notifications to the Browser with Server-Sent Events

Created by Opera, Server-Sent Events standardizes Comet technologies. The standard intends to provide you with native, real-time updates through a simple JavaScript API called EventSource, which connects to servers that asynchronously push data updates to clients via HTTP streaming. Server-Sent Events uses a single, unidirectional, persistent connection between the browser and the server.

Unlike the WebSocket API, Server-Sent Events and the **EventSource** object use HTTP to enable real-time server push capabilities within your application. HTTP streaming predates the WebSocket API, and it is often referred to as Comet or server push. The exciting part here is that the Server-Sent Events API intends to standardize the Comet technique, making it trivial to implement in the browser.

What Is HTTP Streaming?

In a standard HTTP request and response between a web browser and a web server, the server will close the connection once it has finished processing the request. HTTP streaming, or Comet, differs in that the server maintains a persistent, open connection with the browser.

It is important to note that not all web servers are capable of streaming. Only evented servers such as Node.js, Tornado, and Thin are equipped to incorporate an event loop that is optimal for supporting HTTP streaming. These nonblocking servers handle persistent connections from a large number of concurrent requests very well.

A complete discussion of evented versus threaded servers is beyond the scope of this book, but that being said, in this hack I will provide a very simple evented server implementation example to get you started. I am providing simple browser-based JavaScript to connect to the server, and a server-side implementation using Ruby, Thin, and Sinatra.

For the record, this is also very easy to do with Node.js. Keep an eye on the companion Git repositories for an update in the future.

Ruby's Sinatra

The Sinatra documentation describes itself as a "DSL for quickly creating web applications in Ruby with minimal effort."

This text has focused primarily on Node.js (HTTP server) and Express.js (web application framework) to quickly generate server-side implementations for hacking out functionality. It would be a disservice to not mention Ruby, Rails, and Sinatra in the same or similar light as I have Node.js in this text.

Although learning Ruby is another learning curve, in the larger scheme of programming languages it is a less daunting curve than most. And as most die-hard Rubyists will preach, it is arguably the most elegant and fun to write of all modern programming languages.

Ruby on Rails, and its little brother Sinatra, are also great web application frameworks to start with if you are new to web application development.

Much like Node.js and Express.js, Sinatra makes building small server implementations nearly trivial. So for the context of *HTML5 Hacks*, this allows us to focus our efforts on programming in the browser.

For now, let's build a simple HTTP streaming server using Sinatra. To get started with Ruby on Rails or Sinatra, check out the great documentation available at rubyonrails.org (*http://guides.rubyonrails.org/getting_started.html*) and sinatrarb.com (*http://www.sinatrarb.com/intro*), respectively.

Alternatively, you can skip the following by creating a Git clone on the *http://github/html5hacks/chapter9* repository and following the instructions.

Building Push Notifications

Our goal in this hack is to build a simple streaming server and use the `EventSource` object to open a persistent connection from the browser. We will then push notifications from one admin browser to all the connected receivers. Sounds simple, right? Let's get started.

A Simple HTTP Streaming Server

First we will open a file and name it *stream.rb*. Then we will add the following:

```
require 'json'
require 'sinatra'
```

Next, we'll set up a public folder, and set the server to use the evented Ruby server, Thin:

```
set :public_folder, Proc.new { File.join(root, "public") }
set server: 'thin'
```

Now we need to set up two routes for serving our two pages: index and admin. We will use ERB as our templating language. The details of ERB are beyond the scope of this book, but our use is very minimal. For more on ERB go to ruby-doc.org (*http://ruby-doc.org/stdlib-1.9.3/libdoc/erb/rdoc/ERB.html*).

```
get '/' do
  erb :index
```

```
end

get '/admin' do
  erb :admin
end
```

We'd like to timestamp each notification, so here is a very simple function definition:

```
def timestamp
  Time.now.strftime("%H:%M:%S")
end
```

We also want to set up two empty arrays: one to hold the connections and the other to hold our notifications.

```
connections = []
notifications = []
```

Now, for the routes: when our browser loads its page, we have JavaScript running which will use the **EventSource** object to connect to a URL at *http://localhost:4567/ connect*. (More on **EventSource** later.)

For now, you can see the magic of the evented HTTP stream. The connection is held open until a callback is fired to close the stream.

```
get '/connect', provides: 'text/event-stream' do
  stream :keep_open do |out|
    connections << out

    #out.callback on stream close evt.
    out.callback {
      #delete the connection
      connections.delete(out)
    }
  end
end
```

Finally, any data that is posted to the **/push** route is pushed out to each connected device:

```
post '/push' do
  puts params
  #Add the timestamp to the notification
  notification = params.merge( {'timestamp' => timestamp}).to_json

  notifications << notification
```

```
  notifications.shift if notifications.length > 10
  connections.each { |out| out << "data: #{notification}\n\n"}
end
```

As I said before, you can just follow the instructions at the Git repository to pull down and build this code. Or if you have been following along, launch a Terminal, navigate to the directory where your code is, and run the following:

```
$ ruby stream.rb
```

Figure 9-15 shows the Sinatra server starting up.

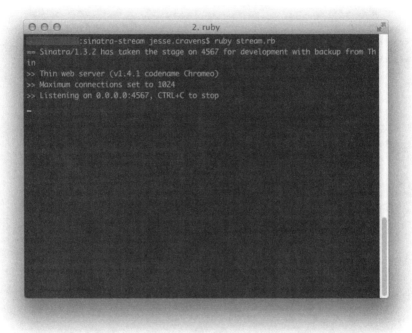

Figure 9-15.
Starting the Sinatra server

All right, now we have our Sinatra app up and running with custom routes to handle incoming requests from our browser.

If this doesn't make complete sense yet, just hang loose. In the upcoming subsections, the rest of the items will start to fall into place.

Setting Up the HTML Pages

We will be building two pages: one for the admin to push out notifications, and the other for the connected receivers to receive the notifications. Both of these "views" will share the same layout, as shown here:

```
<html>
  <head>
    <title>HTML5 Hacks - Server Sent Events</title>
    <meta charset="utf-8" />

    <script
src="http://ajax.googleapis.com/ajax/libs/jquery/1/jquery.min.js">
</script>
    <script
src="http://ajax.googleapis.com/ajax/libs/jqueryui/1/jquery-ui.js">
</script>
    <script src="jquery.notify.js" type="text/javascript"></script>
    <link rel="stylesheet" type="text/css" href="style.css">
    <link rel="stylesheet" type="text/css" href="ui.notify.css">

  </head>
  <body>
        <!-- implementaion specific here  -->
  </body>
</html>
```

The admin page will contain an `<input>` tag and a simple button:

```
<div id="wrapper">
    <input type="text" id="message" placeholder="
Enter Notification Here" /><br>
    <input type="button" id="send" data-role="button">push</input>
</div>
```

Our receiver pages will display a simple piece of text:

```
<div id="wrapper">
  <p>Don't Mind me ... Just Waiting for a Push Notification
from HTML5 Hacks.</p>
</div>
```

By launching one browser window to *http://localhost:4567/admin* we should now see our admin form (see Figure 9-16).

Figure 9-16.
The initial admin page

Navigate to *http://localhost:4567* in your browser and you should see what's shown in Figure 9-17.

Figure 9-17.
The initial index page

Adding a Bit of jQuery

We need to add a bit of JavaScript to attach an event listener to the send button. This snippet will prevent the default submission of the form and post the notification object to the server as JSON.

Notice the URL **/push** maps to the route we defined in our Sinatra app:

```
$('#send').click(function(event) {
    event.preventDefault();

    var notification = { notification: $('#notification').val()};

    $.post( '/push', notification,'json');
})
```

Now, let's open five browser windows: one admin at *http://localhost:4567/admin* and four more receivers at *http://localhost:4567* (see Figure 9-18).

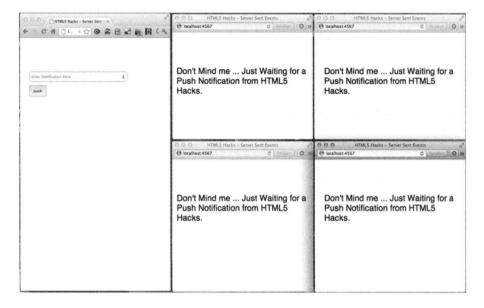

Figure 9-18.
Opening five browser windows

Looking good. Now it's time to set up our `EventSource`.

EventSource

The EventSource API is a super-simple JavaScript API for opening a connection with an HTTP stream.

Because our receiver pages are just "dumb" terminals that receive data, we have an ideal scenario for Server-Side Events. If you wanted bidirectional communication to occur, there are numerous WebSocket examples within this chapter.

Earlier, when we discussed the Sinatra app, you saw how to expose a route for the browser to connect to an HTTP stream. Well, this is where we connect!

```
var es = new EventSource('/connect');

es.onmessage = function(e) {
  var msg = $.parseJSON(event.data);

    // ... do something
}
```

Now we can add a simple notification with the available data:

```
var es = new EventSource('/connect');

es.onmessage = function(e) {
  var msg = $.parseJSON(event.data);

    // ... Notify
}
```

And here is the final script for the admin:

```
$(function() {
  $('#send').click(function(event) {
    event.preventDefault();

    var notification = {message: $('#notification').val()};

    $.post( '/push', notification,'json');
  })
});
```

Installing jQuery.notify

For our push notifications we will use Eric Hynds' great jQuery plug-in, jQuery-notify (*https://github.com/ehynds/jquery-notify*).

In order to display the notification, we'll need to include some markup on the receiver page:

```
<div id="container" style="display:none">
    <div id="basic-template">
        <a class="ui-notify-cross ui-notify-close" href="#">x</a>
        <h1>#{title}</h1>
        <p>#{text}</p>
    </div>
</div>
```

This creates a hidden **div** tag in the bottom of the document (see Figure 9-19). We are not showing the CSS that uses **"display: none"** to hide it, but you can see more by examining the source code in the companion Git repo.

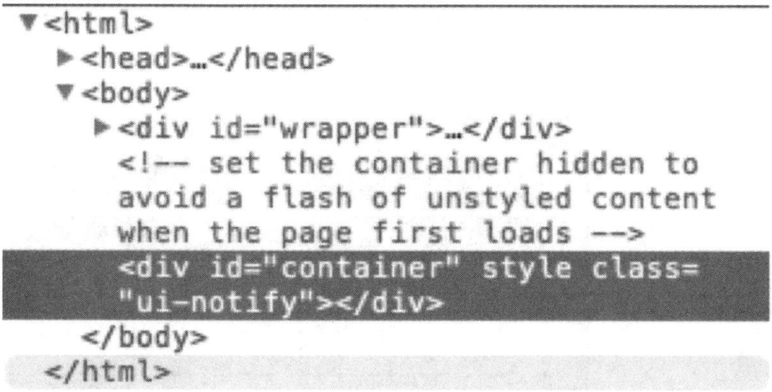

```
▼ <html>
  ▶ <head>…</head>
  ▼ <body>
    ▶ <div id="wrapper">…</div>
      <!-- set the container hidden to
      avoid a flash of unstyled content
      when the page first loads -->
      <div id="container" style class=
      "ui-notify"></div>
  </body>
</html>
```

Figure 9-19.
Hidden div tag

In order for jQuery.notify to initialize, we must first call the following:

```
$("#container").notify({
        speed: 500,
        expires: false
    });
```

Here is the final script for the receiver:

```
$(function() {

    $("#container").notify({
        speed: 500,
        expires: false
    });

    var es = new EventSource('/connect');
    es.onmessage = function(e) {

      var msg = $.parseJSON(event.data);
        $("#container").notify("create", {
            title: msg.timestamp,
            text:  msg.notification
        });
    }

})
```

It's that simple. The EventSource API is minimal and plugging it into a web framework such as Sinatra or Node.js is straightforward.

Now, as we submit notifications from the admin page, our receiver pages are updated with timestamped notifications, as shown in Figure 9-20.

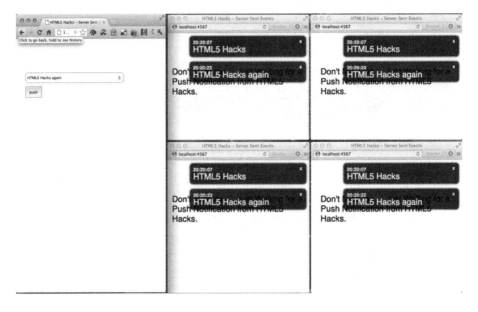

Figure 9-20.
Pushing notifications to the connected browsers

HACK 75 Configure Amazon S3 for Cross-Origin Resource Sharing to Host a Web Font

Cross-Origin Resource Sharing (CORS) is a specification that allows applications to make requests to other domains from within the browser. With CORS you have a secure and easy-to-implement approach for circumventing the browser's same origin policy.

In this hack we will explore hosting a web font on a cloud drive. In order to do so, we will learn how to configure an Amazon S3 bucket to accept requests from other domains.

If you are not already familiar with web fonts and `@font-face`, refer to Hack #12.

In the next section I provide a bit more background on Amazon S3 and the same origin policy, before we get into the details of CORS.

What Is an Amazon S3 Bucket?

Amazon S3 (Simple Storage Service) is simply a cloud drive. Files of all kinds can be stored using this service, but web application developers often use it to store static assets such as images, JavaScript files, and stylesheets.

For performance improvements, web developers like to employ Content Delivery Networks (CDNs) to serve their static files. While Amazon S3 is not a CDN in and of itself, it's easy to activate it as one by using CloudFront.

A *bucket* refers to the directory name that you choose to store your static files.

To get started let's set up an account at Amazon and navigate to the Amazon Management Console (*http://console.aws.amazon.com*); see Figure 9-21.

Figure 9-21.
S3 Management Console

If we click on Create a Bucket we should see the prompt shown in Figure 9-22.

Let's name the bucket and choose a region (see Figure 9-23). As I stated earlier, you can choose a region to optimize for latency, minimize costs, or address regulatory requirements.

We will go ahead and name our bucket none other than "html5hacks." You should now see an admin screen that shows an empty filesystem (see Figure 9-24).

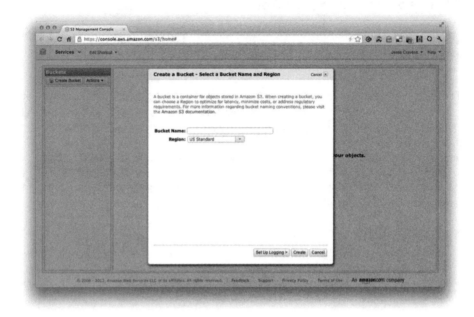

Figure 9-22.
Creating an S3 bucket in the S3 Management Console

Well, that was simple. So why are we doing this? Let's start with some simple browser security—something called the *same origin policy*.

Same Origin Policy

As the browser becomes more and more of an application platform, application developers have compelling reasons to write code that makes requests to other domains in order to interact directly with the content. Wikipedia defines same origin policy as follows:

> In computing, the same origin policy is an important security concept for a number of browser-side programming languages, such as JavaScript. The policy permits scripts running on pages originating from the same site to access each other's methods and properties with no specific restrictions, but prevents access to most methods and properties across pages on different sites.[1]

As stated in Wikipedia's definition, the same origin policy is a good thing; it protects the end user from security attacks. But it does cause some challenges for web developers.

[1] *http://en.wikipedia.org/wiki/Same_origin_policy*

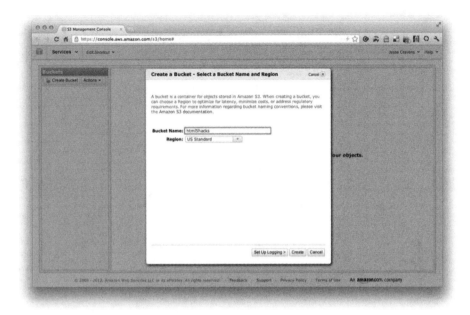

Figure 9-23.
Naming an S3 bucket in the S3 Management Console

This is where CORS comes into the picture. CORS allows developers of remote data and content to designate which domains (through a whitelist) can interact with their content.

Using Web Fonts in Your Application

There are a number of ways to use a web font within your web pages, such as calling the @font-face service, bundling the font within your application, hosting the web font in your own Amazon S3 bucket (more on this later), or converting the file to Base64 and embedding the data inline in a `data-uri`. By the way, the last technique is similar to the one outlined in `Hack #13`.

Each of these techniques has limitations.

- When calling the @font-face service you are limited to the fonts within the particular service's database.
- Bundling the font within your application does not make use of HTTP caching, so your application will continue to download the font file on every page request. Furthermore, you cannot reuse the font within other applications.

Figure 9-24.
The html5hacks S3 bucket

- Hosting the font in an Amazon S3 bucket works great, except with Firefox, which enforces the same origin policy on all resources. So the response from the remote server will be denied.
- Converting the font to Base64 adds additional weight to the stylesheet, and does not take advantage of caching.

An exploration into the different types of web fonts is beyond the scope of this hack, so I will assume that you have already selected the web font *BebasNeue.otf*.

You can download free and open fonts from sites such as dafont.com.

Uploading Your Font to Your Amazon S3 Bucket

Now, all we have to do is to upload the font onto our filesystem in the cloud (see Figure 9-25).

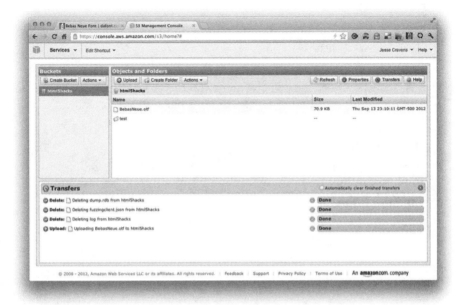

Figure 9-25.
An uploaded BebasNeue font

Adding the Web Font to Your Web Page

In order to add a web font to our page, we need to add a single stylesheet to an HTML page.

Here is our page. Let's call it *index.html*, and add a `<link>` tag pointing to our base stylesheet, *styles.css*.

```
<html>
  <head>
    <title>S3 - font</title>
    <meta charset="utf-8" />
    <link rel="stylesheet" type="text/css" href="styles.css">
  </head>
  <body>
    <h1 class="test">HTML5 Hacks</>
  </body>
</html>
```

In our *styles.css* let's add the following and point to our uploaded file. Also, let's assign the font to our H1 header via the **test** class name.

```
@font-face { font-family: BebasNeue; src:
url('https://s3.amazonaws.com/html5hacks/BebasNeue.otf'); }
```

```
.test {
  font-family: 'BebasNeue';
}
```

Now we'll open a browser and point to our newly created HTML page. In Opera (see Figure 9-26), Safari, and Chrome our header tag is being styled correctly.

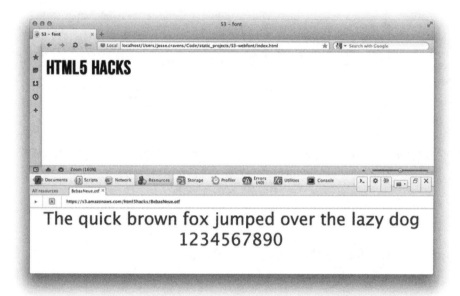

Figure 9-26.
Opera browser showing the BebasNeue font

But if we view it in Firefox, we are having issues (see Figure 9-27).

If we examine the request for our font in the Chrome Dev Tools Network tab, we will see that the response from the server is empty (see Figure 9-28).

What gives? Well, by default, Firefox will only accept links from the same domain as the host page. If we want to include fonts from different domains, we need to add an `Access-Control-Allow-Origin` header to the font.

So, if you try to serve fonts from any CDN, Firefox will not load them.

What Is CORS?

The CORS specification uses the `XMLHttpRequest` object to send and receive headers from the originating web page to a server that is properly configured in order to enable cross-site requests.

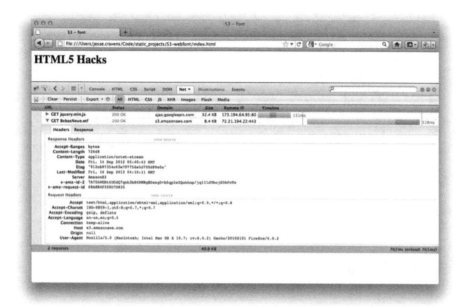

Figure 9-27.
Firefox browser failing to show the BebasNeue font

The server accepting the request must respond with the `Access-Control-Allow-Origin` header with either a wildcard (`*`) or the correct origin domain sent by the originating web page as the value. If the value is not included, the request will fail.

Furthermore, for HTTP methods other than **GET** or **POST**, such as **PUT**, a *preflight request* is necessary, in which the browser sends an HTTP **OPTIONS** request to establish a handshake with the server before accepting the **PUT** request.

Fortunately, after enough backlash from the development community, Amazon made CORS configuration available on Amazon S3 via a very simple XML configuration.

Let's get started.

Configuring CORS at Amazon S3

You should already be at your Amazon Management Console (*http://console.aws.amazon.com*). Click on Properties→Permissions→Edit CORS configuration, and you should receive a modal prompt.

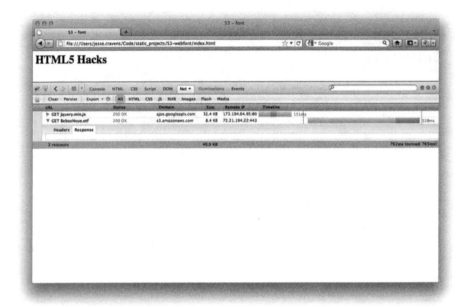

Figure 9-28.
Firefox browser showing an empty response

The configuration can accept up to 100 rule definitions, but for our web font we will only need a few. For this example we will use the wildcard, but if you are doing this in production, you should whitelist the domains to prevent others from serving your font from your S3 account on their own web pages. It wouldn't be the end of the world, but it might get costly.

The first rule allows cross-origin **GET** requests from any origin. The rule also allows all headers in a preflight **OPTIONS** request through the **Access-Control-Request-Headers** header. In response to any preflight **OPTIONS** request, Amazon S3 will return any requested headers.

The second rule allows cross-origin **GET** requests from all origins. The * wildcard character refers to all origins.

```
<CORSConfiguration>
<CORSRule>
   <AllowedOrigin>*/AllowedOrigin>
   <AllowedMethod>GET</AllowedMethod>
 </CORSRule>
</CORSConfiguration>
```

So, let's add our new configuration to our Editor and save (see Figure 9-29).

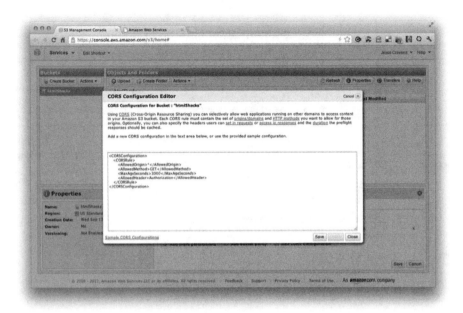

Figure 9-29.
Configuring CORS in the S3 Management Console

Now, let's return to Firefox and reload the page. We should now see the header font styled with our BebasNeue web font, as shown in Figure 9-30.

There is much more to learn about CORS, most notably, HTTP **POST** usage with certain MIME types, and sending cookies and HTTP authentication data with requests if so requested by the CORS-enabled server. So get out there and starting creating your own CORS hacks.

HACK 76 Control an HTML5 Slide Deck with Robodeck

Robodeck uses an HTML5 Sencha 2.0 mobile remote control web application to enable you to control a Deck.js HTML5 slide deck presentation via web sockets and XHR. Robodeck runs on Node.js, uses the Express.js application framework to serve the HTML, JavaScript, and CSS, and uses Socket.IO for web socket support. Robodeck also demonstrates the use of the HTML5 Geolocation APIs.

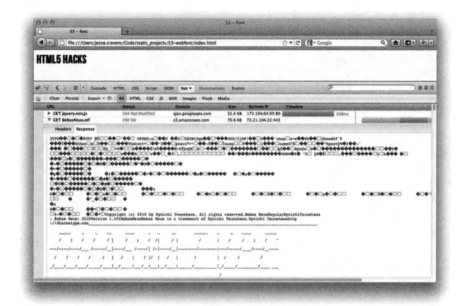

Figure 9-30.
Firefox browser successfully showing the BebasNeue font

Have you ever wanted to build a presentation using just HTML5, JavaScript, and CSS, that rivals the visual capabilities of PowerPoint and Keynote, or deliver that presentation by navigating to a URL with your web browser? How about controlling that presentation with your mobile device? Or have others log in to your presentation and make updates, such as their location, while you are presenting?

Robodeck is a culmination of HTML5 hacks, all wrapped up in one framework. It is a project hosted at GitHub, and demo'ed at Heroku (see Figure 9-31), that provides a starting point for building such presentations. This hack will walk through the creation of this framework.

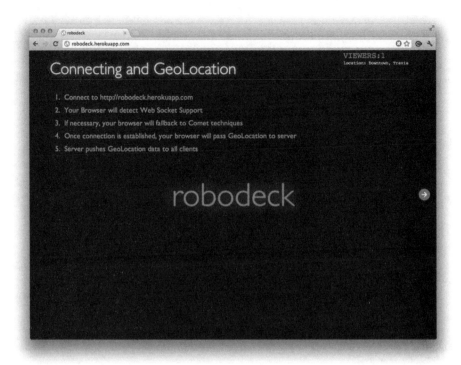

Figure 9-31.
Robodeck demo hosted at Heroku

This hack exposes you to both the server-side implementation and the client Java-Script in more detail than the previous hacks. The beauty of Node.js is that we can write and maintain our application code in one language: JavaScript. This simplicity makes Node.js the ideal implementation for getting started with web sockets.

Deck.js

Deck.js (*http://imakewebthings.com/deck.js/*) is one of many HTML5 presentation frameworks that use JavaScript and CSS3 2D/3D transitions and animations to create elegant presentations for the Web without the need for PowerPoint or Keynote. Robodeck uses Deck.js because of its powerful API, which makes it simple to advance slides and perform other actions on the deck. A more detailed look at the API is available online (*http://imakewebthings.com/deck.js/docs/*).

Let's download Deck.js to a location on our computer (see Figure 9-32), and wait until we have a basic application built before we move these files to the appropriate directory.

Figure 9-32.
Deck.js home page

Node.js and Express

We will use Node.js as our simple web server to handle requests and responses from the browser, and the Express framework to deliver the HTML and markup to the browser.

This hack assumes you already have Node.js installed. If you don't, follow the fantastic documentation already provided at nodejs.org.

To get started navigate to your *projects* directory from the command line and execute the Express application generator. For more information on generating applications with Express, see Hack #83.

```
$ cd your-projects-directory
$ express robodeck
$ cd robodeck
```

Now you can list the files in your directory with the `ls` command:

```
$ ls
Procfile      README       app.js        node_modules    package.json
    Public        routes      views
```

You should now have the files and directories necessary to build and run a simple Node.js/Express application.

First, we need to include the necessary modules in our manifest file, *package.json*:

```
{
    "name": "robodeck"
  , "version": "0.0.1"
  , "private": true
  , "dependencies": {
      "express": "2.5.8"
    , "jade": ">= 0.0.1"
    , "socket.io": "latest"
    , "useragent": "latest"
    , "googlemaps": "latest"
  }
}
```

You can see here that we have included a few modules to build this project. We have already introduced Express, but we will also use Jade as our HTML metalanguage. For more information on Jade see Hack #85.

We also include Socket.IO, which we will touch on in the next section, and Google Maps to enable a web service for doing reverse geocoding. There will be more on our geo-location implementation in an upcoming section within this hack, and the Geolocation APIs were also covered extensively in Chapter 6.

Once we have our manifest filled out, we will use the Node Package Manager to install the modules:

```
$ cd robodeck
$ npm install
$ node app.js
Express server listening on port 3000
```

And finally, we will launch a browser and navigate to *http://localhost:3000*. Figure 9-33 shows the result.

Figure 9-33.
Initial Express application

Establishing Routes

We now have the beginnings of a basic Express web application. Let's open the *app.js* file and take a look. We can see that our basic Express app is only accepting requests from one URL scheme, the root. This is why we get the basic response when we navigate to *http://localhost:3000*.

```
// Routes

app.get('/', routes.index);

app.listen(3000, function(){
  console.log("Express server listening on port %d in %s mode",
app.address().port, app.settings.env);
});
```

In order to support two separate applications, we need to accept incoming requests from two separate URLs: one for our Deck.js application which will continue to use the root URL, and another that we will create for our Sencha 2.0 mobile application. For simplicity, we will use *http://localhost:3000/x*.

We will also need to accept **XMLHttpRequest**s from our Sencha 2.0 mobile application: one from the URL *http://localhost/next* to advance the slide deck, and the other from the URL *http://localhost/prev* to slide the deck back.

Hack #84 is dedicated to the concept of building routes in Node.js. So if you want the complete lowdown on how routes work, read that particular hack. If not, you can copy the following code into your *app.js* file:

```
app.get('/', function(req, res) {
    routes.desktop(req, res);
});

app.get('/x', function(req, res) {
        routes.iphone(req, res);
});

////////// ACCEPT XHR CALLS FROM REMOTE MOBILE APP

app.get('/next', function(req, res) {
  console.log('NEXT- ' + 'server time: ' + getTime() + ',
client time: ' + req);
  send(JSON.stringify({ "cmd": 'next' }));
});

app.get('/back', function(req, res) {
  console.log('PREV ' + getTime());
  send(JSON.stringify({ "cmd": 'prev' }));
});
```

Now, we have established four independent routes for incoming requests.

In our *routes* directory we will house an *index.js* file that will contain the logic for responding to the routes:

```
exports.desktop = function(req, res){
  res.render('desktop', { layout: 'basic' });
};

exports.iphone = function(req, res){
  res.render('smartphone', { layout: 'mobile' });
};
```

Here, we have told Express where to look for the views that will build the HTML markup to return to the client browser, based on the particular route called. Notice that there are four routes, but only two layout views.

This is because two of our routes, **/next** and **/previous**, will not need to return a response in the form of HTML markup. Those routes will, in turn, generate a web socket message that will be sent only to the clients that are listening. The clients that have connected at the root URL and received the desktop view will also receive a script tag with a Socket.IO script that instructs the client to listen for incoming web socket messages. In the callback of that subscriber event handler, we will call the Deck.js APIs, which will perform the CSS transition on the slide deck.

Building Desktop and Mobile Views

So let's build out our two views.

Chapter 10 provides more information about Jade views. But for the sake of this hack, we can use the following code to create two layouts and views: one for our mobile application and the other to display our Deck.js application.

As you will recall, we designated two views in our routes: desktop and iPhone. Each view uses a different layout view as well. You can think of the layout as the container and the view as the internal markup included within the container.

First, let's take a look at the desktop view's basic layout:

```
!!!
html
  head
    title robodeck
    link(rel='stylesheet', href='/stylesheets/style.css')
    link(rel='stylesheet', href='./deck.js/core/deck.core.css')
    link(rel='stylesheet',
href='./deck.js/extensions/goto/deck.goto.css')
    link(rel='stylesheet',
href='./deck.js/extensions/hash/deck.hash.css')
    link(rel='stylesheet',
href='./deck.js/extensions/menu/deck.menu.css')

    link(rel='stylesheet',
href='./deck.js/extensions/navigation/deck.navigation.css')

    link(rel='stylesheet',
href='./deck.js/extensions/scale/deck.scale.css')
    link(rel='stylesheet',
href='./deck.js/extensions/status/deck.status.css')

    // Style theme. More available in /themes/style/ or create your own.
    link(rel='stylesheet', href='../deck.js/themes/style/neon.css')
```

```
// Transition theme.
// More available in /themes/transition/ or create your own.
link(rel='stylesheet',
href='../deck.js/themes/transition/horizontal-slide.css')

script(src='../modernizr.custom.js')
script(src='../socket.io/socket.io.js')

body.deck-container
  != body
```

You can see the inclusion of the Deck.js CSS and the Socket.IO JavaScript dependencies declared within the markup. Now we'll work on the desktop view, which will be included inside the basic layout. This is where we will begin to use the declarative markup needed to create our slides for Deck.js. You will see that each slide is indicated by using the HTML5 section tag with a CSS class attribute of **slide**.

```
// Create any number of elements with class slide within the container
section.slide
    h1 robodeck
    h2 Interactive Demo - Connecting and GeoLocation
    ol
        li Connect to http://robodeck.herokuapp.com
        li Your Browser will detect Web Socket Support
        li If necessary, your browser will fallback to Comet techniques
        li Once connection is established,
your browser will pass GeoLocation to server
        li Server pushes GeoLocation data to all clients

section.slide#remote
    h1 HTML5 Rocks
    h2 Interactive Demo - Remote Control Pub/Sub
    ol
        li We connect to the same application with a Sencha 2.0
HTML5 Mobile Web app
        li We advance the deck by publishing NEXT or PREV command
messages to the server
        li All connected clients are subscribing to the commands
        li Client JavaScript then controls the deck

section.slide#thanks
    h1 Thank You!
    ol Interactive Demo - the end.
```

This markup provides three slides. Navigate to your browser and use the right-arrow key to advance the deck to the second slide. Figure 9-34 shows the second one that includes the title "HTML5 rocks." Notice the hash tag on the URL: *http://localhost:3000/#remote* matches the `id` `remote` indicated in the second slide.

We have also included a section that will be updated once a web socket message is sent indicating the current total clients connected, and the geolocations of each of those clients (more on this later).

```
footer
div#clients
    p#viewers
    div#locationsWrapper
        p#locations
    p#tweets
```

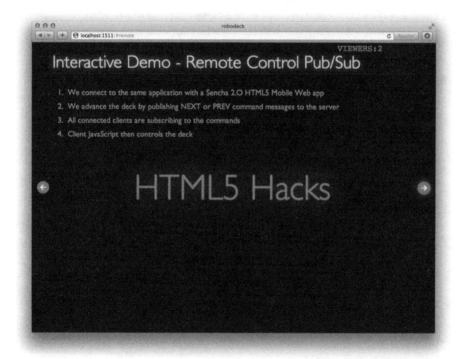

Figure 9-34.
Robodeck second slide

The Deck.js JavaScript dependencies are included in the basic.jade view toward the bottom of the page. This is for performance reasons, to ensure that the markup is loaded before the scripts begin to load and execute.

```
script(src='../jquery-1.7.min.js')
script(src='../deck.js/core/deck.core.js')
script(src='../deck.js/extensions/hash/deck.hash.js')
script(src='../deck.js/extensions/menu/deck.menu.js')
script(src='../deck.js/extensions/goto/deck.goto.js')
script(src='../deck.js/extensions/status/deck.status.js')
script(src='../deck.js/extensions/navigation/deck.navigation.js')
script(src='../deck.js/extensions/scale/deck.scale.js')
```

And finally, we will need to instantiate the Deck.js deck by calling:

```
script
    $(function() {$.deck('.slide');});
```

Now for the mobile route, we will need the mobile layout, which will contain the re-sources required to respond to requests from mobile devices. Remember, mobile devices should access the application from localhost:3000/x in order to receive the mobile-optimized application.

In the mobile layout, we will include the following markup skeleton:

```
!!!
html
  head
    title robodeck mobile
    // sencha 1.0
    // link(rel='stylesheet',
href='../javascripts/sencha/resources/css/sencha-touch.css')
    // script(src='http://maps.google.com/maps/api/js?sensor=true')
    // script(src='./javascripts/sencha/sencha-touch-debug.js')

    // sencha 2.0
    link(rel='stylesheet',
href='app/lib/touch/resources/css/sencha-touch.css',
title='senchatouch', id='senchatouch')
    link(rel='stylesheet',
href='app/css/style.css', title='android', id='android')

    script(src='app/lib/touch/sencha-touch.js')
    script(src='app/app/app.js')
    script(src='app/app/views/Viewport.js')
    script(src='app/app/views/Home.js')

    // other
    script(src='./modernizr.custom.js')
```

```
// script(src='./socket.io/socket.io.js')
```

```
body.deck-container
    != body
```

The mobile layout contains all of the Sencha 2.0 dependencies to create the HTML5 mobile web application.

The smartphone view is injected within the mobile container and is intended to be for nontablet web clients. We could also have tablet-specific views, or we could use CSS3 media queries to respond to the different viewports by configuring our markup with metadata (more on CSS3 media queries in Hack #16).

For now, we will keep it simple and return the same view to all clients accessing the localhost:3000/x URL.

Because of the way Sencha 2.0 works, nothing is needed inside the smartphone view. All of the code necessary to generate a Sencha 2.0 app is included within the Java-Script files already included in the mobile layout view. This approach differs from other similar frameworks such as jQuery Mobile, but this "JavaScript as the kernel" design is what makes Sencha 2.0 unique and popular among some JavaScript developers. We will discuss Sencha in more detail in an upcoming section.

For now, we will continue to support the empty smartphone.jade view in case we want to include some other scripts in the future, such as the Socket.IO client, or switch to jQuery Mobile.

Public Files

Just as in the web socket hacks provided earlier in this chapter, in order to achieve communication through web sockets you must maintain code on both the server and the client. You should also have a */public* directory within your application that will hold all of the static resources for your application.

To begin let's move our Deck.js JavaScript files into the */public* directory so that we can access our basic presentation from the browser. Our directory structure should now look like Figure 9-35.

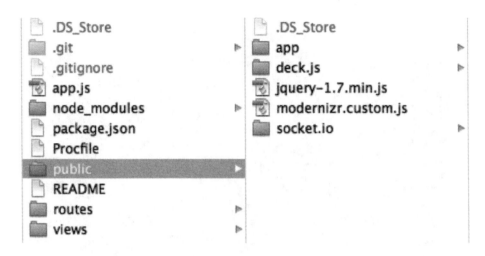

Figure 9-35.
Adding Deck.js to the public directory

Polyfill WebSocket Support with Socket.IO

Socket.IO aims to make real-time apps possible in every browser and mobile device, blurring the differences between the different transport mechanisms.

For more on polyfills, refer to this book's Preface or to Hack #55.

In order to provide real-time connectivity on every browser, Socket.IO selects the most capable transport at runtime, from among those in the following list, without it affecting the API:

- WebSocket
- Adobe Flash socket
- Ajax long polling
- Ajax multipart streaming
- Forever iFrame
- JSONP polling

Figure 9-36 shows the Socket.IO home page.

Figure 9-36.
Socket.IO home page

Fortunately the Node.js community has made it extra simple to include Socket.IO within your application and to be up and running with a web socket server in no time.

We already installed the `socket.io` module in the beginning of this hack, so now we will require it and begin to use the API.

To get started we need to open our *app.js* file and add the following before the `app.config` and `app.routes` calls:

```
// Clients is a list of users who have connected
var clients = [];

function send(message) {

  clients.forEach(function(client) {
      client.send(message);
  });
}
```

Here, we create an array of clients and a special send function that will iterate through the array of connected clients and send them a message.

Now we'll add the following **app.listen** (1511) declaration:

```
app.listen(process.env.PORT || 1511);

var sio = io.listen(app);
sio.sockets.on('connection', function(client) {

  clients.push(client);
  send(JSON.stringify({ "clients": clients.length }));

  client.on('disconnect', function () {
    var index = clients.indexOf(client.id);
    clients.splice(index, 1);
  });

});
```

Here, we begin to create our Socket.IO implementation on the server.

Notice that we are passing the **Express** app object to the **listen()** method of the Socket.IO application so that both will be listening on the same port.

We then set up an event handler to handle the client connection event. Next, we push the unique client to the **clients** array and send an initial web socket message, containing the current number of clients connected.

Also, notice that the client will be removed from the **clients** array when a disconnect event is fired, ensuring that the client total remains accurate.

This is our first web socket message, and it is used within the Deck.js desktop view to update the UI with the number of clients viewing the Deck.js presentation.

One other dependency is required for this UI update to actually work, and that is the addition of the Socket.IO library on the client side.

Adding the Socket.IO Client JavaScript to Our Views

Now, back to our */public* directory that holds all of our static resources. This is where the client-side JavaScript will live that creates the **WebSocket** object that will make the initial request to the server requesting an upgrade to the WebSocket Protocol. This client JavaScript will also establish the publish-and-subscribe system that will handle and send messages over the network.

Here we will create */socket.io* for our *socket.io* files alongside our *deck.js* files.

Let's download the *socket.io* client JavaScript files and place them in the */socket.io* directory. Our directory structure should now look like Figure 9-37.

Figure 9-37.
Adding the socket.io client JavaScript to the /public directory

Finally, let's add some JavaScript to our basic.jade view to enable Socket.IO to begin listening for messages from the server:

```
script
    var socket = io.connect();

    socket.on('message', function (data) {

        var json = JSON.parse(data);

        if (json.clients) {

            // update the DOM
            $('#viewers').text('viewers:' + json.clients);

        }

    });
```

Once a message is retrieved with a **clients** property, we access the DOM with jQuery and update the Viewers section with a current value.

You can test this functionality by opening a number of tabs within your browser, or even separate browser instances anywhere on your network that has access to localhost:3000 and access to the presentation at the root URL *http://localhost:3000*. Each instance will receive a web socket message and update all connected clients with the client total (see Figure 9-38).

Figure 9-38.
Real-time updates of client data

Adding Geolocation APIs and Reverse Geocoding with the googlemaps Module

Now that we have an application that is retrieving web socket messages, let's add additional data (the clients' longitude and latitude) by leveraging the Geolocation APIs available within your browser, and the Node.js googlemaps module to reverse-geocode the client's location based on the two-part data.

We will then send the new location returned from the Google lookup service back to the client for a dynamic update within the browser.

First let's add the necessary code to the client. Within our *basic.jade* file, we will use the Geolocation APIs available in the browser to prompt the user for access to her location. All browsers have slightly different prompts; in Safari the prompt looks like Figure 9-39.

Figure 9-39.
Apple Safari requesting geolocation

For more details and code snippets see Hack #59.

Setup for Mobile and Install of Sencha 2.0

Sencha Touch 2 is a high-performance HTML5 mobile application framework that enables developers to build fast and impressive apps that work on all mobile web browsers. For the purposes of this hack, we have chosen the framework for this very reason. Just as we chose Socket.IO for its cross-platform, real-time communication support, we also want our mobile remote control application to be able to run on as many devices as possible.

Communicating from the Remote Control

As our final piece of functionality, we need the ability to advance our slide deck by sending one-way requests in the background over **XMLHttpRequest** from our client applications connected at *http://localhost:3000/x*. To do this we want to utilize the Sencha 2.0 HTML5 mobile web application framework.

Our UI will contain a Forward button and a Back button (see Figure 9-40).

Figure 9-40.
Robodeck mobile built with Sencha 2.0

In the views section you saw that we included all the dependencies necessary to build a Sencha 2.0 application. In order for those links to access the correct files we need to download Sencha 2.0 (*http://www.sencha.com/products/architect/download/*) and install the files in the */public* directory. Our */public* directory will now look like Figure 9-41.

Figure 9-41.
Adding Sencha 2.0 to the /public directory

Now we will only need to update two files from within Sencha's app directory to use Sencha's declarative syntax for building applications.

First we will open the *app.js* file located in the *app/app* directory and create a new **Ext.regApplication**. Now we'll define the namespace in the **name** property and use the **launch** method to declare the entry point to the application.

```
Ext.regApplication({
    name: 'robodeck',
    launch: function() {
        this.views.Viewport = new this.views.Viewport();
    }
});
```

Let's open the *Viewport.js* file located in the *app/app/views* directory and configure the viewport. All of this should be fairly straightforward; for detailed information refer to the Sencha documentation (*http://docs.sencha.com/touch/2-0/*).

The key declaration to notice is the creation of the **Ext.TabPanel** called **Viewport**:

```
robodeck.views.Viewport = Ext.extend(Ext.TabPanel, {
    fullscreen: true,
    layout: 'card',
```

```
tabBar: new Ext.TabBar({
    dock: 'bottom',
    ui: 'dark',
    layout: {
        pack: 'center'
    }
}),

initComponent: function() {
    //put instances of cards into app.views namespace
    Ext.apply(robodeck.views, {
      Home: new robodeck.views.Home(),
    });
    //put instances of cards into viewport
    Ext.apply(this, {
      items: [
            robodeck.views.Home
        ]
    });
    robodeck.views.Viewport.superclass.initComponent.apply
(this, arguments);
    }
});
```

Finally, in the *app/app/views* directory, we'll open *Home.js*, where we will define our own custom xhr() function and call it from within the click handler of our two custom buttons, Forward and Back.

```
var server = 'http://' + document.location.host;

function xhr(url) {
  var request = new window.XMLHttpRequest();
  request.open('GET', url, true);
  request.send();
}

robodeck.views.Home = Ext.extend(Ext.Panel, {

  ...

  items: [
    {
      xtype: 'button',
      text: 'Forward',
        handler: function(){
```

```
                console.log('pressed -- Next');
                xhr(server + '/next');
        }
    },
    {
        xtype: 'button',
        text: 'Back',
            handler: function(){
                console.log('pressed -- Back');
                xhr(server + '/back');
        }
    }
    ],
    ...
});
```

And that's really all we need to send **XMLHttpRequest**s at the click of a button within our Sencha 2 mobile application.

Finally, remember the routes we set up in the beginning of this hack to accept the requests to the URLs *http://localhost:3000/next* and *http://localhost:3000/back*? Now we can make use of them. Once the request is received, we trigger a web socket **send()** method:

```
app.get('/next', function(req, res) {
  send(JSON.stringify({ "cmd": 'next' }));
});

app.get('/back', function(req, res) {
  send(JSON.stringify({ "cmd": 'prev' }));
});
```

In our connected clients we listen for the message, and if it has a **cmd** property we dynamically call that command from the **$.deck** object:

```
socket.on('message', function (data) {
    var json = JSON.parse(data);
    ...
    if (json.cmd) {
        console.log('cmd: ' + json.cmd);
        console.log("CMD MESSAGE");

        // call deck.js api
```

```
        $.deck(json.cmd)
    }
    ...
});
```

All connected clients should see the move forward and backward, given the button clicks of the mobile remote application.

HACK 77 Inspect a Socket.IO Connection to Determine If It Is Native or Emulated

Chrome Developer tools can help with debugging network traffic. You can also disable web sockets to demonstrate the power of Socket.IO polyfills.

In this hack we'll investigate the power of Socket.IO. Earlier, I explained that Socket.IO provides the ability to polyfill socket support for browsers that don't have a socket implementation enabled yet. In previous hacks we used the Chrome Developer Tools to inspect WebSocket information.

One way to test the ability of Socket.IO to fall back to another mechanism is to go into the Chrome Dev Tools console and enter `WebSocket = undefined` (see Figure 9-42).

Figure 9-42.
Turning off WebSocket support in Chrome

Then, if you click in the Network tab, you'll notice that the browser has closed the WebSocket connection and fallen back to XHR-polling. You will see HTTP requests being sent on regular intervals to check for any updates (see Figure 9-43).

HACK 78 Build a Simple SPDY Server with node-spdy

SPDY is a protocol created and used by Google to reduce web page load time. It doesn't replace HTTP; rather, you can use it to compress and simplify HTTP requests.

Let's start this hack with a disclaimer: this hack will be short and simple. An exploration of SPDY is simply too large for this book. Besides, we have already exceeded 400 pages!

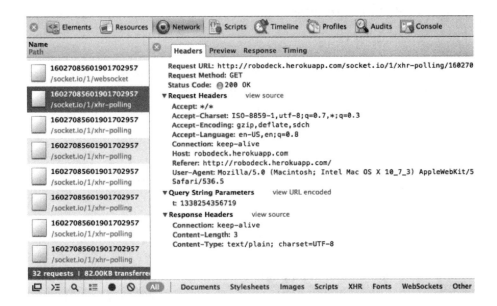

Figure 9-43.
XHR-polling polyfill from Socket.IO

That being said, SPDY is too important to the future of web technologies and the HTML5 connectivity layer to not be mentioned.

So, the goal of this hack will be to get you up and running with the very basics of SDPY, and add another tool to your tool belt.

node-spdy

To serve up our simple SPDY implementation we will default to Node.js as we often have throughout this text. We will make use of Fedor Indutny's node-spdy.

You can pull down the hello_world example from GitHub (*https://github.com/indutny/ node-spdy/tree/master/examples/hello_world*).

Let's go ahead and `git clone` the entire directory, and then navigate to the hello_world example:

```
$ cd your-code-directory
```

```
$ git clone git://github.com/indutny/node-spdy.git
```

Now we'll navigate into the directory and run `npm install`:

```
$ cd node-spdy
$ npm install
```

Now we can start our SPDY server:

```
$ node app.js
```

We are up and running on port 3232.

Let's navigate to *https://localhost:3232/*, and we should see "Hello World" (see Figure 9-44). Be sure to include the "https://" in the URL, or your request will not be accepted.

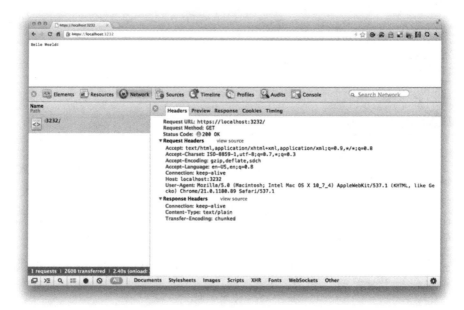

Figure 9-44.
Simple "Hello World" from node-spdy

We made a simple request, and the server responded with "Hello World." You are not going to see a major improvement to your response because it is just too simple.

SPDY shines when you use it with applications that make a large number of connections and transfer significant amounts of data. The string "Hello World" hardly falls into that category of applications.

What's Next?

Well, that's it. I warned you in the disclaimer. This should be enough to get you started. Try adding some logic that creates an abnormal number of requests or passes large payloads. Hook up a performance tool and see if you can tell the difference. Stay tuned in the html5hacks.com/blog for updates on SPDY.

10

Pro HTML5 Application Hacks with Node.js

Up to this point, this book has provided a sample collection of hacks that cover a large portion of the HTML5 feature suite. But what about building professional HTML5 applications?

As you can see in the latter chapters of the book, some of the HTML5 specifications are advancing the technologies at the connectivity layer. In order to begin creating hacks that examine those specifications, we need to employ a web server. We also want to be able to write our markup quickly and deploy our changes easily. The Node.js tool set makes these concepts simple and easy to learn. Node.js is also written in JavaScript, so we can use the same programming language in both the browsers and the server.

It is certainly arguable that other programming languages and web frameworks, such as PHP and Ruby on Rails, provide similar environments, but for the purposes of creating "quick and dirty" hacks to exercise new HTML5 APIs, there is no better choice than Node.js.

The hacks in this chapter will guide you all the way through to having an HTML5 boilerplate starter app that can be easily deployed to a remote server. If you so desire, you can even skip ahead to the final hack and download a starter kit for building professional HTML5 applications in Node.js.

HTML5 Application Design Considerations

In addition to providing hacks that teach you the basics of using these cutting-edge tools, this chapter will also touch on some of the most common modern HTML5 application design challenges presented to developers today, including considerations for the mobile web, client-side performance optimizations, cross-browser compatibility, and DRYing (Don't Repeat Yourself) up your code base.

Why Node.js?

First, let's start with one of the most hyped technologies of late, Node.js. We didn't select this server for the hype surrounding it. We selected it for the following key reasons:

- Node.js provides an HTTP server, so we can serve files.
- Node.js also exposes a JavaScript API, so we can use the same programming language on the server and client to build applications.
- There are a number of tools that make deployment of Node.js apps simple and fast. Since our goal is to create hacks, we will leverage as many of these tools as possible.

Installation

I won't go into great detail on how to install Node.js. For a local setup, just go to *http://nodejs.org/#download* to download an installer.

If you want to install via a package manager go to *https://github.com/joyent/node/wiki/Installing-Node.js-via-package-manager*.

The official documentation for installation, given the specifics of your local environment, is available at *https://github.com/joyent/node/wiki/Installation*.

Once you have installed Node.js, open a terminal and check your installation.

Installing on Mac OS X via Homebrew

If you are using a Mac, perhaps the easiest way to get up and running quickly is to install via Homebrew (*http://mxcl.github.com/homebrew/*). Once you have Homebrew, installation is as simple as running the following:

```
brew install node

user$ node -v
v0.4.7
```

HACK 79 Deliver "Hello Html5" to the Browser

With this classic "Hello World" hack you'll be able to use Node.js to handle requests from browsers and respond with content.

Let's get a handle on our first HTTP request and response with Node.js. We'll start as simple as possible: we'll use the example "Hello World" application from nodejs.org.

To get started, we only need to navigate to an empty directory within our filesystem and create an empty file, such as *server.js*.

We'll add the following to the file:

```
var http = require('http');
http.createServer(function (req, res) {
 res.writeHead(200, {'Content-Type': 'text/plain'});
 res.end('Hello Html5\n');
}).listen(1337, "127.0.0.1");

console.log('Server running at http://127.0.0.1:1337/');
```

Now we can execute the code with the file by running the following from the command line:

```
$node server.js
```

Let's walk through what is going on here. At the top of the file there is a **require** method which is part of Node.js's Dependency Module Management System that follows the CommonJS specification. Once the HTTP module is included, we can call **http.createServer()** and pass it a function that accepts a **request** and a **re sponse** object as parameters. Each object has its own set of methods and properties. Later, we will examine them a little more closely by logging both the request and the response to the console.

```
http.createServer(function (req, res) {
 res.writeHead(200, {'Content-Type': 'text/plain'});
 res.end('Hello Html5\n');
}).listen(1337, "127.0.0.1");
```

Here you can see that **writeHead()** is used to return a response code and write the contents to a buffer, along with the object that contains the response headers. The **end()** method then accepts a string.

The last item to notice here is the **listen()** method chained onto the end of **crea teServer()**. Once **createServer()** has completed and returned, the next method in the stack is **listen()**, which is passed to the port number to listen on. The **crea teServer()** method returns an object that inherits the **http.Server** prototype.

Those are the basics of setting up and running a Node.js server.

Before we print out our request, let's turn off the logging of the additional request for *favicon.ico*, so the console doesn't print the two requests made from the browser. This will make our logs slightly easier to read.

```
var http = require('http');
http.createServer(function (req, res) {
```

```
// control for favicon

if (req.url === '/favicon.ico') {
  res.writeHead(200, {'Content-Type': 'image/x-icon'} );
  res.end();
  console.log('favicon requested');
  return;
}
else {
  console.log('REQUEST: ' + req);
  console.log(req);
  res.writeHead(200, {'Content-Type': 'text/plain'});
  res.end('Hello Html5\n');
}

}).listen(1337, "127.0.0.1");

console.log('Server running at http://127.0.0.1:1337/');
```

In this hack, we are interested in understanding the very basics of HTTP and how Node.js helps us build web applications quickly and easily.

We will begin by examining the HTTP **request** and **response** objects. To simplify, think of the request as an input and the response as an output.

The server and the HTTP module will process the incoming request, and return a response based on all the parameters and information included in the incoming request.

Here is the **request** object:

```
{ socket:
  { fd: 8
  , type: 'tcp4'
  , secure: false
  , _readWatcher: { callback: [Function], socket: [Object] }
  , readable: true
  , _writeQueue: []
  , _writeQueueEncoding: []
  , _writeQueueFD: []
  , _writeWatcher: { socket: [Circular],
callback: [Function: _doFlush] }
  , writable: true
  , _writeImpl: [Function]
  , _readImpl: [Function]
```

```
, _shutdownImpl: [Function]
, remoteAddress: '127.0.0.1'
, remotePort: 50722
, server:
  { connections: 2
  , paused: false
  , pauseTimeout: 1000
  , watcher: [Object]
  , _events: [Object]
  , type: 'tcp4'
  , fd: 6
  }
, _outgoing: [ [Object] ]
, __destroyOnDrain: false
, ondrain: [Function]
, _idleTimeout: 120000
, _idleNext:
  { fd: 9
  , type: 'tcp4'
  , secure: false
  , _readWatcher: [Object]
  , readable: true
  , _writeQueue: []
  , _writeQueueEncoding: []
  , _writeQueueFD: []
  , _writeWatcher: [Object]
  , writable: true
  , _writeImpl: [Function]
  , _readImpl: [Function]
  , _shutdownImpl: [Function]
  , remoteAddress: '127.0.0.1'
  , remotePort: 50726
  , server: [Circular]
  , _outgoing: []
  , __destroyOnDrain: false
  , ondrain: [Function]
  , _idleTimeout: 120000
  , _idleNext: [Object]
  , _idlePrev: [Circular]
  , _idleStart: Fri, 10 Feb 2012 05:46:34 GMT
  , _events: [Object]
  , ondata: [Function]
  , onend: [Function]
  , _onOutgoingSent: [Function]
```

```
    }
  , _idlePrev: [Circular]
  , _idleStart: Fri, 10 Feb 2012 05:46:34 GMT
  , _events:
    { timeout: [Function]
    , error: [Function]
    , close: [Function]
    }
  , ondata: [Function]
  , onend: [Function]
  , _onOutgoingSent: [Function]
  }
, connection: [Circular]
, httpVersion: '1.1'
, headers:
  { host: 'localhost:1337'
  , connection: 'keep-alive'
  , 'cache-control': 'max-age=0'
  , 'user-agent': 'Mozilla/5.0 (Macintosh; Intel Mac OS X ...'
  , accept: 'text/html,application/xhtml+xml,...'
  , 'accept-encoding': 'gzip,deflate,sdch'
  , 'accept-language': 'en-US,en;q=0.8'
  , 'accept-charset': 'ISO-8859-1,utf-8;q=0.7,*;q=0.3'
  }
, url: '/'
, method: 'GET'
, statusCode: null
, client: [Circular]
, httpVersionMajor: 1
, httpVersionMinor: 1
, upgrade: false
}
```

A Little Background on HTTP[1]

When the Node.js HTTP server module accepts a request from a client such as your browser, it creates a new object to hold all the information. If you look into the object you will see a number of important properties: URL, methods, and headers.

---

[1] "The Hypertext Transfer Protocol (HTTP) is an application protocol for distributed, collaborative, hypermedia information systems.[1] HTTP is the foundation of data communication for the World Wide Web." (Wikipedia (*http://en.wikipedia.org/wiki/Hypertext_Transfer_Protocol*))

Understanding these three properties will get you started in understanding the basics of HTTP and web servers.

URL

A Uniform Resource Locator (URL) is a reference to a resource available on the Internet. You can think of it as an address to documents and other resources.

The first part of the URL (or the text before **://**) is the protocol identifier. It tells the client (most often a web browser) which protocol to connect with. In this particular case, HTTP is the protocol (http://). The next part is the resource name (or the text after **://**), which contains an IP address or a domain name.

A URL is one type of Uniform Resource Identifier (URI); it is a more general term associated with numerous types of addresses that refer to objects on the Internet.

Methods

HTTP defines methods (sometimes referred to as *verbs*) to indicate the desired action to be performed on the identified resource. What this resource represents, whether preexisting data or data that is generated dynamically, depends on the implementation of the server.

In this example, the connecting browser uses the `GET` method to request a string of text that contains "Hello Html5."

Headers

HTTP headers make up the parameters passed as a message in an HTTP transaction. The message is made up of a group of fields, which are formatted in a colon-separated associative array. The data format is a string, which makes the data easy to view and debug.

Another property that is of interest to HTML5 is the `upgrade` property. As mentioned in Hack #76, you will see that we make requests using the `Upgrade` method.

In this example, the `upgrade` property is set to `false`. As I mentioned earlier, the creators of HTTP were forward-thinking enough to build in a way for the browser to request an upgrade to a different protocol. This is the handshake mechanism for WebSocket.

If you would like to examine the object further, read the official API documentation of the `request` object (*http://nodejs.org/api/http.html#http_class_http_serverrequest*).

And now, let's print out our `response` object to the console:

```
var http = require('http');
http.createServer(function (req, res) {

console.log('RESPONSE: ' + res);
console.log(res);

}).listen(1337, "127.0.0.1");

console.log('Server running at http://127.0.0.1:1337/');
```

Once the server has processed all the information included in the request, and has run through the logic included within the web framework, it creates a **response** object.

Here is the **response** object:

```
{ socket:
  { fd: 9
  , type: 'tcp4'
  , secure: false
  , _readWatcher: { socket: [Object], callback: [Function] }
  , readable: true
  , _writeQueue: []
  , _writeQueueEncoding: []
  , _writeQueueFD: []
  , _writeWatcher: { callback: [Function: _doFlush],
socket: [Circular] }
  , writable: true
  , _writeImpl: [Function]
  , _readImpl: [Function]
  , _shutdownImpl: [Function]
  , remoteAddress: '127.0.0.1'
  , remotePort: 50807
  , server:
    { connections: 2
    , paused: false
    , pauseTimeout: 1000
    , watcher: [Object]
    , _events: [Object]
    , type: 'tcp4'
    , fd: 6
    }
  , _outgoing: [ [Circular] ]
  , __destroyOnDrain: false
  , ondrain: [Function]
  , _idleTimeout: 120000
  , _idleNext:
```

```
    { fd: 8
    , type: 'tcp4'
    , secure: false
    , _readWatcher: [Object]
    , readable: false
    , _writeQueue: []
    , _writeQueueEncoding: []
    , _writeQueueFD: []
    , _writeWatcher: [Object]
    , writable: true
    , _writeImpl: [Function]
    , _readImpl: [Function]
    , _shutdownImpl: [Function]
    , remoteAddress: '127.0.0.1'
    , remotePort: 50805
    , server: [Circular]
    , _outgoing: [Object]
    , __destroyOnDrain: false
    , ondrain: [Function]
    , _idleTimeout: 120000
    , _idleNext: [Object]
    , _idlePrev: [Circular]
    , _idleStart: Fri, 10 Feb 2012 06:07:08 GMT
    , _events: [Object]
    , ondata: [Function]
    , onend: [Function]
    , _onOutgoingSent: [Function]
    }
  , _idlePrev: [Circular]
  , _idleStart: Fri, 10 Feb 2012 06:07:35 GMT
  , _events:
    { timeout: [Function]
    , error: [Function]
    , close: [Function]
    }
  , ondata: [Function]
  , onend: [Function]
  , _onOutgoingSent: [Function]
  }
, connection: [Circular]
, output: []
, outputEncodings: []
, _last: false
, chunkedEncoding: false
```

```
, shouldKeepAlive: true
, useChunkedEncodingByDefault: true
, _hasBody: true
, finished: false
}
```

If you would like to examine the object further, read the official API documentation of the `response` object (*http://nodejs.org/api/http.html#http_class_http_serverresponse*) at.

The request and response are held in memory as JavaScript objects. In Hack #80 and Hack #81 we will do some hacking on these objects.

HACK 80 Detect the User Agent String Within the Request Object

You can interrogate the HTTP `request` object to find valuable information about the client user agent.

As you can see, quite a few properties are included in Node.js's `request` and `re sponse` objects. In Hack #79 we explored a few of them. Here, we will focus on the request headers and extract the user agent string in order to determine the type of client device that originated the request.

User agent sniffing is a common practice, especially with the recent explosion in the use of the mobile web and the fragmentation of mobile web browsers. So this is a very relevant hack when building HTML5 web applications.

Sometimes it is necessary for application developers to know the type of client device that is making a request for data. If the data is available after parsing the user agent headers, the application can then query a lookup web service that contains detailed properties about the particular device. Properties such as screen size, camera access, and hardware acceleration, just to name a few, can then be used to build conditional logic around which assets and markup are returned to the client.

It has long been considered a bad practice to sniff user agents from within browser JavaScript, so this makes this design decision a controversial one among developers. Although server-side device detection or user agent sniffing is a somewhat common practice, many frontend developers see it as an unnecessary practice. The continued maturity of client-side JavaScript frameworks and native browser APIs is quickly changing the design of many mobile-ready web applications. Concepts such as responsive web design (that makes use of CSS3 media queries and object detection) have made it possible to alter content using JavaScript and CSS3 within the browser without the server needing to be aware of the type of client that has made the request.

In most cases, a balanced approach is most optimal, allowing both the server and the client to provide the functionality they do best.

For now, we will start simple by hacking a user agent string from the node `request` object and then demonstrate that we can make logical decisions based on simple device data in our `response` object.

Within our main *server.js* file, we will add a very basic user agent parsing script. From within the code block where we `console.log` the `request` object, we can pull out the user agent property from the request headers. Also, let's create a global object called `DeviceData` to namespace our data.

```
var ua = req.headers['user-agent'],
DeviceData = {};
```

Now that we have the user agent string, we can use regular expressions to parse it for information pertinent to our goal.

First, we can test for `mobile` within the string and set the `mobile` property of `DeviceData` to `true`:

```
// Mobile?
if (/mobile/i.test(ua))
  DeviceData.mobile = true;
```

While we are at it, let's test for Apple products:

```
// Apple device?
if (/like Mac OS X/.test(ua)) {
  DeviceData.iOS = /CPU( iPhone)? OS ([0-9\._]+) like Mac OS
X/.exec(ua)[2].replace(/_/g, '.');
  DeviceData.iPhone = /iPhone/.test(ua);
  DeviceData.iPad = /iPad/.test(ua);
}
```

We now have the basics of device detection. Obviously, this is a simplified example of a production-ready system. In a production system, the application would most likely pass the user agent string to another application that fronts a database, or to a third-party web service. The application or web service could then look up information, log errors, collect analytics, or make updates to the current data.

HACK 81 Use Node.js's Response Object to Respond to the Client with Device-Specific Data

You can use the `response` object in Node.js to display client-specific information in the browser.

Now that we have hacked our **request** object, let's tackle the response. We can begin by calling the **writeHead()** method and passing the **success** response code, along with the **Content-Type** set to **text/plain**. This is a pretty standard response. Then we will call the **end()** method and pass it a specific string based on the properties we added to our global **DeviceData** object.

```
res.writeHead(200, {'Content-Type': 'text/plain'});

  if (DeviceData.mobile) {
    res.end('Hello Html5\n Request from a Mobile Device');
  }

  if (DeviceData.iOS || DeviceData.iPhone || DeviceData.iPad) {
    res.end('Hello Html5\n Request from an Apple Device');
  }

  else {
    res.end('Hello Html5\n Request from some other Device');
  }
```

So our final *server.js* file looks like this:

```
var http = require('http');
http.createServer(function (req, res) {

  // control for favicon
  if (req.url === '/favicon.ico') {
      res.writeHead(200, {'Content-Type': 'image/x-icon'} );
      res.end();
      // console.log('favicon requested');
      return;
  }
  else {
    // console.log('REQUEST: ' + req);
    console.log(req.headers);

    var ua = req.headers['user-agent'],
  DeviceData = {};

    // Mobile?
    if (/mobile/i.test(ua))
    DeviceData.mobile = true;

    // Apple device?
    if (/like Mac OS X/.test(ua)) {
      DeviceData.iOS = /CPU( iPhone)? OS ([0-9\._]+) like Mac OS
```

HTML5 HACKS

```
X/.exec(ua)[2].replace(/_/g, '.');
    DeviceData.iPhone = /iPhone/.test(ua);
    DeviceData.iPad = /iPad/.test(ua);
  }

  res.writeHead(200, {'Content-Type': 'text/plain'});

  if (DeviceData.mobile) {
    res.end('Hello Html5\n Request from a Mobile Device');
  }

  if (DeviceData.iOS || DeviceData.iPhone || DeviceData.iPad) {
    res.end('Hello Html5\n Request from an Apple Device');
  }

  else {
    res.end('Hello Html5\n Request from some other Device');
  }
};
}).listen(1337, "127.0.0.1");

console.log('Server running at http://127.0.0.1:1337/');
```

HACK 82 Use the Node Package Manager to Add a Web Application Framework As a Third-Party Module

Adding modules to Node.js applications is simple with the Node Package Manager (NPM). Adding the Express web application framework to your application is as simple as adding it to your application manifest and installing it via NPM.

First, we need to understand how Node.js handles third-party modules. NPM is the package management system written for Node.js. Inspired by Linux package management systems, it helps by automating the process of installing, upgrading, configuring, and removing third-party modules from your computer and Node.js applications. NPM maintains a remote repository of version and dependencies information that application developers can query and pull modules from to include in their applications.

Since version 0.6.3 (stable), Node.js now ships with NPM. Let's double-check:

```
user$ npm -help
```

With NPM we get a simple tool for managing packages of modules. Let's see the basics.

First we'll update the *package.json* manifest file to include our first third-party dependency:

```
{
  "name": "html5hacks-node"
, "version": "0.0.1"
, "private": true
, "dependencies": {
    "express": "latest"
  }
}
```

Now we'll use the **d** parameter to install the dependencies from our *package.json* manifest:

```
user$ npm install -d
```

We now have added our first module to our code base and we should be able to access the latest version of the Express web framework to enhance our application.

HACK 83 Use the Express Application Generator to Bootstrap Your App

Express's application generator executable helps you build the skeleton for your application from the command line.

Why Use Express?

In earlier hacks we were operating on the **request** and **response** objects using only the HTTP module. Node.js ships with another "core" module called Connect that provides an additional layer of functionality on top of HTTP.

The HTTP module's **createServer** method returns an object that you can use to respond to HTTP requests. That object inherits the **http.Server** prototype.

Connect also offers a **createServer** method, which returns an object that inherits an extended version of **http.Server**. Connect's extensions are mainly there to make it easy to plug in middleware. That's why Connect describes itself as a "middleware framework."

Express does to Connect what Connect does to the HTTP module: it offers a **create Server** method that extends Connect's **Server** prototype. So all the functionality of Connect is there, plus view rendering and a handy DSL for describing routes. Ruby's Sinatra is a good analogy.

The quickest way to get started with Express is to utilize the executable Express to generate an application. First we'll create the app:

```
$ npm install -g express
$ express /mydir && cd /mydir
```

OR

```
$ npm install -g express
$ mkdir mydir
$ cd mydir
$ express
```

This will generate the following application skeleton in the directory you designate:

```
create : .
create : ./package.json
create : ./app.js
create : ./public
create : ./public/javascripts
create : ./public/images
create : ./public/stylesheets
create : ./public/stylesheets/style.css
create : ./routes
create : ./routes/index.js
create : ./views
create : ./views/layout.jade
create : ./views/index.jade
```

Let's take a closer look at the *app.js* file. This is what you get by default:

```
/**
 * Module dependencies.

 */

var express = require('express')
  , routes = require('./routes');

var app = module.exports = express.createServer();

// Configuration

app.configure(function(){
  app.set('views', __dirname + '/views');
  app.set('view engine', 'jade');
  app.use(express.bodyParser());
```

```
  app.use(express.methodOverride());
  app.use(app.router);
  app.use(express.static(__dirname + '/public'));
});

app.configure('development', function(){
 app.use(express.errorHandler({
   dumpExceptions: true,
   showStack: true }));
});

app.configure('production', function(){
 app.use(express.errorHandler());
});

// Routes

app.get('/', routes.index);

app.listen(3000);
console.log("Express server listening on port %d in %s mode",
app.address().port, app.settings.env);
```

But let's break this down into the bare essentials to get running:

```
// 1. Declare our Module Dependencies
var express = require('express')
 , routes = require('./routes');

// 2. Instantiate an Express Server
var app = module.exports = express.createServer();

// 3. Configure the Application
app.configure(function(){
 app.set('views', __dirname + '/views');
 app.set('view engine', 'jade');
 app.use(express.static(__dirname + '/public'));
});

// 4. Set up Routes
app.get('/', routes.index);
```

```
// 5. Listen on Port 3000
app.listen(3000);
console.log("Express server listening on port %d in %s mode",
app.address().port, app.settings.env);
```

Now we can install dependencies:

```
$ npm install -d
```

and start the server:

```
$ node app.js
```

HACK 84 Build a Custom Module to Handle Routing

Modularize the handling of requests made to your application within your own custom module.

In our main *app.js* file, we will make a few changes. First, our generator already created a new module that will isolate all our routing logic.

For the sake of demonstration, and in case you have the need to use static HTML files, we will disable the layout engine and configure Express to serve static HTML files from the */public* directory. We will also turn off layout support.

Here is the *app.js* file:

```
var express = require('express')
  , routes = require('./routes');

var app = module.exports = express.createServer();

app.configure(function(){

  // disable layout
  app.set("view options", {layout: false});

  app.use(express.static(__dirname + '/public'));

  // make a custom html template
  app.register('.html', {
    compile: function(str, options){
      return function(locals){
        return str;
      };
    }
  });
});
```

```
});

// Routes
app.get('/', function(req, res){
 res.render("index.html");
});

app.listen(process.env.PORT || 3000);
console.log("Express server listening on port %d in %s mode",
app.address().port, app.settings.env);
```

The **routes** module contains the file *index.js*, which contains our routing logic:

```
exports.index = function(req, res){
 res.render('index', { title: 'Index' })
};
```

And here is a basic *index.html* file containing the markup:

```
<!DOCTYPE html>
<html lang="en">
 <head>
   <meta charset="utf-8">
   <title>HTML5 Hacks</title>
 </head>

 <body>
   <p>HTML5 Hacks</p>
 </body>
</html>
```

Now, we have created our first module and we are using routes to serve markup to the browser. As your application grows, you will need to continue to modularize its functionality so that your *app.js* file does not become difficult to maintain.

HACK 85 Configure Express to Use a View Engine

Configuring Express to render views with a view engine provides flexibility and simplicity to our HTML templating approach.

In Hack #84, we disabled the layout engine and configured Express to serve static HTML files. The next logical step is to begin simplifying and optimizing our views strategy. A common coding best practice is to keep our code DRY (Don't Repeat Yourself). We will hack that together here. While we are at it, we will also briefly introduce a metalanguage called Jade and demonstrate that we can configure Express to use as an alternative to HTML. There will be more to come in our next hack about Jade and Stylus. Then we will begin to take witness of the productivity gains provided by these tools.

For now, let's look at our new changes.

Here is the *app.js* file:

```
var express = require('express')
  , routes = require('./routes');

var app = module.exports = express.createServer();

app.configure(function(){
  app.set('views', __dirname + '/views');
  app.set('view engine', 'jade');
  app.use(express.static(__dirname + '/public'));
});


// Routes
app.get('/', function(req, res){
  res.render("index.html");
});

app.listen(process.env.PORT || 3000);
console.log("Express server listening on port %d in %s mode",
app.address().port, app.settings.env);
```

The **routes** module containing the file *index.js* still contains the same routing logic:

```
exports.index = function(req, res){
  res.render('index', { title: 'Index' })
};
```

But now we have an *index.jade* file containing the markup in a less verbose, simpler syntax:

```
!!! 5
html(lang='en')
head
  meta(charset='utf-8')
  title HTML5 Hacks
body
  p HTML5 Hacks
```

In the next few hacks, we will take a closer look at Jade and her sister language, Stylus.

HACK 86 Use Jade Layouts to DRY Up Your Application's Views

DRY (Don't Repeat Yourself) is a common software design idiom. This hack will demonstrate this best practice in your views.

To manage our markup and CSS within our Express application, we will be using two fantastic tools: Jade and Stylus. Jade is a dynamic metalanguage that compiles to HTML. Stylus is a dynamic metalanguage that compiles to CSS. As with the other tools, we will not go into great detail, as this is not an API reference book.

Our reasoning for selecting these "shortcut" languages is simple. We want to ensure that our hacking environment remains organized and doesn't become unwieldy. If you are already writing HTML and CSS, the learning curve for these technologies will not be steep. The time you will save in the long run will make their use worth the time and energy you will spend learning to use the tools.

There are other similar metalanguages, such as HAML, Less, and Sass, of which you may already be familiar. These tools are somewhat different, but the concepts are the same.

Before we jump into our hacks, we will need to get somewhat acquainted with the Jade syntax.

You had a taste of the simplified syntax in the previous hacks, but if you would like to get a little deeper, see the official Jade website (*http://jade-lang.com/*) and the official documentation (*https://github.com/visionmedia/jade#readme*).

In Hack #85, we set up a basic app utilizing Jade. We introduced the concept of DRY (Don't Repeat Yourself). Now, we will hack together a few more views, a basic layout, and a few partials to demonstrate this important concept. Both layouts and partials are techniques to "include" markup dynamically in order to aggregate multiple *.jade* files into one output.

First, we need another route. In our main *app.js* file, let's add the following:

```
app.get('/', routes.index);

app.get('/example1', routes.example1);
```

In our *index.js* file, let's add a new example route:

```
exports.index = function(req, res){
  res.render('index', { title: 'Index' })
};
```

```
exports.example1 = function(req, res){
  res.render('example1', { title: 'Example1' })
};
```

And finally, in our *views* directory, we can add a new *basic.jade* file. Now, when our request is made for *http://localhost/example1* content will be returned from that particular *example1.jade* file.

If we continue to add more routes and corresponding views, our new files will without a doubt contain duplicate markup, duplicate assets, and so on. Well, that is not very DRY. This is where *layouts* and *partials* come into play. Think of the layout as the shared container, and partials as any duplicate content that should be included within the internals of a view.

So let's create a *layout.jade* file to contain all our shared container information, such as our head, our title attribute, and all our JavaScript and CSS dependencies:

```
!!! 5
html(lang='en')
head
  meta(charset='utf-8')
  title HTML5 Hacks
  meta(name='description', content='')
  meta(name='author', content='')
  // Styles
  link(href='assets/css/bootstrap.css', rel='stylesheet')
  script(src='assets/js/application.js')
body
!= body
```

Now, the markup returned from the view will be injected into the body of the document via the != body call. Here is the *index.jade* file:

```
P HTML5 Hacks
```

Now view your application at *http://localhost:3000*, and you will see your two files, *layout.jade* and *index.jade*, aggregated together and output to the browser (see Figure 10-1).

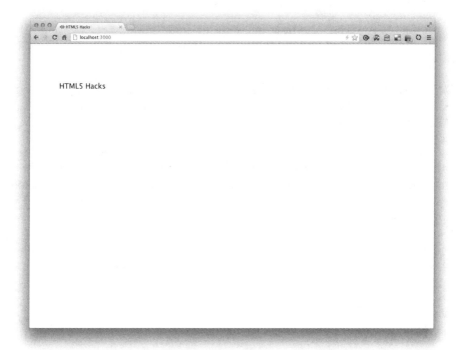

Figure 10-1.
Initial simple view

Layout is turned on by default, but if you ever have the need, such as in Hack #84, you can turn it off with the following configuration:

```
// disable layout
app.set("view options", {layout: false});
```

HACK 87 Use a Jade Partial to Create a Common Navigation Bar in Your Views

Now you can reuse content within your views through the use of partials.

To demonstrate this capability, let's inject some shared content, such as a navigation bar, by creating a file named *nav.jade* and placing it into our *views/partials* directory:

```
ul.nav
  li.active
    a(href='/example1') Example1
```

```
li
  a(href='/example2') Example2
li
  a(href='/example3') Example3
```

We will also need to update our main *app.js* file, with our new routes:

```
app.get('/', routes.index);

app.get('/example1', routes.example1);

app.get('/example2', routes.example2);

app.get('/example3', routes.example3);
```

Now we need to build the three new example files. We'll start with *example1.jade*:

```
p Example 1
```

then another simple file, *example2.jade*:

```
p Example 2
```

and finally the last one, *example3.jade*:

```
p Example 3
```

Here is the layout with the call to **partials/nav** included:

```
!!! 5
html(lang='en')
head
 meta(charset='utf-8')
 title HTML5 Hacks
 meta(name='description', content='')
 meta(name='author', content='')
body
!= partial('partials/nav')
!= body
```

Our browser should now look like Figure 10-2.

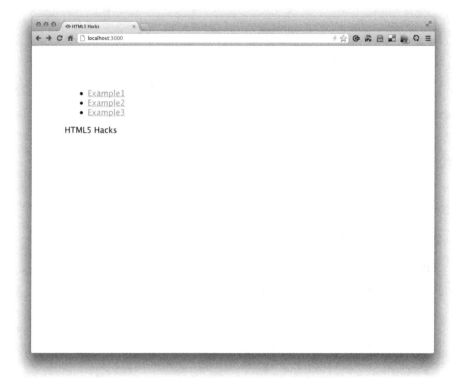

Figure 10-2.
Navigation partial

As we navigate through the application by clicking the links within our navigation bar, we will see that we are now sharing the layout and the navigation partial with each example page. This hack is a very simple demonstration of how to keep our assets organized, as you might imagine that as your hacks grow in size and complexity, following this approach should serve you well.

Before we depart from our exploration of Jade, let's finish up with one more hack that will demonstrate the power of our new template engine.

HACK 88 Use Jade Mixins to Populate Your Views with Data

Jade mixins are another tool in your toolkit that you can utilize in your views to reduce code bloat. You can use mixins to help iterate through data from a web service, from a database, or in memory.

Let's say we have a complex object being stored in memory or being persisted in a database. We would like to print out a few lists to display the data stored in this object.

To do this, we will use mixins. The power behind this feature is that we can now pass objects to our views, iterate through the data, and dynamically display its properties onto the screen. With mixins, we can pass parts of data as objects, nest mixins within mixins, and keep our code tidy, concise, and DRY.

First, let's take a look at passing a complex object from our route to our view. You may wonder why we are working with a complex object. Typically, the objects returned from most web service APIs have multiple levels of nesting. This is also typical of a data blob we might access from a NoSQL database such as MongoDB, CouchDB, or Redis. In our hack, we will emulate data returned from a Frozen Yogurt Shop application. For now, let's hardcode the object and pass it as the second argument to our **response** object's **render** method.

```
exports.example3 = function(req, res){
 res.render('example3', {
"name": "Yogurt Shop Daily Data",
"toppings":
    [
            { "id": "5001", "type": "Walnuts" },
            { "id": "5002", "type": "Jelly Beans" },
            { "id": "5005", "type": "Cherries" },
            { "id": "5007", "type": "Powdered Sugar" },
            { "id": "5006", "type": "Chocolate Sprinkles" },
            { "id": "5003", "type": "Chocolate Syrup" },
            { "id": "5004", "type": "Cocunut" }
    ],
"yogurts":
            [
            { "id": "5001", "type": "Tart", "flavors":
                [
                    { "id": "5001", "type": "Green Tea" },
                    { "id": "5002", "type": "Euro" },
                    { "id": "5005", "type": "Orange" }
                ]
            },
            { "id": "5002", "type": "Sweet", "flavors":
                [
                    { "id": "5001", "type": "Vanilla" },
                    { "id": "5002", "type": "Chocolate" },
                    { "id": "5005", "type": "Mexican Bean" }
                ]
            },
            { "id": "5005", "type": "Cake", "flavors":
                [
                    { "id": "5001", "type": "Cherry Cheesecake" },
```

```
                      { "id": "5002", "type": "Apple Fritter" },
                      { "id": "5005", "type": "Carrot Cake" }
               ]
          }
     ]
  })
};
```

Now, we should have access to the data in our view via the `locals` object. In order to iterate through this data and display it in our view, Jade provides some very helpful features. One of those is mixins.

Wikipedia defines a mixin as "A class that provides a certain functionality to be inherited or just reused by a subclass, while not meant for instantiation (the generation of objects of that class). Mixins are synonymous with abstract base classes. Inheriting from a mixin is not a form of specialization but is rather a means of collecting functionality. A class or object may 'inherit' most or all of its functionality from one or more mixins, therefore mixins can be thought of as a mechanism of multiple inheritance." —From Wikipedia page on mixins (http://en.wikipedia.org/ wiki/Mixin)

Our *example3.jade* file can now utilize this functionality (see Figure 10-3):

```
h2 Yogurts and Toppings

mixin toppings(data)
 ul.data
   - each item in data

      li= item.type

h2= name

h3 Toppings
mixin toppings(toppings)
```

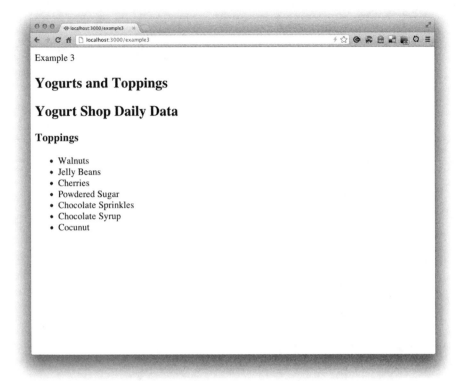

Figure 10-3.
Basic list

Now we can add more logic to our *example3.jade* file. We can also nest a mixin within another mixin.

```
h2 Yogurts and Toppings

mixin toppings(data)
 ul.data
   - each item in data

     li= item.type

mixin yogurts(data)
 ul.data
   - each item in data

     li= item.type

mixin flavors(data)
```

```
ul.data
  - each item in data

    li= item.type

mixin yogurts_nest(data)
  ul.data
    - each item in data

      li= item.type
      mixin flavors(item.flavors)

h2= name

h3 Toppings
mixin toppings(toppings)

h3 Yogurts
mixin yogurts(yogurts)

h3 Yogurts with Flavors
mixin yogurts_nest(yogurts)
```

Through the power of the Jade metalanguage and some of its robust features, we are able to create clear and concise markup to manage our views (see Figure 10-4).

HACK 89 Set Up Expressive, Dynamic, Robust CSS with Stylus

Stylus makes CSS for your Express application easier to write and maintain.

As mentioned earlier, Stylus is a dynamic metalanguage that compiles to CSS.

The feature set for Stylus is exhaustive, so we will have to pick and choose the best for the scope of the following hacks. This is not Grandma's CSS; Stylus provides a slew of support to the laborious task of writing CSS selectors. Again, a metalanguage like Stylus will always be optional, but the benefits will be apparent once you dive in.

First, let's add the Stylus module to our current application. In this hack we will simply include Stylus and compile a *.styl* file to *.css*.

```
var express = require('express')
  , routes = require('./routes')
  , stylus = require('stylus');
```

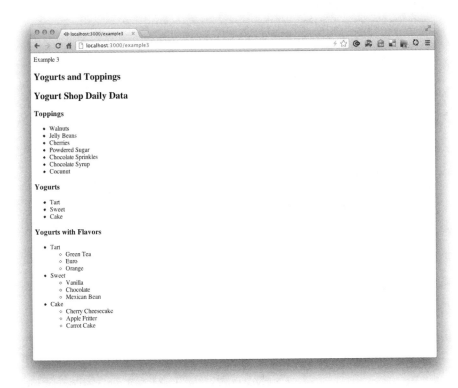

Figure 10-4.
Topping and yogurt lists

```
var app = module.exports = express.createServer();

app.use(stylus.middleware({
  debug: true,
  src: __dirname + '/public',
  dest: __dirname + '/public',
  compile: compileMethod
}));

function compileMethod(str) {
  return stylus(str)
    .set('compress', true);
};

// Configuration
app.configure(function(){
  app.set('views', __dirname + '/views');
```

```
app.set('view engine', 'jade');
app.use(express.bodyParser());
app.use(express.methodOverride());
app.use(app.router);
app.use(express.static(__dirname + '/public'));
});

// Routes
app.get('/', routes.index);

app.listen(3000);
console.log("Express server listening on port %d in %s mode",
app.address().port, app.settings.env);
```

Here is a new *style.styl* stylesheet, where we will leverage our new syntax:

```
body
  font 12px Helvetica, Arial, sans-serif
  background #D6396E
  text-align left

ul
  list-style none
```

If we switch back to our *style.css*, we will notice that our stylesheet is being compiled at runtime:

```
body{font:12px Helvetica,Arial,sans-serif;background:#D6396E;
text-align:left}
ul{list-style: none}
```

We now have an app up and running on Node.js with Express, Jade, and Stylus working together to render output to the web browser (see Figure 10-5).

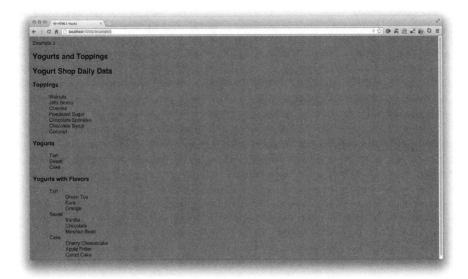

Figure 10-5.
Styled topping and yogurt lists

HACK 90 Include HTML5 Boilerplate As Your Default Starter Template

Use HTML5 Boilerplate, the professional, frontend, developer-based HTML/CSS/ JavaScript template, for a fast, robust, and future-safe site.

HTML5 Boilerplate has evolved into the de facto standard for developing a baseline to address the most common issues and considerations needed to build professional web applications today.

We will be taking a deeper look at some of the items in the exhaustive list of reasons why we should be using a boilerplate to start any HTML5 hack or production-ready application. Go online to see the full list (*http://html5boilerplate.com*). The developers involved have committed exhaustive research into each of these areas, and this boilerplate has evolved into a fantastic collection of best practices.

The approach you take to including HTML5 Boilerplate within your project varies depending on your environment. Let's start with the simplest way, and then we can integrate it into our Node.js applications using Jade and Stylus.

Begin by downloading the archive file (*http://github.com/h5bp/html5-boilerplate/ zipball/v3.0.2*).

Now open the *index.html* file and you will see the following boilerplate HTML markup:

```
<!doctype html>
<!—
paulirish.com/2008/conditional-stylesheets-vs-css-hacks-answer-neither/
-->
<!--[if lt IE 7]>
<html class="no-js lt-ie9 lt-ie8 lt-ie7" lang="en">
<![endif]-->
<!--[if IE 7]>    <html class="no-js lt-ie9 lt-ie8" lang="en">
<![endif]-->
<!--[if IE 8]>    <html class="no-js lt-ie9" lang="en"> <![endif]-->
<!--[if gt IE 8]><!--> <html class="no-js" lang="en"> <!--<![endif]-->
<head>
  <meta charset="utf-8">

  <title>HTML5 Hacks</title>
  <meta name="description" content="">

  <!-- Mobile viewport optimized: h5bp.com/viewport -->
  <meta name="viewport" content="width=device-width">

  <!-- Place favicon.ico and apple-touch-icon.png in the root
directory: mathiasbynens.be/notes/touch-icons -->

  <link rel="stylesheet" href="css/style.css">

  <!-- More ideas for your <head> here: h5bp.com/d/head-Tips -->

  <!-- All JavaScript at the bottom, except this Modernizr build.
       Modernizr enables HTML5 elements & feature detects for
optimal performance.
       Create your own custom Modernizr build:
www.modernizr.com/download/ -->
  <script src="js/libs/modernizr-2.5.3.min.js"></script>
</head>
<body>
  <!-- Prompt IE 6 users to install Chrome Frame. Remove this
if you support IE 6.
  chromium.org/developers/how-tos/chrome-frame-getting-started -->
  <!--[if lt IE 7]><p class=chromeframe>Your browser is
<em>ancient!</em> <a href="http://browsehappy.com/">Upgrade to a
different browser</a> or <a
href="http://www.google.com/chromeframe/?redirect=true">install
Google Chrome Frame</a> to experience this site.</p>
  <![endif]-->
```

```
<header>

</header>
<div role="main">
  <p>Welcome to HTML5</p>
</div>
<footer>

</footer>

<!-- JavaScript at the bottom for fast page loading -->

<!-- Grab Google CDN's jQuery, with a protocol relative URL;
fall back to local if offline -->
  <script
src="//ajax.googleapis.com/ajax/libs/jquery/1.7.1/jquery.min.js">
</script>
<script>
  window.jQuery || document.write('
  <script src="js/libs/jquery-1.7.1.min.js"><\/script>')
</script>

<!-- scripts concatenated and minified via build script -->
<script src="js/plugins.js"></script>
<script src="js/script.js"></script>
<!-- end scripts -->

</body>
</html>
```

For the sake of this hack, I have removed some of the less significant code and comments as they are out of scope. An entire book could be written about the issues and considerations being addressed within this template. We will focus on the items that are most related to HTML5; this will certainly be enough to get you started.

Open *index.html* in your web browser, and you will have a starting point for your HTML5 hacks. Let's take a closer look at the seven most relevant aspects of this boilerplate:

<doctype>

As mentioned in Hack #01, our HTML5 <doctype> declaration is included for us.

Conditional-stylesheets

Conditional-stylesheets were developed to overcome CSS rendering bugs in a number of highly adopted browsers. Since not all browsers correctly implement the CSS specifications released by the W3C, writing cross-browser CSS can be complex. The Conditional-stylesheets approach helps to ensure that your site renders consistently across as many popular browsers as possible, and alleviates some of the pain for frontend engineers.

The concept originated from the method of conditional commenting for Internet Explorer, and has since evolved with input from other frontend engineers. You can follow the evolution at paulirish.com (*http://paulirish.com/2008/conditional-stylesheets-vs-css-hacks-answer-neither*).

The solution predates the HTML5 Boilerplate but has become an important tool to use when starting to build an HTML5 application, thus the reason for its integration into the boilerplate.

Modernizr

Modernizr provides a starting point for making the best websites and applications that work exactly right no matter what browser or device your visitors use.

Included with Modernizr are media query tests and the built-in YepNope.js micro library as `Modernizr.load()`, as mentioned in Hack #55, Hack #63, and Hack #76.

Chrome Frame

Google Chrome Frame is an open source plug-in that integrates Google Chrome into Internet Explorer. With Google Chrome Frame, you get Chrome's V8 Java-Script Interpreter, HTML5 canvas tag support, and other open web technologies not available in Internet Explorer.

Header and footer elements

A mentioned in Hack #02, our template gives us header and footer elements by default.

Google CDN's jQuery

jQuery is a commonly used utility library that essentially extends the capabilities of the browser. It is cross-browser-tested to handle any differences across browser experiences.

A CDN is a Content Delivery Network that aims to solve the problem of network latency for static resources such as stylesheets, images, and JavaScript.

Optimized JavaScript

Our JavaScript should be concatenated and minified via build scripts, and also included at the bottom of the page. These are three of the basic rules for highly optimized web pages made popular by Steve Souders. For more information, visit stevesouders.com (*http://stevesouders.com/hpws/rules.php*).

Integrating with the Node.js/Express Application

Unfortunately, this only provides a benefit for hacking on HTML5 features that are not dependent on communication with an HTTP or WebSocket Server. In order to have a fully capable application that can be deployed to a remote server, we need to integrate this boilerplate into our basic web application that we built in the beginning of this chapter.

Fortunately, I have done most of the heavy lifting for you, by setting up a project and deploying it to GitHub. If you are familiar with Git, pulling down this code is as simple as:

```
$ git clone git@github.com:html5hacks/chapter9.git
$ npm install
$ node app.js
```

Now that you have the app running, let's update the *index.jade* and *layout.jade* files to reflect what we have learned from HTML5 Boilerplate. Here are our original *.jade* files—*layout.jade*:

```
!!! 5
html(lang='en')
head
 meta(charset='utf-8')
 title HTML5 Hacks
 meta(name='description', content='')
 meta(name='author', content='')
 // Styles
 link(href='assets/css/bootstrap.css', rel='stylesheet')
 script(src='assets/js/application.js')
body
!= partial('partials/nav')
!= body
```

and *index.jade*:

```
P HTML5 Hacks
```

After adding the additional markup and script declarations from our boilerplate we end up with this:

```
!!! 5

//if lt IE 7
    html(class="no-js ie6 oldie", lang="en")
//if IE 7
    html(class="no-js ie7 oldie", lang="en")
//if IE 8
```

```
        html(class="no-js ie8 oldie", lang="en")
    // [if gt IE 8] <!
    html(class="no-js", lang="en")
        // <![endif]

    head
     meta(charset='utf-8')
     title HTML5 Hacks
     meta(name='description', content='')
     meta(name='author', content='')
     meta(name='description', content='')
     // Styles
     link(href='css/style.css', rel='stylesheet')
     script(src='js/libs/modernizr-2.5.3.min.js')
    body

      // [if lt IE 7]><p class=chromeframe>Your browser is
    <em>ancient!</em> <a href="http://browsehappy.com/">
    // Upgrade to a different browser</a> or <a
    href="http://www.google.com/chromeframe/?redirect=true">install
    // Google Chrome Frame</a> to experience this site.</p>
    <![endif]

      header
      != partial('partials/nav')
      div(role="main")
      != body
      footer
      // JavaScript at the bottom for fast page loading
      // Grab Google CDN's jQuery, with a protocol relative URL;
    fall back to local if offline

      script(
    src='http//ajax.googleapis.com/ajax/libs/jquery/1.7.1/jquery.min.js')
      script
    window.jQuery || document.write('
    <script src="js/libs/jquery-1.7.1.min.js"> <\/script>')

      script(src='js/plugins.js')
      script(src='js/script.js)
```

As you can see, having our markup, styles, and script declarations in .*jade* files makes managing this template a less complex endeavor.

Become an HTML5 Hacker

The title of this chapter is "Pro HTML5 Application Hacks with Node.js" because at this point you should be ready to build production-deployable applications that use many of the HTML5 specifications you learned in the other chapters of this book.

The intent was to celebrate and share in the hacker tradition by presenting you with step-by-step hacks targeted at transforming your current tools into a suite of tools that are sure to have set you on your way to becoming an HTML5 Guru.

Now, go get started—you should have everything you need to quickly create and deploy your own HTML5 hacks!

For more information visit *http://html5hacks.com/join*.

Index

We'd like to hear your suggestions for improving our indexes. Send email to index@oreilly.com.

J

K

L

M

WOFF (web-only font format), 61
word-wrap attribute, 71
writeHead ( ) method, 446
ws Module, 358
WYSIWYG editor, 227–230

X

XHR-polling polyfills, 432
XHR2, 242

Y

YepNope.js, 250, 300
YUI date picker, 24
YUI slider utility, 29

Z

zebra stripe data tables, 86
ZIP files, 258
zip.js library, 258

About the Authors

Jesse Cravens is a senior engineer at frog, where he works with the world's leading companies, helping them to design, engineer, and bring to market meaningful products and services. He possesses a deep background in web application development and has recently been focusing on single-page web application architecture, the mobile web, and HTML5.

He previously held senior development and technical management positions at USAA, leading a team of mobile application developers in the planning, designing, development, testing, implementation, and maintenance of USAA's industry-leading iOS, Android, Blackberry, and mobile web applications for their eight million members deployed worldwide.

Jesse holds a B.A. in Art from Rice University and a master's degree in Curriculum and Instruction from the University of Texas at San Antonio. He currently resides in Austin, TX, with his wife and two children. He can be reached at jessecravens.com.

Jeff Burtoft is an HTML5 Evangelist for Microsoft, where he has the pleasure of working with the HTML5 community every day. He is also a blogger at HTML5Hacks.com (*http://html5hacks.com*) and has personally released several Hybrid Mobile Applications into some of the popular mobile app markets.

Jeff has been in the web development community for over 10 years. His work experience is varied, with positions such as web master of a startup company and multimedia consultant for the Department of Defense. Jeff has also spent over five years working as the principal front-end engineer for a Fortune 500 Company in San Antonio, TX. Jeff has a B.A. in Rhetorical Studies from Duquesne University and a certification in Latin American Business from Inter-American University in San Juan, Puerto Rico. Throughout the years, Jeff's first love has been the web: HTML, JavaScript, CSS, and now HTML5.

Jeff lives in Bellevue, WA, with his wife and three children. In his free time, he enjoys writing mobile apps and playing video games with his kids.

Colophon

The text, heading, and title font is Benton Sans; the code font is Ubuntu Mono.

Have it your way.

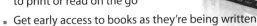